JOURNALISM

Theory in Practice

Edited by
Suellen Tapsall and Carolyn Varley

OXFORD

UNIVERSITY PRESS

253 Normanby Road, South Melbourne, Australia

Oxford University Press is a department of the University of Oxford.
It furthers the University's objective of excellence in research,
scholarship, and education by publishing worldwide in

Oxford New York
Athens Auckland Bangkok Bogotá Buenos Aires Calcutta
Cape Town Chennai Dar es Salaam Delhi Florence Hong Kong Istanbul
Karachi Kuala Lumpur Madrid Melbourne Mexico City Mumbai Nairobi
Paris Port Moresby São Paulo Singapore Shanghai Taipei Tokyo Toronto Warsaw
with associated companies in Berlin Ibadan

OXFORD is a registered trade mark of Oxford University Press
in the UK and in certain other countries

National Library of Australia
Catalogue-in-publication data:

Tapsall, Suellen Maree.
    Journalism: theory in practice.

    Bibliography.
    Includes index.
    ISBN 0 19 550997 8.

    1. Journalism. I. Varley, Carolyn. II. Title.

070.4

Edited by Edward Caruso
Indexed by Geradine Suter
Cover designed by Stephen Horsely
Typeset by Solo Typesetting, South Australia
Printed through Bookpac Production Services, Singapore

Contents

Preface

Journalism in Australia is struggling with a crisis of identity, image, and function. What is a journalist, and does journalism make a difference? Can it reclaim public confidence and restore the shine to its tarnished image? Do the news media matter any more? Is there such a thing as a public-service role or function for journalism?

This crisis is exacerbated by such forces as the concentration of media ownership, diminishing competition, economic constraints, and rapid technological change. Amid this onslaught lie questions about the basic underlying principles of journalism.

Journalism practitioners, students, and educators need to enhance their understanding of the institution of journalism and its place in society. It is no longer enough (if indeed it ever was) to simply *do* journalism or *be* a journalist. Those committed to a news that matters must develop better ways of assessing, evaluating, and articulating the purpose and practice of journalism.

Journalism academics and practitioners are contributing individually and sporadically to an acceleration in the quality and quantity of journalism research and discussion, internationally and in Australia, and to the development of a body of knowledge and a range of tools that might be harnessed to this end. This research and discussion is moving journalism theory and practice beyond an unhealthy polarisation that had developed between some journalism and media/cultural studies theorists. Professional practitioners have looked on with disdain, bemusement, and, at times, hostility, as media theorists have attempted to analyse, critique, and explain the environment in which news is gathered, processed, and published. The post-modern notion that there is no *one* truth has sat uneasily on the shoulders of those who believe their fundamental role is the pursuit of truth. The resulting development of a 'them and us' mentality has weakened journalism and media/cultural studies, at times preventing a discourse that could contribute to the growth of knowledge in both areas of study and practice. Perhaps one of the most frustrating elements for journalism proponents has been the ease with which media/communications studies has generated (and regenerated) its own language — both to explain and justify its existence and to examine the role and place of media industries — yet news practitioners have struggled to find words to adequately describe exactly what it is they do and why it is important.

An articulation and clarification of their roles and of the theoretical construct in which they operate is essential if journalists are to fulfil a useful function in society. Such examinations need to go beyond simplistic explorations of whether journalists are ethical and honest, to begin to build a platform for meaningful discourse.

This book examines journalism purposes, practices, and processes in an attempt to lay a solid foundation for such a platform. It is not simply an account of the daily practice of journalism, but focuses on the functions of journalists and journalism. Most importantly, this book integrates theory and practice, recognising both as essential threads in the fabric of journalism. Any approach that disregards either facet is insufficient, as the whole is greater than the sum of its parts.

For ease of navigation, this book is divided into seven sections. Each chapter within those sections explores a different aspect of the section's theme. In this manner the book aims to present a multi-dimensional view of journalism theories and practices.

Definition: Journalist attempts to define the contemporary Australian journalist. Drawing on primary and secondary research, it examines how the journalist's role has changed over time. It discusses how Australian journalists perceive their role — actual and ideal — and the issues that impact on them. To whom are they responsible, and to whom should they be responsible? How hopeful are they about the future of journalism?

Making journalism work presents a range of theoretical lenses through which journalism can be perceived. It examines the implications the imperative of commercial viability has for the news media. It explores journalism as commodity, cultural activity, public conversation, and work. How is the commercialisation and commodification of the media affecting news practitioners and consumers? Is journalism still the 'fourth estate'? Is the journalist's role to 'comfort the afflicted or afflict the comfortable'? Is journalism a craft or a profession?

Truth or dare considers notions of truth and their impact on journalistic practices. What is truth, and how important is it? What difference does the journalist's notion of truth make to their reporting practices? This section also argues that, in order to present the *whole* story, journalists must dare to move beyond reactive reporting and engage in deeper avenues of enquiry. It presents a theoretical framework that prompts the journalist to ask the *right* questions and step outside the boundaries of simplistic levels of enquiry.

Notions of truth are further explored in *In the eye of the beholder*, which moves from issues of practice (how to tell more of the story using the tool of enquiry, for example) to issues of perspective. Whose truth is promulgated in the mainstream media? How do daily news practices perpetuate the preconceptions held by journalists and their audiences, and how are the voices of 'others' — indigenous people, the socially disenfranchised, those on the 'fringe' of society — silenced or overlooked?

Upsetting the inverted pyramid examines emergent responses to perceived inadequacies in daily news forms and practices. Both literary and public journalism require journalists to discard their attachments to traditional notions of objectivity. Literary journalism opens up a treasure chest — or, some say, a Pandora's box — of story-telling devices. But do fictional techniques have a place in the telling of factual stories? Public journalism sees journalists and news organisations acting as a mediating force for community debates. Is there a place for journalists to take an active role in the stories they present and the issues they cover?

Moral minefields, legal landmarks considers journalism's moral and legal rights and responsibilities. How should journalists balance the interests of the public and the *public interest*? It looks at the ethical and legal tightrope that stretches between an individual's right to privacy and the media's right to publish. This section then considers emerging problems as local laws struggle to respond to the technological and commercial might of global media organisations.

Finally, *Technological talespinning* looks at technology and the predictions that traditional news media are doomed. Will the Internet and on-line journalism result in the death of older forms of print and broadcast news? What possible future does journalism have in a converged, digital environment?

Journalism: Theory in Practice aims to provide a starting point for journalists, academics, students, and critics to begin a discussion and re-evaluation of the role and function of contemporary Australian journalism. It comes at a time when professional cynicism is high and public confidence is low. This is the time to assess the present and map the future of journalism in the changing context of communication in the twenty-first century.

Acknowledgments

In the mid- to late-1990s, we were privileged to participate in ongoing and thought-provoking conversations about journalism in two supportive and challenging environments — at Queensland University of Technology and through the Journalism Education Association.

It is a given that any acknowledgments that we make here will be by nature incomplete. That said, we thank our peers and mentors in the Journalism Education Association for their willingness to engage in various dialogues about the future of journalism and their passionate commitment to improving the quality of journalism and journalism education in Australia.

We also thank our colleagues at QUT and in the School of Media and Journalism for their support in 1994–98, particularly head of school Professor Stuart Cunningham. It was our privilege to work with fantastic students and a quality staff, all willing to invest considerable time and effort to provide the best possible environment for learning and the development of personal and professional skills.

This book would have been impossible without the commitment of the contributing authors and of Oxford University Press, and our publisher Jill Lane.

Finally, our heartfelt thanks to our partners Bruce Connell and Andrew Tapsall, and our children — Sidonie and Maginnis Connell, and Bethsaida, Amaraiah, Jezaniah and Zarah Tapsall — for their patience and forbearance as we continually worked on our contribution in the midst of shifting both families thousands of kilometres from home.

Contributors

Leo Bowman lectures in journalism at the Queensland University of Technology. He started his journalism career in 1978, and has worked on regional daily newspapers and ABC radio and television. He has a Masters degree in Public Policy and has written course material for delivery to regional newspaper journalists throughout Australia. Bowman has served as a federal councillor of the Media, Entertainment and Arts Alliance (MEAA), and has been on the Alliance's Queensland executive since 1989.

Rhonda Breit lectures in journalism at Deakin University. She graduated from Melbourne University law school in 1980 and practised law for four years before embarking on a career in journalism. She has twelve years' experience as a journalist and has completed a Graduate Diploma in Media, Communications, and Information Technology Law (Melbourne University).

Jacqui Ewart is a journalism lecturer at Central Queensland University. She worked as a journalist in regional newspapers for six years before moving into the media and communication field and working as a media manager for Queensland Health (five years). She completed a Master of Arts (Aboriginal Studies) through the University of South Australia. Her research interests lie in the representation of indigenous Australians in the media, as well as access to media for indigenous Australians. This research is leading into areas that examine the role of the media in making regional identity. Other research interests include new technologies and their effect on work place practices in newspapers.

Cratis Hippocrates BA MJourn (Qld) is Group Editorial Training Manager with John Fairfax Publications Pty Ltd. He is Adjunct Professor of Journalism at Queensland University of Technology and is co-ordinator of the Public Journalism project.

Martin Hirst has lectured in journalism at the University of Western Sydney, Nepean, and Charles Sturt University in Bathurst. A broadcast journalist who previously worked for news organisations including the ABC, he has a strong interest in developing community radio news. Hirst's current research is looking at journalism as work. His PhD is titled *Grey Collar Journalism: The Social Relations of News Production*. Hirst is also involved in community radio.

Lynette Sheridan Burns is head of the Department of Communication and Media Arts at the University of Newcastle, where she has co-ordinated the Journalism program since its inception in 1992. Sheridan Burns has worked as a journalist or editor for numerous metropolitan and regional daily newspapers and continues to freelance. She has published widely in the area of educational strategies for developing professional integrity in journalism students. In 1999, she and colleague Paul Scott won The Australian Award for Educational Publishing for journalism curriculum materials. She was elected president of the Journalism Education Association for 1999–2000.

Dr Michael Meadows teaches journalism at Griffith University. He worked as a print and broadcast journalist for 10 years before moving into journalism education. His research interests include journalism practices, media representation of Indigenous affairs, community media, and Indigenous media.

Mandy Oakham is the area co-ordinator of journalism at Deakin University. Her first book, *Don't Bury the Lead*, was published early in 1997. Prior to her arrival at Deakin in 1995, Oakham was the head of journalism at East Surrey College in England. As well as completing her Masters degree at London University, she also acted as consultant to the *Argus* Newspaper Group and was an examiner for the National Council for the Training of Journalists. Oakham has worked as a journalist on newspapers and magazines in Australia and London.

Mark Pearson BA DipEd Mlitt LLM is Associate Professor of Journalism and Head of Communication and Media Studies at Bond University, Queensland. A former press secretary, a journalist on regional, suburban, and metropolitan newspapers, and a section editor on the national daily, the *Australian*, he has been teaching media law to students and regional journalists for the past ten years. He is the author of *The Journalist's Guide to Media Law* (Allen & Unwin, Sydney, 1997) and co-author of *Breaking into Journalism* (Allen & Unwin, Sydney, 1998).

Ian Richards is senior lecturer in Journalism at the University of South Australia in Adelaide, where he teaches print journalism and journalism ethics. A former newspaper journalist, he has a wide range of journalistic experience extending from leader writing to covering Aboriginal Affairs for a metropolitan daily newspaper. He has worked and studied in Australia and the United Kingdom, is a past president of the Australian Journalism Education Association and is studying part-time for a PhD in the field of journalism ethics.

Matthew Ricketson has been a journalist since 1981, with the *Age*, the *Australian*, and *Time Australia* magazine. In 1994 he won the George Munster national award for freelance journalism. He is a senior lecturer and course coordinator of Journalism at RMIT University. He has used and written about freedom of information laws since 1985. His journalistic biography of Australian children's author Paul Jennings will be published by Penguin in 2000.

Angela Romano lectures at the Queensland University of Technology and worked as a news professional in Australia and Indonesia for more than a decade. She is co-ordinator and senior researcher with the Public Journalism Project. She won national and international prizes for excellence in academic research for articles based on her doctorate on journalism and politics in Indonesia.

Sharon Tickle BSc (UK), BA (Honours), MA Research, lived in the United Kingdom, United States, Japan, Malaysia, and Indonesia from 1976 to 1995 in the course of careers in nursing and the fitness industry. She was a freelance journalist for seven years producing news and features for Asian publications and was the Australian correspondent for an Indonesian newspaper from 1996–1998. Tickle worked with ABC Queensland in 1997–1998 to produce a series of cross-media community journalism projects and was senior researcher for the Public Journalism Project in 1998. Tickle has been teaching journalism at Queensland University of Technology since January 1998. She is undertaking MBA studies, majoring in Change Management and Communications.

Suellen Tapsall is senior lecturer in journalism at Murdoch University, and co-ordinates the journalism program. She moved into journalism education and training after working for more than a decade in print and broadcast news in Queensland. Tapsall co-authored the 1998 report *New Media and Borderless Education* and worked with the same team on the follow-up DETYA Evaluations and Investigations Project, *The Business of Borderless Education*. Her Masters thesis, *Technological talespinning*, examined technological determinism and the impact of technology on higher education. In 1997, Tapsall received one of QUT's prestigious awards for Outstanding Academic Contribution for excellence in the area of teaching performance and leadership. Her research interests include defining journalism, computer-assisted reporting, the Internet, virtualisation and globalisation of education, use of technology in teaching, technological literacy, information policy, journalism theory, and technological determinism.

Carolyn Varley began a career in journalism in 1980, spending most of her time in print newsrooms in Australia and England. She worked as chief of staff in various Australian newsrooms before moving into journalism education in 1994. Varley has also worked as a consultant with regional newspaper groups, delivering professional training courses. She holds a Masters degree in journalism ethics, and is working towards a PhD in the same field. Varley was a principal investigator on the *Definition: Journalist* project while lecturing in Journalism at the Queensland University of Technology.

Abbreviations

ABA	Australian Banking Association
ABA	Australian Broadcasting Authority
ABC	Australian Broadcasting Corporation
AJA	Australian Journalists Association
AOL	America On-line
APC	Australian Press Council
ATSIC	Aboriginal and Torres Strait Islander Commission
BBC	British Broadcasting Corporation
CIT	communications and information technologies
APN	Australian Provincial Newspapers
FOI	freedom of information
HREOC	Human Rights and Equal Opportunity Commission
MEAA	Media, Entertainment and Arts Alliance
PBL	Publishing and Broadcasting Limited
PJ	Public Journalism Project
PR	public relations
QUT	Queensland University of Technology
SBS	Special Broadcasting Service
SPJ	Society of Professional Journalists
TNCs	transnational corporations
URP	Urban Jungle Pack
VLGA	Victorian Local Government Association

Part 1

Definition: Journalist

The study of journalism demands a definition of what a journalist actually is. A stereo-typical journalist — whether the positive 'Clark Kent–Superman' image or the less whole-some Mike Moore of *Frontline* fame — no longer exists. The journalistic environment has altered almost beyond recognition, and continues to evolve rapidly; however, our understanding of what or who a journalist is has not progressed at the same pace. This section attempts to define the contemporary Australian journalist, as distinct from jour-nalists of different eras and locales. It examines how the journalist's role has changed over time, and discusses how Australian journalists perceive their roles and the issues that impact on them. The section draws on the ground-breaking Definition: Journalist research project, which involved surveys of a range of journalists and in-depth interviews with journalists identified as leaders in their fields. While there is no single definitive explanation of what — or even who — a journalist is, this section aims to serve as a springboard for the study of journalism in the contemporary Australian context.

1   What is a journalist?

SUELLEN TAPSALL AND CAROLYN VARLEY

> What is a journalist? An alcoholic in training. Well sort of. A journalist is a bundle of energy (hopefully) who finds out about the kind of things most people *want* to know about, and has to look for the kinds of things most people *should* know about. Sometimes they get old and die, sometimes they get shot, sometimes they get out young. Most just get maligned. (a third-year Queensland University of Technology journalism student)

It used to be simple. If you wanted to know what was going on in the world, you picked up the paper, listened to the radio, or turned on the television. An eloquent, debonair, father-figure would authoritatively explain some complex political decision or the latest outbreak of hostilities in a country many hours away.

Journalists have long been the subject of books, movies, and television series. Up until a couple of decades ago, the stereotypical view was of predominantly male, hard-living, hard-drinking, larrikin-types, fingers stained by nicotine and typewriter ink, and with a pencil stuck behind one ear. They could be obnoxious know-it-alls, but that was what society seemed to want — and expect.

Now it is no longer quite so clear what a *typical* journalist is — or what job they are supposed to be doing. The stereotypical journalist is not a focus of admiration and respect, and is likely to be despised by the public as someone about on par with a politician or used-car salesman.

So why bother attempting to define the contemporary Australian journalist? And who cares anyway?

Journalists need to know what their role is in order to decide whether they are acting appropriately, correctly, or ethically. Journalists who believe their function is to tell the truth — *the whole truth and nothing but the truth* — might be expected to act in a different manner to those whose objective is to strengthen society, or work for public benefit. A *watchdog* is likely to have different targets in sight of his or her pen than a *recorder of history*. The defining of the role of a journalist — or indeed roles, as there is no law that says the journalist will play only one part in the drama of society — will dictate what qualifications, skills, and personal attributes journalists have now or need in the future.

Intending journalists need to know and care what they are about to get into. In today's rapidly changing technological environment, significant discussions are taking place around the importance of lifelong learning, transferable skills, and generic attributes. Specific skills are quickly outdated. Employers no longer just want graduates who know how to use a digital editing system or write a simple news story. They want graduates who can think and adapt, who are creative and have initiative, and who can take the skills and techniques they have learnt and apply them in new situations. They want graduates who can learn how to learn, and who are willing to keep doing so (Cave 1998, Richardson 1998, Walsh 1998, Hippocrates 1999). In a sense this is nothing new for those in the journalism business, who have tended to become superficial knowers-of-all and specialists in little. And, in the current pressured environment of news, it could be argued that journalism graduates need to know not just how to be a journalist — but *why* they should be one (King 1997).

The public also needs to care about what a journalist is and what journalists do. Otherwise news consumers may not be able to recognise or distinguish between good news, bad news, and no news. Perhaps some of the blame for the public's huge dissatisfaction with the performance of journalists (Morgan 1995) is the lack of understanding of the profession, its practitioners, and its function. This lack of understanding is not some vague, nebulous feeling that journalists or those in the media industry can ignore. It has tangible and definitive impacts, such as the public's willingness to trust (or readily *dis*trust) news-gatherers, and falling newspaper circulations.

So what is a journalist and has the function of journalists changed at all? More to the point — what are the qualities and attributes of a contemporary Australian journalist? What pressures impact on their working lives? And how is a journalist different from other information workers? This chapter draws on the *Definition: Journalist*[1] research project that encompasses a quantitative survey of journalists working for Queensland daily news organisations, and qualitative interviews with reporters and editors in major television, radio and print news in Sydney and Melbourne. The *Definition: Journalist* project was undertaken by journalism lecturers and researchers Carolyn Varley and Suellen Tapsall at the Queensland University of Technology in 1998.

The project noted that little attention had been focused in Australia on the underlying principles of journalism, despite the fact that the profession was undergoing rapid evolution. It sought to determine if those principles were also evolving, and to develop a philosophy of journalism by defining the roles and attributes of journalists. The researchers argued that such a philosophy was essential if industry participants were to make informed decisions on issues such as professional practice, ethics, education, and technological change.

A journalist is . . .

It is easier to identify the things that contemporary Australian journalists *do* than to clearly label the functions and roles of journalism. This may be understandable given the traditional inability of news-gatherers and reporters to articulate their functions. Not surprisingly, attempts to define what a journalist is often take one of two opposing approaches — either failing to progress beyond the doing, or addressing elements of news practice in such theoretical terms that it is difficult to relate the theory to the practice. Such approaches can be seen in the work of Hartley and Windschuttle. On the more theoretical side, Hartley (1995) has previously described journalism as the 'sense-making practice of modernity', asserting that journalists, like cultural theorists, 'reduce the world to a text' (*Media Report* 1998b). On the other hand, Windschuttle (*Media Report* 1998b) argues that journalists go out into the 'external real world . . . find out what's going on . . . do empirical investigation . . . then try and report that as truthfully and objectively as you can'. The American-based Society of Professional Journalists (SPJ) also falls into the *doing* end of the spectrum, with its tenet that the principles of professional journalism are to tell the truth, minimise harm, act independently, and be accountable (Geimann 1996). Still primarily in this category, the AJA section of the Media, Entertainment and Arts Alliance (MEAA) highlights respect for truth and the public's right to information as 'overriding' or 'fundamental' principles of journalism. The preamble to the new code of ethics goes on to define journalists:

> Journalists describe society to itself. They convey information, ideas and opinions. They search, disclose, record, question, entertain, comment and remember. They inform citizens and animate democracy. They give a practical form to freedom of expression. They scrutinise power, but also exercise it, and should be responsible and accountable. (MEAA 1999)

Like the preamble, King's description of journalists combines both the social function and the practical aspects of the role. Journalists find the truth; try to interest and engage readers, listeners, or viewers; act independently and question society; support society's wider values; communicate clearly; and strive to be fair in their reporting (King 1997).

The *Definition: Journalist* Survey respondents defined journalists (in order of frequency) as news workers, information workers, gatherers, reporters, entertainers, historians, researchers, explainers, probers, and writers. Less frequent responses included journalists as editors, communicators, storytellers, producers, and presenters. Coming a distant last in the definition stakes — as distinct from the codes of ethics, which place these as cornerstones of news practice — journalists were defined as objective, truthful, accurate, and fair.

Peter Cave, then presenter of the ABC's *AM* program, suggests there are 'fancy' answers to the question 'but the simple answer is a journalist is an intermediary between the people who want to know information and the sources of information ... at the same time, the journalist is a filter of information ... and that's where the danger lies' (Cave 1998). That filter function is even more important for journalists who work with international news, according to Helen Vatsikopoulos (former host of SBS's *Dateline* program), who also sees journalists as communicators and conveyors of information: 'but ... a very important part of that is to analyse and to set certain events in context ... to inform people about the human aspects of conflict and struggle overseas ... you tend to see a news snippet and people don't know the context of it' (Vatsikopoulos 1998).

Attempts to define journalists are made more difficult by the complex nature of their function and the huge diversity in news or pseudo news products, programs, and publications. The most obvious — and superficial — response to the question 'what is a journalist' is that he or she is someone who is employed as such in the news media. However, new media forms and increasing diversity in information-processing roles, combined with a range of pressures such as commercialisation and others discussed in more detail later in this chapter and in this book, make this a less than helpful definition. There is no longer — if there ever was — one colour, shape, or size of a 'typical' journalist. As Walsh (1998) asserts 'there are almost infinite varieties ... at one end there's journalism as entertainment, and at the other end ... there's journalism as very dense, hard-edged information'. However, it may be possible to identify a core set of skills, attributes, and theoretical constructs that are common to those performing journalistic roles — in whatever setting that work occurs. One such defining element appears to be the issue of public responsibility.

To whom are journalists responsible — and to whom should they be?

A journalist is an 'odd mixture of a super-optimist and a total cynic' (Richardson 1998), a cocktail caused in no small part by the constant tightrope news practitioners walk between the reality of their daily work and their own idealised notions of what a journalist should be. Nowhere is this schizophrenic tension more evident than when reporters are asked to whom they *are* responsible — and to whom they believe they *should be* responsible. Reporters working in Australian newsrooms, especially those working in regional areas or for smaller publications, told the *Definition: Journalist* project they are responsible to their employers (60 per cent of survey respondents), to the public or community

(20 per cent), and to their audience (15 per cent). However, *more than 90 per cent* believed they should be responsible to the public and community, then to themselves, and next to their audience. Osmond (1998) says it is important to acknowledge an obligation to journalists' employers 'because for serious scale print media to survive, there has to be backing for it'. Cave agrees that journalists are responsible to their employer for their pay and that 'it's always going to be a factor'. He argues that reporters working for the ABC and Channel 9 might be expected to produce different types of stories, but that does not make one superior to the other:

> They are just a different type of journalist. You can argue philosophically which sort of journalist is the best sort of journalist, but if you were employed by *60 Minutes* to do a certain sort of job, and the people who watch *60 Minutes* expect a certain sort of result, you probably are fulfilling your responsibility both to the people who consume your journalism and your employer. (Cave 1998)

Reporters and editors working for major metropolitan news organisations, cushioned to some extent by the size of their news organisations and the extensive public reach of their news products, appeared to find less of a gulf between the real and the ideal.

> My feeling would be that in doing the best that you possibly can for your readers, that is also doing the best that you possibly can for your employer. But the first thought in your mind is for the readers, and . . . unless you have a huge ego, I don't think you can operate as a journalist unless you have at the back of your mind 'I have a right to ask this question, go into this person's house, or this or that intrusive thing, because I, in some way, am acting on behalf of the wider community'. If you thought to yourself 'I have a right to do whatever it is, burst into someone's home or something, or look into somebody's, private affairs because Mr Murdoch wants me to', I don't think you could do it. I think you've got to have that sense that there is some sort of overarching public good that you're working for. How could you justify yourself otherwise? (Richardson 1998)

Walsh also suggests there is 'not a lot of conflict' between responsibility to the public and to the employer, although he argues that it depends on the publication, and its definition of audience. He notes that the concentration of media ownership in the print media in Australia does put pressure on journalists, as 'there's no depth of employment'.

> You're insecure. If you get the sack from Fairfax there's only one place left to work, and you've got no bargaining power. It's a jungle and you'd be silly not to recognise the faults. I think it's absolutely certain it makes people overcautious and

oversensitive. It's a natural function of the existing order — not something you approve of, something you live with. (Walsh 1988)

Individual journalists whose popular currency or own name 'brand' is of sufficient stature might be better equipped to withstand such pressures. Political reporter Margo Kingston, who prides herself on not playing the establishment game, states that while she is responsible to her readers to be accurate, honest, and not hypocritical, her responsibility to herself is of primary importance:

> This is not a very popular view, I don't think, but I make my decisions about what I'm prepared to do. I'm prepared to move a long way from what I'm comfortable with, to meet my boss's demands, but I'm not prepared to go all the way. And that is a luxurious position to be in ... it sounds like I'm suggesting that I'm a superior journalist because I say 'no'. The fact is, I'm a lucky journalist, that I'm allowed to get away with saying 'no'. Most journalists, if they say 'no', they're out. But if I wasn't allowed to say 'no', then I wouldn't be a journalist, because I wouldn't feel that my integrity was intact. (1998b)

The public service nature and function of public broadcasters is more explicitly understood (and usually explicitly stated in the relevant legislation that sets out their mission and function). As a result, journalists working for public broadcasters are also likely to find less of a gulf between their responsibility to their employers and to the public. It is not likely, for example, that they would be directed to cover stories in a particular way (Vatsikopoulos 1998) — but these journalists walk a fine line between delivering news that is important and still holding the interest of an audience.

> ... You have to be picking up the slack. You have to be doing the stories that aren't going to rate sexily, but that are still worthy. But at the same time, I think the problem that public broadcasters fall into is that they think that if they do a worthy story, they can just ignore entertainment and those types of values that make good and watchable television. (Sales 1998)

Journalists working for public broadcasters might face fewer conflicts over the notion of their *public interest* function, but they are more likely to be confronted with tensions over reporting in the *national interest* (Smyth 1999). Thus, during the Gulf War, the ABC was directed by the government to broadcast certain types of information to Australian troops travelling by boat to participate in the conflict. On another occasion, the Federal Government intervened to stop ABC news programs from using a specific 'expert commentator'.

Journalists have a responsibility not just to those they write *for*, but also to those they write *about*. Sales, a political reporter with ABC Television in New

South Wales, argues she probably feels most responsible to the sources, or 'talent', in her stories:

> ... depending on who the talent is, of course. I think when you're representing someone's viewpoint, and putting it out to thousands and thousands of people, you are responsible to that person to show a fair and accurate representation of what they've told you. I think that is really paramount ... In terms of responsibility to the public, that's definitely a factor, because that's the whole thing of what your job is. So for me, I suppose I'm always thinking about things like trying to make my stories understandable, and to make complex things understandable, so that you can help people to have an understanding of these sorts of processes. (1998)

It is this ideal of a 'public' responsibility that should separate journalists from other *information presenters* such as radio and video disc jockeys or *information workers* such as public relations (PR) professionals and education and information officers for corporate, public, or government organisations. The PR practitioner is seen to be delivering a message that in some way promotes the employer or client. In the same way, information and education officers for specific organisations are also primarily responsible for delivering organisation- or industry-specific information.

> ... it's what the PR person will exclude, the information that they won't put in their press release, which puts them in a completely different category, because they are motivated by purely commercial reasons. You could say that 'we work in commercial television' but that's different, unless you're a Channel 9 reporter who's doing a story about Channel 9 ... even if you say Amnesty, even if you say Greenpeace press releases ... they'll always give you the line they want to promote. (Vatsikopoulos 1998)

The often-subliminal attachment to the public responsibility ideal, as problematic in practice and theory as it may be, might be the only differential between the journalist and other information workers who also endeavour to convey information and ideas in an understandable and accessible manner to the public.

What then, are the skills and attributes necessary for the contemporary Australian journalist?

Skills and attributes

A journalist needs to be much more than a good writer. Based on *Definition: Journalist* survey responses, the top skills and attributes identified as necessary for a contemporary Australian journalist (in rank order) are:
- communication skills;
- a questioning, curious, and inquisitive mind;

- writing abilities;
- news sense;
- knowledge of computers, technology-literate;
- listening skills;
- general knowledge;
- empathy, patience, and understanding;
- a sense of working for more than self (the notion of a public responsibility);
- language skills;
- interviewing skills.

Other attributes mentioned — but far less frequently than those above — include the ability to meet deadlines, thinking/knowledge analysis skills, resourcefulness and persistence, truthfulness, accuracy, and integrity.

Vatsikopoulos suggests the combination of a questioning mind and good communication skills is essential, as is a 'bullshit filter'.

> If you've written a story or produced a story that only you understand and a couple of academics ... then you're not doing your job properly. It's being able to condense, and also having the sort of common sense to know when someone is feeding you a line, or to know that when you're getting a certain press release from a certain faction that you have a certain amount of background knowledge to be able to say 'that's not true'. (Vatsikopoulos 1998)

News sense and language skills are also vital ingredients when it comes to distilling multiple pieces of information into newsworthy bites, without losing the sense, balance, or complexity of the news event, but while providing some sense of the big picture. But what is news sense and can you learn it? Richardson suggests it is a 'sense of the market' that can take a long time to develop (if it ever does). Denovan says whatever news sense is, journalists will continue to need it:

> Always a journalist is going to have to see what the story is. I see people go out and come back — they'll go to a news conference or something, and they won't come back with a story. They haven't got that ability ... The more I'm in this business, the more I feel that it's (news sense) almost innate ... I think that to a degree, you have to have this flair for it. And if you haven't got that flair for it, and it's not sort of almost second nature to you, I don't think it's something you can teach someone. (1998)

Richardson (1998) suggests good journalists also have a 'hunger to get information, a hunger to find out the truth ... to always get more'. The ability to cope under pressure, to deliver good copy and generate good stories at short notice, and to survive the daily adrenaline rush of impending deadlines is also important (Denovan 1998, Walsh 1998, Sales 1998, Kingston 1998b).

One key attribute, which does not appear in the survey responses but was mentioned repeatedly in personal interviews, is that journalists need to be tough and have thick hides. In this age of media management, 'if you run a story that people don't like you personally cop abuse . . . so you have to be able to not take that personally' (Sales 1998). Kingston argues that journalists need a persona that demands answers and that exudes confidence about their ability to ask for answers.

> It's psychological — you've got to be tough . . . and the other reason you've got to be very tough is not only have you got to get the story, but you've got to wear the pain, which is just relentless if you're writing in controversial areas. You've got to be prepared to accept that many people will despise you. (1998b)

The real-world perspective of what it takes to be a successful journalist, as discussed here, differs markedly from one ideal discussed at a 1998 Poynter Institute conference in the United States. That model, a ten-block pyramid, features ethics at its peak, with news judgment ('. . . knowing when *not* to put the President's sex life on Page One') and reporting as the cornerstones. Other skills include cultural competence, civic competence, visual literacy, technological competence, numerical competence, narrative and language, and analysis and interpretation. The civic and cultural areas deal with reporters' knowledge of their communities, and knowledge and understanding of the different cultures within their communities. Those attending the conference argued that journalists must know maths — including reading and manipulating data on a spreadsheet or database — and must also be able to use word processing, spreadsheet and database software, as well as the Internet and e-mail.

Exact combinations of skills and attributes obviously vary according to the duties of the individual journalist and the requirements of his or her workplace. Journalists working in the broadcast media, for example, need to be able to tell stories and communicate through effective and creative use of sound and vision, while those working in an online environment need high levels of technological literacy. They must be able to take information and package it according to their target audience, the publication they work for, and their personal style — all within an environment that is, in itself, the subject of immense and conflicting pressures.

Pressures

Commercialisation of the news media is a recurring theme in this book, and it should come as no surprise that aspects of the business of news continue to provide major causes of concern for Australian journalists. Walsh (1998) calls it 'the tyranny of the bottom line'. A lack of resources in news organisations, as reflected in down-sized newsrooms, shrinking budgets, funding problems, business considerations, time constraints (due to lack of staff), technology (addressed later in this chapter), and the concentration of media ownership are major concerns. One survey respondent begged for more resources 'to investigate items fully rather than just merely scratching the surface'. 'Too many station owners see newsrooms as a "cost only unit"' and there is an 'obsession with economic influence on editorial judgment', others complained.

These factors are contributing to the growth of what some call the *battery hen* model of news, with journalists cloistered in their newsrooms, which they seldom leave, and fed on a high-fibre diet of paper press releases and phone interviews that they regurgitate into space-filling news (Walsh 1998, Richardson 1998). These journalists increasingly come to rely on *dial-a-quote* sources — spokespeople who are used repeatedly because they can be counted on to quickly deliver a promising sound bite on the topic of the day. Smaller newsrooms, shrinking budgets, and the concentration of media ownership have also seen decreasing numbers of people actually covering news events and gathering copy, both in Australia and overseas. The closure of overseas bureaus and growth in network/group affiliations, along with the advent of news supergiants, has normalised the *CNN-isation* of news, further reducing the number of voices or perspectives reporting on any one issue. In the global village, news organisations are retreating into parochialism, with more and more reliance on copy supplied from a pooled or limited number of news-gathering sources (Cave 1998, Kingston 1998b, Sales 1998, Vatsikopoulos 1998, Walsh 1998).

> Even the ABC these days takes CNN, and it's very easy for a producer . . . at Gore Hill to sit there and put together a story using CNN pictures, and using the CNN script as the basis of what they do, rather than what we would have done a few years ago in having our own correspondent there. (Cave 1998)

While the bureau accounting of the story tends to be considered as good as the real thing (witness the sports reporters who write news stories based on sitting up all night and watching the satellite coverage of events such as Wimbledon), the news agenda is soon driven by the media feeding off itself in a selective and limited cycle:

> . . . You can't be treating it literally because you should know that every medium has its own tricks and its own hidden defaults. And it's going to be a selective process. I mean, how many cameras are there looking at the tennis court and how are the feeds from each of those cameras mixed? This is all highly selective, and arbitrary in its own way, even if you have highly skilled operators. And there are things that they will miss, that actually happened there on the tennis court. So you can't pretend that a camera or a set of cameras run by a director is a complete account of the particular reality. (Osmond 1998)

Journalists continue to struggle, too, with falling audiences for their news products. News organisations have attempted to combat the slide in news consumers by *dumbing down* serious stories and increasing the entertainment quotient of the news (Vatsikopoulos 1998, Richardson 1998, Walsh 1998). It is a 'desperate way in which to maintain or keep your circulation up' (Walsh 1998). The result is more organisations competing to be the same, and the loss or diminution of certain types of stories:

> Stories where you're dealing with articulate people, and people of a certain socio-economic class and so on, I don't think they suffer. It might be that the stories where you need to reflect the voices of people who aren't comfortable talking on the phone or can't be reached — that sort of thing — I mean naturally those voices are to some extent disenfranchised, I suppose. But I think the fall-off in quality is more in things like intangibles, the atmosphere of a story, the flavour that you'll get into a story. (Richardson 1998)

This combination of trends — the dial-a-quote and battery-hen approaches to news-gathering, and the CNN-isation and dumbing down of news — 'threatens the whole future of journalism' (Walsh 1998). Journalism is no longer as attractive an endeavour as it once was. Journalists with the knowledge, intelligence, and commitment necessary to successfully report business news, for example, can earn a greater income in the corporate world, while political spin doctors or PR professionals generate much greater salaries than most senior journalists of the same experience level. The degradation or devaluing of the 'eye-witness' or in-the-field reporting skills is also frustrating for those with a passion for nosing out the news. Indeed, Sales asks, would the big stories of the past twenty years have ever been told, or have got a run, in an environment in which most organisations simply re-package 'the same stuff coming off the same feed' and seldom go out on the road? 'It also means you literally don't have that eye-witness account, which is sort of what journalism is all about' (Sales 1998). Trying to access public figures in an era of media management further compounds the problems: 'it is really, really hard to break through that barrier . . . of protection that surrounds key players' (Sales 1998).

These pressures translate into what *Definition: Journalist* survey respondents labelled as some of the worst aspects of the job. They complained about not having enough time to write good stories, with longer working hours, greater demands and low pay rates. The pressure was on to produce something with a tangible sales impact rather than for the greater good. Morale was low in newsrooms, resulting from the combination of workplace pressures and the low public perception of journalists. Journalists questioned the dumbing down of news and the strengthening symbiotic relationship between journalists and PR practitioners.

Technology

Technology and technological change is a significant issue affecting the work of Australian journalists. Richardson (1998) says technology has changed 'hugely', altering the practice of journalism 'in a way that's made it more superficial in some ways'. Technological change has introduced a new layer of tools and techniques into the media, adding to the work of journalists, and not making it less complicated. In regional print newsrooms, for example, technology has reduced the layers of filters between the gathering and writing of the news and its publication — with sub-editors now devoting the majority of their time to desktop manipulation of digital text. Along the way, those sub-editing staff unable to adjust to the new digitised typesetting environment became casualties of technological change, leading to a loss of valuable experience from the sub-editing tables and the newsroom floor.

> The standard of sub-editing — for example, of text editing, and the arts of headline and caption writing — I think those skills are declining because of the technical complexity of page design software ... sub-editors become page designers ... content becomes less and less important, whereas for a traditional journalist the content is what matters, and what should be given priority. (Osmond 1998)

On-screen editing and publishing systems deify those who can use them. At the same time, the increasing computerisation and digitisation of news systems have brought deadlines forward, reducing the margin for late-breaking stories, while simultaneously reducing options when it comes to choice of content, as the demands of the technology overshadow journalistic or creative considerations.

> It's not helping us, it's hindering us ... it's all so structured. You know, it used to be free. And new technology has not made us free, it has imprisoned us. We can't fight its demands. We can't talk to it about its demands. It has its demands and we must obey. (Kingston 1998b)

Technology has made its impact on broadcast journalism as well. Satellite phones, laptop computers, the Internet, and digital audio recorders and cameras allow instantaneous field-to-newsroom contact from most parts of the world. Despite the improved access provided by such technologies, many news organisations succumb to the temptation of taking 'pre-digested news from big sources', such as CNN, because it is an easier option (Cave 1998). However, technology is being used to compensate for the lack of personnel in overseas and remote news bureaus, with fewer, but more mobile, staff using better transport systems and improved technology in the field in an attempt to provide adequate news coverage.

New technologies have made it easier to process broadcast news vision. More images can be shot and there is a faster turnaround with the ability to go live-to-air or to edit quickly and broadcast late-breaking news stories (Sales 1998). However, this speed of information is not something the news media have fully adjusted to, as evidenced by the controversy surrounding the 1999 mass murders at Columbine High School, in Littleton, Colorado, when the news media was criticised for broadcasting potentially life-threatening information while the siege was unfolding.

The Internet is an invaluable addition to the contemporary journalist's toolkit, providing a means of worldwide publication, information, and communication. While it has increased the options and sources of news available for a global audience, it has yet to be fully embraced by journalists, news organisations, and media managers. It is providing valuable additional employment for those with journalistic skills — and opening up new avenues of publication for journalistic 'wannabes' who may be doing journalistic 'work' but in a context that might bear no resemblance to that of the thinking, caring, ethical, professional reporter.

Further discussion of technology and the news media can be found later in this text.

Challenges

Another problematic aspect of attempts to define what journalists are centres on the generalist versus specialist question. Traditionally, most journalists were, as said previously, knowers-of-all things and specialists in very little. As discussed in Chapter 7 'The importance of enquiry', the claim to professionalism rested in *knowing what to ask* rather than a specific body of specialist knowledge. But this, too, is changing. At one end of the spectrum, the generalist journalist is alive and well, and multiple skills, attributes, and competencies are essential job requirements. The journalist-cum-editor-cum-sub-cum-photographer is likely to continue to be the mainstay of regional and smaller newsrooms. But the growth in specialist and niche publications and the death of mass markets is also generating increasing specialisation. Newspapers are no longer the mass media papers 'of record'. The only mass media remaining are national television networks (Cunningham et al. 1998, Walsh 1998). It is possible to broadcast to the world, but is the world interested? Apparently not (Sales 1998, Kingston 1998b, Vatsikopoulos 1998).

> My experience, in the time I've worked in news, especially in commercial TV, is it's just getting more and more parochial, like they care less and less about what's happening in the world, and more about what's happening in your street. (Sales 1998)

The trend in large metropolitan papers to create sections that reflect the interests of different groups of readers is further evidence of the failure of the newspaper as a mass medium. While the 'traditional generic form of the newspaper' has been maintained, 'it's become increasingly hollow' (Osmond 1998). Today's average newspaper appeals to a 'confederation of different constituencies' (Walsh 1998), rather than a single audience.

> Nobody reads the paper from front to back, you know that some people like to read sport, some people might read the business section, others read the Good Living section. Consequently, what you're doing with a modern newspaper these days is you're running what 10 or 15 years ago would have been 10 or 15 different newspapers ... and because you've got this functional relationship between circulation and advertising, you've got to constantly go out hunting for new constituencies to lock up and to maintain your advertising base. (Walsh 1998)

Journalists as authoritative sources — commentators, specialists, and analysts — are in demand from publications that are also endeavouring to align themselves with a clearly defined market audience. Walsh, a self-confessed 'dinosaur' in the news business, suggests if journalists want to stay in the business they:

> ... have to find an area which actually sort of really keeps your curiosity level up. It's got to be intellectually challenging to you — you've got to specialise to survive, in the end. I mean there are too many generalists out there, and I'm really talking in a way in commercial terms. Say, if you want to survive personally and maximise your outcomes, the only thing you have is your brand name — that's yourself. So you have to establish a brand name recognition in your peer group ... the most difficult area in establishing a brand name is quite frankly to be a jack-of-all-trades, because there are very few people who are expert at everything ... Also I might say on the other side, on the demand side of the equation, is that the people out there that you're writing for, or that you're selling your wares to, they're educated to a much higher level than they were in the past, and so consequently their demands for quality are much higher than they ever were in the past. (Walsh 1998)

Kingston argues there is a more fundamental and wide-ranging issue involved:

> Economic rationalism ... basically dismembers its institutional loyalty, and so you go down to the individual as the product ... so it is becoming harder and harder to maintain loyalty to the brand, and I have enormous loyalty to my brand, the *Sydney Morning Herald* brand. But that's quite old-fashioned.

Osmond says he would like to believe that journalism still has a function of a communal and democratic kind, and as a result both generalists and specialists are necessary.

> You've got to have the generalist philosophy, which says basic journalistic training can be applied to any field, regardless of the content. But then you've got to get a bit more realistic and concede that the world is very complicated, and there are highly specialised and highly technical fields all around us. You have to either know or learn to understand the particular frame of reference of any of those specialised fields. That's the point at which generalists' skills may break down, because ... it requires knowing a specialised field on its own terms and within its own discourse, being able to work within the discourse, but also to translate it into a more general kind of intelligibility. (1998)

Sales agrees that journalists' work is getting more specialised and targeting more niche markets to the extent that:

> ... if I was finishing school now, and I knew what I know now, I wouldn't do an undergraduate journalism degree. I'd do an undergraduate economics degree or science degree and have a specialty, and then do a postgraduate journalism degree. And I think it's getting to the stage where you'll only be able to get a job as a journalist if you have another specialty. But in terms of what that actually means for publications, like whether for example we'll start getting news bulletins just on business news and that sort of thing, I'm not sure. Because again, for things to rate well enough to have a life in the commercial world, they do have to try and appeal to as many people as possible. (1998)

Conclusion

So what is a contemporary Australian journalist? It is obvious that in the information age, the ability to convey information, communicate, and make knowledge accessible is in high demand. As a result, there are many different types of information workers fulfilling various communicative functions and using what traditionally have been considered journalistic skills to do so. Ultimately, the essence that distinguishes journalists from these other information brokers might be the commitment to the public good and the notion of a responsibility that goes beyond self and employer. This commitment will need to be balanced with a commitment to truthfulness, accuracy, and personal and professional integrity, and a realistic appreciation of the current dependence of journalists on the news organisations' bottom line.

Technology has provided a great leap forward and the access of people to information has never been easier. However, navigating through this deluge of information takes skill and journalists have a role to play as facilitators of this process. There is no simple definition of what a journalist is, although this text sets out to consider some of the characteristics of contemporary Australian journalists, and to situate within a holistic theoretical approach some of the processes and practices they interact with on a daily basis. Ultimately, as Walsh states, technology is 'creating an *information rich* society, (but) journalism to a large extent grew up on the fact that we were an *information poor* society, so people were prepared to pay for the scarcity factor. That's no longer the case. You've got to be a little more nimble in your thinking'.

Case study

In 1999, Sydney radio identity John Laws was the subject of several inquiries following revelations that he had signed a million-dollar-plus deal with Australian banks to promote the 'whole' story about the extremely profitable corporate giants (*Media Watch* 1999, Cameron and Lagan 1999). Laws, a nationally syndicated Australian broadcasting icon based at 2UE, denied claims the Australian Banking Association (ABA) deal was linked to perceived changes in his on-air opinions about the bank, or that there was any problem in his, and the station's, failure to publicly announce the deal. Subsequently, several other radio announcers, including Alan Jones (2UE), Howard Sattler (6PR), and Jeremy Cordeaux (5DN), acknowledged their involvement in cash sponsorship deals. According to Meade et al. (1999), Sattler had a 'long-running agreement with Optus', but not one that would 'affect his editorial independence'. While Laws acknowledged the banks had paid him a 'lot of money', he said the secret deal had not affected his editorial content or programming — and that there was no conflict of interest or any reason for concern:

> He (Laws) said it was 'rubbish' that the payment from the bankers' association raised ethical concerns. 'I'm not a journalist and I don't pretend to be a journalist. I'm an entertainer . . . here isn't a hook for ethics'. (Cameron and Lagan 1999)

Radio Station 2UE subsequently imposed limits on announcers' cash-for-comments deals and Laws and the ABA ended the agreement. Later, Laws defended himself, saying the attacks on his integrity had been savage and undeserved, and inviting his listeners to return to the 'truth' of the issue:

> For a long time now, and you know it, I have been critical of the big banks and I've let them know on this radio program and we've hit them and hit them hard. Other people have hit them harder, mind you, but you've heard me do it, and the banks believed, and they have every right to believe, that I wasn't getting the full story and because I wasn't getting the full story you weren't getting the full story either.
>
> They wanted to make their voice heard on this radio program and collectively it was agreed that that should happen. Seemed fair, didn't it? So together, the banks, their agent and the radio station devised the segment of our show we call The Full Story, which incidentally has been enjoyed by a couple of million people around Australia, but I suppose that's beside the point.
>
> But it was all pretty simple, pretty straightforward. We told you the first half of a good Australian yarn about people and places, then the banks came up with facts and figures in answer to my criticism or in a reply to your criticism and there's certainly been plenty of that, and then after that we finished the story. Of course, the banks paid for it. I mean, that's how commercial radio works. It's how I make my living, it's how I've made my living for 46 years. (*SMH* 1999)

The findings of the Australian Broadcasting Authority inquiry into the issue, handed down early in 2000, did not shed any light on whether talk-back radio falls into the category of *news and current affairs* or *entertainment*, and whether those hosting on-air talk shows should be held to the ethical standards of journalists. It did find that 2UE breached the Broadcasting Services Act five times by not properly identifying political matter, and breached the Commercial Codes of Practice 90 times (ABA 2000a). The ABA identified 60 breaches of Clause 2, which concerns the need to present news accurately and fairly, to distinguish news from comment, and to ensure relevant facts are not withheld; and 30 breaches of Clause 3, which requires that broadcasters ensure advertisements are not presented as news programs or other programs. ABA deputy chairman Gareth Grainger said after the findings were released that the Australian public had:

> an interest in ensuring that radio services that include news and current affairs programs provide fair and accurate coverage. And when

information or current affairs commentary could be affected by con-
tractual commitments that bind the licensee or presenter, the public
should be informed of such arrangements. This is the public interest
that lies at the heart of the commercial radio inquiry. (ABA 2000a)

In March 2000 the ABA finalised the imposition of two conditions on
2UE's radio commercial licence. The station is required to maintain a
regime of on-air and off-air disclosure of certain commercial agreements
between presenters and their sponsors, and to conduct a compliance program to ensure presenters and staff are aware of their obligations under
the relevant Act and codes of practice (2000b). Second, 2UE is required
to distinguish advertisements from other program matter.

Twelve months after the cash for comments controversy first hit the
headlines little else had changed. Both Mr Laws and Mr Jones continued
with their on-air programs. Some of their sponsorship deals had ended,
others continued.

DISCUSSION QUESTIONS

1 Does the public see a difference between *journalists* and political commen-
   tators/on-air radio hosts like John Laws and Alan Jones? Should programs
   and publications, which deal seriously with news and current affairs issues, be
   required to adhere to journalistic standards of ethics and practice?
2 What do you think a journalist is? What expectations and presumptions do
   you bring to news-gathering?
3 Is there a central core of activities or issues that you believe defines 'true' journalism?

Further reading

Committee of Concerned Journalists 1997, *Changing definitions of news*,
   http://www.journalism.org/lastudy.htm, 27 September 1999.
King, J. 1997, 'Principles, professionalism and philosophy', *Australian Journalism Review*,
   vol. 19, no. 1, pp. 19–33.
Poynter Institute 1998, *Competence in the Newsroom: A Poynter Conference*,
   http://www.poynter.org/comp/comp_index.htm, 24 September 1999.

Notes

1   Funded through the Queensland University of Technology 'New Researchers' Scheme.

Part 2

Making journalism work

Journalism is a commodity, a cultural activity, a public conversation, work, and much more. This section presents a range of theoretical lenses through which the discipline and work of journalism can be perceived. It traces the evolution of contemporary journalism, explores the impact of media commercialisation and commodification on news practitioners and consumers, examines the notion of journalism as the 'fourth estate', ponders the journalist's role — to 'comfort the afflicted or afflict the comfortable' — and delves into the ongoing discourse about journalism's place on the trade–profession continuum.

Are journalists fearless seekers of truth and justice or powerless purveyors of products? This section looks at the perceived and actual roles of journalists, at the conflict of interest found at the intersection of market theory and journalism theory, and at the impact of market research and cultural subjectivity on news values. It reflects on the transformation of journalism from a public conversation to an independent activity, and the impact this has had on the journalist's accountability to news consumers. And it questions the future prospects of journalism in the face of a merging of the editorial and commercial functions of news organisations.

2

Comfort or curse?

LYNETTE SHERIDAN BURNS

> News is what someone, somewhere, wants concealed. Everything else is advertising. (Jervis 1987, p. 62)

It was once said that the role of a journalist was to 'comfort the afflicted and afflict the comfortable'. Today, comfort still preoccupies news editors but the intention is to keep a carefully defined audience in its 'comfort zone', thus ensuring its continued support. Images of the world are not so much reflected as refracted to reinforce the identified consumer's pre-existing worldview with all its imbedded cultural values and prejudices. Why? In the 1970s, then metropolitan daily editor Derryn Hinch was wont to induct cadet journalists (including the author of this chapter) with the words 'You want to know if a paper's first priority is to inform, educate or entertain? It's none of these. Its first priority is to continue to exist'. As journalism is tailored to serve the market, will it provide a clearer picture of the world or only one that satisfies and reassures the dominant groups in society? As news becomes more explicitly a commodity, is it losing its value as a source of 'objective' information'? Media magnate Rupert Murdoch called it 'different papers for different publics', but where does all this leave the journalist's role as a voice for, say, social justice?

Perceptions about journalists

There is no doubt that in the late 1990s, journalists were facing the worst press they have ever had. So routinely did journalists rate with used car salesmen in surveys of public perceptions of honesty that such findings rarely sparked a reaction from either the media or the public. Michelle Grattan addressed the loss of faith with the public in her 1998 monograph, *Editorial Independence: An Outdated Concept?* She describes how the culture of commercialism feeds community cynicism about journalists:

> Journalists are under unprecedented criticism for everything ranging from alleged bias and lack of balance to inaccuracy and negativism. The readers — customers — have lost the feeling of special identification with the papers they buy. They have become goods, better or worse, no longer institutions. (1998, p. 21)

Underwood denounces today's journalists as little more than process workers manipulating information for commercial purposes:

> The reporter was once, at the most basic level, communicating with an audience. But in today's high concept journalism, where the most complex ideas must fit into a black and white box, reporters are no more than assembly line workers packaging information. (1993, p. 146)

Underwood argues that the modern emphasis on marketing a news product inevitably gives rise to a situation 'where the manufacture of a product is carefully calculated ... to hit as many of the audience's emotional hot buttons as possible ... Editors know by the mid-morning meeting what the stories will say; the reporters' task is to fill in the blanks' (Underwood 1993, p. 145).

Part of hitting the 'right buttons' is to stimulate and 'heat up' the audience while keeping within its 'comfort zone', where the world is ultimately reassuringly familiar. This means representing the society in a way that agrees with identified world views and values of the dominant audience and 'preserves the myths that a society deems precious' (Underwood 1993, p. 17). It also leads to journalism that never dares 'afflict the comfortable' and often blames the 'afflicted' for their troubles. Journalists find themselves only telling people what they think they are already thinking. Ewart (1997a) describes what respondents in her survey of journalists called 'the breakfast test', where any story that might 'put a reader off their breakfast' is deemed unsuitable for publication. In the central Queensland town where the survey was conducted, this might include any story suggesting community discrimination against the Indigenous population. The overall effect is to create a climate where journalists cease to challenge or confront the audience, unless it is over an issue where the public's position is transparently obvious, such as society's opposition to child abuse. As Underwood notes, 'this leads to fairly safe, less controversial, sociological investigative stories', but mitigates against reports on many important issues, such as 'asking how Exxon got to be bigger than five or six countries in the world' (1993, p. 19).

The role of journalists versus what journalists actually do

Never has there seemed to be a greater disparity between the traditional representations of journalists (as found in literature) and public opinion. Fictional representations (see Gaunt 1990) emphasise the independent fearlessness of a writer armed with truth, but modern descriptions cast journalists as mere cogs in the mass production of public consent. Journalists are portrayed with certain characteristics throughout Western literature, including a tendency to lonely cynicism born of too much exposure to man's inhumanity to man. The journalist, accustomed to being an outsider, fears no one and cannot be corrupted in the pursuit of truth, whatever the temptation. Always ready to drop everything in pursuit of a 'story', the journalist is always on the move, seldom pausing too long to reflect, and 'tells it like it is', whatever the personal cost. In Australia, the popular tradition of the journalist is also as a somewhat undisciplined larrikin. He (and it is a *he*, despite the statistical reality that the majority of journalists are female) has seen it all at least twice. He is a pub philosopher who likes nothing more than bringing the mighty to account, or championing the cause of society's powerless. Grattan speculates on the fate of such journalists in today's media.

> When I joined *The Age* there was a character on the paper called Jack Darmody. Darmody drank like a fish, inconveniently went AWOL, got into huge rows with the then editor Graham Perkin on the floor, in front of everyone; and loved or hated his colleagues more or less on whim. God knows what the 'human resources' experts would make of a Jack Darmody, or quite how the management consultants would react to his work practices. (1998, p. 6)

Central to the idealised view of what a journalist is, is the notion of independence and the ability to report anything in the public interest. The model journalist then, according to Underwood (1993, p. 170) is someone who resists all attempts at control. ' . . . He observes the law, rendering unto Caesar what is Caesar's, but morally is his own man. Even his boss can't touch him . . . Freedom can be preserved only if that lonely journalist is unfettered, acting on the basis of his own reason, sensitivity and commitment.' Contrast this with the views of Hirst (in Chapter 4), and McManus's (1994, p. 203) assertion that journalists are peddlers of a commodity called information that is marketed to commercial advantage, without reference to the individual's 'own reason, sensitivity and commitment'. McManus argues that journalists are not independent professionals, but employees, and therefore are not as free to follow professional norms. Unlike doctors, lawyers, architects and others, journalists are not paid by those who consume their services. Their practice is neither licensed nor disciplined by their peers, nor are they or their workplaces accredited as professional. McManus argues that the crucial difference is that professionals serve clients — acting on their own interpretation of the client's best interest — while employees serve the market, accepting the customer's interpretation of what is best. The most important customer — and in journalism, it is the advertiser — is always right. McManus argues that the commodification of news as a product for sale to advertisers means that quality is measured by profit — advertising revenue generated.

Koch (1990) also found that journalists, rather than communicating independently with an audience, work for companies whose primary purpose is to make profit for the company owners. The key stakeholders in the company's profit-seeking endeavours are other corporations who seek to increase their own profits by selling products to people who buy 'news'. This, more than anything, weakens the editorial independence of journalists to make 'unfettered' news judgments.

> A reporter or editor in a profit-maximising media firm who subordinates market standards to those of journalism may be tolerated about as long as a counter clerk at McDonald's who refuses to sell fried food. (Koch 1990, p. 23)

In practice, the confrontation is played out in countless ways. In country newsrooms it might be arguments over 'advertorials' — paid advertisements disguised as news stories or community service announcements. It is also found in the cross-promotion of media interests — the magazine story that happens to be front-page news on the day the magazine hits the stands. And it is definitely present when the editor discreetly pulls a story about alcohol abuse from a page containing liquor advertisements. As journalist and author Craig McGregor recalls in *Soundtrack for the Eighties*:

> When I was a cadet reporter on the *Sydney Morning Herald*, we were lectured on the virtues of objectivity, detachment and lack of bias (unless you were writing about a subject in which your proprietor was involved, in which case you were expected to show a certain pragmatic common sense). (1983, p. 135)

McManus, Koch and others claim that the move over the past 10 years to market-driven journalism has fundamentally changed the daily role of journalists in making the news. Whereas once a reporter investigated and then interpreted an event, it is argued that these days facts are selected in advance to meet a predetermined interpretation of the information. Underwood's 1993 study supports this view, finding that newspaper 'design and packaging needs' favour predictable stories that reduce journalists to the roles of researchers (1993, p. 163).

Underwood (1993, p. 142) found that while news proprietors were careful to maintain the rhetoric of journalistic independence, actual practice was rather more compromised by commercial reality. He concluded: 'news workers soon learn by "osmosis" the boundaries of their freedom and the rewards of performing their tasks in a routine manner'. Certain large advertisers are not scrutinised too closely, certain sources are preferred over others. A journalist who receives a list of advertisers along with the brief to write a feature about trends in interior design does not have to be told who to call for interviews. Underwood argues that journalists can, in theory, cover almost anything they wish, but the reality is that they simply follow routines.

In a sense, the dual rhetorics of commercial imperative and journalistic ideal-ism combine to support a culture of rationalisation that ultimately 'exonerates' journalists who succumb to the market. For example, a news editor who tailors the evening bulletin to fit a pattern of 'hard' and 'soft' news that has been unchanged for thirty years hotly denies that the news is 'constructed' or manipu-lated to reflect a certain world view. But he is happy to acknowledge his preoccu-pation with the audience's 'comfort zone' and shares his Queensland colleague's concern about the consumer's digestion. 'You don't want to be putting the view-ers off their dinners,' he tells young journalists. Altschull describes how some journalists reconcile the contrast between what they might do and what they most often do by assigning the first with the romantic qualities of a heroic but impossible dream:

> Nothing gratifies the individual journalist more than a successful challenge to power, even as Don Quixote rejoiced in tilting at windmills. There is built into journalism the possibility of inducing change and of helping to create a world that is more just and peaceful; it is this possibility that has fired and continues to fire the imaginations of journalists everywhere on earth. Political and especially eco-nomic reality, however, severely circumscribes these possibilities. (1984, p. 273)

White takes a broader view of the role of journalists. While acknowledging the important role of the media as a political watchdog in Western countries, she hints that idealised images of journalists telling people what they need to know, whatever the consequences, are unrealistic.

> We have to remember that journalism, good or bad, is not only one thing. And in a sense, we've been looking at a particular view of what journalism is and what it should do ... There is another thread, and it has always been with us ... We keep saying 'Oh newspapers are doing this now' or 'Radio's doing this now' but there has always been a thread of entertainment. (White 1998)

Journalists as entertainers

The shameless pursuit of an identified market is hardly new in journalism. As Grattan (1998) puts it: 'When we talk about commercialisation, we must of course recognise that newspapers have always mostly existed to make a profit. No profit, no paper except in a tiny minority of papers'. In fact, it may be argued that the commercial imperative that seems so at odds with the aspirations of a free press is at the very core of the media's independence from government con-trol, thus securing its role as a social watchdog. Biographer Hugh Cudlipp credits Alfred Harmsworth, later Lord Northcliffe, with creating feature journalism

Proponents of market theory argue that the market protects itself against exploitation and that it is intrinsically democratic because it is based on the free choices of the buyers and sellers. This defence was used in 1995 when *A Current Affair* producers pointed to sky-high ratings when called to account for a live-to-air interview with two child hostages. Just as the unrestrained market brings consumers better computers and cars at lower prices, market theory promises more interesting news that responds to the audience's needs and wants, or perishes in the competition. Northcliffe, who created the 'independent' press by funding his newspapers with advertisements, was also the first to foresee conflicts of interest with the aspirations of journalism when he said:

> It is not pleasant to think that . . . newspapers are now for the first time in their history entirely subordinate to advertisers. I see no way out of this impasse, other than by maintaining a great daily net sale and thus keeping the whip hand of the advertiser. (Cudlipp 1980, p. 82)

What Northcliffe had, and modern proprietors lack, was a captive mass market with scant other opportunities for cheap daily entertainment. Today the mass market is diverse and demanding, and the clamour of popular media competing for its attention is bigger than ever in history. Underwood (1993, p. 3) proposes that the application of market theory to the management of media is symptomatic of an historical trend toward commodification — the creation of a monetary price and market for virtually every aspect of human existence. This, he argues, inevitably creates 'the tension between representing reality as accurately as humans can, and misrepresenting it in favour of those who control the production process'.

Effect of the market on journalists

The most obvious effect of commodification of audiences on the role of journalists is that increasing reliance on market research has diminished the traditional role of 'professional' journalists as arbiters of which news and events are newsworthy. Underwood found that ' . . . managers are telling journalists to let the public decide what becomes news by paying attention to what kinds of reports are most highly valued in the marketplace.' Grattan agrees that journalists are losing the 'whip hand' described by Northcliffe:

> The contextual background is the continued blurring of the line between information and entertainment in the media, and the newspapers' battle to hold their market against long-term decline in circulation. The struggle to maintain the market has led to increased uncertainty within newspapers about what their role is and should be in the modern media kaleidoscope. (1998, p. 3)

This anxiety about holding on to a shrinking audience has led to what Underwood (1993), McManus (1994) and others describe as 'market-driven journalism', as opposed to *traditional* journalism which provides:

> ... information about current issues and events designed to provide the greatest increase in understanding for the largest number of citizens that the resources of the media firm permit. Such content serves the public good. By contrast, market journalism is information about current issues and events designed to serve the profit-maximising interest of the firm, often, but not always, at the expense of the public's need to understand its environment. (Underwood 1993, p. 184)

McManus describes the way in which market-driven journalism infiltrates the news selection process.

> From a market perspective, broadcasters and to a lesser extent newspapers are better off with more generalised stories such as consumer-oriented features and human interest pieces that arouse emotional response, even if the result is news that fails to help consumers make sense of current events. (1994, p. 89)

Profit-oriented modern media managers are nothing new (Gaunt 1990, p. 146). What is new is that technical innovations introduced by profit-conscious media management, such as networking of resources and consolidation of mastheads, seem inevitably to be producing greater homogeneity of news content. Or, as Silk (1991) puts it: 'Corporate executives never find it easy to acknowledge that the public interest may not be identical to their company's ... what could be more in the public interest than for publishers to do everything in their power to protect newspapers' profitability?'

Underwood (1993, p. 144) found that commodification fundamentally changes the role of journalists, so that they are less likely to delve into and behind stories, and more likely to follow routines and proformas. Presentation, planning, packaging and promotion become more important than content, and even articles promoted as in-depth or investigative scarcely skim the surface of issues and events, contributing little to public knowledge.

The dominance of the market-driven need for audiences to be 'comfortable' with news judgment does not need to be stated explicitly in newsrooms. As Underwood discovered

> ... Better to let the staff know, in informal ways or through the marketing structure of the news coverage, that it is safer simply to write about the news in ways that are pleasing to readers — or to advertisers or powerful people in the community or the publisher, to be more exact ... In this market-driven world of easy-to-digest events, news increasingly becomes almost a parody of the term. News is

no longer something 'new' but instead becomes a commodity that can be passed off as something new or original. (1993, p. 142)

Market-driven journalism places as much emphasis on presentation as it does on content, and predictability is favoured over flexibility to ensure advertisers get a reliable product. Grattan is one who sees it as a victory of style over substance:

> Most papers are increasingly design-driven. Design is used to try and attract readers, especially the young and those who want their newspapers to look like magazines. It has become another tyranny on newspapers. The imperative of design, sometimes in the hands of non-journalists, has complicated their construction and made deadlines more important than flexibility ... the stories have become shorter. They are often lacking in detail and journalists often lacking in expertise, just when it can be argued that many of the people who buy newspapers are likely to want more of both. (1998, p. 3)

McManus (1994, p. 89) notes that journalism is seldom cost-effective because it can be time-consuming and expensive and offers a return that is hard to quantify: 'If a station seeks to maximise profit, less care may be taken with information. And just as the interesting topic may replace the merely important, the interesting source and quote may replace the informative source and quote.' Another way in which the 'realities' of journalism impact on the daily lives of journalists is their ability to give the degree of attention to their reporting that they professionally consider necessary. The reality is that fewer staff and earlier production deadlines mean that journalists are less independent in their research than ever before. As journalist and educator Sally A. White told the ABC's *Media Report* in March 1998:

> I think when we're discussing what journalists are and what they do, we forget their general information role. I think one of the problems ... is the fairly recent, last 20 years or so, professionalisation of information. It's information management, if you like, which journalists and management, newspaper or media management, are complicit in, in that it makes it easy for them to get what they want.

Paletz and Entman (1982) reached the same conclusion — that journalists work in bureaucratic organisations characterised by hierarchy, division of labour, and routinisation of working procedures. They found that where the primary objective was efficiency in the gathering, describing, and transmitting of news, the result was reliance on official sources and homogeneity of reporting. Warren (1995) reported that 80 per cent of stories in the Australian media were generated by publicity releases provided to media outlets. McManus offers a simple explanation.

... It is less costly to rely on other news providers such as wire services and on press agents to learn of community events and issues than to hire adequate staff to infiltrate the community. Such passive discovery, however, creates potential for manipulation of the public agenda by sources powerful enough to hire press agents and manufacture events. (1994, p. 88)

Reliance on news sources — and this extends to the broadcast media in the form of radio 'grabs' and video news releases — can also be manipulated to affect the news agenda in a way journalists seem unable, or unwilling, to resist. Newsroom influences, such as deadlines, space, and staffing, place heavy constraints on those journalists responsible for news selection. As a result, journalists tend to take the line of least resistance and select those news items that are the easiest to find and edit.

The routine use of the same information by journalists is another way in which news is homogenised — the same language appears across a variety of news media to describe events a certain way. Or, as expatriate Australian journalist John Pilger noted during an appearance on ABC-TV's *Media Watch* (7 September 1998) during the acrimonious national wharves dispute: 'What does productivity on the wharves mean? It means more profit for Corrigan and company (the employer).' It is here, in the constant representation of the 'taken-for-granted world' that individual journalists exercise the greatest individual power to define what a journalist is.

Journalists and world view

In the induction and training of journalists in newsrooms, novices are exhorted from the beginning to always keep sight of the audience. Young journalists are encouraged to hone their developing 'news sense' by testing the value of a news angle against the interests of a mythical citizen. 'Imagine you're talking to Mrs Smith down the street,' the news editor advises, 'and write the story from the perspective of what she would be most interested in.' In the newsroom tradition, the audience is made up of people much like the journalists themselves. Editors claim to 'know' their readers' tastes, because they are the same as the editor's own. Or, as a metropolitan editor told the afternoon news conference one day in 1995 after the newspaper had run a series on homelessness: 'I don't want any more losers in the paper. Our readers aren't losers.' The effect of this culturally subjective approach is found in what does not get into the media as much as it is in what does go in. For example, Western societies are generally portrayed as white, Christian, nuclear families bound by marriage, despite years of statistical evidence to the contrary. Aboriginal and Asian faces do not figure in common representations of Australian society, and Jewish, Islamic and Asian religious traditions do not attract the same media attention as Christian ones, flying in the face of the demographic make-up and devotional habits of the population.

Stuart Hall (1992) uses the term hegemony to describe the way the media reinforces, more than reflects, the leading-class ideology. Koch describes the ubiquitous nature of news as 'a window on the world':

> ... but like any frame that delineates the world, the news frame may be considered problematic. The view through the window depends upon whether the window is large or small, has many panes or few, whether the glass is opaque or clear. (1990, p. 20)

Hall denounces the 'window on the world' analogy for the media's function. Rather, he argues, the real role of the media is 'production of consent' rather than 'reflection of consensus'. His central position is that journalists never deliver a single meaning but a 'plurality of meanings, in which one is preferred and offered, over others, as the most appropriate' (McQuail 1994, p. 367). In such a scenario, the media plays a crucial role in whether a strike on the wharves is represented as a defence of workers' rights or a minority group holding the public to ransom. The position from which the journalist observes the 'facts' unfold determines the presentation of the 'truth'. This truth is, in turn, a calculated reinforcement of the position thought to be held by the audience. As Schattschneider (1960) points out: 'The definition of the alternatives is the supreme instrument of power.' Underwood agrees that journalists are not impartial observers.

The effect of cultural hegemony on the daily work of journalists is in the self-censorship it engenders in reporting. Stories are written from only one, often narrow, point of view. Alternative outlooks are ignored or dismissed. Those who challenge or confront the preferred image of society are marginalised or not heard. But Hall makes it clear that Western journalists are not *controlled* in the conventional sense. Instead, as McQuail (1994, p. 367) explains: 'just as native speakers may not understand the syntax or grammar of their language, so reporters and commentators don't recognise their bias toward the status quo'.

This bias is often reflected in the language of journalism discourses. For example, a journalist who consciously seeks to avoid racism in his or her reporting may have no problem using, and thereby applying a culturally specific meaning to a phrase such as 'Aboriginal crime' to refer to a concrete range of activities. In the same way, a foreign correspondent chooses to describe combatants in a foreign war as 'anti-government rebels' or 'freedom fighters' in accordance with the dominant ideology. It is in the faintly patronising tone of the voice-over of an ABC-TV report on a music festival described in pale comparison to the 1960s Woodstock. It is the difference between 'hooligans congregating' and 'citizens gathering' at a local park. It is the TV story on health problems among metropolitan Aborigines that is accompanied by images of dirty children in a remote bush camp.

Most often, though, the influence of cultural hegemony is evidenced in the stories that are not reported, or in stereotypical or deviant representations of groups outside the dominant ideology. For example, the 1991 *Royal Commission into Aboriginal Deaths in Custody* found that Aboriginal people continued to be portrayed in the media as 'problems' with an emphasis in reporting on health and crime problems and a lack of attention paid to community and corporate achievements. The Commissioner found that the consistent misrepresentation reinforced misconceptions and inaccuracies about the situation facing Aboriginal people, despite the presentation of contradictory facts.

Cohen observed that the media's greatest power was not in telling people what to think, but what to think about:

> ... the world will look different to different people, depending on the map that is drawn for them by writers, editors and publishers of the paper they read. (1963, p. 13)

Hall and others also argue that journalists always give some 'spin', conscious or otherwise, to the news of the day, but acknowledge that journalists retain some control in this process. Their activities are not determined by hegemonic influences. In fact, the 'reality' of any journalist's working life is most likely to be shaped by the images held by the individual and the organisations for which they work. On an individual level, the role and image of the journalist is affected by the details of their own experience — their training; the size, type and culture of organisation(s) worked for; editorial pressures; and personal idiosyncrasies. Journalists' view of themselves 'as disseminators, interpreters, investigators or adversaries' depends on 'the society they live in, the image of the press in general, and the image of the organisation in which they work' (Gaunt 1990). Hall argues that because hegemony is consented to, it is never guaranteed. It may be argued that the current loss of faith between media and audiences reflects 'withdrawal of consent'.

Conclusion

So what is a journalist? A fearless seeker of truth and justice or a powerless purveyor of products? Gaunt (1990, p. 142) ponders the dilemma facing journalists who aspire to live up to the definition of journalism as 'not just another business' (Schultz 1994). Is the delicate balance between legitimate business objectives of the media and their duty to society disappearing? If Northcliffe's 'whip hand' has passed to commercial interests, can independent editorial opinion survive? Has profit become the gatekeeper in the news selection process?

Gaunt, Hall, Koch, and others suggest that any understanding of the world can only be impoverished by the imposition, however willing, of one 'global' media world-view that reflects the interests and aspirations of a minority of the Western world. The question is what, if anything, individual journalists can do to regain the community high-ground, to reassert the profession as a voice for the powerless in society. The answer lies in lifelong activities of those who claim the title journalist. Every individual journalist at some point chooses the words they use to describe the world. Each is equally empowered to be part of the problem or part of the solution. Their power lies in what Chomsky called 'manufacture of dissent' (Cronau 1995, p. 24), the bringing to public attention of images and facts that have the potential to 'afflict' those otherwise untouched by them.

An example of this can be found in the 1997/98 reporting of *Bringing Them Home, the report of the National Inquiry into the Separation of Aboriginal and Torres Strait Islander Children from their Families*, which became commonly known as the Stolen Generation report. Prior media experience dictated that the coverage of this report would be marginalised due to the commonly held belief that 'black faces turn away white readers' (Smythe 1998, p. i). Added to this was the political sensitivity of the issue, with the Prime Minister and others seeking to question the validity of the report through subtle manipulation of the language of the debate, such as the persistent use of the term 'so-called' to describe the Stolen Generation. A study by Mervyn Smythe and Associates found that the media coverage was almost opposite to that predicted. As well, the language used by individual journalists in their reports was significant to the overall thrust of the coverage. The study — which looked at coverage in ten daily newspapers, metropolitan radio services, and metropolitan TV services — found:

> There is a spectrum of words and phrases which can be used to differentiate between belief and scepticism, between acceptance and rejection of the material that is being reported. In the reporting of the Stolen Children report, words such as 'claims' or 'alleged', which preserve a sceptical distance from the material, are used quite rarely. Much more frequent are words such as 'reveals', 'exposes', 'uncovers' among the common and more neutral words such as 'said', 'commented' etc. ... Further, given that there is a body of opinion that the children were 'rescued' or 'taken for their own good', the words used to describe the separation policy reflect the extent to which that view has been adopted by the writers/editors. Overwhelmingly, the words used to describe the policy and its results have been unfavourable, and often damning. (1998, p. v)

The Smythe report concludes that, against the predicted trends, the coverage of the Stolen Generation sought to 'afflict' the 'comfortable' members of white Australian society who previously chose to doubt the reality of institutionalised abuse of indigenous people. The effect was powerful. It was achieved by careful use of language to challenge, rather than reinforce, the political rhetoric being espoused on the issue at the time.

In the same way, individual journalists have the power to resist the 'easy' story that is fed to them by obliging media relations personnel. Each has the power to choose a different interviewee, to seek another point of view before writing. Each has the power to choose their own words to describe events, rather than duplicate what is provided to them in a media release. And many journalists, well aware of the constraints under which they work, find ways to write stories they can be proud of. In most media organisations, reporters have some say in stories they cover. Today's journalists, with their editors or despite them, must find ways to fit challenging ideas into conservative news agendas. With determination and an eye for a good angle, the newsroom culture can work to a journalist's advantage. The crucial factor is the individual's willingness to accept responsibility for the kind of journalism they write, and therefore the kind of journalist they are. As Underwood concludes:

> In an era when the bottom line limits the vision of so many news room managers, it's more important than ever for reporters to remember that they shouldn't define their job only the way their bosses define it for them. (1993, p. 170)

In the final analysis, whether a journalist or editor is compromised or challenged by the competing commercial and social obligations of the craft remains in the control of the individual. Good journalism will disappear if journalists give up and declare themselves what Epstein (1974) called 'agents for others'. Journalists who seek to absolve themselves of social accountability by declaring themselves 'in the business of selling news' find a strident and long-established culture of rationalisation ready to comfort those fleetingly afflicted with conscience about what they *do*. Those who take up the challenge to explore the world, tell all, and perhaps even make some sense of what they learn, will find they too have the power to profoundly affect what they *do* and therefore what they *are*.

Case study: the writer, the actor and the musician

A PARABLE FROM THE REAL WORLD

Once there were three school friends who had very different aspirations.

One dreamed of being a writer, someone whose prose shed light on the human condition. Her friend thought she might be an actor, touch an audience and live a thousand different lives. And the third, well, he just wanted to play bass guitar, immerse himself in the world, maybe write some songs.

When the friends reached the end of high school, each set off to follow the dream. The writer won a journalism cadetship with a major Sydney newspaper; the actor almost went to NIDA (the National Institute for Dramatic Art), but decided to study archaeology instead; and the musician bought a one-way ticket and set off to see the world.

Fast forward roughly 10 years, and the writer is a senior journalist on her third metropolitan daily newspaper and has started doing a journalism degree part-time. The actor has returned from archaeological digs in Jordan and joined SBS-TV, where she has gone from a job in the library into a job as a newsreader. Within a year, she is reading the prime-time news bulletin on commercial TV. The musician, meanwhile, has finally returned from his travels, and taken a job on *The Land*, an agricultural newspaper, where he edits stories about stock prices and sheep dip.

Fast forward another 10 years, and the writer is teaching journalism in a university and 'keeps her hand in' with a bit of part-time editing. The actor has left a career in TV science journalism, and now, among other things, freelances as a documentary scriptwriter and narrates an internationally popular children's television show. And the musician? He's an ABC-TV foreign correspondent reporting from one of the world's hot spots.

How did that happen? Are they all journalists? Only one did a cadetship and was trained as a journalist. Is anyone who earns money from reporting a journalist? Is a person who reads a script as much of a journalist as someone who does his or her own research? And if they were all journalists, are they still, given that the former cadet now teaches? And what of the actor — was she a journalist or a talking head? Is the musician the only real journalist because he's a foreign correspondent? Is it just coincidence that he finds no shortage of guitar players among his peers? Is experience as a foreign correspondent equivalent to, or greater than, a university qualification in journalism?

Perhaps the answer lies in the convergence of their lives rather than the differences. What they had in common, all along, was a desire to engage the world, to touch people. The actor, in her incarnation as an archaeologist, was digging up information about people's lives and sharing it. The musician, in his music, travels, and now journalism, also seeks to understand the world a little better. And the writer is still reporting what she's found as she seeks to provide some insight into the challenges of journalism to new groups of students.

So perhaps that's what a journalist is, stripped of the commercial pressures and the lofty aspirations. A journalist is someone who wants to know,

COMFORT OR CURSE? 39

who believes there are answers, and wants to find them. All journalists seek in some way to touch an audience, to make some sense of what they discover in the world, and share the news.

DISCUSSION QUESTIONS

Draw some examples of reporting from your local media — print, radio, and TV:

1 Why was each story published/broadcast?
2 Consider the language used in the story. What can you tell about the intended audience from the way the story is put together?
3 Consider where the stories came from. Are they sourced to a company or organisation?
4 Is there any form of advertising in the story? Is it disguised?
5 Consider the same event as covered by different news media. What are the similarities and differences in the coverage?

Further reading

Underwood, D. 1993, *When MBAs Rule the Newsroom: How Markets and Managers are Shaping Today's Media*, Columbia University Press, New York.

Adam, G. Stuart. 1993, *Notes Towards a Definition of Journalism: Understanding an Old Craft as an Art Form*, The Poynter Institute for Media Studies, St Petersburg, Florida.

Grattan M, 1998, *Editorial Independence: An Outdated Concept?*, Australian Journalism Monographs, no. 1, Department of Journalism, University of Queensland.

3

A return to practice: reclaiming journalism as public conversation

MICHAEL MEADOWS

The Western form of modern journalism emerged around the turn of the century, coming out of public-sphere activities where disparate members of the emerging entity called 'the public' met to discuss politics, sport, gossip — in other words, experiences of the everyday. Typically, people tended to gather in public houses like pubs and cafes, and these became important meeting places of ideas — and sites from which newspapers reporting public conversations emerged. Journalism of the day reported directly on this public-sphere activity and, because of the limited nature of what then constituted 'the public', could be held directly accountable by readers. In this way, modern journalism began as a cultural practice that was both *of* and *for* the public. Although this public sphere activity was influenced, in varying degrees, by the self-interest of businesses like newspapers (McManus 1994, p. 200) and the restrictions imposed by race, class and gender, it nevertheless was crucial to the historical formation of 'the public' (Carey 1997a, p. 236).

With the expansion of communication and transport technologies, and the onset of the 'post-modern' age of information technology, journalism has been transformed into something else. The rise of journalism as an independent professional endeavour has disrupted its traditional links with the public. It is now almost indistinguishable from other forms of writing, such as fiction and public relations (Carey 1997c, p. 329). This is why Turner (1996) can accurately describe television current affairs reporting in the 1990s as 'post-journalism'. The transformation of journalism from a public to an independent activity has effectively displaced the lines of accountability that traditionally linked journalists with their readers, and later, their listeners and viewers. As Carey (1997a, p. 238) reminds us, public spaces were places where public opinion was formed, and the press that emerged at this time 'reflected and animated public conversation'. In contrast, modern journalism *forms* public opinion rather than reports on it.

Carey (1997b, pp. 129–33) suggests important elements that influenced the movement of journalism away from its earlier, publicly accountable form — the emergence of national media, the growth of minority or alternative media, and the creation of the professional communicator. Professional communicators — like reporters, editors, artists, and public relations practitioners — were traditionally different from other communicators like writers, novelists, and scholars because the former dealt with messages that were not necessarily related to their own thoughts and perceptions (Carey 1997b, pp. 132–3). It is this important element that set them apart. But these distinguishing features have begun to disappear in the age of information technology. As it becomes more difficult to distinguish between journalism organisations and those that produce entertainment, so forms of writing — once distinguishable — have become blurred. As Carey suggests (1997c, p. 329), 'The membrane separating journalism and the novel and short story, fact and fiction, has been pierced, and these forms and many others flow into one another'.

Along with the emergence of the so-called information society, the practice of journalism was caught up in the rise of middle-class professionalism — with journalists, alongside doctors, lawyers, and social workers, forming national groupings (Carey 1997a, p. 242) (see Hirst, Chapter 4).

The emergence of modern journalism practice as 'independent' was a natural outcome of this historical process. It developed from the earlier idea of media institutions being seen as 'the fourth estate' — independent of the other three 'estates' of the judiciary, executive government, and parliament. But what of the public? In pursuing fourth-estate status, the media have claimed for themselves the position of adversary — a watchdog — relying on notions such as objectivity and professionalism to support this stance. In the process, the public has been excluded and this is reflected in continuing popular disdain of the media and journalism. Schultz (1998, p. 29) acknowledges the 'remarkable exercise in political lobbying and marketing' pursued by the press in assuming the authority of the fourth estate. And she suggests this as 'an abject lesson for other industries seeking to reinvent themselves as institutions'. This may be an abject lesson more in the sense of how to alienate 'the public' than in building the 'more meaningful, reflective alliances' needed for journalism to reclaim the public's interest (Schultz 1998, p. 238).

Journalism should be seen as part of the broader process of making culture — or 'imagining', to use Benedict Anderson's term. If journalism is viewed as a cultural practice, it enables us to think about how it might be reformed so that it may again be both *of* and *for* the public.

Objectivity emerged at this time as a central pillar of journalists' claim to independence. It became 'a defensive measure, an attempt to secure by quasi-scientific means a method for recording the world independent of the political and social forces that were shaping it' (Carey 1997a, p. 245). Allied with objectivity was the emergence of journalism as a profession. Despite the debate over this notion, professionalism is an enduring idea to which Carey has applied this insightful critique:

> ... the great danger in modern journalism is one of a professional orientation to an audience: the belief, usually implicit, that the audience is there to be informed, to be educated, to be filled with the vital information and knowledge whose nature, production and control rests with a professional class. The knowledge is defined, identified, presented based upon canons of professional expertise over which the audience exercises no real judgment or control. And in this new client–professional relationship that emerges the same structures of dependency are developed that typify the relations of doctors, lawyers and social workers to their clients. (1980, p. 6)

Zelizer (1992) suggests that journalists have used critical incidents such as the Kennedy assassination and the Gulf War to legitimise their claims to professionalism and to counter questions around the credibility of television news. She asserts that journalists use critical events as a way of legitimising their practices and that this is *a* major — perhaps *the* major — driving force. As a result of their approach to reporting the 1991 Gulf War, journalists 'adapted to altered boundaries of journalistic practice in two ways: imitation and surrender' (Zelizer 1992, p. 76). While this and other critiques of modern journalism and its adoption of notions such as the fourth estate, objectivity, and professionalism is lucid and savage, it nevertheless remains the 'bulwark of liberty' in our time — and no-one has yet come up with something better (Carey 1997a, p. 250). Rather than 'reviving' the fourth estate, as Schultz suggests, perhaps it needs to be re-examined in terms of how it has shaped modern journalism. One productive way of doing this might be to consider journalism as a cultural practice and the media as a cultural resource.

The media as a cultural resource

Antonio Gramsci, writing from his own experiences as a journalist in Italy in the early part of the twentieth century, identifies the importance of the media — 'publishing houses, political newspapers, periodicals of every kind (1988a, p. 380)' — describing them as the 'most dynamic part' of the ideological structure of society. Ideology, in this sense, refers to the ideas and assumptions about society and its practices that tend to predominate at a particular time. The way in which social policy in Australia has tended to be couched in economic terms over the past ten years is an example of this. It is almost impossible now to talk of social justice without having to argue it in the language of the corporations. Why shouldn't 'users' pay for social services? This, of course, assumes that all users of social services are in a position to pay.

Despite the powerful role played by the media in legitimating ideas and assumptions — that the economic frames all social activity — Gramsci acknowledges that the media take their place alongside other cultural institutions which influence public opinion — libraries, schools, associations, clubs, trade unions, churches, parliament, and the courts (Gramsci 1988a, pp. 380–1). The media and journalism are part of the array of institutions and practices that form culture. This approach to analysing the role of media and journalism forms the basis of this chapter's argument.

Gramsci saw journalism as a cultural practice that could act to 'draw out and elaborate' elements of critical awareness and 'good sense'. He defines 'good sense' as the best ideas of an era or populace. He argued that 'good sense' is already present in people's 'common sense' — the widely held ideas and assumptions that are seen as 'natural' or 'immutable' and generally taken for granted. 'Common sense', Gramsci argued, cannot be challenged because the 'facts' are considered 'obvious' (Gramsci 1988a, p. 323; Culhane 1998, p. 25). The term 'common sense' has been defined in terms of ideology — effectively, a set of commonly held ideas and assumptions, which enable particular ideas to predominate (Hall 1981; 1982; 1983a). It was in his *Cultural Writings* that Gramsci developed these ideas in relation to journalism.

In adopting this framework, Gramsci proposed an ideal kind of journalism — 'integral journalism' — that aims not only to satisfy all the needs of its public, but also to create and develop these needs, to arouse the public and to 'progressively enlarge it' (Gramsci 1988a, p. 383; Holub 1992). This is journalism practice that engages its audience in an activist, democratic sense — looking at inspiring a readership, 'to make it think concretely, to transform it and homogenise it through a process of organic development that can lead it [the readership] from simple common sense to coherent and systematic thought' — or 'good sense' (Gramsci 1988a, p. 385). This resonates with Carey's notion of journalism as 'a public conversation' and, in turn, with Jay Rosen's idea of public, civic, or community journalism. Gramsci's 'integral journalism' suggests opportunities to critically challenge some of the 'common sense' notions of news values that seem influenced more by economic imperatives than reflecting public concerns. It is by considering journalism as a cultural practice that we can examine, and re-examine, its cultural role. Gramsci was interested in the 'tactical orientation and usages' of cultural activities like journalism and ways they 'present themselves for identification and target audiences' (Mercer 1989, p. 10).

This approach offers concrete strategies for approaching the cultural practice of 'doing' or 'making' journalism. If journalism is a cultural practice and media organisations are cultural resources, Gramsci's idea of hegemony (intellectual and moral leadership) equates to one of 'cultural resource management' (Mercer 1989, p. 9). Journalism, then, is a cultural practice that plays a crucial role in the process of consensus formation or, as Mercer (1989, p. 9) defines it, 'cultural resource management'. Focusing on journalism in this way allows a more effective analysis of its role in the formation of culture.

Cultural forms, like the media, and cultural practices, like journalism, continue to make a significant contribution to the way in which we 'imagine' ourselves and our communities. Applying the concept of the nation as 'an imagined community', Anderson argued:

> It [the nation] is *imagined* because the members of even the smallest nation will never know most of their fellow-members, meet them, or even hear of them, yet in the minds of each lives the image of their communion. (1984, p. 15)

Anderson continues with this theme, explaining that:

> ... the convergence of capitalism and print technology on the fatal diversity of human language created the possibility of a new form of imagined community, which in its basic morphology set the stage for the modern nation. (1984, p. 49)

Journalists and journalism played (and continue to play) a crucial role in this process of 'imagining' through the cultural form of print technology, superseded in the twentieth century by broadcasting and now, information technology (Anderson 1984, p. 49). As Gramsci (1971) suggests and Hall (1983a) elaborates, the process of winning consent for particular ideas and assumptions — hegemony — is a constant struggle over meaning. This dynamic process means there is rarely ever a single meaning — or truth — that might be conveyed to 'the public' through a news story (as discussed in Chapter 6, which considers the post-modern debate on the notion of truth). There will inevitably be a range of interpretations of a story that, through culture-forming activities such as conversation and access to other sources, is eventually shaped into meaning. While journalists argue that they merely reflect society, over time, this process can, and does, create inaccurate images that are remarkably durable. For example, the role of the twentieth-century press has been paramount in constructing images of Indigenous populations in Australia and North America — they have been patronised, romanticised, stereotyped, and ignored by most of mainstream society (Meadows 1995, Weston 1996). Weston concludes:

> To be sure, journalism has reflected the images and stereotypes prevalent in the popular culture. But it has done more. The very conventions and practices of journalism have worked to reinforce that popular — and often inaccurate — imagery. (1996, p. 163)

So journalism might be theorised as a cultural practice that 'makes sense' of existence (Mercer 1989). Journalism plays a pivotal role in the strategic management of cultural goods, like the media, in the process of the formation of the 'imagination' and thus, consensus and culture.

Journalism as a cultural practice

Fundamental to this argument is the notion of journalism as a cultural practice that effectively manages the flow of information and ideas in society. While journalism does not work alone in the 'imagining' process, it plays a dominant role. Hackett and Zhao (1998, p. 224) usefully argue that journalism should be seen as 'a form of public communication for sustainable democracy'. Using a Foucauldian framework, they approach journalism as a 'discursive regime' — a collection of statements and ideas — in which it is possible to define 'how power is imbricated with knowledge ... indirectly and internally through the criteria and practices that govern the production of statements'. They identify a set of practices with which to analyse journalism but suggest that there is no single monolithic model — different purposes and constituencies need different types of journalism (Hackett and Zhao 1998, p. 233). But they conclude that there are important common practices that are required to 'make journalism' within the shifting notion of the public sphere:

> Journalists have a common interest with labour, the alternative media, non-governmental organisations, and critical social movements in revitalising a culture of publicness, in placing the issue of media structure on the political agenda, in supporting public policy that would counterbalance the negative impacts of unimpeded market logic on communication, and, above all, in developing new institutional bases for journalism orientated towards the public interest. (1998, p. 236)

In her recent work with the alternative press in Australia, Forde (1997, 1998) argues that journalism in that sector represents a crucial activity that extends contemporary ideas of the public sphere and democracy. Carey stresses the necessity of linking the principles of journalism with those of the democratic process:

> ...journalism naturally belongs with the political theory which nurtures an understanding of democratic life and institutions; with literature from which it derives a heightened awareness of language and expression and an understanding of narrative form; from history which forms the underlying stratum of its consciousness; and from art which enriches its capacity to imagine the unity of the visual and verbal world. (1993a, p. v)

Adam extends this argument, taking thinking about journalism into the realm of the imagination. He suggests that journalism embraces and gives a place to notions of commentary, judgment and criticism:

> Journalism is a form of expression that is an invention. It is a creation — a product of the Imagination — in both an individual and a cultural sense. It is a form of expression in which the imaginative capacities both of individuals and a culture are revealed. The idea here is that although individual journalists speak individually in journalism, they speak through a cultural form that, although it is an invention, they did not invent. (1993, p. 13)

Adam, a journalism educator, stresses the importance of linking journalism skills such as judgment with knowledge of other disciplines to enable journalists to have a deeper understanding of the 'forming principles of public policy'. He concludes that just as 'democracy calls for citizens with judgment ... the need to preserve democracy calls for journalists with judgment' (1990, p. 69). In making this case, Adam reminds us that the world — through cultural practices such as journalism — is 'born in our imaginations':

> It is to say that experiences of ... consciousness ... [are] the work of the Imagination in both its rudimentary and its artistic incarnations. It means that the transfer of consciousness from one human being to another through a story, any story — from a journalist to an audience, in other words — produces the forms of public consciousness that make collective existence possible. What is initially private becomes public; and so in journalism society is born and reborn every day. (1993, pp. 17–18)

Adam draws on the work of Anderson (1984), which highlights the crucial role played by journalism in the process of 'imagining' society and the public's place within it. This power of the 'imaginary' can work in various ways: take the coverage of crime, for example:

> ... the more stories people read about crime, especially of events they can't control, the more likely they are inclined to think crime is out of control, which will produce more stories and generate interest in legal reform, a condition promoting the production of crime news in the first place. (McCormick 1995, p. 155)

Sources selected by journalists play a crucial role in giving rise to how society is 'imagined'. Hall et al. (1978) identify the symbiotic relationship between journalists and their sources and the deference to the status quo. Australian research provides support for this process, particularly in relation to the cultural construction of identity and how Indigenous people are excluded from mainstream definitions of culture (Meadows and Oldham 1991; Mickler 1992; Goodall 1993; Meadows 1994a; Trigger 1995; Ewart 1997b; Mickler 1997a, 1997b). But this creative process is always a struggle over meaning with contradictions always in evidence. This is clear from Griffin's insightful research into the representation of Indigenous affairs in press photographs. It reveals a tendency for positive representations in contrast with a generally negative tenor of stories unaccompanied by such visual imagery with the two discourses working in apparent contradiction of each other (Griffin 1998).

While journalism is a creation in the broader cultural sense, it might be further defined as:

> ... a form of expression, the templates of which have been invented and developed in the English-speaking world since the second decade of the seventeenth century. It is a form of expression that ... resides in the cultural storehouse where we put the procedures and techniques for creating public consciousness. It is the aspect of culture that inspires and directs the work of every journalist. (Adam 1993, p. 20)

Another common way of defining journalism is to describe it in terms of what it produces — news. The problematic definition of news is enough to challenge this approach. Even journalists cannot agree on what is news (Baker 1980). News, for Adam (1993, p. 26), is often nothing more than the last thing that happened in a chain of events. Dwelling on notions of 'what is news' alone does little to help in extending this argument. People have been buying and selling information in the form of news only for about 150 years. The common form of news is diminishing in importance as a result of the communications revolution, being replaced with two different commodities — information and entertainment (Bird 1997, pp. 18–19). Turner (1996) identifies this 'post-journalism' move to infotainment by Australian television current affairs programs and its detrimental impact on journalism practices. Herman and McChesney's study of global media systems suggests that this is indeed a global phenomenon with strong tendencies for advertiser preference towards infotainment rather than public-service programming, all in accord with market logic (Herman and McChesney 1997, p. 188). How do such trends impact on the practices of journalism? So far, journalists have shown 'remarkably little ability' to speculate constructively about their role in the new age of information technology (Desbarats 1996, p. 261).

For the most part, journalists are not highly conscious of the explanatory techniques they use, but Adam (1993, p. 45) identifies five principles of journalistic design from which all journalists draw — news and news judgment; reporting or evidentiary method; linguistic technique; narrative technique; and method of interpretation or meaning. These principles or practices offer not only a methodology for analysing journalism, but also a template for journalism education (Meadows 1997b).

A common critique of the analysis of journalism is that it tends to take the newsroom as a starting point and argues for its worth in terms of what it *does* rather than what it *is*. Adam (1993) suggests that broadening the analysis to include 'journalism's more ambitious forms' reveals what is missing from 'everyday' journalism. His five principles foster a better critique of journalism. They facilitate assessment of the quality of news judgment in a journalistic piece, the authority of its facts, the clarity and originality of the language, the utility and success of its narrative technique, and the degree to which the journalist has penetrated and thereby interpreted the materials he or she has brought to light (Adam 1993, p. 46).

So journalism is a form of expression that is the product of something called the 'Imagination' — the spontaneous consciousness-forming faculty of individual human beings. It is the 'Imagination', conceived of as a property of culture, that connects the imagination of individuals to society's consciousness-forming projects. It is an influential cultural practice — 'the primary method of framing experience and forming public consciousness of the here and now' (Adam 1993, p. 45).

Journalists as intellectuals

Another way of theorising journalism and journalists is to draw from Gramsci's idea of the intellectual in society. Gramsci's writings from the 1930s, collected in *The Prison Notebooks*, emerged at the time of the rise of Fascism in Italy. Gramsci, who was imprisoned for his anti-fascist views, acknowledges the cultural importance of the media of the time — publishing houses and presses — in assuming a public leadership role. He defines journalists as intellectuals, performing crucial cultural functions, but who work alongside other intellectuals such as doctors, pharmacists, teachers, and priests. But one of Gramsci's tenets is that journalists — because of the role of the media as an important cultural resource — play a key role in producing consensus on particular issues (Holub 1992, p. 158). Like other intellectuals, journalists express a set of values that, although tending to support the status quo, have always facilitated relationships between a range of publics and elites as part of the process of hegemony (Craig 1997, p. 9; Palmer 1998, p. 389). While this relationship with the public has become problematic (as already outlined), journalism and its role as a cultural activity can be defined in this way. Gramsci was writing before the rise of the professional, a status that journalists have claimed for themselves. But his notions of journalism and of the journalist as an intellectual are more akin to the current ideas incorporated in public journalism than mainstream practice.

Renate Holub (1992, p. 26) argues — using Lyotard's understanding of 'the ubiquity and irresistible presence of global power' — that knowledge producers like journalists must move within the limits of the media's technological order, 'directed by the systemic and self-regulative nature of the system itself'. This is, in effect, what Carey has argued about the way in which journalism has been shaped by its self-imposed fourth-estate status. Holub (1992, p. 26) observes: 'In this scenario, we as western intellectuals cannot but reproduce the inherent laws of the system when engaging in the reproduction and dissemination of knowledge'. Lawson (1998, p. 83) acknowledges the repressive impact of transnational media conglomerates on their intellectuals: 'Journalists feel themselves frustrated midgets, scrambling hysterically around in the shadows of the Titans, or else they fully internalise the ideology of entirely individualistic careerism (it must be said that it's very hard not to do)'. This would seem to limit the possibility for resistance but, fortunately, drawing from Gramsci, Holub offers an alternative.

The age of information technology has brought with it not only the possibility of extending global power structures, but also the opportunity to subvert them by increasing the possibility of global democratisation (Holub 1992, p. 28). The cost of access to information technologies such as radio, television, and the Internet is decreasing rapidly and it is this, she argues, that might offer the possibility for intervention. With better access to computer software, it is possible for community groups to produce their own publications. Of course, the chance of challenging the transnationals is all but impossible, given the high start-up cost of a new newspaper, radio, or television station, for example, in Australia. And Holub, like many others, acknowledges that the age of information technology has done little to change the economic conditions of many social groups. The gap between developed and developing countries continues to widen. But she stresses that the impulse for democratic change does not arise from privilege — it emerges from disadvantage.

If journalists are intellectuals playing a critical role in applying a set of cultural practices in particular ways, then there seems much that could be achieved beyond the mundane reporting of the everyday; beyond a routine reliance on institutional sources; beyond the shallow view that journalists merely 'reflect reality'; beyond a reliance on a flawed notion of the fourth estate and the limiting effects of objectivity and professionalism.

Conclusion

Political journalist Margo Kingston (1998a) remarks that Australian journalists in the late 1990s entered a 'terrorist phase of survival' because of the impact of the concentration of media ownership and pressure on the remaining 'independent' media such as Fairfax (publishers of the *Age*, the *Sydney Morning Herald*, and the *Australian Financial Review*), and the national broadcasters, the ABC and SBS. She argues that journalists need to adopt a kind of 'intelligent subversion' to work effectively in this environment. In a similar vein, Paul Chadwick (1998a) suggests that journalism needs to learn how to communicate more effectively with the public, by recognising the 'language of the corporations' in order to counter the threat to democracy that the current Australian mediascape presents. This is not possible without acknowledging the contradictory frameworks that constitute communication and economics. As Carey (1997d, p. 64) indicates, economics is the practice of allocating scarce resources whereas communication is the process of producing meaning from a resource that is anything but scarce. Experiments with public, civic, or community journalism — call it what you will — similarly aim to improve communication between journalists and their communities, with mixed results. A crucial element seems to be the commitment of individual editors or publishers rather than the idea itself (McManus 1994, p. 210–11; McGregor, Comrie, and Campbell 1998). Public journalism professes admirable aims, but how effective can these experiments be when journalists and journalism maintain perceptions that naturally set them apart from 'the public'? (For a discussion of the merits of public journalism, refer to Chapter 11.)

Modern journalism must move beyond its myopic claim to fourth-estate status and its accompanying adversarial, watchdog role. While this has played and continues to play a central role in the democratic process, public alienation and the lack of 'conversation' reflected in the work of today's journalists does little to contribute to a more inclusive conception of culture as 'a whole process of living' (Williams 1977). If journalism is seen as a cultural practice made up of sub-sets of practices — making news judgments, reporting, applying particular linguistic and narrative techniques, and of interpreting information or meaning — then it is possible to re-think modern journalism in terms of what it does ('making' the world and 'making' journalists) rather than in terms of what it is (part of the fourth estate, independent, professional, objective, standing up for 'the public's right to know', and so on). Considering journalism as a cultural practice also avoids conflating it with technology or communication, or ignoring its essential links with the democratic process. This means that journalism practices should be seen as anything but self-justifying — they must be contingent on the social consequences they provoke in the formation of democracy. Until there is a return to the forms of 'public conversation' from which modern journalism emerged, there seems little hope of journalism and journalists regaining a credible place in the public imagination and, by association, in the process of the formation of culture.

Case study

In April 1986, an article appeared in *People* magazine quoting a senior sergeant of police at Cairns Police Station who described Aboriginal people as 'coons', 'boongs', 'black bastards', and 'dingoes'. In response, the Aboriginal people of Cairns marched on the police station, demanding the policeman's sacking. They also lodged a complaint with the Australian Press Council.

In the following two months, twenty-eight news stories were published about the incident in newspapers from Cairns to Launceston. The offensive words and many of the other allegations against Aboriginal people made by the police officer were re-published. In none of the stories did journalists attempt to examine the truth or otherwise of the policeman's reported statements. The Press Council dismissed the complaint and the police officer was later promoted.

In the aftermath of this incident, Michael Meadows visited Cairns as an ABC radio news journalist in an attempt to get another perspective on Indigenous affairs in the deep north. His contact in Cairns, a Murri woman who ran a hostel for homeless men, invited him to visit her to discuss possible story ideas. When Meadows arrived at the hostel, he was met by fifteen members of the Cairns Aboriginal community seated around a table and was invited to join them for a 'cuppa'. They spoke for 30 minutes about anything but the reason he was there.

'It was clear that they were checking out my credibility by trying to find a place for me in their own social structure,' Meadows said.

'When we discovered a mutual friend — a senior political figure — one of the group quietly left the room. He made a telephone call to the politician concerned who vouched for my credibility. When the Aboriginal man returned to the room, without more than a few words being spoken, the meeting broke up.

'It became clear that the people present, all representatives of various Indigenous community organisations in Cairns, had already determined my timetable and had even worked out how I would travel from one location to another. They had set the agenda. They spoke about the issues they felt were important.'

During the subsequent compilation of four 20-minute radio documentaries based on that visit, Meadows spoke to some of these people in Cairns by telephone to clarify points and to explain how the programs would be put together. He made some changes to the script following these discussions but nothing that compromised the quality of the final cut.

'It seemed to me at the time that this interaction had strengthened the stories — and increased my own confidence that I had accurately presented their views,' Meadows said.

'It was a valuable lesson for me in learning how to *listen* to sources and being prepared to follow *other agendas*.

'Some years later when I became aware of moves to make journalism more accountable in the United States, it seemed to me that Indigenous people in Cairns had already taught me about the implicit meaning of 'public journalism' and its potential to improve journalism practices. It seemed to me to be the kind of dialogue that should be part of everyday journalism practice, regardless of the cultural context.'

DISCUSSION QUESTIONS

1 How does James Carey argue that journalism could have once been considered to have been 'a public conversation'? What did he mean by this description?

2 What are the main arguments advanced in this chapter suggesting that journalism has moved away from its traditional roots?

3 What are the main points raised by the author in arguing that journalism can be seen as a set of cultural practices?

4 How effective do you think the idea of journalists as 'intellectuals' is in postmodern society?

5 How has the so-called 'information age' changed the nature of journalism?

6 What are the five principles of journalism identified by Stuart Adam in this chapter? Use these to analyse a news story of your choice to gauge how effective they are in defining what journalism is.

Further reading

Adam, S. 1993, *Notes Towards a Definition of Journalism: Understanding an old craft as an art form*, The Poynter Papers: No. 2, The Poynter Institute for Media Studies, St Petersburg, Florida.

Forde, S. 1998, 'The development of the alternative press in Australia', *Media International Australia*, no. 87, pp. 114–33.

Herman, E. and McChesney, R. 1997, *The Global Media: The New Missionaries of Corporate Capitalism*, Cassell, London.

Holub, R. 1992, *Antonio Gramsci: Beyond Marxism and Postmodernism*, Routledge, London.

Mickler, S. 1998, *The Myth of Privilege: Aboriginal Status, Media Visions, Public Ideas*, Fremantle Arts Centre Press, Fremantle.

Munson, E.S. and Warren, C.A. (eds) 1997, *James Carey: A Critical Reader*, University of Minnesota Press, Minneapolis.

4

Journalism in Australia: hard yakka?

MARTIN HIRST

More and more the owner of the big daily is a businessman who finds it hard to see why he should run his property on different lines from the hotel proprietor, the vaudeville manager, or the owner of an amusement park. (Edward Alsworth Ross 1910, in Brennan 1995, p. 75)

As we move into the twenty-first century the media looks, and tastes, vastly different to its counterparts of 100 years ago, or even a decade ago (Carey 1993b, Schultz 1994, Guerke and Hirst 1996, Schultz 1998). Despite that, it is still big business, 'essentially a moneymaking scheme, dependent on one hand upon its popularity with the public, on the other hand upon the money market' (Rogers, cited in Salcetti 1995, p. 54). The giants of the communications industry, News Corporation, Reuters, and CNN, are at the forefront of economic, cultural, and political globalization (Carey 1993b, Alleyne 1997, Boyd-Barrett and Rantanen 1998).

Is it any wonder that the public-service values of journalism are under pressure from the interlocking commercial interests of the media moguls? Carey (1993b, p. 6) writes that the communication cycle follows the pattern of business cycles in the capitalist economy, a 'long revolution' that contains 'moments of decisive alteration in existing social relations amidst longer periods of stability and stasis'. The new millennium may present one of these altering moments.

Bob Franklin argues that the 'retreat from investigative journalism' and the reporting of hard news to the preferred territory of 'softer' or 'lighter' stories, has led the news media into the 'entertainment industry' where stories 'which interest the public' are replacing 'stories which are in the public interest'. Franklin calls this new type of infotainment news 'newszak', a term coined by conservative British social critic Malcolm Muggeridge (Franklin 1997, p. 4).

Franklin is horrified by the seemingly unstoppable rise of 'newszak'. He cites three 'unprecedented and significant' signposts that herald the new age of info-tainment journalism:

- the shifting balance in favour of entertainment in the news media;
- the disappearance of foreign and political news in some media;
- the trend towards infotainment affecting broadsheets as much as tabloids and the public, as well as the private broadcasting sector. (Franklin 1997, p. 6)

Franklin does not mention it, but there is a fourth signal of this tendency: much of the information available through the Internet is of this 'newszak' variety. The exceptions are 'serious newspaper' sites, but even they have a large percentage of 'lifestyle' material posted on the Web. There is no doubt that journalism is changing, but is it change for better or worse, and what is driving the change?

These questions can be addressed by looking at journalism as work — as a labour process with its end result the commodity 'news', which is then marketed, sold, bought, and consumed. As these questions involve change over time, an historical approach to journalism as work provides useful insights. The approach taken here is broadly that of historical materialism, a Marxist framework (Hirst 1993, 1998a) that seeks 'to link the individual practices and behaviours of the newsrooms to the broader structural conditions which interact with, and impact upon, those practices'; in particular 'some form of theoretical engagement with that economic or commercial base' on which modern journalism stands (Oakham 1998, pp. 25–9).

From fourth estate to fortress Wapping

The relatively modern institution of journalism had its beginnings in the radical pamphleteers of the French and American revolutions, and the struggle to remove the 'tax on knowledge' that many governments imposed on the news magazines of the seventeenth and eighteenth centuries. This monumental struggle for 'freedom of the press' is well documented, but freedom from the newspaper tax was quickly replaced with a press beholden to the interests of the rich and powerful people that came to own it (Hollis 1970, Walker 1976, McQueen 1977, Bowman 1988, Engel 1996, Hartley 1996, Williams 1997, Schultz 1998). As Williams (1997, p. 5) points out, the history of journalism and the news media can only be fully appreciated if one takes into account 'the countervailing pulls on the mass media' exercised by public opinion on one hand and 'powerful institutions in society' on the other.

Cryle's (1997) case study of status among journalists in colonial Australia and Pearl's *Wild Men of Sydney* are two examples of histories that factor this contra-diction into their narrative accounts. As Cryle insists:

> A distinctive challenge for the journalism historian is to steer a balanced course between the uncritical genre of journalistic reminiscence, on one hand, and the wholesale dismissal of journalists which appear in official accounts on the other. (1997, p. 176)

By the 1860s, once literacy levels began to increase during the industrial revolution, daily newspapers, which relied mostly on advertising revenue to survive (Williams 1997, p. 6), started to proliferate to meet the needs of a reading public (Hardt and Brennen 1995, p. vii). Prior to this, the paper's publisher was often also the writer, proofreader, typesetter, and printer, but the industrial revolution also saw newspaper production revolutionised. Newspapers became less the mouthpiece of individual and politically motivated proprietors and more industrial conglomerates. 'The market did its job very well. Within twenty years radical newspapers had virtually disappeared' (Williams 1997, p. 6).

As this process gathered pace in the late nineteenth and early twentieth centuries, journalists discovered that 'the division of labour and the subsequent standardization of occupational practices did not result in a better work life, but in a struggle for economic and professional survival' (Hardt and Brennen 1995, p. x). Williams identifies this period as the beginning of the continuing struggle over 'editorial freedom' between editors and owners (Williams 1997, p. 7). According to Braverman (1974, p. 251), this timeframe coincides with the consolidation of monopoly capitalism, during which the 'modern structure of capitalist industry and finance began to take shape' and capital began to harness 'science' for 'the more rapid transformation of labor into capital' (p. 252). Work, for the first time, became highly mechanised.

The first round of 'mechanisation' in the workplace also began to affect journalists. News-workers were 'increasingly bordered, and in turn valued, by their technological place in the production process of gathering, writing and producing news' (Salcetti 1995, p. 49). Salcetti's comments refer to the Industrial Revolution, but technology is never constant, and changes in the technologies of news-gathering, writing, and dissemination have changed work practices in the same way that the assembly line revolutionised the mass production of manufactured goods. The technology of television has also impacted on the journalistic role and function of newspapers. According to Simons (1999, p. 13) technology, instead of making news more immediate, has made newspapers more like reflections and annotations of the previous night's TV news, which those in newspaper production have little time to watch. Of course, it also works the other way. Commercial television reporters will often take their lead from the front-page splash in the morning tabloids. Radio has also become a medium that 'breaks' new stories, particularly when politicians make a point of announcing or confessing on talkback.

As Schultz (1989, 1994, 1998) argued, the journalistic values of democratic liberalism — characterised as 'the fourth estate' — are compromised by the need of the media industry to show a profit for those who invest in news just as they might invest in 'widgets'. In his 1996 novel *The Fourth Estate*,[1] Jeffrey Archer has one of his characters express this view: '"The truth, the whole truth, and anything but the truth", said Townsend, smiling. "Just as long as it sells papers"' (p. 11).

Townsend appears to be based on News Limited's Rupert Murdoch and the novel's other protagonist, Armstrong, is a thinly disguised caricature of the late Robert Maxwell. In Archer's story the two men are engaged in a life and death struggle, not to produce a better newspaper, but to be the richest and most powerful media baron. In the novel, the men are under no illusion that first and foremost they are capitalists, and they behave accordingly. The reporting staffs on the fictional newspapers they control are pawns in a global chess game, hired and fired as necessary to maintain a competitive edge over the rival media capitalist.

In the 1940s, the fictional Keith Townsend spends time 'apprenticed' to another publisher where he observes: 'Surely in the end, however massive a paper's circulation was, the principal aim should be to make as large a return on your investment as possible' (Archer 1996, p. 150). Townsend 'expressed the view that the shop floor at the *Express* was overmanned by a ratio of three to one, and that, while wages made up its largest outgoings, there could be no hope of a modern newspaper group being able to make a profit. In the future someone was going to have to take on the unions' (Archer 1996, p. 150). This was, of course, what Murdoch did at Wapping in 1986.

Australian author and journalist George Johnston painted a fairly bleak picture of a Melbourne newspaper office in the 1930s in his famous novel, *My Brother Jack*. The offices of the fictional *Morning Post*, most likely representing the Melbourne *Argus* where Johnson worked in the 1930s (Sekuless 1999, p. 89), are described as 'warrens of little rooms and airless cubby-holes divided by frosted glass and mahogany', where the classifieds were composed and the accounts settled (Johnston 1964, p. 187). The fictional reporters' room was larger and grander:

> ... divided into two main rooms on either side of the chief-of-staff's glassed-in box ... fifteen subs [sat] around a huge elliptical table, all wearing green eye-shades and stooped over ... as if they were all slightly cowed by the basilisk presence of Mr. Farnsworth, who had been there as chief sub for as long as anybody could remember ... and he had a row of lead-based spikes in front of him, and to his left the teleprinter and the gawping, faintly hissing mouths of the pneumatic tubes. (Johnston 1964, p. 189)

Fifty years later things were not all that different at News Limited's Holt Street headquarters in central Sydney:

> The News Limited building [was] noisy, dirty, overcrowded, chockablock with deadlines and a Mahogany Row more interested, we thought, in profits than prose. (Krause 1999, p. 7)

Johnston was writing about journalism at a time when the 'mechanisation' of news production in Australia was beginning to catch up with the rest of the world and to impact on 'the role and work duties of newspaper reporters and increasing capitalization–commercialization of the newspaper industry' (Salcetti 1995, p. 51). In the first half of the twentieth century the teleprinter, the telephone, and the telegraph all impacted on news-gathering. When the first telegraph connected Australia to Europe in 1859, the London-based Reuters news agency became the monopoly supplier of cable news to Australia and New Zealand (Rantanen 1998, pp. 35–48). The news agencies have always been active players in the introduction of new technologies to news-gathering and dissemination. Reuters was instrumental in the laying of telegraph cable in the second half of the nineteenth century and one of the first to take full advantage of satellite technology in the twentieth (Boyd-Barrett 1998, pp. 32–3).

British journalist and author Raymond Snoddy (1992) suggests the introduction of the telephone means that journalists stay in the office 'rather than getting out and meeting the people they're writing about' (p. 144). Of course, in the late twentieth century the fax machine and the Internet are strengthening this tendency to news-gather from the reporters' room, rather than the street. Schultz (1998) reports studies that show up to 90 per cent of news is generated from media releases that are distributed by fax, or even on videotape (see, for example, Ward 1991 and Zawawi 1994). Snoddy argues this tendency 'has put pressure on standards' because, as a former senior Fleet Street editor said, of the 'emphasis on competition and circulation battles' (Montgomery, cited in Snoddy 1992, p. 145). There is no doubt that editors and senior journalists recognise that work practices have a direct impact on news values, the veracity of a story, and the quality of the reporting.

Tom Wolfe was one of the founding fathers of American 'new journalism' in the late 1960s. He began experimenting with new styles at the *New York Herald Tribune*, partly as a reaction to the work routines and conditions of daily news (Hirst 1998b). He describes the newsroom in the early 1960s as 'one big pie factory' (Wolfe 1975, p. 16) and remembers it being painted 'industrial sludge', the same colour as the floor in the tool and die works, 'a grim distemper of pigment and filth'. This decor would have been familiar to Wolfe's contemporaries in other American newspapers and around the world: 'Most newspapers were like that,' Wolfe writes, '[t]his setup was instituted decades ago for practical reasons' (1975, p. 16).

While he does not elaborate the reasons, it is not hard to surmise that the industrial conditions reflected the needs of the newspaper proprietors and the physical conditions of newspaper production. Most newspaper offices today are *probably* considerably cleaner than the *Tribune*'s, but the basic open plan remains: 'There were no interior walls' (Wolfe 1975, p. 4) and the reporters labour at computerised workstations rather than in serried ranks at battered Remingtons. A breakthrough study of technology, environment, and workplace design in the Australian context (Dombkins 1993, pp. 29–51) looked at the organisational structure of the *Sydney Morning Herald* as it was in 1962 and 1992. Dombkins notes that journalists' roles have changed and they are necessarily multiskilled:

> The traditional mandatory shorthand, although still used, is not as essential [as in 1962]. News sense is still the main skill. Journalists now need word processing skills, not just adequate typing skills. Promotion is now based more on ability than seniority. Training has moved from the traditional craft-based training through the cadetship system to university training and a limited cadetship. (1993, p. 36)

In 1992 the Fairfax organisation was in the process, once again, of updating its computer system for reporters and subs — with obvious knock-on effects for the blue-collar trades (plate-making, and so on). Dombkins noted that computerised copy control 'provided owners and senior management with the power to control journalistic output', but added that 'through industrial action' journalists were able to resist to a point, while productivity per journalist increased by 15 per cent (1993, p. 48). A further compelling argument for the idea that journalism is basically process work can be found in Barbara Garson's *The Electronic Sweatshop* (1988), which documents the transformation of white-collar work into repetitive manual labour via the technology of computer terminals:

> In the nineteenth century the phrase 'factory hand' suggested an interchangeable part or a tool to be used as needed ... So far there's no equivalent white-collar phrase like 'hourly brain' or 'piecework pencil' to describe the fast-growing class of consultants, freelancers, and executive temps. But there is a new ethic arising both toward them and among them. (1998, p. 226)

This same trend is also evident in newspapers, particularly in Britain in the decade since Rupert Murdoch moved his English newspaper empire to the London industrial suburb of Wapping. In *The Fourth Estate*, journalists on the fictional *Globe* newspaper complain to Keith Townsend about the poor working conditions in the new plant: 'Once they were inside, few of them cared for the production-line atmosphere, [or] the modern keyboards and computers which had replaced their old typewriters' (Archer 1996, p. 421).

Not only are British newspapers replacing full-time reporting staff with cheaper freelance writers (Snoddy 1992, Franklin 1997, McNair 1998), but Murdoch's newspaper 'factory' in the London suburbs resembles the classic Fordist industrial structure. According to Mathew Engel (1996), Wapping remains 'a weird and dispiriting place: inside more like Ford's Dagenham plant than the traditional happy chaos of a newspaper office' (p. 305). Snoddy wrote of Murdoch's 1986 move to Wapping:

> Most of the unions were left outside the gates at Wapping. Journalists were able to enter their copy directly into computer terminals, and, after editing on screen, their articles were automatically turned into print by a computerized typesetter. (1992, p. 14)

Murdoch's eventual success at fortress Wapping created a climate in which other newspaper proprietors moved against their own journalists and printers. Robert Maxwell sacked one-third of his workforce and so did United Newspapers, publishers of the *Daily Express* and other papers (Snoddy 1992, p. 14). As Snoddy notes, despite, or perhaps because of, 'the revolution in technology and industrial relations, the big media barons are virtually as powerful as they ever were' (1992, p. 15). Their power is exemplified in the way they treat those who work for them. The cost-cutting and the attacks on wages and conditions are typical facets of capital–labour relationships, particularly when the bottom line is under threat. To this extent the media is just like any other business and journalists just like other workers — ultimately expendable.

Engel's comparison to the Ford automobile assembly plant is also interesting from another angle. Much current thinking in media and cultural studies takes for granted the so-called 'post-Fordist' model. That is, the notion that repetitive, manual work no longer dominates 'late capitalism'. In the 'information age' of post-modernity, the traditional model of the labour process, it is argued, no longer has the power to explain social reality. 'It was OK for Marx in the nineteenth century,' the critics say, 'but it's now as outdated as the "Model T" Ford that Henry designed his factory to build.' The evidence seems to contradict this view.

There is general consensus among Engel, Franklin and McNair that journalism is a commodity when it lands on the news-stand — in the same way that the finished car is a commodity when it hits the showroom — but there is little clarity about what this actually means. It is obvious to most commentators that it implies 'a number of market-led restraints' (McNair 1998, p. 109), but to others it means the unfettered circulation of ideas: 'we are speaking of a market, offering choice' (Horne 1994, p. 9). But often this 'choice' is very limited — a

It would seem, though, that journalists are workers, but perhaps with grey collars, rather than the traditional blue (manual) or white (intellectual) collars. In this schema, workers are active participants in the creation and reproduction of the conditions under which they labour — a process of constant class struggle with its attendant victories and defeats. This 'rank and file' approach to industrial sociology can be distinguished from Emile Durkheim's argument in *The Division of Labour in Society* (1933), which focuses on the corporation as social institution and primary definer of relations of production.

The process of 'proletarianisation' — where work once considered 'white collar' is pushed more and more into a 'grey-collar' class location (Braverman 1974) — is also relevant here. For example, educational requirements for a journalism cadetship have risen from the completion of high school to completion of a three-year university degree, reflecting what Braverman describes as an 'extension of mass education' that has 'increasingly lost its connection with occupational requirements' (1974, p. 439). The result in journalism is that newsworkers are being pushed into accepting (or resisting) lower standards of pay and conditions. This idea is supported by Garson's (1988) thesis of the second Industrial Revolution by which the office of the future is being transformed into the factory of the past. This would suggest that the wage relationship between journalists and their employers creates its own tension and continuously pushes media workers to the *consciousness* of their real *class location* as workers in a capitalist production process (Callinicos and Harman 1989).

The 'rank and file' approach to theories of journalism is not fashionable in academic circles, but it is well articulated by Hanno Hardt and Bonnie Brennen in their introduction to *Newsworkers: Towards a History of the Rank and File* (1995). Hardt and Brennen are highly critical of 'mainstream' histories of the press that 'present ideologically predisposed accounts that fail to consider the issues of work and class' (p. vii). Instead, they argue 'for a reconceptualization of press history as a history of work' (p. ix).

A recent contemporary discussion of British journalism that comes closest to a rank and file history is Matthew Engel's *Tickle the Public: One Hundred Years of the Popular Press* (1996). Engel worked on Fleet Street for twenty-five years, many of them at *The Guardian*, and distances himself from academic historians 'with no direct experience at all of the practice of journalism' (Engel 1996, p. 9). According to Engel, distortion is a 'by-product of the way news is gathered, written, subbed and "altered" on its journey through the newsroom'. The very industrial processes of newspaper production create 'the distorting mirrors of the seaside' from which 'the image comes out elongated or compressed' (Engel 1996, p. 272).

Windschuttle provides a useful working definition of news production as a labour process, noting that 'it has become increasingly difficult to confine the concept of the "working class" to blue-collar workers, or to characterise all white-collar workers as "middle class"' (1988, p. 349). Windschuttle ends his brief explanation of journalists' class location by noting that:

> On any meaningful notion of 'class' as a concept related to *the social relations deriving from the system of production* in a capitalist society like ours, journalists are not 'middle class' — nor, for that matter, are they part of any 'new petit bourgeoisie' ... Journalists work for wages, [and] are part of the *white-collar working class* or, if you like, they are *professional workers*. (1988, p. 351) [*emphasis added*]

Braverman's work supports this view. Newsworkers produce both a service and a commodity, and as such theirs is productive labour for the capitalist, 'since both are forms of [the] production of commodities ... the object of which is the production not only of value-in-exchange but of surplus value for the capitalist' (Braverman 1974, p. 410).

The social and industrial attitudes of journalists

If journalists are grey-collar workers, why does the ideology of professionalism and the perception that news-workers are middle class persist so strongly? The answer resides partly in the fact that capitalism is a resilient social system and that ideology can exert a strong grip over the minds and actions of even the most rational human being. It is easy to extrapolate that 'the consciousness of journalists is inextricably linked with their ongoing professional practices' (Oakham 1998, p. 31).

As noted by Breed (1955) and other media sociologists (for a good exposition of this argument see Meadows 1998a, pp. 1–23), the ideology of professionalism can help mask the raw economic relationships (the relations of production) that bind journalists to the production process. Bob Franklin suggests that even greater social control can be exerted on journalists in tough economic times. Regulation, competition, and technology have tightened profit margins in the media industry. These economic forces 'have altered the social and demographic character of the profession', restructuring reporters away from investigative journalism into something 'more akin to a glorified clerk'. In this climate of change and uncertainty: 'Serious news journalism has been replaced by newszak' (Franklin 1997, p. 49).

At least two surveys of journalists' attitudes were carried out in Australia between 1991 and 1993 (Schultz 1992a, Henningham 1993, Schultz 1998). They are broadly in sympathy, in that both studies indicate that journalists tend to be to the left of the political spectrum. They also indicate that media workers take their jobs seriously; are 'modest, public spirited and serious' and that 92 per cent of respondents to one survey felt the most important element of their job was 'uncovering and publicising problems' (Schultz 1992a, pp. 5–8; 1998).

Breed carried out a similar, smaller, survey in the 1950s. He found that American journalists, even at the height of the Cold War, held 'more liberal views' than their employers (1955, p. 108). Like Breed's, the Schultz survey also examines the issue of newsroom control and her results appear to validate the ideas of Breed, Tiffen (1994) and Windschuttle (1988) about bureaucratic models of news organisation and newsgathering.

However, it does not automatically follow that journalists will attempt to influence the news agenda. The Schultz survey (1992a, pp. 5–8) found that 54 per cent of graduate journalists 'believe that journalists determine the news agenda', compared to 79 per cent of those who entered the profession as secondary school leavers. There could possibly be an age and generational differential here too, with older journalists perhaps more conservative (Breed 1955, p. 108). Despite acknowledging this, only 17 per cent said that advocacy 'was in any way typical of their work' (Schultz 1992a, pp. 5–8). About 71 per cent said that their work was much more likely to be characterised by a commitment to impartiality. Schudson's review of the American literature seems to confirm this. He writes that journalists are 'avowedly and often passionately committed to their ideology of dispassion, their sense of professionalism, their allegiance to fairness or objectivity as it has been professionally defined' (1997, p. 16).

It seems that the social and political views of journalists have not shifted much from Breed's conclusion that they are more liberal than media barons, though Schudson notes that several studies 'find leading American journalists not so much liberal or conservative as apolitical' (1955, p. 16). An Australia-wide survey, conducted in 1992 by the Department of Journalism at the University of Queensland, reports that journalists on political rounds tend to be 'left leaning' (Henningham 1993, p. 21). Thirty-nine per cent of journalists surveyed described themselves as 'at least a little to the left', 16 per cent to the right and 41 per cent 'middle of the road' (Henningham 1993, p. 21).

The Henningham survey also indicates differences in opinions between journalists in different organisations. Fifty-nine per cent at Fairfax and 50 per cent at the Australian Broadcasting Corporation (ABC) and the Special Broadcasting Service (SBS) described themselves as 'left of centre', compared to Packer (29 per cent), News Ltd (38 per cent), and Australian Provincial Newspapers (45 per cent). The most right-wing workplaces were News Ltd (20 per cent), Packer (18 per cent), APN (14 per cent), SBS and ABC (8 per cent) and Fairfax (6 per cent).

If most journalists are fairly liberal in their views and politics, then what social group do they identify with? Schultz argues that journalists are more likely to come from middle-class backgrounds and to have completed a tertiary degree (1992). This has not always been the case. Typical of 'newspapermen' of the early twentieth century, Raymond Swing was the son of a college professor, but did not complete college himself. Instead he first worked as a barbershop cashier and a clerk in retail and steel manufacture before landing his cadetship with the

Cleveland *Press* earning $10 a week; enough 'to rent a modest room, provide modest meals, pay for laundry, and supply me with a little pocket money' (Swing 1964, pp. 17–19).

Does the contemporary reliance on 'graduate' cadets mean that journalists are part of the 'new middle class'? Apparently not. Journalists, under Braverman's model, are workers, albeit in an office environment rather than the traditional blue-collar factory. However, as Braverman notes, 'the work processes of most offices are readily recognizable, in industrial terms, as continuous flow processes . . . the flow of documents required . . . punctuated by personal interviews and correspondence [that] serve merely to facilitate the flow of documentation' (1974, p. 312). This perfectly describes the workflow in a large news organisation, whether a wire service, newspaper, magazine, radio, or television station.

Conclusion

What difference does it make if journalists are labourers rather than middle-class professionals? A significant difference — to journalists themselves, the news output, the news-gathering process, and the news the public receives.

If journalists are conscious of themselves as workers it could have important implications for their own 'world view'; that is, how they imagine the world to be. The most immediate and obvious impact would perhaps be noticed in the reporting of industrial disputes. Journalists, as workers, would be more inclined to be sympathetic to the union point of view and less inclined to simply parrot the ideology that strikes are inherently bad and ultimately against the general 'public interest'. As conscious members of the working class, journalists might be more inclined to see the opposing interests of workers and bosses as an issue to be explored, rather than buried in a consensus view.

Following on from this it stands to reason that as conscious members of the working class, journalists might decide that there is a news value of 'class interest' that should be taken into account in the writing process. This has implications for the way that, for example, politics might be reported. The (now hidden) class nature of political parties — Liberal favours big business and the interests of capital, Labor has strong historic ties to working-class organisations through its links with the union movement — would be more apparent in the way that news is framed. On a more general level, issues of class would be moved from Hallin's (1986, 1994) 'sphere of deviance' into the sphere of 'limited controversy' and might therefore be more widely discussed. A class-based view of journalism might also have implications for the way journalism and the notion of the 'public sphere' are theorised. It would undermine the 'fourth-estate' view of journalism in favour of a more radical model of class politics. Ultimately, it might lead to what Antonio Gramsci might describe as a form of 'organic' journalism — news reporting that is intrinsically tied to the life experience of a working-class audience. On the other hand, one might argue that class-conscious journalism would not sell so well to advertisers who rely on reporters' assumed commitment to the economic, political, and social values of the 'free market' system.

What might happen if a system of 'workers' control' became the norm in newsrooms and if journalists controlled the news-gathering process itself? A newsroom in which news values, angles, and stories are democratically decided on the 'shop floor' might be a very different place to a newsroom where Warren Breed's social control is exercised by managers more in tune with the commercial needs of the organisation (as a capitalist enterprise) than with the needs of a working-class audience. For example, there might be less emphasis on reporting parliament, and more emphasis on reporting from the *pavement*, rather than the *penthouse*. The lives and experiences of *ordinary* people might be more highly valued and the interests of communities more highly appreciated than at present. The closest current example is the concept of *civic* journalism, which is very much an American phenomenon and thus tied to the ideology of partial citizenship common to Western liberal democracies. A class-conscious civic journalism would be a much more radical tool of social change and might mean that journalistic interventions in popular political debate would be more influential and decisive than at present.

On a day-to-day basis the news that the public receives would be noticeably different if journalists were more class-conscious. There would be less news about the 'big end' of town and more about the daily lives of 'real' people in the suburbs and factories. There might also be a shift in the types of stories considered for investigative journalism and certainly in the way in which major stories about politics and economics are covered.

It is possible to argue that a fully developed working-class journalism would be of more public service and lead to more public good than the reporting that passes for informed social critique today. It is hard to predict the ultimate impact such a move might have on the nature of journalism, but one might argue that class-conscious journalism is better journalism.

Case study: Keep left — why journalism should take sides

What happens when journalists choose to report within a class-conscious or political framework, as opposed to treading the more mainstream middle-class 'objective' line?

John Pilger's ground-breaking reporting of Cambodia in the 1970s is an enduring example of this type of reporting, despite opposition from those who disagree with his work. One of Pilger's most recent documentaries, about Australian racism towards Indigenous people, was pilloried in the mainstream media when a couple of 'errors' were picked up and used to blast his whole thesis. Pilger's work makes him an important contemporary figure in the centuries-old tradition of radical journalism. It wasn't until the emerging middle class got its hands on the printing presses in the nineteenth century that newspapers changed from agitation and propaganda to a more 'objective' and commercial blend of advertorial, advertising, and sanitised 'news'. The most famous of socialist journalists is George Orwell. He's best remembered for *Nineteen Eighty-Four* and *Animal Farm*, but his reportage, reviews, and commentaries are also well worth reading. In a famous piece called 'Why I write', written at the end of the Second World War, Orwell explicitly takes the side of the English working class and argues for a journalism committed to radical solutions to the world's problems. It's also important to put on record that, far from being anti-socialist tracts, both *Nineteen Eighty-Four* and *Animal Farm* are solid critiques of the emerging cult of Stalin that wrecked the international socialist movement from the 1930s on.

Australian journalist Wilfred Burchett was also vilified, perhaps with a little more reason. He was, after all, an unreconstructed Stalinist. Burchett was the first reporter in the Japanese city of Hiroshima after the Americans dropped the nuclear bomb in 1945. He was the only journalist to report the Korean War as an imperialist adventure into Asia, instead of parroting the line that it was a Cold War redoubt against Communism. The Menzies government confiscated Burchett's Australian passport and he was declared *persona non grata* in his own country.

Paul Foot, a contemporary journalist who writes for British tabloid papers, holds a leading position with the largest group to the left of the Labour Party in England, the Socialist Workers' Party. A collection of Foot's journalism, *Words are weapons*, contains some inspiring examples of good crusading reportage.

Martin Hirst is a self-confessed Trotskyite agitator who worked in the Canberra Press Gallery in the early 1990s. A member of socialist groups for more than 25 years, Hirst was active in the Australian Journalists' Association, and held executive positions in the ABC and SBS house committees, and in the ACT branch while working in Canberra.

He occasionally had to face hostility from employers, particularly when leading industrial action in newsrooms.

His political stance also attracted the attention of a right-wing Liberal MP, who wrote to Hirst's employer and demanded he be sacked. The politician had seen evening news footage of Hirst chanting and waving a red flag during a national ACTU-co-ordinated union day of action.

Hirst sees a need for activist reporters and budding Pilgers. He says they need to stick to their principles, be active in the union and always be super-critical.

'My biggest concern about journalism today is the fact that for most reporters the pressure of time and resources leads to sloppy reporting,' Hirst said. 'The quick grab with the leader or expert has replaced the investigation and questioning that's at the heart of all good journalism. Collectively, the media takes the easy option, and assumptions that are purely ideological go unchallenged.'

DISCUSSION QUESTIONS

1   The assembly-line production process involves work being divided into a series of repetitive steps with individuals only responsible for a small part of the final product. An automobile plant is a good example — one worker adds the wheels while another fits the engine. How does this model impact on reporters working in the newsroom?

2   Is Bob Franklin's 'newszak' analysis of British journalism relevant to the media in other countries or regions?

3   How relevant today are historical, biographical, and fictional accounts of journalism, such as George Johnston's *My Brother Jack* and Raymond Swing's memoirs? Identify other sources of historical documentation of journalism and the lives of reporters.

Further reading

Franklin, B. 1997, *Newszak and News Media*, Arnold, London.
Hardt, H. and Brennen, B. (eds) 1995, *Newsworkers: Toward a History of the Rank and File*, University of Minnesota Press, Minneapolis.
Johnston, G. 1964, *My Brother Jack*, Fontana Modern Novels, London.
McNair, B. 1998, *The Sociology of Journalism*. Arnold, London.
Wolfe, T. 1975, *The New Journalism*, with an anthology edited by T. Wolfe and E.W. Johnson, Picador, London.

Note

1   In this chapter, the author refers to several fictional accounts of journalism, one based loosely on known history and the other autobiographical. This may seem an unusual process in an academic text, but it is a legitimate use of 'primary source material' that has been pioneered by Bonnie Brennen (1995) as a way of gathering 'insights into aspects of media history that have not been explored previously' (p. 75). Brennen provides a compelling series of arguments for accepting 'newspaper novels', often written by former and practising journalists, as 'realistic representations of the newspaper world' (1995, p. 80).

5

Journalism: beyond the business

KATRINA MANDY OAKHAM

We have to teach these new journalists to be small business people supplying a product to people. They have to learn how to plan for their job. As roundspeople they have to be very organised, they have to be thinking about the calibre of that round, they have to appreciate that they are competing for space in the paper and they need to appreciate that they have to get a round early in their career. They have to understand the nature of their organisation and they have to understand all aspects of news production and practice. (the training manager of one of Australia's leading newspaper groups)

The revolution is here. Journalists are no longer the public's watchdogs or privileged members of the fourth estate. They are business people producing a product for market. Australian journalist Michelle Grattan characterises the latest revolution to hit journalism as the seemingly unstoppable rise of 'commercialism' as a 'core value' (1998, p. 1). Grattan cites the current trend towards making journalists shareholders in their own companies as just one worrying feature of this revolution. Of course revolutions have come and gone in journalism. Journalists have experienced many so-called technological revolutions, the rise of the Internet being the latest. But the revolution to be discussed in this chapter is the most profound, and will redefine journalism. This revolution is the almost complete merging of the editorial and commercial functions of news organisations and the consequent merging of the role played by journalists within those organisations.

Grattan (1998, pp. 1–2) spells it out: 'the editors-in-chief of all four major Fairfax papers . . . have been appointed "publishers" so that they all have one foot firmly planted in each of the journalistic and management camps.' And in the Murdoch domain, she argues, the 'Chinese walls between editorial and management have traditionally been less substantial.'

Schultz (1998, p. 145) defines the revolution thus: 'In the dance of the giants that characterises the corporate news media in the late twentieth century, maximising turnover, profits and scale is the primary obligation and itself the key to political influence.' Television journalist Jana Wendt describes the mix of journalism and commercialism as a 'potent cocktail' and former editor-in-chief of the *Australian* Paul Kelly states that 'demands for commercial success are having a negative impact on quality journalism' (Schultz 1998, p. 145). Former Fairfax executive John Alexander, in delivering the 1998 Andrew Olle Lecture, argued that one of the biggest threats to quality journalism was what he described as 'news management', while at the same time calling for a new generation of 'commercially savvy editors' (Alexander 1998).

This revolution is not confined to Australia, as Herman and McChesney state: 'In addition to the centralization of media power, the major feature of the global media order is its thoroughgoing commercialism.' (1997, p. 1) The ultimate effect of this globalisation, they argue, is the 'implantation of the commercial model of communication' (1997, p. 9).

Theorising the commercial drivers of modern journalism

The actual implications of this revolution for the practice of journalism are discussed elsewhere in this book. The primary concern of this chapter is the need for a credible theoretical framework to deal with the increasingly commercial or economic imperatives that drive modern journalism. This chapter establishes the nature of the commercial spirit that now dominates journalism, before discussing previous attempts to theorise the nature of journalism and then moving to propose a new revised Marxist framework that can encompass modern journalism.

In 1842, Marx wrote: 'The first freedom of the press consists in its not being a trade' (Chibnall 1977, p. 206). Marx recognised that journalism was about more than its commercial operations. But today, in the incredibly complex world of transglobal capital, it is not clear what journalism is or is not. Attempts to theorise journalism remain controversial.

Readers of this chapter watching developments in Australian journalism, as the next generations of Packers and Murdochs take hold of their media domains, might view journalism as simply just another capital acquisition to divert the attentions of these new bloods. Be it a newspaper or a casino, does it really matter except in the balance sheets? It is surely hard not to conclude that the economic imperative that drives journalism has been born again, enlivened and voracious. But voices of denial still ring loud and clear. Journalism is more than just an economic exercise, they cry, quoting C.P. Scott of 1921: 'It is a business like any other business ... but it is much more than a business, it has a moral as well as material existence and its character and influence are determined by the balance of these two forces' (Schultz 1998, p. 136).

Clearly modern journalism does incorporate to some extent all of the above
— expression, consensus formation, and a commitment to reporting the truth
— but none of these perspectives engages with the rampant commercialism that
now drives journalism.

Franklin, in his state-of-play analysis of the British media, paints the following
picture of the modern journalistic landscape:

> Journalism's editorial priorities have changed. Entertainment has superseded the
> provision of information; human interest has supplanted the public interest; meas-
> ured judgement has succumbed to sensationalism; the trivial has triumphed over
> the weighty ... Traditional news values have been undermined by new values: info-
> tainment is rampant. (1997, p. 4)

As discussed elsewhere in this book, Franklin argues that news has been
replaced by 'newszak', which he defines as news as a product designed and
'processed' for a particular market and delivered in increasingly homogeneous
'snippets' that make only modest demands on the audience. Newszak is news
converted into entertainment (1997, pp. 4–5).

Herman and McChesney (1997, p. 109) confirm that in the era of Newszak
'the superiority of the market and the profit motive as the regulator of all
branches of communication is taken as a given'.

Which theory of journalism?

Given the complexities of modern journalism, it is clear that there is a need for
a broader theoretical pluralism to be introduced to the discipline. Those who
attempt to theorise must develop a stronger and livelier willingness to engage
with the theoretical developments taking place in other disciplines.

One of the founders of the sociology discipline, C. Wright Mills, argued for
a theoretical imagination to link the personal, individual issues to the 'public
issues of social structure' (Mills 1959, p. 14). In the same way, the individual practices and behaviours of the newsrooms should be linked to the broader structural conditions that interact with, and impact on, those practices. Mills argues
'there is always the urge to know the social and historical meaning of the individual in society and in the period in which he has ... his being' (1959, p. 14).
Journalists need to be able to articulate that meaning. Journalism is clearly a
world full of relativities and subjectivities, full of the vagaries of individual psy-
chologies, professional idioms and ideologies. These present many obstacles for
the would-be theoretician; however, any theory of journalism has to do two
things:

1   It has to be able to take account of the primarily commercial context in which
journalism is practised.

2 It has to be able to take account of the professional ideologies, beliefs, ways of doing, and ways of making meaning that operate among the practitioners of journalism.
   Why is this necessary? To return to Mills:

> ... every self-conscious thinker must at all times be aware of — and hence be able to control — the levels of abstraction on which he is working. The capacity to shuttle between levels of abstraction with ease and with clarity, is a signal mark of the imaginative and systematic thinker. (1959, p. 43)

So how can a journalism theory 'shuttle' between these two levels of abstraction, the commercial context of journalism, and the worldviews formulated by journalists?

A new Marxist theory of journalism

One way might be through a revival of the Marxist project. This theoretical framework delivers the conceptual tools capable of facing such rampant commercialism. Modern journalism could provide the theoretical laboratory for such a revival, while also presenting an opportunity to address some of the alleged deficiencies of Marxist theory. This new version of Marxism would differ from that vigorously rejected by Windshcuttle (1998), providing a model that does not reduce journalists, or their audiences, to 'passive dupes'. This new model could move beyond those proposed by political economists and stand against charges of economic determinism.

A Marxist approach to journalism traditionally has been associated with the political economy model. It is indicative of such a narrow approach to the interpretation of the Marxist framework that commentators, such as Franklin, actually write as if the two are interchangeable:

> The Marxist or political economy approach to journalism suggests that the production of news and other journalistic products is structurally constrained by economic and political factors, especially the private and increasingly concentrated ownership of media industries. (1997, p. 37)

This version, in its crudest form, argues that because the media are owned and controlled by capitalist interests, these outlets are geared to the production of dominant capitalist ideologies, which in turn mystify class relations and produce a false consciousness among the working class. However, this approach has been accused of failing to articulate how this ideology operates at the level of 'concrete practice' (Chibnall 1977, p. 210).

Franklin neatly summarises the other problems and deficiencies inherent in this approach:

- journalists are perceived as lacking any autonomy;
- content is ideologically biased towards certain groups in society, and journalists are therefore seen as agents in helping to create a false consciousness about the inequalities in capitalist societies;
- ownership and control are confused.

Schudson (1991) argues this 'ignores the observable fact that reporters often initiate stories of their own, that editors rarely meet with publishers, and that most working journalists have no idea who are on the board of directors of the institutions they work for' (in Berkowitz 1997, p. 10).

There is also a culturalist critique of this model, which argues that:

> News cannot be understood as merely a function of media ownership, nor as a consequence of journalists' professional routines, but reflects the impact of cultural and ideological influences on 'relatively autonomous' journalists working in media organisations whose reporting is structured by cultural and ideological influences ... rather than by hierarchical supervision and control. (Franklin 1997, pp. 44–5)

These opposing views position journalists as either primarily controlled by economic forces or the commercial considerations of their employing organisations, or primarily controlled by ideological forces or forces of their own professional and cultural consciousnesses.

The problem of ideology

One of the continuing critiques of the Marxist framework is that everything outside the perspective is reduced to 'false consciousness'. Marxists such as Althusser, who attempted to deal with the problem of ideology, have been dismissed by commentators such as Windschuttle (1998) as mere proponents of indoctrination. Chibnall (1977), however, sees potential for placing journalists among the functionaries and operatives of the 'ideological state apparatuses' and he argues for more explication of that role. Journalists have to be studied not only as the agents of ideological transmission, but also as embodiments of a particularly resilient professional ideology. As Hall (1983b) argues, Althusser moves away from seeing audiences or journalists as dupes suffering false consciousness to ask what the process is by which people come to internalise ideology. Drawing on Althusser's discussion of the role of teachers within the education systems, Chibnall argues it would be wrong to look at this role for journalists in terms only of being 'naïve accommodators' or 'willing collaborators' (Chibnall 1977, p. 213).

Herman and McChesney (1997, p. 35) argue that the triumph of 'TNC (transnational corporation) power' is not only the triumph of political and economic power, but 'extends to basic assumptions and modes of thought; that is, to ideology. To no small extent the stability of the system rests upon the widespread acceptance of global, corporate ideology'. They suggest there is 'a strong tendency in corporate ideology to identify "freedom" with the mere absence of constraints on business' (Herman and McChesney 1997, p. 35).

They are also clear, however, that this ideological power is not complete.

> ... journalists' performance cannot be ascribed in toto to structural factors ... On some types of stories and in some contexts, reporters are able to do first-rate work, despite corporate control of the industry. (1997, pp. 192–3)

Bourdieu (1998, p. 19) argues that journalists wear 'special glasses' to facilitate the incorporation of the economic imperatives of their work into a broader worldview and their place in it. Those glasses and the ways in which they are worn must be constantly under scrutiny. It is specifically this domain of ideological work that can be overlooked by a strictly political economy approach.

Hirst argues for his own rejuvenation of a Marxist analysis of journalism, albeit of the political economy approach, viewing journalism as both 'assembly line' work and as artistic endeavour. He concludes that journalism must be understood first as a labour process producing a cultural commodity according to the rule of capital, and second as a form of popular reality that has both 'explicit and implicit ideological functions' (1998a, p. 49). A crucial third dimension should be added to this analysis to encompass, and indeed celebrate, the role of agency in journalism. Journalists as workers do produce ideological goods for consumption in the market place, but they also carry out their own ideological activities that incorporate their real conditions of production.

A political economy approach explains journalism as a commodity but fails to integrate elements of journalism as cultural activity or autonomous acts of consciousness. These factors, and others not related to the economic, also must be considered in attempting to theorise journalism.

The issue of determination

Determinism remains a controversial aspect of attempts to apply Marxist theory. Determinism has a 'complex range of meanings' but maintains its special significance because 'it bears on several significant tendencies in modern thought' (Williams 1988, p. 98). Determinism in 'its most widely-used sense' assumes 'pre-existing and commonly "external" conditions that fix the course of some process or event' (Williams 1988, p. 98).

The problem is that such determinism can be seen as overruling any individual acts of will or individual consciousness and therefore appears to negate the role of the individual and any possibilities of change or alternative outcomes. To devise a credible Marxist theory of journalism, one must establish how the economic base (that is, economic factors) can play a determining role in an activity that clearly encompasses other important social, cultural, and political factors. This is the core problem. As Marx said, journalism is about more than just a trade and journalists see themselves as being more than just tradespeople churning out a product for market.

Franklin explains it this way: the 'economic structure of society' (that is, the base) has 'significant implications' (issue of determination) for the 'social, political, legal and cultural spheres' (that is the superstructure) (1997, p. 38). But Franklin's discussion fails to address the controversial issue of just how significant this 'significant implication' is. Why is the issue of determination so important? Its significance can be likened to the rise of the feminist movement and the consciousness-raising movement. Feminists of the time argued that until women could name the problem, that is, patriarchal oppression, they could not become active and set about solving the problem. The same could be said of journalism: until the problem with modern journalism is named then it will not be confronted directly. Peripheral problems such as ownership, ethical standards, and audience apathy will become the convenient moral scapegoats that can be named and hunted while the underlying cause, commercial imperatives, remain unquestioned.

The work of Gramsci opened up thinking around this issue of determination. Gramsci demonstrated through his concept of hegemony that dominance is never guaranteed and dominant positions have to be won and negotiated. In other words, the commercial mode of thought now dominating journalism can be challenged. Meadows articulates a resonance between Gramsci's ideas on what an 'integral journalism' could be like and the newer forms of public journalism now emerging.

Journalism, at least in the Western world, is practised within a commercial context so the starting point for a journalism theory has to be some form of theoretical engagement with that economic or commercial base. A more constructive way of looking at this relationship is one of determination in the first instance, and not the last instance, thus moving away from the imposition of a heavily deterministic model. If the economic base operates only in the first instance, there is an allowance for those obvious interruptions to that determination to occur, be they editorial, ethical, political, or social.

Hall (1983b, p. 84) helps us understand this more fluid notion of determinacy as the 'setting of limits, the establishment of parameters, the defining of the space of operations, the concrete conditions of existence, the "giveness" of social practices, rather than in terms of the absolute predictability of particular outcomes'.

If the economic context of journalism is visualised as a perimeter fence with gaps, then it might be easier to understand how other factors can, at times, intervene and affect the practice of journalism, while at the same time recognising that the commercial context (the 'fence') is the paramount force.

It might be useful to consider an example of how interventions in the journalistic process appear to overrule the economic context as the key determinant in journalistic practices. Consider the relationship between Victoria's former Kennett government and the *Age* newspaper. Grattan (1998) set the scene: '...in Melbourne, Bruce Guthrie, who had engaged in a hot shooting war with Victorian Premier Jeff Kennett, was replaced as editor in August 1997; despite apparently rising (though heavily subsidised) circulation, Kennett had lobbied constantly, privately and publicly, for Guthrie's demise.'

Here is a situation where, on the surface, the economic needs of this particular news organisation were being met — circulation was rising — but political forces and political allegiances appeared to be the paramount consideration. Just over a year later, Errol Simper, writing in the *Australian* (an economic rival of the *Age*), condemned the fact that the *Age* had failed to run a story about the reconciliation of Kennett and his wife Felicity. 'The fact is that Kennett has told the media he didn't want the story to run and Melbourne's media, including Gawenda (editor of the *Age*), had complied. When Jeffrey Gibb Kennett makes telephonic communication with the Melbourne media it listens' (the *Australian* 9 October 1998, p. 6).

By any news criteria the story had interest and there were possible political implications from the reconciliation. Was the news organisation allowing political considerations to overrule its economic imperative; that is, to produce stories that would sell?

A story about the reconciliation was published in the *Age* the same day of the Simper column under a byline of state editor Ewin Hannan, but with a note from the editor that read:

> The *Age* was aware of the fact that the Premier and his wife were attempting a reconciliation some weeks ago. We were contacted by the Premier's office and asked not to publish any story about the reconciliation because the Kennetts were not yet ready to go public. Given that there were no public interest issues involved, and the Kennetts were concerned about the effects on them of publicity about their reconciliation, we decided not to publish the story. (the *Age* 9 October 1998, p. 3)

The distinction drawn here between genuine public interest and mere public curiosity may have been acceptable if the *Age* had not published the following month a page 3 non-story about the movements of a certain young, attractive, ex-fiancée of Jamie Packer (Ms Kate Fischer). She was described as 'Australia's very stunning, very tall and very sexy Kate Fischer', who was looking for work in Hollywood. The article was complete with a large photograph emphasising certain body proportions in the best of tabloid traditions.

Media commentator Paul Chadwick exposes the hypocrisy in both camps:

> When Lachlan Murdoch calls his hounds off James Packer and Kate Fischer, we see only a variation of A. J. Liebling: freedom from the press belongs to those who own one ... If owners can silence their journalists about these matters, over what weightier matters do they exercise the same power? Recent events demonstrate the falsity of the media claims that the owner's power is mythical, neither practicable nor practised. We concentrate that power in fewer hands at our peril ... It (media ownership) is a property right, and when editorial independence is granted by owners to journalists, it is power delegated, not ceded. Even if truly independent of owners, journalists must be accountable both to the people they cover and to the audiences. (Chadwick 1998b)

Here Chadwick is defining the problem in classic Marxist terms; that is, the problem is that the means of production rests in limited capitalist hands and yet even he makes a distinction between the obligations that journalists should have to 'the people they cover' and accountability to their 'audiences'. In making such a distinction it could be argued that even Chadwick is recognising the inevitability of that overriding commercial or economic determinant.

It is also interesting to note that in July 1998 journalists at the Leader newspaper group in Melbourne went on strike in response to a management plan to give Premier Kennett a monthly column. Management justification of the column was couched in professional rhetoric (ideology) about the extreme newsworthiness of the Premier. The journalists returned to work with their sense of professional integrity perhaps restored, but the columns still appeared.

These examples demonstrate the continuous 'leakages' from the political superstructure into the journalistic process; however, the primary determinant is the commercial interests of the newspapers' owners.

Ethno-Marxism

In the face of the escalating economic demands being made on the practice of journalism, it would be easy to leave the Marxist conceptual framing of journalism at the level of commodity production. However, with their increasingly loud claims of professionalism, it would seem journalists believe they are more than just commodity producers.

The Marxist approach proposed in this chapter henceforth will be referred to as ethno-Marxism. It emphasises the active involvement of men and women in making their own history, their own reality. This theoretical perspective allows for more attention to the way in which news-workers make their own meanings and ideologies, and produce their own ways of doing that cluster around the central notion of autonomy. Ethno-Marxism is a synthesis of Marxist theory and an ethno-methodological approach 'borrowed' from sociology. It was this perspective that sought to expose the core dilemma of sociology, which in its attempts to theorise its object of study (society) negated the role of the subject.

The innovation of social action is an important consideration for any theoretical project.

Ethno-methodology takes its name from two sources:

- *ethnography*: being the descriptive study of any society in terms of its culture and the ordinary style of collective life that is established through that culture;
- *methods*: the ways in which the members of a society draw on the knowledge which that culture places at their disposal to describe and characterise the world they inhabit.

Ethno-Marxism enables the study of the ways in which the members of a particular social group, in this case journalists, draw on the knowledge that their sub-culture places at their disposal to describe and characterise the world they inhabit. In other words, there are constituting schemas of meaning and interpretation that account for the structures and practices of journalism, and the processes by which journalists bring these into being must be addressed. This approach stresses the rational accomplishment of social actors. Its incorporation could deliver the theory of consciousness that Marxism is often accused of failing to produce.

This incorporation need not rule the crucial forces of production and relations of production; that is, the conditions that impact on this consciousness. Just as Gramsci's theory of hegemony demonstrated that consciousness can not be abstracted from a context of power relationships, so it can be argued that the consciousness of journalists is inextricably linked with their ongoing professional practices. Through this incorporation, as Smart (1976) argued, there is a way of reconciling subject/object, theory, and practice. Smart, arguing for a reconstitution of the Marxist project using the tenets of phenomenology, puts a convincing case for the merger of the two approaches:

> When investigation proceeds at the ideological level alone then consciousness, ideas, language, belief, values and cultural factors in general are taken to be the primary and most specific elements of human society, material relations of production generally being excluded from consideration. Alternatively, if attention is devoted to the material level alone there is the danger that the social relationships of human beings to society and nature will be reduced to a 'presocial or asocial fact'. (1976, p. 162)

Ethno-methodology provides a way to enter the world of making meaning. Listening to the ways in which subjects articulate their own responses and how they interact through language is a key way to study the role of agency in the newsrooms. As Zelizer explains:

> Journalists ... create community through discourse that proliferates in informal talks, professional meetings and trade reviews, memoirs, interviews on talk shows,

and media retrospectives. Through discourse, journalists create shared interpretations that make their professional life meaningful; that is, they use stories about
the past to address dilemmas that present themselves while covering news. (in
Berkowitz 1997, p. 27)

It could be argued that a truly dialectical Marxist approach already incorporates both the material and ideological levels. However, further attention needs
to be paid to the specific task of meaning-building on which ethnomethodology
focuses.

For example, consider a researcher attempting to study how cadet journalists
are socialised into the norms and ideologies of the profession. One approach
would be to take the political economy method as outlined by Hirst (1998a)
and look at these cadets as labourers in the commercial production of news.
However, to take this approach alone might fail to recognise that these cadets
have clear senses of their own engagement with their socialisation process, and
that they carry out work which builds their own worlds of meaning.

In other words, work being done here at the level of active agency would not
have been accounted for without the addition of another conceptual layer to this
primary Marxist approach. While Marxism gives the conceptual tools to deal
with the interaction of both structure and agency within the newsroom, it does
not, in its political economy form, give the facility to properly access the level
of agency.

Hall (1983b) argued that Marx demonstrated the translation of economic
categories to ideological categories, for example, in the way that the oppressive
realities of capitalist market structures could be translated into political and ideological discourses of free enterprise and individualism. Thus the realities of running commercially viable news organisations with minimal staffing can translate
through a lack of hierarchies and minimum supervision, to adamant declarations
of autonomy by journalists. The construction of these ideological notions of
autonomy is carried out at the level of agency.

False consciousness is false in that it 'is an inadequate explanation of a process'
(Hall 1983b, p. 73). This is important because it prompts a recognition that journalists can experience real freedoms in their work and are not just suffering from
false consciousness.

By using ethno-methodological tools of language and verbal cues, researchers
are in a better position to try to explicate processes of meaning construction
within newsrooms. Getting to this level will hopefully allow future research to
study the professional or occupational imperatives highlighted by Chibnall,
which operate in the practice of journalism. In this way, he argues, media representations can be seen as being 'the product of conscious decisions made by
thinking actors within a framework of imposed limitations' (1977, p. 216). He
concludes:

Professional communicators are not simply puppets on strings pulled by capitalists. Nor do they necessarily feel oppressed by the power of the machine they serve. They are men and women who exercise choice and construct their own realities within the constraining parameters set by their ideal and material interests and their professional stock of knowledge. (1977, p. 224)

This new synthesis produces a theory that can accommodate: economic context (base) + cultural, political, and editorial interventions (superstructure) + individual ideologies (consciousness); that is, B + S + C = ethno-Marxism.

In other words, this is a Marxist framework that genuinely incorporates the journalistic perspective and everyday journalistic practice. Being able to elucidate all these levels is the task of journalism theory. If there is no systematic theoretical approach to future research, how will it ever move beyond mere description, and how will it ever effect paradigm shifts? Without a critical theoretical base, research and education in the journalism discipline would be forced to adopt an empirical approach based only on observation or experience, locking it into normative straitjackets. Ethno-Marxism, while recognising the ultimate power of the economic context of journalism, encourages the incorporation of the realities occurring at the level of practice and is able to illuminate that practice.

Conclusion

Concerns about the future of journalism are very real. There is no doubt that future generations of journalists will have to be very savvy commercial operators or, in another sense, very proficient small business people. The question is whether they will be anything more than these corporate operatives. There is, and will continue to be, scant time for consideration of theory or concepts in newsrooms. However, the insidious nature of the commercial forces driving and redefining journalism, and the true nature of their impact on the next generation of journalists must be critically elucidated. Journalism is primarily an economic activity, but is carried out by individuals in a world of meaning produced by their social and cultural and, at times, political activity. One of the most important features of a Marxist framework is its inherent optimistic strain; that is, within any system there is always a 'kernel' of contradiction that opens up the possibilities of change.

Even with the virulent commercialisation now dominating journalism, there are still acts of resistance to that dominance by journalists. Resistance is possible if journalists can be encouraged to think beyond just the 'doing' of journalism.

Case study: the anniversary, the award and the nomination

In the course of a week's phone calls the chief of staff of a country newspaper is faced with three different requests for coverage that cause her
problems.

The first call is from the local Safeway store celebrating its 40th year
of operation in the town. Tacked on to this request for coverage is the
gentle reminder that the store is of course a very regular advertiser with
the newspaper group.

The second call is from the local hotel, which operates a major gaming
franchise, informing her that the venue has just won an international award
for success in its operations. The hotel is also a very regular advertiser in
the newspaper group.

The third call is from the town's major video outlet, which is an owner-
operated franchise, informing her that the owner of the store has just been
nominated as the most successful operator in the State.

The chief of staff feels there is a potential ethical problem arising out
of these three scenarios and raises the problem of 'to cover or not to cover?'
at her morning team meeting, which includes the editor and advertising
manager, as well as other senior staff.

After the meeting the chief of staff is left to make the final decision.

She decides to use news values as the judgment criteria. Basing her
decision entirely on what will make a 'good yarn' she decides that the paper
will cover the success of the video operator as the owner is a well-known
local making a contribution to the local economy.

Both the hotel and the supermarket are contacted by advertising reps
offering them a special deal that could incorporate coverage of their
material, but that would be clearly designated as advertising.

What does this real-life scenario tells us about the day-to-day operations
of journalists within a commercial context?

Clearly, the economic or commercial determinant was a factor in the
decision-making process of this chief of staff. She was clearly aware of the
problems arising from offending two of the newspaper's major advertisers.
However, she also identified the conflict with her editorial responsibilities
as chief of staff to ensure the news value of the stories being covered by her
reporters.

Although ultimately 'contained' by the perimeter fence of the capitalist
mode of production, this journalist was able to use a professional 'tool'
— her news judgment — to make an editorial decision that she was

able to act on. A 'site for resistance' to the commercial determinant was energised.

Cynics may of course note that the advertisers did get enhanced coverage, albeit at a cost!

DISCUSSION QUESTIONS
1 Do you think that journalists have any real freedoms and, if so, what are they?
2 Would the establishment of an international media-monitoring watchdog alleviate the problems created by the increasingly commercialised news organisations?
3 Can you envisage a non-commercial model for journalism, and how would this operate?

Further reading
Curran, J. and Gurevitch, M. 1996, *Mass Media and Society*, Arnold, New York.
Franklin, B. 1997, *Newszak and News Media*, Arnold, London.
Hall, S. 1983, 'The problem of ideology: Marxism without guarantees', in B. Matthews (ed.), *Marx 100 Years On*, Lawrence and Wishart, London.
Schultz, J. 1998, *Reviving the Fourth Estate: Democracy, Accountability and the Media*, Cambridge University Press, Melbourne.
Smart, B. 1976, *Sociology, Phenomenology and Marxian Analysis*, Routledge and Kegan Paul, London.

Part 3

Truth or dare

Truth is central to the process and practice of journalism, but what is truth, and how important is it? Some view truth as a self-evident fact, an obvious and definable entity waiting to be revealed or discussed. Others question whether it is ever possible for journalists to present their audiences with accurate representations of issues and events. This section provides an overview of a range of understandings of truth, and asks what difference the journalist's notion of truth makes to reporting practices. It also asserts that in order to present the *whole* story, journalists must dare to move beyond reactive reporting — and seek deeper truths. It presents a theoretical framework that prompts the journalist to ask the *right* questions and step outside the boundaries of simplistic levels of enquiry. Enquiry must progress beyond the purely knee-jerk reactive type of reporting (passing on the news of a car crash or rise in taxes), through an analytic phase (why has this happened, who is responsible?), and on to a reflective stage (what does this event say about our society?). A recognition of how to progress through these phases of enquiry equips journalists with the basic tools to tell stories as completely as possible, and to avoid the temptations of accepting incomplete coverage as the 'truth' or 'end of the story'.

The real problem for the 'new' journalism is that there is no longer even the pretence of balance between these two forces. The central question that needs to be addressed is: what is journalism and what conceptual tools can be used to arrive at a satisfactory theoretical explanation of its modern form?

Australian theories of journalism

Current theoretical thinking on journalism in Australia could be divided into four major 'camps':

- journalism as commodity (see Sheridan-Burns and McKee, Hirst);
- journalism as autonomous consciousness (see Meadows and Ewart);
- journalism as cultural activity (see Meadows);
- journalism as 'empirical facts' (the Windschuttle version).

All these strands offer something, but this chapter does not intend to be either relativist or pluralist in its approach. One factor above all else has to be accounted for in any theoretical explanation: that is, the economic imperative that appears to dominate thinking about journalism. Journalism as a commodity will provide the major focus for this chapter, but at this stage it might be useful to summarise the alternative visions outlined above.

> . . . journalism, Adam argues (1993, p. 45), is a form of expression that is the product of something called the 'Imagination' — the spontaneous consciousness-forming faculty of individual human beings. It is the 'Imagination', conceived of as a property of culture, that connects the imagination of individuals to society's consciousness-forming practices. (Meadows 1998a, p. 15)

Meadows (1998a, pp. 6–7) further argues that this 'consciousness-forming activity' can be used as a cultural resource: '. . .we can define journalism as a set of practices, which enables consensus formation . . . by focusing on journalism as a cultural resource enables a more effective analysis of its role in the formation of culture.'

The Windschuttle (1998) version of journalism could be dubbed the 'separatist' version in which journalists carry out their work in some form of economic, political, and cultural vacuum. Windschuttle articulates his vision of journalism as such:

> First, journalism is committed to reporting the truth about what occurs in the world. Journalists go out into society, make observations about what is done and what is said, and report them as accurately as they can. They have to provide evidence to verify and corroborate their claims and they have to attribute their sources. Journalism, in other words, upholds a realist view of the world and an empirical methodology. Second, the principal ethical obligations of journalists are to their readers, their listeners and their viewers. Journalists report not to please their employers or advertisers, nor to serve the state or support some other cause, but in order to inform their audiences. (1998, p. 11)

6

The truth, the whole truth, and nothing but . . .

SHARON TICKLE

The sceptical public's perception of journalistic practice, exemplified by the old chestnut 'Don't let the facts get in the way of a good story', is far removed from the benchmark Australian journalism has set for itself. The preamble of the Australian Journalists Association section of the MEAA Code of Ethics opens with: 'Respect for truth and the public's right to information are fundamental principles of journalism'.

Between these two extremes lies the everyday reality of the working journalist — a reality shaped by time pressures, market forces, law, work culture and practices, human frailty, and the journalist's experiences. As for the public, convincing individuals who have been battered by the tabloid press that 'truth in journalism' is not an oxymoron is becoming increasingly difficult. And in this digital age of textual and visual manipulation, can the consumer ever be certain they are seeing the 'real thing'?

Terms of reference

Examining truth in journalism is an exercise in what social scientists call *boundary–work rhetoric* (Winch 1997, p. 3); that is, it is an attempt to draw a boundary between journalists' discourses and their routine practices, and those of other professional communicators. This attempt highlights the differences between news work and entertainment work to support the argument that journalists still have an important role to play in interpreting reality as honestly as possible for their audiences.

It is axiomatic that any interpretation of reality is mediated by language. Language is an imprecise communication tool that can by turns become an instrument of peace or war. For example, take the use of one word by an

Australian Prime Minister in the 1990s. Malaysian Prime Minister Mahathir bin Mohamad decided not to attend the APEC summit in Seattle in November 1993. The then Prime Minister of Australia Paul Keating, asked by the Australian press for his reaction, said Mahathir was being 'recalcitrant'. Mahathir and the Malaysian media took this as a very negative characterisation and began a diplomatic freeze that did not thaw until John Howard replaced Keating as Prime Minister in 1996.

Trying to pin down universally agreed meanings of words is fraught with problems. Most often the different meanings invested in words are a result of different experiences. Another case in point is that of Washington's Ombudsman David Howard, who had been quoted in the media as describing his approach to budgetary restraint as 'niggardly'. The word 'niggardly' (stingy or parsimonious) is listed above the racial slur term 'nigger' (Negro, or any member of a dark-skinned race) in the dictionary, but the two words have widely different meanings. The uproar over Howard's use of the adjective cost him his job. Semantic difficulties notwithstanding, what is important for journalists is that people *do* strive for commonality of understanding. This is one of the reasons the news media were created and why they continue to play such an important role.

By trying to achieve a common understanding of external reality — what the AJA code of ethics calls 'describing society to itself' — journalists face the task of truthfully representing in words, numbers, sound, and pictures, events that have occurred at a particular time and in a particular place. They do this as part of their covenant with the public, which invests in them the authority to tell the news as accurately and completely as possible. This chapter is concerned only with the type of reportage known as 'hard news'; that is, the timely reportage of new information via traditional print media, television, and radio, as well as through the newly converged technologies of digital television, digital radio, and the Internet. For a discussion of the use of fact versus fiction techniques in other forms of non-fiction writing, see Chapter 10.

Grattan (1998, p. 3) suggests commercial pressures are causing an infotainment take-over of newspapers. In time, traditional news will become extinct. Media studies theorists say that the media product known as news is a 'social construct' because 'language does not describe reality, it actually constructs it' (Turner 1993, p. 219). Hartley (1996, p. 201) takes this further when he states that 'journalism, democracy, politics, government, as well as being what common sense says they are, *are also fantasies*'. That discussion is taken up in this book by Meadows in Chapter 3.

Whether one subscribes to these notions or not, pragmatic news-gathering is still the bread and butter of journalists' work, and editors-in-chief will, for the foreseeable future, expect journalists to produce fact-based, authoritatively sourced news stories. Queensland Newspapers' editor Chris Mitchell put it succinctly at a media forum in Brisbane on 3 September 1998: 'If a journalist can't tell the difference between fact and fiction, they shouldn't be in the job'. This is, interestingly, the same man who hired the *Courier-Mail* columnist Helen Darville–Demidenko and then fired her when she admitted using, without attribution, material from the Internet in her weekly column. Darville–Demidenko was already infamous for masquerading as a Ukrainian Australian to promote her first novel, *The Hand That Signed the Paper*, which won Australia's prestigious Miles Franklin award.

The tensions between news media producers, journalism educators and cultural studies theorists concerning the notion of 'truth-telling' have been considerable. News media producers reject claims that they cannot represent the truth in their news stories, while cultural theorists say that it is futile to try to represent the truth because it is a situational and subjective construction of reality. Even the cultural studies proponent Hartley (1996, p. 3), who has criticised vocational journalism education in the past, concedes that journalism is useful as 'a huge store of sense-making' and that journalists "translate' specialised knowledge into common knowledge' (1996, p. 26). For information to make sense, the audience must have some faith that what it is presented with has some basis in reality. This then is the journalist's task. What is outside the scope of the news journalist, and will not be directly addressed in this chapter, are propaganda, public relations, fiction, opinion, and commentary.

Truth from Plato to Foucault

An understanding of what truth means in contemporary society must consider the way in which Western philosophers and Judaeo–Christianity have viewed it and its relationship with epistemology (the theory of knowledge) over the centuries. This review is limited to the Western philosophical tradition and the Judaeo–Christian tradition because current Australian journalistic theory and practice is predicated on these two overarching systems of viewing human existence. It is necessary also to touch on cognitive psychology for insights into how the human mind processes information and makes judgments.

The philosophers of antiquity and the Middle Ages were all *realists*. They believed that there were absolute truths (unconditional or perfect truths) and people could know and understand something in the past or an event that occurred even though they did not witness it. For example, realists would have no difficulty accepting the veracity of the Holocaust from eye-witness accounts.

There were different schools of thought about whether truths could be *universal* (true for people everywhere and for all time). Plato said a universal truth could be realised as a transcendent ideal independent of the concrete thing itself, while Aristotle argued universality was inherent in the thing or idea itself. This is the difference between the notion of gravity as a universal truth, independent of the concrete thing itself, and the idea of gravity being inherent in the object.

The spiritual dimension Plato and Augustine added to this thesis was that man could know truth by being illuminated directly from within by the knowledge of transcendent ideas. This led Thomas Aquinas to try to resolve the arguments over the nature of knowledge by stating that: 'ideas had three kinds of existence: as exemplars in the mind of God, as intelligible forms in things, and as concepts in the human mind formed by abstracting from things' (Tarnas 1991, p. 187).

Judaeo–Christianity's foundational thinking is that the first absolutely certain truth is that of our existence and the second is the inevitability of our death. These truths are held to be *absolute* and *universal*. It follows that since at least two absolute and universal truths have been identified, it is beholden on the believer to search for others.

In the modern era, the mid-1600s, the so-called *continental rationalists* (because they clustered in Holland, France, and Germany) — such as Descartes, Spinoza, and Leibniz — held that the mind alone, through its recognition of clear, distinct, and self-evident truths, could achieve certain knowledge. In a journalistic sense the continental rationalists would agree with the realists that after material evidence of the occurrence of the Holocaust had been tested and found to be congruent with eye-witness accounts, then it could be accepted as true.

The continental rationalist position was at odds with the *British empiricists* of the seventeenth century Enlightenment era, the most prominent of whom were Bacon, Newton, Boyle, and Locke. These men believed that all things must first be experienced by the senses, otherwise they remained speculations only. The British empiricists' position on the Holocaust would be to only accept the absolute veracity of the Holocaust if they had been present to witness it and if the events could be replicated.

The rationalist, realist belief that science could attain certain knowledge of general truths about the world was increasingly displaced by an empiricist position, typified by Karl Popper, who suggested that science cannot make known the real structure of things: it can only, by empirically testing hypotheses, discover probable truths.

The post-modern perspective, which developed from the early 1900s, owed much to Friedrich Nietzsche. Nietzsche (1844–1900) was a radical perspectivist who argued that reality and knowledge were constantly changing, who privileged concrete reality over fixed abstract principles, and who was convinced that no single established thought system should govern belief or investigation. It follows that, for the post-modernist, all truths and assumptions must be continually subjected to direct testing with the understanding that knowledge is relative and fallible, rather than absolute or certain. The post-modern view of reportage of the Holocaust would be that it could only ever be an incomplete, subjective account limited by the ability of the journalist to represent reality.

The analysis of language has contributed most to a delineation of the post-modern intellectual position. In this regard Tarnas (1991) credits principally the work of Nietzsche in analysing the problematic relation of language to reality; Pierce's semiotics (positing that all human thought takes place in signs); de Saussure's linguistics (the relationship between word and object, signifier and sign is arbitrary); Wittgenstein's analysis of the linguistic structuring of human experience; Heidegger's existentialist-linguistic critique of metaphysics; Sapir and Worf's hypothesis that language shapes the perception of reality as much as reality shapes language; Foucault's genealogical investigations into the social construction of knowledge; and Derrida's deconstructionism (which challenges the attempt to secure meaning in any text).

The secular post-modern perspective that has held sway recently (although it must be said that, given the rationale for post-modernism, there cannot be just *one* perspective) rejects previous efforts to find a unifying or totalising theory of knowledge in favour of the thesis that all human thought is ultimately generated and bound by an infinite number of idiosyncratic cultural–linguistic forms of life. Thus human knowledge is inherently chaotic and is the historically contingent product of linguistic and social practices. No interpretation of a text can claim decisive authority — there are as many truths as there are readings of the text. Since there are no uncontested versions of the truth, the most one can hope for is 'to be temporarily useful or edifying, emancipatory or creative — though it is recognised that in the end these valuations are themselves not justifiable by anything beyond personal and cultural taste' (Tarnas 1991, p. 400).

The post-modern condition has been criticised as being dogmatically relativist, detached, and sceptical, and in its extreme form paralysingly nihilist (a nihilist is an extreme sceptic, one who denies that there is an objective basis for truth or that existence is real). Of concern is that if one accepts the nihilist philosophy of nothingness — that life is merely an occasion for sensations and fleeting experiences — then it makes no sense to try to explain events or phenomena, to describe the past, or to predict the future. Certainly it places journalists in an invidious position. If journalists subscribe to post-modernism, whose truth are they going to tell? Will it be through their own heuristic strategy (intuitive, trial-and-error approach), or will they choose to internalise the norms dictated by work practices modelled by their employer and peers? Alternatively, will journalists replace their own cultural–linguistic schema with one they perceive their reader/viewer/listener would prefer and deliver the truth skewed to suit the audience? Post-modern journalists charged with representing the Holocaust would have great difficulty saying anything of lasting significance and would run the risk of offending a large section of the community because they see all accounts as equally valid and would not, for example, privilege a Jewish survivor's account over an SS officer's.

Reasoning and judgment

Cognitive psychologists have examined two general styles of reasoning present in the process of drawing conclusions from evidence — a process that is the daily grind of the news reporter. These are:

- *deductive reasoning*, which relies on inferring from general principles that are then applied to specific facts to reach logically correct conclusions; and the converse
- *inductive reasoning* (the basis of the empirical method), which is based on inference from specific facts that are then combined to draw general conclusions that have different levels of plausibility.

A simple example of deductive reasoning in journalistic practice is the thought process: 'Heroin is an illegal drug in Australia, therefore people who sell heroin are breaking the law. The person just brought into the court is a convicted heroin dealer, therefore he or she is a criminal'. This is a logically correct conclusion.

A simple example of inductive reasoning in journalistic practice might be: 'Police report that there has been an increase in the number of sex workers soliciting customers from the street. Sex workers who operate from the street tend to be heavy users of illegal injectable drugs. The amount of illegal drug usage in the area frequented by the sex workers will go up — this can be judged by the increase in the number of needles given out at the local needle exchange'. This is a plausible inference to make.

It is easy to see that conclusions drawn from both logical deductive and logical inductive reasoning may be valid (logically correct), but they may not necessarily be sound (true) and they certainly cannot do justice to the particular person or event unless many other factors are taken into account.

Investigators Holland, Holyoak, Nisbett and Thagard (1986) propose an integrated framework for understanding inductive reasoning that draws from philosophy, psychology, and computer science. They note that people seem to synthesise their experiences to form various general, flexible rules regarding their observations. They posit that people use these rules to construct mental models (representations) of their environment that allow them to make tentative predictions about what to expect in a given situation as a basis for interacting with the environment. Through interaction the individual learns exceptions to the rules, modifies them and forms new rules (in Sternberg 1995, p. 358).

Applying this mental model paradigm to the journalist, it is predictable that a journalist covering a newsworthy event will make use of both deductive and inductive reasoning to make sense of that event. They will draw conclusions from verifiable evidence — the who, what, when, where, why, and how of the event — and will use their established mental models to assist them to make sense of an ambiguous or novel situation.

Journalists must also exercise their judgment; that is, they must select from among many choices the crucial elements of the story and structure it appropriately. Psychologists call judgment 'decision-making processes' and have theorised that most decision-making does not occur under ideal conditions. While it strives for optimal decisions, it falls far short. They have identified several decision-making models including utility maximisation theory (the goal of human action is to seek pleasure and avoid pain); game theory (decisions have game-like aspects); heuristic strategies (such as cognitive short-cuts based on perception of probabilities); biases; overconfidence; and the fallacy of composition (what is true of the parts of a whole must be true of the whole as well). These models go some way towards explaining how imperfect decisions are made.

Case studies

Truth can mean very different things to different people and the cognitive strategies journalists use to uncover the truth may or may not be effective. There are several cases in which the news media got the story horribly wrong. The following discussion of three such cases illustrates what can happen to subvert the 'truth-telling' processes of the different news media.

Technology and truth: Martin Bryant's eyes

When Martin Bryant's colour photograph appeared on the front pages of major Australian newspapers following the mass murder at Port Arthur, Tasmania, on 28 April 1996, the public got its first look at the face of the alleged killer of thirty-five people. The young man with the long blond hair, dressed in jeans and a white sweater, and looking to the camera, did not have the stereotypical appearance of a mass-murderer. But there was something odd about one of the photographs. In the *Australian*, Bryant's blue eyes had a slightly demonic look that did not appear in reproductions of the same print in other newspapers. Why?

After the discrepancy was raised publicly, the *Australian* claimed that the photo had been digitally enhanced simply to make the image clearer, not to make Bryant look less appealing.

It is arguable that the adage 'the camera doesn't lie' was never true. The camera has always been a tool that attempts to both represent and to manipulate reality. With the advent of digital technology, media workers are now, more than ever, under pressure to improve/distort the image. The demand may come from within the organisation (publisher, editor) or from outside (advertiser, politician). Just as Dustin Hoffman, playing the movie producer Stanley in *Wag the Dog*, directs a film editor to 'punch in a calico cat' to replace a bag of corn chips a young 'war victim' carries in her arms as she flees a burning building, so news media workers are subjected to pressures to 'produce' a news event that wrings the maximum impact or the required angle from the available elements of text, sound, and vision.

In at least one incident the digital manipulation of a photo appears to have been politically motivated. On 14 November 1999 Malaysia's leading Chinese language newspaper *Sin Chew Jit Poh* published a photograph of Prime Minister Mahathir standing next to Deputy Prime Minister Abdullah Ahmad at a function. The file photo had been digitally doctored to remove the previous Deputy Prime Minister, Anwar Ibrahim, who was on trial for sex charges and corruption, and replace him with the new Deputy Prime Minister.

When the alteration was revealed by a website, the newspaper's editor-in-chief wrote to the website to apologise for the alteration, which he said was 'a violation of a cardinal principle of journalism'. He said the junior sub-editor responsible for the substitution had done it because he felt that, as Anwar Ibrahim was no longer in the governing party, '. . . his presence in the photograph was inappropriate'.

It is believed the manipulation was aimed at reducing Anwar Ibrahim's media exposure prior to the general elections. While an apology by the newspaper was posted to the website that uncovered the photo fraud, none was printed in the 250 000-circulation newspaper, leaving most readers none the wiser. It is arguably a short step from the sub-editor's desire to reflect reality to the construction of reality by digitally altering images.

Callahan (1998, p. 5), in his litany of digitally manipulated photos published by the mass media, cites one of the worst offenders as *The New Weekly*, which in 1994 ran a striking cover photo of a man carrying a crying child with bushfires raging behind him. The photo was used to illustrate a news story and was in fact produced by superimposing a photo of a man carrying a child over another image of a fire. Digitally enhanced or manipulated pictures are frequently labelled as 'photo illustrations', but just as often no disclosure is made.

Television: two cameramen — two 'truths'

The documentary *Primetime War* (1997) by Noam Shalev and Yosi Leon illustrates how an event can be interpreted and represented very differently by two people. The program follows Palestinian cameraman Jimmy Michael and Israeli cameraman Alon Bernstein, long-time friends and colleagues, as they go about their work. They are contracted by the BBC and other networks to shoot footage of the ongoing drama in Israel and the disputed territories. Bernstein is sceptical that the vision they send for broadcast tells anything like the truth about the situation in Hebron or Jerusalem. He is convinced that, merely by their presence, they stimulate violence. Michael disagrees and stands by his claim that the video camera plays an important role by showing the world the violence that is occurring in the struggle between Palestinians and Israelis.

This is one exchange between the two men:

AB   Half of it is just a fake, made for the camera.

JM   I think the lens of the camera can do a lot of things.

AB   I don't think the truth is to be found by us ... just as you don't expect a gun to show you the truth, you don't expect the camera to tell you the truth.

JM   Why not?

AB   Because your camera and my camera show two different things.

The moral dissonance of Bernstein who, although he believes his camera may trigger violence, continues to film, is intriguing but is not the subject of this analysis. What is important is that at the most basic representational level — projecting moving pictures with sound of the same event — the cameramen cannot agree that their film represents the same thing, even though it was shot while they were standing side by side. By the time their vision and sound have been edited and the voiceover added, the news packages will be vastly different. Can either one purport to tell the truth?

Personal integrity and the truth: falls from grace

Former associate editor Stephen Glass admitted he made up most of his ground-breaking stories for the *New Republic*; Jonathon Broder, a reporter for the *Chicago Tribune*, was fired for plagiarism; *Boston Globe* columnist Patricia Smith admitted she made up quotes and sources; and Matt Drudge has readily confessed that he often published stories in the *Drudge Report* that he suspected were not true. One of these landed Drudge in court facing a US$30 million defamation suit. Drudge protests that he is not really a journalist, but what he practises, putting news stories on his web page, *is* journalism. Glass's was the most stunning fall from grace. Over a three-year period he wrote prolifically — feature articles, investigative pieces, and columns. Most of these have been found to contain fabricated elements such as fake companies and individuals (Robertson 1998).

When journalists are unable to represent reality to the best of their ability because of overwhelming external influences, they may be viewed as hapless hacks operating in a cold, commercial system. Or they are pitied when a repressive state ideology decrees the norms under which reporters and editors may publish. But when journalists knowingly fabricate and plagiarise stories in the interests of their own careers, they take the profession to another place. What these four individuals have in common is that they took ethics out of the unwritten news equation and replaced it with self-interest. Good journalism requires balanced, factual, important new information presented in context, plus ethics, to produce a good news story. Without respect for the truth-seeking process — compromised, incomplete, and situational as it may be — news reportage is nothing but gossip and hearsay with high production values.

Challenges and opportunities

Journalists are making do with less. Shrinking budgets and longer shifts are the order of the day. One inevitable outcome of this is that journalists rarely have the time to methodically pursue a lead over a period of days or weeks. Investigative journalism is just too expensive for today's MBA-educated financial managers, and journalists are likely to have to write three stories in the time that used to be devoted to one. Today's journalists are much more reactive — responding to the steady river of media releases faxed or e-mailed to them at their hot-desking workstation from the public-relations mills in government, corporations, and NGOs.

One survival skill a journalist must develop early on is to be able to rapidly sort the chaff from the grain in the mountain of information available to them. Although lack of time is a common complaint, the digital age has brought compensations. Computer-assisted reporting, the speed and breadth of electronic communication, and the convergence of digital technology to allow the seamless transfer of sound and vision have all been a tremendous boon to journalists as they try to put together the best possible representation of events. Ethical, critical, reflective, and well-trained journalists can capitalise on the new technologies to better do the job of presenting new information in a timely fashion to their audiences.

While journalists have been busily reskilling for the digital age, media consumers have also learnt a thing or two. Today's readers, listeners, and viewers are not passive habit-bound receptors of news. They are media-literate and sceptical, and are just as likely to get their news from a web page as from the morning paper. More than forty years after television was first switched on in Australia, viewers are still loyal to the evening news bulletin, even though that bulletin comprises only a small portion of their total news consumption.

And the producers of media watchdog programs and media columnists whose job it is to critique the media have educated the public to the reality of news reporting, which is that media practitioners often get it wrong. Sometimes this occurs with malice aforethought, but more often inaccurate reporting is due to time pressure, sloppy journalistic ethics, or laziness. Media studies now forms part of the curriculum at high school, so it is no surprise that young people have an increasingly sophisticated appreciation of the news media and their failings. It is surely a positive development to have some of the responsibility for evaluating the reliability and credibility of news reports situated in the media consumer. Educated readers/viewers/listeners should be able to discern when they are being sold the government line, or if a news story is not factual.

'Authorised truth tellers' in the age of digital convergence

The day has already arrived when an individual can be handed a backpack and told to 'go get the story' anywhere in the world or in near space. The backpack would contain a mobile phone, a laptop computer, a hand-held digi-cam, a passport, and a credit card. The new breed of all-in-one digital journalist will cover breaking news stories, acting as journalist–editor–camera-operator–sound-recordist–video-editor–presenter. Whether the beat is Kabul or Canberra, the cyber-journalist will be a one-person shoot-show-and-tell.

Digital television, digital radio, and the Internet are the mass media for journalists in the new millennium. While print will never die, the patient is ailing and it will take a major cash injection from the infotainment industry to upgrade it and keep it alive. The future is about media convergence, cost control, and cross-promotion. Convergence will see the intermeshing of the interface between television, radio, and the Internet so that news content produced in one medium is streamed to the other two. Ink on paper will serve as a limited indelible promotional vehicle until the proposed electronic newspaper becomes a reality (prototypes operate using electronically charged ink and can be updated second to second by reconfiguring the charge). Costs in the new digital media are controlled by minimal staffing, centralising data storage and handling, and cutbacks to technical operators, while cross-promotion allows corporations to maximise programming publicity.

One obvious concern in this scenario is that the tiered structure, which previously existed to sift and sort news, is considerably flattened. When there is only the field cyber-journalist, a chief of staff and possibly one editor/producer per shift, veritas will inevitably suffer. Fact-checking, source-checking, and sub-editing may be skipped altogether, and with the push to a younger staff profile to handle the new technologies, the experience and judgment of older, wiser heads may be irretrievably lost.

Conclusion

In the pursuit of truth in journalism in the digital age there are three timeless maxims that should be adhered to now more than ever. 'Don't believe anything you hear or read until it has been independently verified by the most authoritative sources possible', 'There are as many sides to a story as there are people who want to tell it', and 'There will always be someone who knows more about a subject than you do'. Journalists ignore these at their peril.

Finally, an apt analogy for the individual journalist's pursuit of truth comes to mind: a Japanese children's game. Each player is presented with a glass bowl containing ten glass marbles, an empty bowl, and a pair of lacquered chopsticks. The object of the game is to be the first person to transfer the marbles from one bowl to the other using the chopsticks. Although seemingly impossible at first, success is achievable with a combination of intense concentration and skill developed through practice. Journalism is like that. Although the truth is slippery and journalists seem to have inadequate tools to deliver it, by concentrating on the essential skills and exhaustive practice, they will succeed eventually in their goal of presenting a credible description of society to itself. The journalistic record serves as a store of instant, if imperfect, history that constitutes a crucial element in public and national life.

DISCUSSION QUESTIONS
1 How might an individual's religious or philosophical convictions (or absence of same) impact on their journalistic practice?
2 What would be the key difficulty a news reporter would have with the post-modernists' understanding of truth?
3 What does Grattan claim is the biggest threat to truth in journalism?
4 What principles could be invoked to assist journalists in the digital age to report as truthfully as possible?

Further reading

Grattan M. 1998, *Editorial Independence: An Outdated Concept?*, Australian Journalism Monographs, no. 1, Department of Journalism, University of Queensland.

Robertson, L. 1998, 'Shattered glass at The New Republic', *American Journalism Review*, 16–22 June, <http://ajr.newslink.org/ajrby78.html> 2 September 1999.

Turner, G. 1993, 'Media texts and messages', in S. Cunningham and G. Turner (eds), *The Media in Australia: Industries, Texts, Audiences*, Allen and Unwin, St Leonards, NSW, pp. 203–66.

7

The importance of enquiry

LEO BOWMAN AND STEPHEN McILWAINE

This book explores a range of challenges conventional journalism must confront if it is to survive. One of these is the problem of where information provided by news media begins and ends: what impacts, what expectations, what public responsibilities are created or ignored in converting events and processes into words and pictures. The problem has always existed but has taken on a new urgency. The globalisation of economic life has unleashed a process of social adjustment: where once there may have been an implicit consensus on the notion of the public interest — and what the public was interested in — what constituted the basis of journalistic work, public interest, and the interested public have become ambiguous issues. A fellow-traveller of economic globalisation, the communications revolution that is the Internet allows consumers more readily to consult references other than journalistic texts in the search for the 'facts' about their world. And, as the corporate scramble for multi-media vantage points attests, all news media are being drawn into the Internet vortex. As Merritt (1996) warns, electronic 'information everywhere' is putting journalism into a position of, at least, uncertainty. Journalism practice must change to accommodate this new order of things — just as it has adapted to the new communications systems that were the hallmark of the economic and social changes of the past, systems such as telephone and broadcast media technology. For this change to be effective, journalists need to understand why it is necessary, as well as the theoretical foundations for such new ways of thinking.

Attempts to meet some of the perceived deficiencies in existing journalism practice have resulted in the evolution of 'new' forms of journalism, such as public journalism (discussed in Chapter 11). Stepp (1996) suggests that, to the degree that it seeks to 'fix' journalism, 'public journalism' is a blessing. It offers many specific antidotes to what might be considered today's non-public journalism: involving citizens in the news agenda; divorcing coverage from officialdom and grounding it in people's lives; and clearing away some of the snideness and smugness that have infiltrated the media.

However, although 'public journalism' has assumed a legitimacy in daily publications (Hippocrates 1999, pp. 65–78), the dedication to searching enquiry methods arguably needed to meet the challenge of diversity and difference appears under threat in many of these same publications. Facilities and approaches to story development appear to be declining, with a notable decrease in newsroom staff numbers and article length, and a concurrent increase in 'single-incident reports on public affairs, significant by themselves, but misleading unless balanced periodically by contextual analyses' (Nelson 1994). These constraints lead to a declining emphasis on analytical and investigative journalism, and a preference for factual and descriptive reporting. Schultz (1992b, p. 22) suggests there needs to be a cultural change that places investigation in a context where it is considered part of the day-to-day work of all journalists: 'Recognising that investigative journalism is something that all journalists can do is an important element of demystifying and broadening understanding of "investigative reporting"'.

Setting up the enquiry

In seeking to indicate that all good journalism requires ongoing investigation, Mencher (1987, pp. 236–71) and Itule and Anderson (1991, pp. 340–59) identify several phases of story development. They illustrate that each stage requires a different focus from journalists seeking to provide a truly comprehensive coverage. Mencher's is a three-step process and Itule and Anderson identify four steps, each requiring a qualitatively different approach to the research for, and the conducting of, an interview. Since they are dealing essentially with practical applications, the theory underpinning these structures is discussed only fleetingly. However, the challenges of today require a conceptualisation of this process that allows both for its explication and application.

This theorisation allows journalists more readily to assess the type of enquiry that is needed and, in turn, the sorts of interview questions that are appropriate. It provides a means to assist with the framing of not one but a range of questioning approaches to allow for the fact that there is a range of stories that might be constructed around any given topic.

Journalists, unless they subscribe to the arguments of academic and other critics that they reflect only the views of power and the status quo, maintain that they seek to discover 'truths' about their society and the wider world (as discussed in Chapter 6). Discovering these 'truths' requires the establishment of rules that suggest a rigour like that adopted by social science, which is also unable to justify its uniqueness through possession of a body of special knowledge. Journalists' claims to knowledge rest with the ability to define and investigate a subject rather than with pre-existing knowledge of its substantive properties. Journalists cannot work from a body of static, specific information because the areas they inhabit are so numerous and dynamic. Their credibility as reporters and writers depends on their making the claim that their training allows them to 'know what to ask', enabling them to begin to present an authoritative report to their audience.

Journalism's methods diverge from those of the social scientists in that journalists must work in obedience to extremely stringent time and space constraints that make news commercially possible but which are foreign to the natural progression of social enquiry. As Tuchman (1978) and Schlesinger (1978) observe, news organisations are geared to produce such accounts with requisite speed to meet daily (newspapers) and hourly (broadcast) deadlines. This means that news and reporting (or enquiry) are not synchronous — they have their own timeframes, independent of each other. It is rarely possible for a journalist to tell the *whole* story in any one report. Journalists can tell the story up to and including deadline, using the information they have been able to discover. But, even while reporters are writing, the story and the situation may change. There is always more information — and there is always more than what appears to be available. Thinking of reporting and writing in terms of levels of information provides a basic technique to cope with the practicalities of the news organisation.

The three stages of enquiry

To meet audience needs, the news-gathering process should *always* seek to encompass three levels of reporting, not one or two, as is conventionally accepted. These can be identified as Level 1 or reactive reporting, Level 2 or analytic reporting, and Level 3 or reflective reporting. Take, for instance, a story about a flood or bushfire. The obvious fact first available is that the event is happening. The journalist can report on this event and on observed facts connected to the event — lives lost, property damaged, times, and places. Reactive reporting includes such observations. At this stage, information is obtained from *people* — through press conferences, the premier's press secretary, the head of a police investigative team, and so on — and from *documents*, such as court transcripts and police booking sheets.

Journalists rely on people to tell them or show them these things; they need people in authority or with special knowledge to supply them with the information that enables them to tell the audience what is happening. Reactive reporting concentrates on information that originates from the source and may be controlled by the source. This level of reporting is often good enough for the *time being* — it supplies those readers whose interest is only vicarious with the information they need or want. And it does so within the time constraints of the news industry. But it is obviously not the *entire* story and it increasingly is not the *only* story that audiences require. Journalists should consider bringing new levels of enquiry to bear on the same material.

As a news event continues — as the reactive phase is exhausted (the fire goes out, the flood recedes, or the initial intensity dies down) — there is a need to go beyond reactive accounts and to burrow deeper in order to make more than superficial sense of the event. This is Level 2 or analytic reporting. Journalists are looking for answers to the *how* and *why*. At this stage the roles of institutions and authorities and their officers are examined with a view to answering some deeper questions. Journalists want to know such things as who was responsible for aspects of this event — who is to blame or who is to be praised for their actions before, during, and afterwards. Did the bushfire result from some failure by authorities to take preventative measures and was its spread exacerbated by some failure in communications? Equally important, did the system work as it should? This is not scapegoating or hero-hunting; it is providing audiences, as taxpayers and citizens, with an explanation for what has happened in their sphere of the world.

Finally, journalists must move into Level 3 or reflective reporting. This stage looks at more deep-seated societal trends and approaches that might have set the stage for a particular news event. It goes beyond institutional accounting to consider broad patterns and trends. For example, while the negligence of officials might have contributed to a fire, broader social patterns also might have played a part. An economically driven trend to concentrate city populations in ever-denser areas around risky sites might have greatly increased the likelihood of hazard to people from a major chemical fire. State government reduction of funds for rural fire brigades might have contributed to fire damage in rural residential settlements; but the increasing trend of urban Australians wanting to get away from it all in bush areas with high fire-danger risks might also be a primary cause for loss of life and property damage.

It is ideally possible to combine all three levels in a single piece of reporting or, at least, within the pages of a single edition of a newspaper or in a broadcast bulletin, but it is usual for the levels of enquiry to be dealt with sequentially, not simultaneously. Reporters cannot expect to move from one level to the next if they have not done a full and proper enquiry at the initial level. An incomplete enquiry that fails to explore a range of aspects at this stage means leads to stories at the analytic level remain hidden and important stories go unnoticed. The 5Ws and the H (who, what, when, where, why, and how) should be applied to every significant facet of each level. Any one of these can provide the critical information that is required to move productively to the next stage. Answers from these inquiries may be unconnected or they may be most closely connected. That is where the basis of analytic and reflective enquiry is established.

Journalists producing the most complete account possible at the time of writing address all elements of a report in a text that, to be understood, must be internally cohesive; that is, it has to hang together. The *what* of the report must be related to a *how*, a *why*, a *when*, and so on. These relationships may be tenuous in a reactive (Level 1) report — that is the nature of this level of reporting — but it is the journalist's job at this level to smooth out rough junctions. If this is not done, readers make no practical sense of what is being reported. 'Going with what you've got' means necessity of practice must subjugate the quest for absolute truth. Journalists do not pretend otherwise. They acknowledge that their accounts rarely cover all aspects of the topic, that some statements are open to contradiction, and that accounts proposed as explanations are partial and partisan at the very least. The fundamental reporting practice of direct and indirect quoting shows this: the views expressed are demonstrably those of the person quoted, and not some higher truth.

Satisfying the critics

Acknowledgment of incompleteness does not mean dodging responsibility. It simply means that journalists know they are never able to claim to have told the full story. Tomorrow is another day and, literally, another story. Acknowledgment of incompleteness, though, is not a statement of resignation — it is an active pronouncement, at least among journalists, that there is *more to come*, and it is worth waiting for. Active acknowledgment of incompleteness by journalists in the end protects journalism from unrealistic demands and unfounded and unfair criticism, and buttresses the perceived worth of journalists in results-driven media organisations. Reporters are open to criticism if:
- they treat initial reactive reports as if they were an end in themselves and not the prelude to a wider (yet ever incomplete) enterprise;
- their inquiries become routine and their stories formulaic;
- they construct a neat, orderly reporting technique that imposes order on chaos and says 'that's that'; or
- they do not pursue incompatible or varying accounts.

These approaches confine story focus to the initial accounts, primarily of officials. Without some critical analysis, these preliminary and often perfunctory interviews between journalists and powerful official sources reign supreme.

Although good journalists are aware of these dangers, the structure and culture of news organisations can lead to acceptance of incomplete coverage as the 'end of the story'. Organisational norms, established work practices, lack of time, personal opinions and reactions can persuade journalists to treat inadequate coverage as the end of the line. Journalists might be satisfied with explanations that are trotted out at hastily convened media conferences or media interviews. These 'hot-house' encounters can encourage a predisposition towards an easy and orderly construction of events. Journalists speak to authoritative people, who have access to information. The authority provides, and often controls, access to details of an event and the actions taken in dealing with a situation under enquiry. This is information journalists need, but it is not the *only* information. Nor is this account the only account of the incident. It is primarily a bureaucratic accounting of a person's role in those aspects of the situation they are responsible for, a by-product of their need to be bureaucratically and publicly accountable. This means the story is told from a certain perspective. The information provided might still be true and important. It is simply not *all*. But because much of this account accords with journalists' perceptions of what happened and because some of their preoccupations are necessarily the same (lives, property, damage, costs), such accounts can have a compelling force. When adjusted — through journalistic questioning, for clarification and challenge on some points — and read in conjunction with often collaborative accounts from other agencies, such information can come to be seen by journalists as 'all there is' or 'all that's worth reporting'. A particular version of the story then becomes the story. Journalists who fall into this trap reify the entirely contestable positions of those in power.

Where this is the case, journalists limit themselves to a reactive approach to reporting. Such an approach does not allow work at this level to build the basis for deeper and broader enquiry at subsequent levels. As a result, published accounts are partial and necessarily selective.

Viewed in social science terms, if journalists confine their inquiries to accounts gathered in the reactive phase, these are necessarily restricted by space and time. Spokespeople can describe only what they have seen or know at a certain time and place. They usually are not qualified or authorised to go further. Journalists who make independent inquiries, at this or later stages, take the story into the more sophisticated analytic and reflective stages. Following the Port Arthur mass murder (see Chapter 6), journalists went beyond official descriptions of the incident to ask questions about the killer's mental state and to reveal his ready access to an arsenal of lethal assault rifles and ammunition. This opened the way for analytic and reflective enquiry: a series of how and why questions that ultimately provided a deeper understanding of the implications of the issue for society.

Delving in to Level 2 enquiry

Once journalists fully explore the reactive phase they can then productively move to Level 2 or analytic enquiry. They move from examining the concrete physical realities or the immediate *what* of the news event to ask who was responsible. By implication, they are asking: How well or badly have the institutions authorised to handle these situations performed and why is this so?

Journalists who wish to inquire at this level need to understand the political system that determines institutional responses to problems in the context of the State and nation in which they operate. They must understand the difference between policies and procedures, be able to identify those responsible for day-to-day maintenance of both, and have some idea how change occurs in these realms. There is little point, for example, starting an editorial campaign lambasting a judge for an inadequate sentence in a particular case if the court is constrained by law from making any other judgment. In such a case, in Australia at least, politicians would have to make the requisite changes to legislation.

This understanding of the different elements of the political system will also assist in a more basic way, allowing easier identification of the appropriate sources for a story. However, at the analytic level, contacts are only part of the enquiry. A reporter also needs to ask the right questions of the right people. To get the best out of an analytic interview phase, journalists can structure their interviews around three principles that move from the most concrete, where black-and-white answers might be available, to the most abstract, where the most appropriate course of action is less clear and might be the subject of considerable contention and debate. Using this approach, the best overall coverage would take the interview through three sequential enquiry stages within Level 2 analytic reporting. The journalist should initially examine the procedures that require and regulate action at street level. What rules and regulations govern the situation, and how is their compliance assured? The journalist should then move through the political facilitation of the process. For example, did politicians allocate enough resources to the task? Finally, the journalist should proceed to policy formulation. Does existing legislation or policy provide adequately for the situation in question?

These questions should be accompanied by secondary questions framed around the appropriate who, what, when, where, why, and how elements to get all the information necessary to a comprehensive enquiry at this stage. A familiarity with the appropriate questioning techniques attuned to reporting this stage has become a prerequisite for the practice of a journalism speciality known as 'political reporting'.

Even within these structures, however, there is an acknowledgment that political systems are value-laden and that political policy-making and implementation are not filtered through some objectifying prism. More concrete stories are possible if the issues are clearly identified. At the more abstract levels (examination of political facilitation and policy), journalists enter the realm of argument and opinion in the coverage of debates where the 'correct position' is often a matter of opinion, formed from the audience's interpretation of the report. Thus, in debates on the appropriateness or otherwise of policy on greenhouse-gas emission levels, the government has only to take on the appearance of gathering the relevant information and consulting interested groups to argue that it has observed 'due process'. Once this is done and a rationale for action is formulated and publicised, the appropriateness of the government's action is a matter for interpretation rather than an unequivocal fact.

In these grey areas, political debates will emerge around the correct course of government policy and implementation. In such cases, where news of a dispute over particular issues or policies 'breaks', journalists critically question those involved and 'balance' the coverage through synthesising their report into a single article or a 'spread' on the issue. This sort of coverage gives much useful information and fulfils the object of enquiry at this level. The time-and-resource limitations of news organisations often constrain the simultaneous search for deeper implications and broader enquiry approaches, but the search is necessary, at least at some stage, if journalists are to move beyond the reactive reporting phase.

Unless enquiry moves beyond the analytic framework to the reflective, the presence of divergent and often hotly contested views — with all the accompanying spirited rhetoric — might disguise the fact that the coverage examines only a certain aspect of a much broader question. Where such a specific focus is allowed to remain in place, a range of relevant considerations is left unexamined. It is at this point that social science critics and the proponents of the notion of 'public journalism' converge in their criticism of journalism. They maintain that the journalist-source nexus that is so pronounced at the analytic level excludes the search for explanations elsewhere.

Fortunately, accomplished journalists realise that, at the analytic level, debate about an issue can mask tacit agreements as to the parameters of that debate, despite a range of differing perspectives being presented. The mission of reflective reporting is to expose this perception for the limited construct that it is: a single level of enquiry in a multi-layered process. Journalists should consider other possible solutions and different categorisations of the problem, which might be available outside the discourse of analytic reporting.

Progressing relevant stories to the reflective stage is accomplished through the initial shift of a frame question that sets about the most concrete reappraisal of the preceding debate. The frame question designed to trigger primary research that critically examines the bases of statements made by various sources is: what underpinning propositions are verifiable through a re-examination of the material?

This research area is followed by more abstracted enquiry preoccupations: how might people outside the field of interest and discussion contribute to a more accurate representation of the issue? The frame question prompts journalists to stand back from the debate and investigate the bases of the statements put by various parties. It allows for a checking of the 'facts' they have used and their interpretation of reports and other documents.

This initial primary research can achieve two outcomes. It might query the use or misuse of certain statistics or the interpretation of certain reports or documents. In this way, the self-interested motives of parties to a dispute might be exposed. Alternately, it might allow the material to be read in another way. It is excessively cynical to hold that all uses of material on the public record are suspect: it is possible that equally valid interpretations or aspects have been overlooked. The journalist who examines this material may see different ways of interpreting the same information and insinuate this into the debate through questioning. This might lead to the framing of insightful questions that force participants to reformulate their positions, and, in so doing, provide a better story for their audience.

The above information allows journalists to take a story beyond knowledge controlled by a source. It goes some way towards answering claims that journalists seek to treat the definition of 'knowledge' as residing in powerful individuals.

Journalists still face some of the problems implicit in analytic enquiry. They are still interviewing 'experts' on their own terms. Journalists' lack of substantive knowledge limits their activity to critical questioning of, say, members of the architectural field who might construct debate on the built environment around questions as to the appropriate design standards. Thus, a development-versus-environment debate might focus on the appropriate location and style of a particular development. This concentration on tangible local manifestations of a conflict might ignore the influence of global patterns. It might mask the fact that such disputes are symptomatic of modern patterns of settlement promoted, for instance, by a shift of international finance into developments friendly to tourism and other leisure-based industries. Such macro-patterns contain properties that exist independently of the events they influence and, as such, might manifest themselves simultaneously through a range of similar or different events.

It is such issues that proponents of public journalism claim escape day-to-day political reporting, with its perceived focus on the interaction between powerful institutions and vested interests to the exclusion of citizens and communities. However, these same journalists, or others with a more reflective brief, might reintroduce the subjects of such debate at the local level. These journalists might move on to ask the question: how might people outside this field of interest and discussion contribute to a more accurate representation of what is at issue?

The journalist needs to know not just what primary sources agree or disagree about, but also at least why they agree or disagree, where this stems from, and whether there are a number of different ways of looking at the question.

The scepticism that most journalists develop should provide the starting point for thinking differently about an apparently routine story. Such enquiry might provide an independent hypothesis that could be tested at least to the point that it is practicable: can this question be answered? Is this enquiry beyond my resources? Is it worth the time? Although practical considerations must be taken into account, a systematic routine of probing every story for its potential at each of the three levels would help establish a more reliable and consistent way of satisfying twenty-first-century news consumers.

Conclusion

Changes in technology and audience appear to be dictating a more accountable and more relevant form of journalism practice that heeds news audiences' needs for explanation and involvement in the news process. Journalists need a structured pathway and an understanding of the theoretical foundations of that pathway if they are to move confidently into new and more responsive ways of working. The three-level system of enquiry encourages journalists to seek and explore the countless stories that await telling. It is a simple, sound technique for journalists at all stages of their careers and in all kinds of news outlets.

Case study

On 28 April 1996, thirty-five people were shot dead and twenty others were wounded at Port Arthur, Tasmania. The sole assailant, Martin Bryant, used two high-powered, semi-automatic rifles in the shootings. Bryant was captured after fleeing a house he had set alight.

Media reaction to this extraordinary event was swift and intense, as would be expected. Tasmanian Director of Public Prosecutions Damian Bugg, QC, warned potentially overzealous news organisations of prosecution for contempt of court should they do more than report on the event and subsequent happenings. Journalists were thus confined to Level 1 or reactive reporting, at least in Tasmania, by legal restriction. In other states, however, where the Tasmanian legal jurisdiction does not apply, news organisations rapidly moved to a higher level of investigation of the massacre. At Level 2, analytic reporting, journalists began to ask why was such a known psychiatrically disturbed person able to own an arsenal of firearms? Could the behaviour of Bryant have been predicted by normal community and police scrutiny? Why did Tasmanian law make such firearms so readily available to anyone in Tasmania? Whatever the rights of Bryant, under arrest in hospital, media consumers throughout Australia and throughout the world had a natural and eager interest in how government action or inaction laid the foundations for this shocking event.

Throughout the court appearance and sentencing of Bryant, journalists continued to report at levels 1 and 2, but enquiry was already focusing on the socio-political background to the massacre. At this third level, reflective reporting, the entire gun culture in Australia came under media attention, culminating in the federal government making arrangements with the states and territories to buy back semi-automatic weapons and to restrict their sale and ownership. The de-institutionalisation of people like Bryant became a renewed and, fitfully, important area of journalistic interest. The media have continued to monitor the firearms agreement in its socio-political context as gun laws partly frame party-political stances at state and federal levels.

This enormous event and its consequences demonstrated the natural movement of enquiry from basic to sophisticated levels: people were told what was happening, who could have allowed it to happen, and how the socio-political groundwork for this event was prepared. Acceptance of such natural flow should not obscure the fact that many events at many intensities of impact are worthy of such treatment but often do not receive it. Many events of an apparently routine newsworthiness are treated at levels of analysis that do not satisfy public interest and latent public demand.

Discussion questions

1   Examine your local newspaper. Group stories into reactive, analytic, or reflective categories. What conclusions can you make based on the numbers of stories in each category?
2   Pick out one recent major news issue and track it through the three stages of enquiry. What types of stories were written as the story moved through the three levels?
3   Take one local reactive news story. Plan to move it into analytic and reflective stages. What questions would you need to ask? What people and sources would you need to consult to do this?

Further reading
Bowman, L. 1993, 'Interviewing: establishing the context', *Australian Journalism Review*, vol. 15, no. 2, pp. 123–30.
Bowman, L. 1994, 'How journalists' cultural dispositions affect news selection', *Australian Journalism Review*, vol. 16, no. 2, pp. 25–30.

Part 4

In the eye of the beholder

Truth, like beauty, may be seen to be in the eye of the beholder. This section examines issues of perspective, investigating *whose* truth is promulgated in the mainstream media. It looks at the ways in which daily news practices perpetuate the preconceptions held by journalists and their audiences, cementing stereotypes while overlooking or silencing the voices of 'others' — Indigenous people, the socially disenfranchised, and those on the 'fringes' of society. The section looks at both metropolitan and regional journalism, identifying the latter as playing a unique role in the formation of notions of community — who belongs and who does not. It investigates the impact on reporting of Indigenous issues of concepts of readership, the choice of sources, newsroom policies on what is or is not newsworthy and journalistic routines. The section moves beyond an examination of the challenges of reporting about and for 'others', and suggests concrete strategies journalists can use in attempting to remain fair, accurate, and culturally aware in their work and their reporting of issues.

8

More than skin-deep: Australia's Indigenous heritage

MICHAEL MEADOWS AND JACQUI EWART

This chapter focuses on journalism practices in relation to the reporting of Indigenous affairs. It builds on Chapter 3 to argue the central place that journalism has in 'imagining' society. It argues, too, that journalism, as a set of cultural practices, is inextricably linked to notions of democracy, particularly in relation to public sphere activities. While concepts of the public sphere have come under increasing pressure from an expanding and powerful global media market (discussed in Chapter 14), this does not mean the concept should be rejected. On the contrary, journalism needs to be reorientated to account for this global shift in power relations and the first steps must be taken at the local level.

The role of Australian journalism in the rise — and fall — of One Nation[1] was crucial (Meadows 1997a). And journalism, as an important cultural resource at both the regional and metropolitan levels, did not respond confidently to the opportunities afforded by two 1990s legal decisions with the potential to impact in a profound way on the lives of all Australians. The High Court's 1992 *Mabo* decision[2], followed by the 1996 *Wik* decision[3] have placed settled Australia in a new relationship with Indigenous people — theoretically, at least. But almost before the ink had dried on the judges' published findings, the clamour of critics was deafening — with journalists playing a dominant role in framing the 'debate' (Meadows 1994a, 1998b).

This chapter looks at both regional and metropolitan journalism as it applies to the reporting of Indigenous affairs. There is evidence to suggest that regional journalism has a unique place and role in the formation of identity and the creation of the concept of community. It is this concept of community reinforced by regional media that impacts on notions of identity — who belongs and who does not belong. The majority of Australians have limited, if any, contact with Indigenous Australians (Trigger 1995), and it is often at the regional or local level that non-Indigenous Australians formulate their ideas about Indigenous people.

These ideas are certainly taken up at national level, with media in general playing a significant role in the formation of the everyday, commonsense ideas and assumptions about Indigenous people. Most journalism is about the everyday, even the mundane, and it is at this level that representations of Indigenous people may be the most abiding because it is here that readers are more likely to form connections and commonalties, not with those being represented, but with those doing the representing.

Regional journalism does play a unique role in the formation of the notion of community, helping to unite and connect groups of people. It is dependable in the face of the unpredictable. Metropolitan media cannot provide the same kind of unity because they focus on national and international issues. While metropolitan media may be a linking force between disparate groups of people across the country, they lack the community focus so unique to the regional media, which, therefore, play a key part in the production, construction and maintenance of social reality and relations. Regional journalists have to appeal to the habits and world views of their readers (Cryle 1996). Notions of community, who belongs, and who does not, are formed and cemented at the local level with news acting as a bridge for regional people — a bridge between them and other members of their immediate community, and between them and the outside world.

Framing the news

Studies of the coverage of Indigenous affairs in the Australian news media suggest a lack of ability by journalists — from first contact — to accurately represent 'the other' in anything but stereotypical, patronising, assimilationist, or ignorant terms. Fortunately, there are exceptions. There are journalists who continue to try to expose the ignorance of politicians, the injustices, and the social disadvantage experienced by many Indigenous people in Australia. But in the grand scheme of everyday journalism, these attempts seem to be the exception (Meadows and Oldham 1991; Mickler 1992; Goodall 1993; Meadows 1994a; Trigger 1995; Ewart 1997b; Mickler 1997a, 1997b).

But it is the routine, day-to-day journalism with its steady repetition of stereotypes and ethical breaches, which sets up a framework of understanding about race relations for audiences (Blythe 1988, Ward 1989, Hippocrates and Meadows 1996, Weston 1996, Meadows 1997a). It is the everyday practices of journalism that have helped to enshrine racism at an institutional level in Australia. The media — and journalism — represent key cultural resources where ideas and assumptions about Indigenous affairs are created, worked on, and perpetuated — a process through which society is strategically managed (Hall 1981; Gramsci 1988b, Holub 1992). This is no conspiracy but, as argued in Chapter 3, the media *are* places where members of society 'imagine' others and themselves as citizens with particular rights and responsibilities (Anderson 1984). Journalism is a set of cultural practices that enables this process to take place.

Understanding journalistic practices and how they impact on the representation of Indigenous Australians requires insights not only into those practices, but also into the field in which journalists work, particularly their workplace cultures. It is vital that researchers *talk* to journalists, as well as examine the final outcome of their practices. At the heart of the task of this chapter is the need to discover and understand how journalists describe their own work practices and ideals, and how these lead to Indigenous Australians being represented (or not represented) in particular ways in the media. These practices have been identified in previous studies (Ericson et al. 1987; Hippocrates and Meadows 1996; Meadows 1997) and this chapter provides an explanation of the impact they have on the reporting of Indigenous issues at a regional level. The broad claims made in this chapter about journalistic practices are based on existing research and the journalistic experience of the authors.

This chapter also investigates journalistic practices through an exploration of articles produced by Australia's leading daily newspaper, the *Australian*. The case study includes all news and feature stories published by the *Australian* for the period 5 June to 7 July 1998.

Van Dijk (1991) identifies the need to examine the semantic significance of the text of news stories — their implications and irrelevances, for example — as well as what he terms 'news schema' such as headlines, story introductions, key events, context, history or background, quoted passages, and commentary. This should also include *omissions* from stories, which might be more revealing in some cases. Van Dijk's discursive method — or analysis of the discourse of news — includes an examination of the text, which leads to questions such as why particular choices of language and descriptions are preferred over other possibilities. Applying both ethnographic and discursive approaches enables a deeper understanding of the practices and processes of journalism — in this case, in relation to the representation of Indigenous people.

The journalists

There are several key areas in which journalistic practices — frequently a result of the inculcation of journalists into journalistic culture — lead to constraints when covering Indigenous issues. While some researchers and theorists focus on the influence of management — and even owners — in the type of coverage given to Indigenous issues, a broader understanding of the factors restricting journalism can be achieved by an examination of journalistic practice, particularly everyday routinised practices and their impact on journalism. It is these everyday, routine approaches to reporting on Indigenous issues and people that cement stereotypes and lead to exclusion of Indigenous people in the media. The key problematic areas include journalists' concepts of readership, the use of sources and the granting of authority status to those sources, newspaper policies, and constraints in the routine gathering and writing of news (Meadows and Oldham 1991; Goodall 1993; Trigger 1995; Ewart 1997b).

Readership

One of the predominant factors that influences journalists is readership, or more precisely, ideas about readers — who they are and their cultural and social backgrounds. Understanding how journalists formulate a picture or, as Hartley (1992) suggests, 'a caricature' of readers, is essential in exposing the role journalism has in imagining society. Journalists often claim they are reflecting society in their coverage of news, as they are writing for the reader. However, journalists are more likely to gain their ideas of readership from two sources: their immediate supervisors and colleagues, and their sources. This reliance on a limited pool of people who are authorised knowers (Ericson et al. 1989) has a huge effect on the way journalists report, gather, and write the news. In the process, they reflect the world of the limited group from which they draw their concepts of readership. Logic dictates that journalists and those who manage the media should arrive at concepts of readership through demographic information and reader surveys. However, journalists frequently comment that they have limited or no access to such data.[4] When journalists do manage to access such material, reader profiles are often stereotyped because of identification and categorisation generalisations by marketing and research companies. In regional areas, such limited access to reader profile information can and does lead to the formation of limited concepts and ideas of readers, with journalists likely to describe them as Anglo-Celtic and hard-working rural people (Ewart 1997b).

Hartley's 1992 study found journalists address a media-constructed image of the audience that is really a caricature, interpreting the world of audience as a down-to-earth 'man in the street' or a family sitting comfortably at home, all with some kind of uniform common sense. His case studies and findings illustrate how journalists help the audience to metaphorically understand the world in which they live. It is this imagining of the reader by journalists and their colleagues that assists in the exclusion of Indigenous people from the concept of community, and in the cementing of stereotypes of them.

Sources

Concepts of readership held by journalists influence the way they source, gather, and write news. The abstraction of the audience by journalists and their reliance on authorised knowers for information results in limitations on the coverage of issues, particularly those involving Indigenous Australians. Journalists may see this limited coverage as a way of meeting readers' requirements. For example, Indigenous issues are not considered by journalists and others to be news because they do not appeal to the majority of readers. Yet, the media are a major (if not the only) source of information for many non-Indigenous Australians — and journalists — about Indigenous affairs. Because many journalists have limited contact with Indigenous people, they rarely talk to Indigenous sources about Indigenous issues, which are only considered newsworthy by some newspapers if they can be sensationalised.[5]

The worldview of journalists is defined by the circle of people they move within and includes their newsroom colleagues. More interestingly, it includes those contacts and sources they rely on regularly for news. These regular sources are frequently authority figures such as police, court officials, council officers, and business people, which limits not only the topics that attain genuine news status and therefore are covered as news, but also the angles taken and the views expressed in those stories (as discussed in Chapter 7).

Regional journalists work in an organisational environment and culture of limited resources, low staff numbers, and heightened time and production pressures. The accessibility and credibility of authoritative sources, along with the limitations and constraints facing regional journalists, means they tend to spend large amounts of time cultivating such sources because of their accessibility and credibility. This institutionalised use of sources by journalists legitimises the media as a cultural institution in the eyes of the members of other cultural institutions, who are almost always the sources on which journalists rely. This establishes a kind of two-way process of reinforcement and legitimisation of cultural institutions by each other.

Newspaper policies: what makes news?

The journalistic practice of selecting what makes news plays a major role in the 'imagining' of the community. Research reveals that what makes news and the selection of events and issues for news coverage is controlled by a select group (Ericson et al. 1989; Grabosky and Wilson 1989; Hartley 1992). From the time of taking up a cadetship until they retire, journalists are continuously socialised by their colleagues and editorial management into knowing what issues they should and should not cover. Often this socialisation is subtle. Journalists are not always directly told not to cover a story. Rather, they learn by being steered in other directions by colleagues, or by the editing or rejection of their copy. Journalists take their cues for reporting the news from the editorial hierarchy rather than the community.[6]

There is significant research evidence of the selective application of ethical judgments by journalists (Kiernan 1998). Sometimes this selectivity is designed to suit the unwritten policies of the media about not covering certain issues (such as the traditional avoidance of suicide-related stories). Reporters and editors often cite the potential of a story to exacerbate a crime or harm an individual as a reason for not covering an issue. However, many of the stories that are covered do have such potential, as well as the potential to damage the standing and aspirations of Indigenous Australians. It is not always journalists who decide whether or not an issue is going to be covered — often, editorial managers make such decisions and journalists have little choice in the matter. Few newspapers and other media outlets have a written policy on the coverage of Indigenous issues, but some journalists believe Indigenous issues are covered only if they are sensational or can be sensationalised (Ewart 1997b).

Regional journalists rely heavily on metropolitan media for news leads. Regional journalists follow state and national news closely in an attempt to find newsworthy stories with potential local angles. This reliance on other media for news could be responsible for the lack of spontaneity in regional news, which becomes routinised, setting up an ever-decreasing circle of what can be legitimately considered news by journalists.

Daily routines

Arguably one of the most important elements that affects the way journalists represent and cover Indigenous issues and people is the daily practices involved in producing news. It is these everyday practices, which appear to have no conceivable racist overtones, that are largely responsible for the enshrining of racism within the practices of journalism. These tend to reinforce stereotypes and to restrict the ways in which Indigenous people and issues are treated in the news. This is subconscious or, perhaps, unconscious racism. The first of these practices is news-gathering.

Regional journalists rely primarily on the telephone to gather news. They regularly get second-hand reports of events, limiting both the amount and veracity of their information. This impacts on the reporting of Indigenous events when linked with the limited use of Indigenous sources, as information about Indigenous issues and events is obtained from non-Indigenous people. Thus, journalists often receive unreliable and culturally inappropriate interpretations of Indigenous news. The problem is compounded by the community-based nature of Indigenous organisations, which do not have official offices and so have limited access to telephones. Time and resource constraints mean regional journalists favour those organisations and people they can contact quickly by phone, cementing the exclusion of Indigenous sources, categorised by journalists as 'difficult to get hold of' and 'lackadaisical' in returning phone calls (Ewart 1997b). This reinforces and perpetuates the systematic disadvantaging of Indigenous people's and community groups' social and economic power, with journalism (and the media) becoming a site for the augmentation of the power relations institutionalised by other cultural institutions.

Another aspect of journalism that strengthens racism at the institutional level is the deadline. While deadlines are a vital part of news practice, it is not the slavish adherence to them that is of concern, but journalists' voiced reliance on them as a reason for not obtaining balance or an Indigenous perspective in stories. In Ewart's 1997 study, regional journalists used tight deadlines as a justification for the lack of Indigenous perspectives in stories involving Indigenous people or issues. They argued that this was linked to the difficulty of contacting many Indigenous people by phone.

A third element that contributes to the failure to adequately report Indigenous affairs is the routineness of news — a major issue for regional journalists faced with little immediate 'real' news. Much regional news is rote and can be relied on to occur regularly — council meetings, annual fetes, court sittings, and sporting events. Regional journalists acknowledge they write much of this news before it actually occurs because they come to rely on these stories fitting a particular pattern (Ewart 1997b). Hartley (1992) suggests this facet of news production involves a reliance on habits and conventions established by previous news production.

The introduction of new technology has further limited the ability of journalists to cover certain events and issues as news. Deadlines have crept forward with the arrival of new technology such as newspaper pagination systems. Despite the initial promises offered by such technology, it has not facilitated expanded coverage of local news in regional newsrooms. Instead, it provides regional journalists with another reason for not covering Indigenous issues or gaining Indigenous perspectives on relevant issues. The lack of Internet sites belonging to Indigenous organisations may mean that while government and business views are easily accessed by journalists using the Internet, Indigenous perspectives are not.

Style and presentation also influence the representation of Indigenous people and issues. Those who deal with the media regularly are aware of the house rules and work to them. Those who are not regularly contacted by journalists are often unaware of these requirements, so are less likely to be approached again for information. The set of journalistic expectations and rules that govern the way journalists write and present stories limits their capacity to fully expose the intricacies of an issue. For example, journalists are often forced to 'rationalise' sources — to make a quoted source 'appear to sound rational' when what the person actually said was quite irrational (Ewart 1997b). This process of 'tidying up quotes' leads to a false perception of the source, providing an inappropriate picture of their rationality and authority to speak on an issue. This makes it seem perfectly logical and justifiable for a non-Indigenous source to be the primary source of comment on an Indigenous issue or event.

Treatment of Indigenous issues

Thus, everyday, routinised practices produce agreement within the public consciousness over images of Aboriginality (Trigger 1995). While there is no intention to fabricate or invent stereotypes, it can be argued that journalists and the media reinforce the stereotypes and representations of Indigenous Australians held by the non-Indigenous population.

Journalists consider the issue of 'race' problematic. There are significant disjunctures between their ideals and practices in this area. Journalists rationalise this divide by citing the constraints of their work practices and ethical obligations. Again, they are not intentionally racist; indeed, Loo's 1992 study found that journalists considered blatant racism to be 'repugnant and anachronistic'. However, major contradictions are evident in the treatment of race in a range of stories, particularly those dealing with crime and violence. In a 1997 study, journalists expressed conflicting views about how race was included in crime stories, initially suggesting it was rarely if ever mentioned and then saying all stories contained such information regardless of the person's racial background (Ewart 1997b). A textual analysis of the newspaper involved revealed Aboriginality was clearly referred to in pre- and post-arrest accounts. A perusal of articles from regional and metropolitan newspapers provides further evidence of this practice.

The existence of the MEAA's code of ethics has further complicated the issue of reporting on race. Many journalists report being pressured into acting contrary to the code by editorial management. The 'reality' of gathering and writing news is frequently cited as a justification for journalists' inability to strictly adhere to the code. This self-justification of ethical and professional breaches might skew the audience's understanding of race relations. For example, it is considered acceptable by both readers and journalists to mention a person's ethnic or racial background in a crime-related story, despite the Code of Ethics' admonition not to 'place unnecessary emphasis on race' (Schultz 1994, p. 184).

Journalists approach their work through a value system that positions them as watchdogs on government and as promoters of democracy. This notion of journalism and the media as the fourth estate is a theme discussed elsewhere in this book. The debate is timely, given the increasing public disillusionment with both government and the media. In Ewart's study, journalists and members of the editorial hierarchy argued that this fourth-estate role indicated they had a duty to discuss issues that affected the community and, in some cases, to assist with resolution of those issues. However, in discussing a rift between police and an Indigenous community, senior editorial management suggested that it was *not* the newspaper's responsibility to heal this breach, and that it had nothing to gain from doing so. The staff did believe they had a duty to report the One Nation phenomenon because of the damage it was doing to the economy. Yet the same senior staff and journalists suggested this sense of duty did not extend to in-depth reporting or comment on the arrest of fifty alleged fine defaulters during a funeral at an Aboriginal community (see the case study on page 128). This contradictory approach to issues by the newspaper's management and journalists demonstrates the different status of issues, according to the subject and its relation to Indigenous and other communities.

It is obvious then, that problematic practices affect regional journalists' reporting of Indigenous affairs. An examination of a major national news event sheds light on the manner in which their metropolitan counterparts negotiate the often complex political issues that are intimately connected with Indigenous people.

Reporting the 10-point plan

The Wik people comprise a group of eleven communities living on the western side of the Cape York Peninsula in far north Queensland. Their traditional lands cover a vast area of this region (Stevenson 1997, p. 2). During the 1950s the discovery of bauxite on the Wik lands encouraged the Queensland Government to do all it could to oust the people (Reynolds 1989, p. 88). By 1957, the Government had passed a special Act of Parliament — the *Comalco Act* — effectively handing a 110-year lease to mining company Comalco. The lease covered virtually all of the Wik people's Weipa reserve of more than 600 000 hectares. In 1963, the expansion of mining prompted the Queensland Police Force to remove the Wik people from the settlement of Mapoon. Their homes were bulldozed and burned to the ground. The community was forcibly relocated to Bamaga, several hundred kilometres north. Another mining company, Aurukun Associates, was given a lease over 2000 square kilometres of the Aurukun reserve in 1975, without consultation with traditional owners. Traditional owners have received no royalties from mining reserves, then estimated to be worth $14 billion (Stevenson 1997, p. 3).

Pastoral leases are titles given by the Crown over Crown land. Pastoralists rent the land from the government and are limited to conducting specific activities — primarily managing stock (Love 1997, p. 11). The concept of the pastoral lease was developed as 'a very specific response to the unauthorised movement of "squatters" with their herds and flocks onto back country beyond the limits of early settlement' (Nettheim 1997, p. 5). Reynolds (1996, p. 14) argues that the pastoral lease was also designed by colonial authorities to protect Indigenous people from the onslaught of European settlement. The dubious claims made by some pastoral lease-holders in the 1990s — and dutifully echoed uncritically by many journalists — suggest that leaseholders have the same rights as those who have freehold title over their land. Nothing could be further from the truth. Just 12 months after the 1992 High Court's *Mabo* decision destroyed the legal fiction of *terra nullius*, the Wik, joined by the Thayorre people, lodged a claim in the Federal Court of Australia for native title to 28 000 square kilometres of land on Cape York Peninsula. It included ten pastoral leases (Stevenson 1997, p. 5). Despite the Wik people's desire to use the Native Title Tribunal as a mediator in the case, the Queensland Government moved it to the High Court following an application. On 23 December 1996, the High Court determined that it was possible that native title rights and pastoral leases could co-exist (Stevenson

1997, p. 10). However, the court also found that where there was conflict in the exercise of those rights, native title rights were *subordinate* to those of pastoral leaseholders (ATSIC 1997). It seemed clear enough. While co-existence of rights was possible, where conflicts existed, pastoralists had the upper hand. However, the tenor of media 'debate' following the decision suggested otherwise.

By May 1997, Australian Prime Minister John Howard had formulated what he termed a '10-point plan' — essentially, amendments to the 1994 *Native Title Act* in the wake of the 'uncertainty' created by the High Court *Wik* decision. When the amendments were first presented to the Senate in May 1998, Independent Senator Brian Harradine — who held the balance of power — refused to accept several of the points. Howard threatened to call an early federal election unless the Senate accepted all his proposed amendments. But the bargaining began again in light of the success of One Nation candidates, elected to the Queensland Parliament in June 1997. During an intense period of high-pressure debate — with Indigenous people totally excluded — Harradine changed his stance on several key amendments 'to avoid the anger and horror of a race-based election' (Henderson 1998, p. 1). This about-face enabled the *Native Title Act Amendment Bill* to pass through the Australian Senate on 7 July 1998.

Coverage in the *Australian*

In the month leading to that decision, the national daily newspaper the *Australian* published 41 stories on the 10-point plan (as outlined in Table 8.1).

An analysis of the headlines used in the 41 news/feature stories reveals much about the agenda-setting role of the media. Almost half the headlines focused on the so-called 'deal' over Wik. This approach superseded all others in the study period. From 11 June, beginning with the headline, 'No watering down Wik' (p. 5), the *Australian* limited discussion over the next four weeks within this narrow frame. The 'Wik deal' became the primary definer of what was news in Indigenous affairs.

The results of the Queensland election — where One Nation gained 11 seats — increased the tempo of stories now firmly located within the 'deal' framework. Headlines that followed suggest support for the 'deal' framework:

Table 8.1   The *Australian's* coverage of the 10-point plan 5.6.1998–7.7.1998

Story type	June	July	Total
News/feature stories	21	20	41
Wik context	6	2	8
Advertisement	1		1
Editorials	1	1	2

- PM between Wik and a hard place (15 June, p. 1);
- Wik compromise mooted (19 June, p. 5);
- Harradine rebuffed on Native Title (22 June, p. 2);
- Harradine edges closer to compromise on Wik (27 June, p. 2);
- Harradine holds key to Senate gridlock (28 June, p. 5);
- PM rules out compromise veto (1 July, p. 6);
- Main points of Harradine's negotiations (1 July, p. 6);
- Howard claims Wik victory (2 July, p. 1);
- Brickbats and bouquets for Harradine: Agreement splits blacks (2 July, p. 4);
- The Wik resolution: Harradine out to sell agreement (3 July, p. 4);
- Wary PM warns Wik not yet won (5 July, p. 1).

From this progression, it is clear that Wik had become a major political issue that focused not on the details of the 1996 High Court decision, nor even on the detail of Howard's 10-point plan, but on whether there would be a political victory for the Howard government. The headlines cited here are representative of the stories of this period that effectively set up and adopted the 'Wik deal' as the dominant framework.

Backgrounding

Just eight of the forty-one news and feature stories included background material that provided some explanation of either the 10-point plan or the original High Court decision. There was no detail explaining the relevance of the 10-point plan to previous court actions, or attempt to link the present situation with a history of the treatment of the Wik people by successive colonial, state, and federal governments. This omission of important contextual material has become a common occurrence in Australian newspaper coverage of Indigenous affairs (Meadows 1993, 1994a; Hippocrates and Meadows 1996). This was an important national political issue and yet the *Australian* managed to include only the most minimal background explanation in less than 15 per cent of its stories. It would be surprising if, based on this coverage only, readers of the *Australian* over this period could have listed the key elements of the 10-point plan or those of the original High Court *Wik* decision, or were aware of the historical context of the Wik people's battle for land rights.

Sources

An examination of the sources journalists relied on for their stories during this period supports the contention that the entire period was framed in terms of 'cutting a deal' — any deal — to give John Howard a 'victory'. The number of non-Indigenous sources outnumbers Indigenous voices by a factor of around four to one (as shown in Table 8.2).

Table 8.2   Media bias and sources quoted during the period of Wik debate

Sources quoted	June	July	Total
Indigenous	11	9	20
Non-Indigenous	35	48	83

Given the framing of the debate, this is not surprising, but it should be of great concern. Unfortunately, it reflects a pattern in the Australian newspaper coverage of Indigenous affairs, which has remained unchanged in some outlets for the past 20 years. A study of the *Courier-Mail* and the *Cairns Post* revealed that journalists with these newspapers use Indigenous sources sparingly — even in stories *about Indigenous affairs*. Twenty years ago, around one-third of all sources used in stories about Indigenous affairs were Indigenous people. In the first five years of the 1990s, nothing had changed (Hippocrates and Meadows 1996). This study reveals an even poorer statistic — Indigenous voices made up just 20 per cent of all opinion sought on an issue of deep concern to Indigenous people. Why were Indigenous voices so absent?

One interesting trend that emerged was that the proportion of non-Indigenous sources increased dramatically as the 'deal' came closer to resolution, with Indigenous voices notably reduced in number and prominence. In the first few days of July, twenty-nine different non-Indigenous sources were quoted on forty-eight separate occasions. This was an increase on sixteen different sources quoted on thirty-five occasions in the previous month. In June, nine Indigenous sources were quoted in the *Australian* on eleven occasions. In the first few days of July, when the so-called 'deal' was imminent, just four Indigenous people articulated their concerns on nine separate occasions — seven of these, significantly, came *after* the 'deal' was done. Indigenous people were effectively shut out of negotiations at a political, symbolic, and public level.

Conclusion

Regional journalists and their perceptions of journalism practices provide a starting point from which to examine the broader aspects of reporting on Indigenous people and issues. The claims made in this chapter about regional journalistic practices are based on the limited number of studies that have focused on regional journalism in Australia. It remains a largely ignored area in scholarly research that requires further examination. The examples used here show how specific journalistic practices lead to the framing of news about Indigenous issues. The clear links between regional journalists' approaches and the reporting practices of metropolitan journalists is apparent.

The 10-point plan was a race-relations issue. This was acknowledged internationally, if not in Australia. Late in 1998, the United Nations Committee for the Elimination of Racial Discrimination found that the 10-point plan represented an 'acute impairment' of the land rights of Indigenous people. The Committee expressed concern over the 'compatibility' of the amendments to the *Native Title Act* in terms of the International Convention for the Elimination of All Forms of Racial Discrimination — to which Australia is a signatory. Nothing could be clearer. The *Australian's* coverage of the 10-point plan is an example of how journalism practices can frame particular ideas and assumptions about Indigenous people. The very issue of race became submerged in the intricacies of Australian politics, fanned by an eager press gallery and their willing, accessible sources. There is no doubt that it was an important political story but it was sparked by the other story — the discriminatory treatment of one section of the Australian community. This important issue was lost in a headlong dash by journalists for headlines and their obsession with political intrigue.

It reveals that journalists are reluctant to use Indigenous sources or to engage in any meaningful research, despite apparent easy access to relevant background material. It also reveals a predisposition for journalists covering politics to become trapped by a particular framework. Clearly, this period was dominated by speculation of an early election — even a 'race-based poll' — and the rise of One Nation. While these are important issues that required thoughtful and measured debate, they engulfed the very issue on which newspapers such as the *Australian* based their arguments against having a 'race-based election'. It seems that the people the newspaper claimed to be protecting were the very ones they systematically ignored.

The struggle over journalists' representations of Indigenous affairs is not a recent one. From first contact, Indigenous people — through the early journalism of the period — have been positioned from, and within, the dominant ideas and assumptions of Anglo-European culture. The colonial press expanded and the era of mass media dawned, but not much changed and coverage of issues remains largely anchored within narrow ideological boundaries. As this chapter suggests, the continuing omission of Indigenous people from the news agenda as sources for regional and national news is an enduring example of this. Indigenous people, by and large, have had to be content with a portrayal that is mostly stereotypical, sensational, emotional, or exotic, with an ignorance of the historical and political context in which these images are situated. In a significant number of cases — and as outlined here — the *omission* of Indigenous voices and perspectives from journalistic accounts offers more powerful support for dominant ideas and assumptions than examples of *overt* racism. Attempts by journalists to address the issue of sourcing alone would be a huge step towards enabling a better and more accurate representation of Indigenous affairs in Australia.

A new approach to reporting race relations might take into account such issues as the omission and invisibility of Indigenous people, notions of identity, the implications of deadlines, the use of derogatory and imposed labelling, and the negotiation of conflicts such as the ownership of knowledge in an Indigenous community versus notions of editorial control. It might be, for example, that several people in a community need to be consulted as sources to get a 'good' story. Critics of this more measured approach to journalistic practice suggest that this is a form of censorship or 'political correctness' — a threat to free speech. But it is precisely free speech that is threatened unless *all* sides of a story can be heard and debated intelligently and freely.

The role of journalism as a set of cultural practices in this quest is critical. As this chapter suggests, journalists' claims to professionalism, principally relying on the MEAA Code of Ethics, do not provide an adequate framework for fair representation of indigenous affairs. Journalists need to reconceptualise journalism in terms of how it 'imagines' society within the context of the shift in global and media power (ownership and concentration), and its role as a colonising cultural institution. Such an approach might help explain why daily news practices have such an impact on the marginalised and why the media are key cultural sites in the production and maintenance of stereotypes.

Case study

The following case study examines the factors affecting daily journalistic practice and the reporting of Indigenous issues together with a specific example of the reporting of a story involving Indigenous people and events. It does this to highlight the need for a revitalisation of journalistic practices if journalism is to understand and renegotiate its role as one of the major cultural resources of society, responsible for the cementing of 'common-sense knowledge' (racism) about Indigenous Australians.

Jacqui Ewart reports:

In the lead-up to Christmas 1996, I was at a journalism conference sitting in on a session on the reporting of Indigenous issues in the media. I slipped out of the room to call my husband in Rockhampton and he told me the news of the day: more than 50 Indigenous people had been arrested on outstanding fine warrants at an Aboriginal community near Rockhampton. While not apparently a big news story, its newsworthiness increased exponentially when he told me the 'fine evaders' had been arrested while attending the funeral of a community elder. The following quote from a senior editorial staff member of the newspaper that broke the story helps illustrate the attitudes and practices of journalists in covering such events:

'With the Woorabinda story we opted not to go overboard. We decided there is a perception that the majority of readers don't really care what happened out there. It is our responsibility to report it and we did that. We covered the fact it happened: that they served the warrants and the actual issuing of the warrants we covered as news. There was a blow-out over the fact it happened at a funeral and we did not embroil ourselves in the shit fight that blacks hate police and police hate blacks. It would not have achieved anything. We made a conscious decision based on our circulation; we had nothing to gain circulation-wise by continuing the fight for days and days. We don't think we could achieve anything in healing the rift between police and Aborigines. We should not be used as a vehicle for dirty laundry to be hung out. The only news in the story was the large amount of warrants that were served in the police operation. That is news so we covered it. We took a stance that the police were only doing their jobs.'

While this quote illustrates many of the issues discussed in this chapter, the interviewee might have added that the newspaper had more to lose than gain by following up the actions of the police. What it risked by reporting the human rights violation that occurred when police raided the funeral was the availability of a huge number of stories from police sources. This relationship could have been at risk if the issue had been followed through and police had taken umbrage at the coverage. Here the link between readership — in the interviewee's comments that it was a circulation (read-ership) decision not to follow the issue further — and sources can be clearly seen. In this instance, the newspaper and its journalists showed their reliance on one of the cultural institutions of society (police/law) through their desire not to transgress on the close, symbiotic relationship between that institution and journalism, another cultural institution. It also revealed clearly how journalists work within the economic constraints of a business and that this is an omnipresent conflict of interest. In this case, that tension acted on journalism practices to frame the story as 'un-newsworthy'.

DISCUSSION QUESTIONS

1 Choose a story from a newspaper on an Indigenous issue and identify the sources used and the angles taken by the writer. What factors do you think may have been involved in the preparation of the story?
2 What do you think is missing from the story?
3 What alternative sources and angles would you have used in preparing the story?
4 What questions would you ask the journalist who wrote the story if you were undertaking a small study into journalistic practices and how they affect the gathering and writing of such stories?
5 Many of the elements that influence journalistic practices are ingrained in the day-to-day routines of journalists. How do you think journalists might change their practices to take account of the impact they have on the representation of Indigenous Australians?

Further reading

Anderson, B. 1984, *Imagined Communities: Reflections on the Origin and Spread of Nationalism*, Verso, London.

Ericson, R.V., Baranek, P.M. and Chan, J. 1987, *Visualising Deviance: a Study of News Organisation*, Open University Press, Milton Keynes.

Ewart, J. 1997, 'The Scabsuckers — regional journalists' representation of indigenous Australians', Asia Pacific Media Educator, no. 3, July–December, pp. 108–17.

Goodall, H. 1993, 'Constructing a riot: television news and Aborigines', *Media Information Australia*, no. 68, pp. 70–7.

Hall, S. 1981, 'The whites of their eyes: racist ideologies and the media', in G. Bridges and R. Brunt (eds), *Silver Linings: Some Strategies for the Eighties*, Lawrence and Wishart, London.

Langton, M. 1993, 'Well, I heard it on the radio and I saw it on the television': An essay for the Australian Film Commission on the politics and aesthetics of filmmaking by and about Aboriginal people and things, Australian Film Commission, Sydney.

Meadows, M. 1997, 'Perfect match: the media and Pauline Hanson', *Metro*, no. 109, pp. 86–90.

Mickler, S. 1998, *The Myth of Privilege: Aboriginal Status, Media Visions, Public Ideas*, Fremantle Arts Centre Press, Fremantle.

Notes

1   The One Nation Party was an extreme, conservative political organisation which emerged in Queensland at the 1996 federal poll following the election of independent candidate Pauline Hanson. A Liberal candidate who was disendorsed for her outspoken claims about immigrants and Indigenous affairs, Hanson subsequently presided over a party that saw eleven members elected to the Queensland Parliament in a State election two years later. But Hanson herself failed to be re-elected to Federal Parliament in the the same year — 1998. By early 1999, six of the Queensland Parliament's One Nation members had either resigned from the party to become independents or had left politics.

2   The 1992 High Court's native title decision was named after one of the five plaintiffs, Eddie Mabo. The court battle for native title recognition in law began ten years before the decision was handed down on 3 June 1992. Tragically, Eddie Mabo died of cancer a few months before that day. The judgment established the continuing existence of native title to land in some cases. It effectively overturned the idea that the Australian continent at the time of European invasion was *terra nullius*—an empty land.

3   The 1997 High Court *Wik* decision found that native title could exist simultaneously with a pastoral lease on the same piece of land. While the pastoral lease did not give exclusive possession to pastoralists, where there was a conflict over the exercise of rights, native title rights were subordinate to those pastoral leaseholders. For more information on this decision, see ATSIC's *A Plain English Guide to the Wik Case*, Native Title and Land Rights Branch, Canberra, January 1997.

4   See Ewart's 1997 study of regional journalists for more information.

5   In Ewart's 1997 study, regional journalists indicated they did not have any Indigenous contacts or sources and relied on non-Indigenous people to comment on Indigenous issues and events.

6   Public journalism attempts to address some of these concerns, returning the agenda-setting function to the community.

9

On the fringe: journalism, representation and cultural competence

PAUL SCOTT

> The subtlest and most pervasive of all influences are those which create and main-tain the repertory of stereotypes. We are told about the world before we see it. We imagine most things before we experience them. And those perceptions, unless education has made us acutely aware, govern deeply the whole process of percep-tion. They mark out certain objects as familiar or strange, emphasising the differ-ence, so that the slightly familiar is seen as very familiar, and the somewhat strange as sharply alien. (Lippman 1929, pp. 89–90)

Lippman's observations about the power and ubiquity of influences that invent and perpetuate stereotypes remains as salient today as it was in 1922. Much com-munity, government, academic, and journalistic concern surrounds myriad matters pertaining to media representation of people, places, issues, and events. This concern has often focused on those representations and constructions that have provided distorted impressions of groups and individuals — particularly groups and individuals who are not readily considered part of the 'mainstream' of society.

Media researchers have identified distorted impressions as being significant because they can be linked to the maintenance of economic, political, and cul-tural marginalisation of groups and individuals. Simplified media representations and stereotypes of gender, race, and ethnicity have attracted much attention and critique from media analysts and academics investigating and analysing the role of the news media and its links with the hegemonic legitimation of power and subordination in society. The work of journalists in both news and entertainment media representations can cultivate and legitimise ways of understanding people, places, issues, and events, so both genres are deserving of equal attention.

While it needs to be stated from the outset that there is no single 'magic bullet' or 'quick fix' formula that can be prescribed and applied to ensure that journalists

will shy away from stereotypes, this chapter focuses on how journalists can perpetuate or challenge distorted impressions about groups or individuals on the
margins of mainstream society. It explores issues surrounding journalism and
identity, ideology, representation, marginality, cultural competence, and fair
reporting. It examines some of the challenges journalists face in reporting about
and for 'others', and suggests some concrete strategies journalists can use in
attempting to remain fair, accurate, and culturally competent in their work and
their reporting of issues.

Identity, representation and changing consciousness

When American golfer Tiger Woods described himself as 'Caublinasian' (see
Page 1997) — referring to his Caucasian, Native American, African American,
and Thai heritage — journalists and audiences were forced to consider the nature
of ethnic identity labels, and the subsequent difficulties associated with representation in a contemporary society in which hybrids of culture and identity are
becoming more common. Woods's multidimensional description of himself as
'Caublinasian' challenges ways of thinking about identity, demonstrates the
problematic nature of simplified identity constructions, and stimulates discussion
and debate about representation. As journalism is in the business of providing
descriptions and explanations for readers, viewers, and listeners, this discussion
and debate is equally as relevant to journalists as it is to their audiences. Why
does Woods's racial heritage matter? Is it even important? If so, then to whom
is it important? Is it because Woods excels in a sport few non–Anglo-Celtic players have been able to compete in at the highest levels? How does the story change
if Woods doesn't identify exclusively as African American, but rather as multi-
dimensional in identity? To what extent is the construction of a group or individual's identity more important to the media than it is to those being described?
Why? Perhaps it can be attributed, in many cases, to the way identity labels,
and stereotypes in particular, give form and understanding to those never met
or little known, except through media discourses.

These issues are important to journalists because the construction of individual identity is formed through what Ferguson (1998, p. 82) describes as 'the
recognition and confirmation of relative "sameness", the negotiation of multiple
and often contradictory positions on a range of issues, and from time to time,
the external imposition of undesired or unacceptable norms'. Belay (1996) claims
a significant problem in theorising contemporary society and the effects of
globalisation is the difficulty people will experience in managing the multidimensionality of their own identity and 'cultural self'. If understanding one's
own identity is problematic, then surely there will be just as much, if not more,
difficulty in managing understandings regarding the multidimensionality of
others. For Belay (pp. 342–6), five types of identity will become key signifiers

of self and others: sociological identities (social class, gender, religion, and the like), occupational identities, geobasic (rather than racial) identities, national identities, and ethnic identities.

In the past thirty years, and particularly in the 1990s, there was considerable growth in the consciousness of Australian journalists of the importance of representations pertaining to class, religion, age, sexuality, disability, gender, race, and ethnicity. These representations are now more widely understood to be of significance to the Australian ethos of a *fair go*. If this ethos is ever to be more than a nationalistic platitude and *feel good* slogan, these understandings of the world warrant treatment that is accurate, ethical, and non-stereotypical.

The growth in journalistic consciousness of fair representation has been aided by several factors, including pressure campaigns aimed at media organisations and government by affected groups; educational campaigns targeting journalists; and the introduction of laws, codes, and principles outlawing various forms of discrimination, vilification, and hatred. Other factors influencing journalists' understandings of fair representation include audiences that are better educated, highly media literate, and subsequently more resistant to manipulation. The attention to media representations by agencies such as the Human Rights and Equal Opportunity Commission, the National Women's Media Centre, and the Office of the Status of Women has also contributed to a growing and changing consciousness of journalists.

Journalists themselves are also better educated than they were thirty years ago. Henningham (1998) points to research carried out in the 1960s that found only 5 per cent of journalists working at metropolitan newspapers had a degree. In the 1990s, some 55 per cent of journalists had studied at tertiary level. Debate continues over whether tertiary education equips journalists to better understand the potential effects of their representations than exclusive on-the-job training might; however, it is apparent that journalists have played, and continue to play, a substantial role in analysing modes of media representation.

While the occasional scrutiny of the work of journalists by other journalists is not a new development, there is adequate evidence to support Bacon's (1999, p. 84) observation that the media itself has become a round — and that 'the story of the story is part of the story'. *Mediawatch* on ABC television; *The Media Report* on ABC radio; *Walkley Magazine*, published by the Media Entertainment and Arts Alliance (the MEAA, industrial union for journalists); the insert *Media*, in Thursday's edition of the *Australian*; *Reportage*, published by the University of Technology, Sydney; and the now defunct *Zeitgeist Gazette*, published by Richard Walsh and David Salter, are among prominent programs and publications concerned with critiques of 'the story of the story', and with analyses of media representations of people, places, issues, and events.

Academics such as Gandy (1998) have also identified the importance of the 'story of the story'. He traces this interest as having been ignited by the Black

Power and civil rights movements of the 1960s, and sees these movements as being instrumental in providing confidence for the emergence of identity movements that challenged the manner in which marginalised groups were represented in the mainstream media. He sees this challenge as being particularly pertinent to African Americans and ethnic groups, along with 'social movements that shared a common opposition to oppression and discrimination based on gender, sexual orientation, physical differences and differences in capacity' (1998, p. 71). He believes that one of the most readily identifiable results of this campaign of common opposition to oppression is that it is 'certainly no longer socially acceptable for people to be explicitly racist in public conversation' (1998, p. 72).

Croteau and Hoynes (1997) also see the 1960s as a significant period in challenging dominant media representations of the oppressed and marginalised. They argue that 'since the 1960s, the trend has been towards more inclusiveness and growing sensitivity in media of all types' (p. 142), and that, as a result of this growing sensitivity, 'blatantly racist images of minority groups are no longer widespread in the US media' (p. 143). The corollary of this shift prompts McNair (1998, p. 7) to note there now exists a 'routine journalistic acceptance of sexism and racism as "bad things"'. Such attitudes are obvious in the hostile media coverage directed at the Toyota motor company in Australia when its advertising agency authorised a campaign featuring a naked, pregnant women with text referring to the 'comforts of a wide body' (Ward 1995, p. 254).

Further evidence of these changing attitudes is provided by Mickler (1998, p. 173) who states the exposure of Aboriginal disadvantage in Australia has been 'a steadily increasing journalistic enterprise since the 1960s when the news media started to turn from indifference and ambivalence to interest and indeed sympathy'. There appears to be ample evidence to suggest that in the last thirty years, journalists have contributed to many attitudinal changes in society towards ideologies such as racism and sexism.

However, it can also be argued that a journalist's sympathetic motivation can be problematic because, as Stam and Spence (1983, p. 2) pointed out, some representations 'might at times be as pernicious as overtly degrading ones, providing a bourgeois facade for paternalism, a more pervasive racism'. Weston's 1996 study of Native Americans in the news media found that the sympathy that results in the unquestioning acceptance of information as part of a determination to create positive representations can result in a 'newer version of the noble savage' (1996, p. 148).

Similar concerns arose in the wake of the 1990s' debacle surrounding a proposed bridge development to Hindmarsh Island in South Australia, which a group of Indigenous women believed should not proceed because the land was sacred for reasons presented as being secret women's business (for more information refer to *Background Briefing* 1995, and Jopson 1999). A Royal

Commission in the mid-1990s made a contested finding that the claims of the women had been fabricated. According to Duffy (1998, p. 25), former ABC political journalist Paul Lyneham believed some ABC journalists covering the controversy were determined to create positive representations at the expense of fair and accurate journalism. Lyneham saw the dispute as an example of the problematic juncture of the 'private agenda and value systems of individual journalists interfering on a serious issue ... I complained to ABC executives in Sydney about the cosy, warm, unquestioning coverage ... which I don't think did the truth a great deal of justice'. Duffy claimed the failure to give adequate opportunity for the 'dissident' Ngarrindjerri women (those who did not support the prevention of the proposed development and disputed the claims of secret women's business) to express their point of view demonstrates the ABC 'cannot be trusted to report Aboriginal matters fairly or accurately' (1988, p. 25). He argued the personal ideology of some ABC journalists interfered with their ability to fairly mediate reality or reveal what he saw as the truth. Some years earlier, the Federal Minister for Communications Senator Richard Alston told Radio National that he believed the ABC placed undue emphasis on issues relating to Indigenous people:

> You can often find ABC programs dominated with issues like racism and Aboriginal affairs. Now that's not to say they're not important issues, but you've got to ask yourself why those issues seem to be perennial favourites when there are a lot of other issues around, whether it's unemployment or the general state of the economy. (Radio National, 17 June 1996)

The Hindmarsh Island dispute clearly showed that the facts — and a way of determining, describing, and understanding the facts — was an arena of struggle for competing ideas and ideologies. McNair refers to this struggle as:

> ... an expression and reflection of the ideological 'balance of forces' in a given society, a balance which changes over time, owing at least partly to the exposure which journalism may give to ideas alternative to, even oppositional to, currently dominant ideas. (1997, p. 7)

Evolutionary biologist Richard Dawkins (1989) uses the term *memes* to refer to the non-static nature of ideologies. He sees that ideologies, like genes, are subject to evolution — they survive and reproduce in a manner that is determined by their adaptability and fitness for survival in their particular environment, which itself is subject to other determining factors. Journalists, as agents of the media, have assisted in ideological evolution. McNair sees one example of this shifting ideological terrain exemplified in the way patriarchal ideology:

... has declined and is dying out, as a result of the countervailing force of women's growing socio-economic power and the ideology which legitimises that power. Capitalism survives, indeed goes from strength to strength, but against a back-drop of consensual feminism in which women are in theory, if not yet in practice, the equals of men. How has feminist ideology become consensual in such a short time? The answer lies largely, if not solely, in its acceptance as 'common sense' by the institutions of the media and the people who work in them. (1998, p. 31)

Ferguson (1998) is not as clearly convinced that ideological chasms have been bridged to the point where there can be wide-ranging consensus on what con-stitutes 'common sense'. He argues that we might indeed be in an age of trans-formation of long-standing and widely held ideologies, but hastens to add 'there is little evidence to suggest that it is more than a surface transition. The dis-courses of nationalism, chauvinism, patriotism, and racism are still there and sometimes bubble to the surface or appear in a sanitised or reformist guise' (p. 153).

Mainstream Australian media and the journalists who work for it have played a part in assisting shifts in ideological understandings in wider society, but it is worth noting Ferguson's claim regarding surface transition and asking how, when, where, why, and in what circumstances these discourses 'bubble to the surface'. What are the effects on groups or individuals when they do re-emerge? If there is a general acceptance and supporting evidence to demonstrate the media is not as blatantly racist as it once was, if there is general journalistic accep-tance of sexism and racism as 'bad things', if it is generally agreed the work of journalists in Australia is closely scrutinised by their peers, if we acknowledge there are behavioural codes and enforceable laws to police the actions of jour-nalists and media organisations — then what else is necessary to understand the fair and accurate representation of, for, and about those who are differenti-ated as *other*? Who are those differentiated as *other*?

Common sense, ideology and otherness

There is an inescapable dualism in the democratic public sphere (and of course, in any rational communication process). Specific identities are routinely spoken and written of as being separate or outside the imagined collective or general community of interests while their claims are negotiated. Any constituent part of the whole must be spoken of as *they* (politicians, bureaucrats, unions, capitalists, workers, children, and so on) in the calculation of interest guided by a principle of [the] collective good. (Mickler 1998, p. 126)

The concepts of normality, naturalness, and common sense are central in attempting to understand that which is commonly identified as *other*. These concepts are sometimes used interchangeably and can be utilised to legitimise and privilege certain ideological positions and views in the mainstream of society. Arguing that an emergent view or belief is *common sense* (that is, that mainstream society shares a common understanding of that perspective) can lead to its entrenchment and validation. Such an approach negates any examination of these types of views/beliefs as the end products of ideological positions that have evolved or developed through complex historical factors and relationships between groups or individuals.

The media plays a key role in assisting citizens to determine what is common sense or socially normal through both regular repetition and a preference for particular framings of events. Equally — through omission, neglect, or ridicule — other ideas, lifestyles, or behaviours can either be marginalised or become part of the spectacle of the bizarre. During research that examined numerous case studies of representations of ethnicity in the Australian news media, Boreland and Smith (1996, p. 6) found that 'although engaging in best practice in the approach to most stories, some journalists appear to fail to consider the impact and consequences of their reportage'.

Journalists often become defensive when it is suggested that journalism has ideological dimensions that normalise or naturalise certain positions at the expense of others, and that journalism thus seeks to define consensus. Some journalists view arguments about ideological positioning as of little consequence or relevance to their daily work. They see the work they produce as a reflection of audience interests, norms, and ideas, rather than a matter of ideological positioning. They point to commercial realities as evidence that they have to be able to communicate with a particular audience. Such journalists point to attacks on their work from extremes of the political spectrum as evidence they occupy the pragmatic, middle ground — a kind of ideological-free zone called objectivity, that exists precisely because of the common sense of journalists. Leeroy Betti, Aboriginal Affairs journalist with the *West Australian* newspaper, says he has been accused 'of being a pinko–liberal–bleeding-heart and at the same time I've been accused of being a biased racist' (McKee, 1998, p. 6). Similarly, Matt Price from the *Australian* notes he has been 'congratulated for good reporting and for being a racist — in relation to the same story' (McKee, 1998, p. 6). Croteau and Hoynes point out that ideology, for many journalists:

> ... is something to be avoided, (and so) the journalistic middle ground becomes safe. There is good reason for them to want to occupy this ground. It insulates them from criticism and gives the news a legitimacy with a wide range of readers and viewers who see themselves as occupying some version of [the] middle ground ... In short, the middle ground is ideological precisely because it is a cultural site where commonsense assumptions are produced, reproduced, and circulated. (1997, pp. 172–3)

The argument surrounding ideological positioning is not based on a conspiratorial insistence that journalists are consciously trying to stimulate or perpetuate ideologies among their audiences, although such an argument might sometimes be demonstrable through evidence of consistent and persistent demonising of certain people and places. Ideological positioning seeks more to make clear that the manner in which stories are selected and presented further legitimises a way of seeing and thinking about things as being *either* normal, natural, and common sense *or* deviant, unnatural, and devoid of common sense.

Media theorists' attempts to find an all-embracing theory of ideological dominance by the powerful elite over a subordinate class have largely failed because neither capitalism nor ideology is static. Advanced capitalism in liberal democratic societies has shifted its emphasis from production to distribution and consumption, and the dominance paradigm that characterised much sociological thinking about the role of the media in society has become redundant as a stand-alone theoretical explanation. This is partly because the paradigm was overly reliant on the notion that both the media and journalism perpetuated the status quo of economic, political, and cultural protection for the elite and exploitation of the subordinate. McNair (1998, p. 31) sees the paradigm as impotent because it 'implies a degree of conspiratorial intent, class/sex/ethnic-based unity and ideological stasis which conflicts with the experience of the late twentieth century'. He argues (1998, p. 31) that liberal journalism is predisposed towards capitalism, 'but not towards a rigid capitalism in which relations of domination and subordination are forever fixed and not changing'.

While ideological preferences in the news media are sometimes empirically demonstrable through discourse and content analysis, it is obvious these preferences are not fixed. This allows for the repositioning of ideologies, and journalists are able to challenge ways of thinking about issues — such as, for example, racism and sexism being seen by most journalists as 'bad things'. Again, this is not to completely deny that dominance and subordination have a theoretical role to play in the explanation of the exercising of political, economic, and cultural preferences within a society. Rather, it suggests, a reliance on that position exposes its inability to explain shifts in ideology.

Hall sees the media as not simply reflecting the world back to audiences, but re-presenting it by engaging in practices that define reality. He points out (1982, p. 64) that 'representation is a very different notion from that of reflection. It implies the active work of selecting and presenting, of structuring and shaping; not merely the transmitting of an already-existing meaning, but the more active labour of *making things mean*'. Hall's view is particularly useful in understanding how journalists can make things mean — this is perhaps one of the key differences between *the right to know* and *the desire to show*. It is useful to keep in mind when attempting to understand the construction of otherness.

Otherness is a key idea in understanding issues pertaining to representation and explaining the way in which the identity of groups and individuals can be constructed and perpetuated, and how these constructions can reciprocally shape the identity of those who construct that identity. Said's *Orientalism* (1978) is a seminal text in understanding otherness, as it discusses the influence of representations in both fostering imagining and creating understandings about people who are represented as being different from us. Some scholars (see Ferguson 1998) have pointed out that Said's work is sometimes undermined by sweeping generalisations and a tendency to rely on binary opposites. Yet some of the strengths of Said's thesis include the manner in which it identifies how identities are constructed in unequal relationships to provide the definers of identity with power to exclude the other.

Identities can be constructed through defining what individuals, groups, or nations are not, as much as by corralling what they are. Belonging to a group depends on some common sharing of certain things, characteristics, beliefs, or ideas, as well as defining which characteristics, of all those possible, are privileged as significant. This creates a situation where there can be an identifiable 'us' and an identifiable 'them'. Like ideologies, these situations are not static. They can, and will, change from time to time. Such changes can have political consequences.

Richon (1996, p. 242) points out terms such as the 'Orient and the Occident are not just words, but names, proper names constructing identities that have become territories'. Crang (1998, p. 61) sees the Orient and the Occident as only existing through the Western gaze, 'leaving the subordinate group as "objects" of a knowledge that denies them the right to shape their own identity and uses them as a "negative" pole, being the devalued or disliked elements, around whose exclusion the dominant group's sense of self can be organised'. One of the strengths of the theoretical legacy of otherness is that it has assisted in the explanation of both the ideological dimensions of racism and the demonisation of people and places for the purposes of colonialism and economic exploitation. Shohat and Stam (1994) see that racism is often manifested in the companionship of sexism, classism, or homophobia — all ideologies that can be subject to changing attitudes in societies. Ferguson (1998) points out that a superficial sense of solidarity and an unearned feeling of superiority can be gained by a group (*we*) through an antipathy to another, differentiated group (*they*).

The simplified assignment of an aggregated entity to individuals with broad and diverse lives and views is obviously problematic. For many years journalists, governments, and bureaucrats referred to Aboriginal and Torres Strait Islander peoples as one group or class without recognising the inherent cultural, linguistic, geographic, and personal differences obscured by the label. At the same time, it must be acknowledged that this false singular identification gave

Australia's Indigenous peoples a weight of presence and significance that would have been missing had the individual identities of each group and tribe been the primary identifier. Mickler (1998) sees it as a commonplace of public politics, which journalism renders meaningful, that sectional interests be accorded a 'they' identity.

The constructing of *positive* and *negative* representations of *others*

Arguments around issues of positive and negative representations of others owe a good deal of their methodology to the 'images and representation approach', which Rakow (1986, p. 28) describes as the 'earliest of the contemporary feminist approaches to popular culture'. Its political agenda 'underlines the importance of mobilising public opinion and lobbying governments and regulatory authorities to take legislative action to stamp out sexist stereotypes where the advertising industry cannot bring itself to do so' (Ward 1995, p. 254). This conceptual underpinning has provided focus for much mainstream media research. However, this approach remains flawed because arguments against the use of unreal or negative images of women presupposes there are real or positive images of women available to take their place. Yet what is real or positive varies greatly between readers.

Mickler (1998), in his comprehensive study of the role of the media in manufacturing widely circulating myths about Aboriginal privilege, points out concern regarding the unqualified endorsement of a positive images approach at the expense of other representations. He calls for a reassessment of 'the tradition of the victim', which has at its foundations a belief that, through 'normalising' representations of Aboriginal people via emphasis exclusively on 'positive' representations, somehow a greater understanding of Indigenous disadvantage will emerge within broader society (p. 192).

'Bad news', as Mickler points out, can have 'positive effects beyond its seemingly immediate stigmatisation of those involved ... each representation of "Aboriginal riots", demonstrations, civil disturbances, even with the often prejudicial and sensational treatments given them, heightened the sense of crisis and increased the public visibility of the social crisis' (pp. 193–4). The corollary of an emphasis only on positive representations would mean that the non-Indigenous public would have little idea of the myriad of problems — economic, social, cultural — faced by many Indigenous people.

This can seem confusing for journalists — a kind of 'damned if I do' and 'damned if I don't' dichotomy that makes issues relating to representation of those marginalised by mainstream society both complex and impossible to generalise. In *The Report of the National Inquiry into Racist Violence in Australia*, there is acknowledgment that journalists can play a significant role in the representation of those identified as *other*. However, this is tempered by other findings, which include:

... a general concern about the apparent lack of consistent application of the journalists' principles of fairness and accuracy in reporting of race-related issues. There
has been a tendency on the part of many media outlets to focus on conflict and
extreme views in relation to these issues. The viewpoints of the communities themselves are too often ignored. There are too few stories about positive developments
within minority racial/ethnic groups ... (National Inquiry into Racist Violence
(Australia), p. 372)

Similarly, the Royal Commission into Aboriginal Deaths in Custody highlighted examples of sensational journalistic practice in the reporting of stories
involving Aboriginal people. The Royal Commission's *Regional Report Of Inquiry
Into Underlying Issues In Western Australia* found an emphasis in the media of an
ongoing connection between crime and Aboriginality, and that the police:

... exerted enormous influence on the way the media reports criminal and civil
matters involving Aboriginal people ... There is little doubt that the police and
courts are a key source of stories for journalists and news teams on a daily basis. A
glance through any major Western Australian newspaper will demonstrate that
crime, violence and civil disturbances form a sizeable part of the daily staple of
dramatic news. Likewise, crime and violence are nightly components for television
news, whose format has evolved over the past decade toward news as entertainment
rather than information. (Royal Commission into Aboriginal Deaths in Custody
1991)

The Inquiry found the connection between crime and Aboriginality was
maintained through three readily identifiable relationships between journalists
and the police. First, journalists who work the police round build relationships
with the police force and individual officers who then alert them to stories. The
detail in the information provided by the police to journalists depends on their
relationship — and it is possible to build a good relationship with police by
adopting the police line on an issue. Second, the Perth police media liaison unit
held daily media conferences attended by most large media organisations, and
police provided details of arrests, operations, and what the police saw as wider
law and order issues. Third, the police regularly provided media releases in newspaper copy style. Journalists told the Commission it was 'not uncommon for
police media releases to go straight into the newspaper with little or no alteration' (Royal Commission into Aboriginal Deaths in Custody 1991).

While journalists can point to the workplace realities of time pressures and
deadlines, they need to be aware a commitment to responsible and fair journalism demands they develop a cultural competence and become able to identify
stereotypical representations that perpetuate mythical constructions and demonising of the 'other'. This is not an argument to limit, censor, or gag journalists

from doing their jobs — but it does suggest cultural competence is a necessary aspect of commitment to fair journalism.

Cultural competence and fairness

> Cultural competence creates opportunities to pursue excellence in journalism. It encourages explanations. It enhances understanding. It provides greater access to individuals. It develops more knowledgeable sources. It reflects a more accurate, complete and authentic picture of communities. It builds bridges between different groups. It captures the whole as well as it does the sum of its parts. (The Poynter Institute 1999)

The myriad representation issues faced by journalists interested in the creation of fair representations underlines the need to develop cultural competence and strategies that assist in negotiating complex sets of competing interests. Cultural competence is more than cultural understanding — it requires journalists to become competent in the cultural contexts in which they are working. As this chapter points out, the under-representation or misrepresentation of diverse groups and individuals perpetuates the mythologising of those who are not seen as part of the mainstream of society.

Many journalists are aware that competing ideological interests expose them to the risks of being accused, on one hand, of marginalising groups or individuals and, on the other, of practising the kind of journalism carried out by the pompous, self-righteous, and self-indulgent Thought Police (to borrow from terminology drawn on in Sheehan's 1997 work, *Among the Barbarians*). Sheehan is particularly critical of the 1996 HREOC publication, *The Racial Hatred Act: A Guide for People Working in the Media*. He writes that Australia has an over-abundance of laws that 'give power to control or sanction what people say by legal action, legal threat or professional rebuke' (1997, p. 312). He warns that attempts to stultify, marginalise, and ultimately silence debate on issues pertinent to multiculturalism, immigration, ethnicity, and almost anything involving Indigenous people is a significant threat to individual freedom. He writes that 'of all the political problems facing Australia, the growing power to suppress and constrain freedom of expression is the most sinister' (1997, p. 317).

Sheehan's concern does not negate a general notion of fairness. A 'fair go' remains a potent idea that draws general allegiance in the Australian community. While ostensibly a positive aspect of the Australian ethos, the fair go is a loose, highly subjective notion capable of distortion under pressure. Such distortion occurred when, in attempts to remedy social inequalities, the notion was used by the economic rationalist proponents of the level playing field and the populist opponents of affirmative action and positive discrimination. Their demands for fairness were at the heart of an eruption of anger and resentment that eventually saw significant numbers of Australian voters turn to the One Nation Party.

The fair go sits comfortably in a discussion of social issues, offering a way to discuss cultural sensitivity without reverting to formularised language that can be too quickly characterised, and dismissed, as political correctness. The fluidity of the concept of fairness makes it an ideal platform to confront deeply entrenched racist attitudes — and 'othering' — in a non-threatening and highly productive way.

Communicators of all kinds strive for a style that effectively interacts with the audience. The notion of fairness is also a useful way for journalists to absent themselves from interminable debates about the existence of truth, objectivity, and facts, while they get on with the job of ensuring their work is fair — in that it is free from dishonesty, bias, and injustice, and marked by a relatively high degree of accuracy, balance, and ethical awareness.

Accuracy, balance, and ethics

Within a multicultural society such as Australia, it is often difficult to report on societal transformation when topics relating to sex, race, and religion 'are personal and value laden' (Hurst and White 1994, p. 55). A fundamental line that must be walked by journalists every day is that which separates personal perspectives from what is in the public interest (for a more detailed discussion of public interest see Chapter 12). Defining the public interest when matters of race (and the often-related issue of religion) are involved, is even more difficult, yet it must be done if journalists are to begin to understand how to fairly report stories of the other. It is 'easy to define the public interest' (Hurst and White 1994, p. 57) in many stories relating to politics. Policy issues covered by the media are in the interest of the public, as these decisions affect all individuals, as citizens, alike. However, whose interest is served when media stories on ethnicity and religion are broadcast and printed? Is it the interest of the public generally, or the publics that are reported about, whether Aboriginal, Islamic, Asian, or Greek? Are such reports serving just the interests of journalists seeking to create controversy or to emphasise difference and conflict in order to maximise sales? As Hurst and White ask (1994, p. 57), 'who determines the composition of the public: the media, the regulators, the citizens whose lives are not touched by the issue discussed, or the group directly affected?'

This provides a useful starting point for journalists to consider when any particular story might be about matters pertaining not only to race, but to various representational issues that may involve constructing otherness. Journalists interested in fairness should question why they are doing a story — in a way that will impact on how they do it. It is incumbent on journalists engaged on a story with elements of ethnicity or race to approach the news-gathering and writing process with the same professionalism they would use to investigate, report, and produce any other story.

Accuracy calls for care and precision to produce material that reflects the actual state of affairs. 'Accuracy ought not be an editorial issue' according to Wilson, because 'it is a fundamental value, deserving to be unquestioned and always applied as rigorously as reporters and editors can apply it' (1996, p. 52). Unfortunately, commitment to accuracy can sometimes be cynically manipulated and waved aside within a workplace culture that believes the facts should not be allowed to get in the way of a good story, or a front page by-line. Rather, a culture of precision is required, where accuracy is attained by close observation, detailed note-taking, assiduous filing of material for easy reference, the use of public records to check details, and the confirmation of all points with other sources. It is a practical commitment to the minutiae rather than claiming allegiance to an ideal truth that produces accuracy. Of course, if it is a duty to present actuality, there must be mechanisms available whereby errors can be quickly and freely corrected (Hurst and White 1994).

Balance is produced by the assiduous weighing of actions or opinions. Fair representation of actuality requires journalists to discover the full breadth of facts, to check them against a range of sources, and to present them in an even-handed way that discloses whose interests are served by various statements. This is a high standard because it requires journalists to actively combat their own ignorance or insensitivity by constantly challenging themselves to tell the full story. The attempt 'to get to the bottom' of the story requires interviewing all interested parties and carefully observing their words and actions while being aware of prejudices and preconceptions that get in the way of understanding the story from the interviewee's point of view. Balance is more than just equal space for different sides of the story. More importantly, it is about equal representation of points of view that require a high degree of empathy from the journalist. It is this empathy with diverse points of view that prevents events, issues, and people from being sensationalised, trivialised, or stereotyped in ways that perpetuate mythologies and racist attitudes.

Conclusion

Ethical awareness requires more than a passing knowledge of the rules of engagement. Too often discussions of media ethics get side-tracked into the search for legislation that prohibits the excesses of media practice. While there needs to be a code of practice that ensures journalists do not invade privacy or grief, do not endanger people, do not use their positions for personal gain, and so on, there also needs to be a greater awareness of the journalists' own ethical formation as professionals who strive to do the best they can in all situations. This position accepts that journalists are always growing and learning, and that they have a responsibility to their audience and themselves to develop their understanding and judgement in ways that reflect a commitment to fairness.

The Poynter Institute (1999) posits that the attainment of fairness in the coverage of issues involving those from other cultures is dependent on journalists understanding that they need to attain a level of cultural competence. Coverage that springs from ignorance or is inhibited by fear of the unfamiliar falls short of the basic tenets of ethical media work: that is to be complete, balanced, clear, and, above all, fair. A journalist who wants to be culturally competent leaves the familiar behind and approaches the unfamiliar with curiosity, sensitivity, and respect. Cultural competence creates opportunities to pursue excellence in journalism. It encourages explanations, enhances understanding, provides greater access to individuals, and develops more knowledgeable sources. It reflects a more accurate, complete, and authentic picture of communities. It builds bridges between different groups. It captures the whole as well as it does the sum of its parts. Cultural competence is the cornerstone of best practice in journalism because it draws together the need for accuracy, balance, and ethical awareness in a practical context that provides for a *fair go*.

Case study

In the lead-up to the 2000 Olympics, many Australian athletes were in the news. Some were not just making headlines because of their sports abilities. For athletes including Cathy Freeman, Kyle van der Kuyp and Patrick Johnson there were additional pressures resulting from their Indigenous heritage. Van der Kuyp, an Olympic hurdler, was adopted by white parents and told ABC Radio's *The World Today* (2000) he 'probably went through a few identity problems just trying to figure out as a young kid what is Aboriginal, what does it mean, why am I different?' Van der Kuyp said he believed he has 'gotten over that, and [is] still on a journey of trying to find my biological side and my biological family, but I think I've found myself ... Kyle is an athlete and Kyle's an Aboriginal, I sort of look at it in that order'.

Van der Kuyp said he felt the media spotlight might be on him because of his 'Aboriginality':

If I was just a normal ... white Australian guy ... would I have a profile? Probably not. I want people to know Kyle and not Kyle who's Aboriginal Irish. No one asks me about Irish, but I'm half and half.

DISCUSSION QUESTIONS

1 How might a journalist develop contacts outside of his or her cultural experience?

2   What presumptions do you have about people from other cultures?
3   Why do you think the concepts of normality, naturalness, and common sense are central in attempting to understand that which is commonly identified as *other*?
4   Do all journalists always have an ideological position on people, events, and issues they are covering? Why?

Further reading

Allan, S. 1999, '"Us and them": racism in the news', *News Culture*, Open University Press, Buckingham.

Cunneen, C. 1999, *Racial Stereotypes Kill*, *www.austlii.edu.au/au/other/media/Australian%20Courts/Free%20Speech%20Comentary/1257.htm* 29 November.

Pettman, J. 1999, *On boundaries and institutions* *www.austlii.edu.au/do/disp.pl/au/other/media/Australian+Courts/Free+Speech+Comentary/1258.htm?query=royal%20commission%20into%20aboriginal* 29 November.

Plater, D. 1999, *Guidelines on reporting Aboriginal and Torres Strait Islander issues* *www.austlii.edu.au/do/disp.pl/au/other/media/Australian+Courts/Free+Speech+Comentary/1260.htm?query=royal%20commission%20into%20aboriginal* 29 November.

Part 5

Upsetting the inverted pyramid

The inverted pyramid is a traditional model for newswriting. The 'pyramid' is the structure most often used for narrative or essay-style writing, with an introduction at the top, an array of facts or arguments in the body, and a conclusion at the end. Newswriting's inverted pyramid reverses this order, with the conclusion — or the crux of the story — at the top, followed by a fleshing out and a filling in of less important aspects. The reader who goes no further than the introductory paragraph should have a reasonable grasp of what the story is about, while a lazy sub-editor should be able to cut from the bottom without doing major damage.

This section recognises perceptions that the inverted pyramid and traditional journalism often fail to do justice to news, newsmakers, and news consumers. It examines two forms of journalism that have the capacity to upset the inverted pyramid, moving away from the long-established newswriting form and the traditional who, what, when, where, why, and how introductions. Literary journalism and public journalism have their ardent fans and their staunch critics. Each genre challenges journalism to reassess its role in society. The following chapters present some of the successes and failures of these forms of journalism, and suggest how literary journalism and public journalism can be incorporated into a journalist's toolkit.

10

True stories: the power and pitfalls of literary journalism

MATTHEW RICKETSON

Most consumers of the news media feel ill these days, like children given the run of a milk bar. Dazzled by all the lines of brightly packaged media confectionery, they have eaten and eaten but, instead of feeling better informed or entertained, their stomachs are groaning and their mouths taste strangely sour. The news media's unceasing production of words and images swamps the consumer's sense of scale and meaning. The headline type size used by the *Guardian*, a respectable English broadsheet, to announce the possibility of a minor cabinet reshuffle in 1998 was twice the size used by the popular tabloid *Daily Mirror* to report the sinking of the *Titanic* in 1912 (Jack 1998, p. 13 (see Buford 1993)). If the news media is not screaming urgency at the audience, then it is homogenising and neutering truly tragic or shocking news events. Barely an evening goes by on network television without the brief appearance of a grieving relative. Each interview looks so much like the other that it is almost impossible for viewers to identify with the victim's plight. Alternatively, the most appalling overseas war scenes are parcelled up in 45 seconds and sweetened by a reporter's dully intoned voice-over.

The effect is to gradually dehumanise both the subjects of stories and those who read or watch them. That subjects feel abused has been well documented (Malcolm 1990), feeding in to the common view that journalists are 'bottom-dwelling' scum. The impact on media consumers has received less attention but it appears they feel either disconnected from what they read and watch or see media stories as episodes in a never-ending soap opera. Just as some people treat the characters in television soapies like *Neighbours* as if they were real, so audiences are persuaded to treat real people like Princess Diana as if her life and death were scripted for their entertainment.

Sorting fact from fiction

Many working in the news media feel the stories they produce only glancingly connect with their audience. Some have sought to re-connect by producing civic or public journalism. Some commentators have urged journalists and proprietors to match their power and influence with greater accountability. Another group nods respectfully at public journalism and accountability, then places its faith in providing deeply researched, well-written pieces that use the techniques of fiction to fully engage the reader's mind and emotions. The purpose of this chapter is to describe and analyse a branch of journalism that is more common in magazines and books than in daily news, and is growing in the United States, the United Kingdom, and, to a lesser extent, Australia. Such journalism goes by various names, none wholly satisfying. Literary journalism is the most common; to many journalists it sounds pretentious but at least it conveys the twin aims and arms of the enterprise. This kind of writing was labelled New Journalism in the 1960s, but there were so many arguments about it — this isn't new! this isn't journalism! — that the term fell into disuse even if the activity did not. Truman Capote created a similar furore in 1965 when he described *In Cold Blood*, his account of a multiple murder in the American mid-west, as a non-fiction novel. Journalists were outraged and literary critics dismissive; one snorted that the non-fiction novel was an oxymoronic phrase and a moronic idea (Birkerts 1987, p. 268).

This is an important half-truth. Fiction is fiction and non-fiction is not — but, like the labels themselves, it is simplistic and misleading to define the two activities as mutually exclusive. Journalism and fiction occupy different domains but there has long been a relationship between the two. Journalism is about covering real events and issues and people in the news media; fiction is about inventing stories. The primary task of journalism is to gain accurate information about a news event. A novelist's primary task is to tell a compelling story. The two activities share a core belief in the necessity and virtue of constructing the world into a narrative; journalists actually label their work as stories. Some novelists, starting with Laurence Sterne's gleefully convoluted *Tristram Shandy* in 1760, question whether narratives actually do make sense of the world, just as some journalists puncture the certitudes of news. Janet Malcolm, the American journalist and critic, believes news stories, like folklore and myth, run in firm, undeviating lines. Cinderella must remain good, the ugly stepsisters bad, which is why you will never see the headline 'Second Stepsister Not So Bad After All' (Malcolm 1994, p. 69).

Both journalists and novelists tell stories; however, the difference is that the journalist's story is true. Novelists ask readers to willingly suspend their disbelief. They use coincidence sparingly in plotting, for fear, as Henry Fielding counselled in his great novel *Tom Jones*, of straining the reader's credulity. Conversely, when a true story is told in an extended narrative it carries the power of the real. If it happened, it happened and coincidence be damned, or as the respected American literary journalist John McPhee once said: 'Things that are cheap and tawdry in fiction work beautifully in non-fiction because they are *true*' (Sims 1984, p. 3). As an example, the pardoning of Lindy Chamberlain for the 1980 murder of her daughter in central Australia happened only after a truly remarkable coincidence: a travelling English backpacker, David Brett, tried to climb Ayers Rock (now known as Uluru) at dusk in 1986. He slipped and fell to his death. When police found his body eight days later they stumbled across Azaria's missing matinee jacket, a crucial piece of evidence that would have buttressed Lindy Chamberlain's claim at the trial that a dingo had taken her baby. 'Were it fiction, no new and risky character would appear so late, but the ways of unruly fact drew in David Brett,' wrote John Bryson (1985) in an afterword to the American edition of his groundbreaking narrative account of the Chamberlain case, *Evil Angels*.

Audiences not only accept events that are stranger than fiction but are thrilled by them. Think of the famous mid-1990s confrontation between entrepreneur Alan Bond and his nemesis Paul Barry outside a courthouse. Barry's earlier exposé of Bond on ABC television and in a biography had helped demolish the shaky tax-haven foundations of Bond's empire and reveal his arrested personality. 'Mine's bigger than yours', the former signwriter once boasted to another tycoon about his overpriced acquisition of Van Gogh's *Irises*. In court, Bond routinely resorted to faulty memory to evade prosecutors' questioning. On this particular day as Bond was filmed trudging towards court, Barry came up and showed him his business card, saying: 'Mr Bond, it's Paul Barry from *Four Corners*. You do remember me don't you?' Bond stared balefully at Barry, tore the proffered card into shreds, threw it down and, like an enraged child, melodramatically ground it into the pavement. In a novel such a scene would undoubtedly have been dismissed as cheap and tawdry but because the scene was real, it was hailed as a journalistic masterstroke that skewered Bond before a national audience.

If novelists cannot say to readers 'this happened in front of my eyes', the rest of the canvas is fresh; they are free to invent their fictional world and populate it with anyone and anything they like. Journalists are constrained by the real, too; first, they have to find it, which can be extremely difficult, and then they strive to make sense of the confusion and gaps in true stories. They especially struggle to understand what is going on in the heads of their subjects. To begin with, a rare order of trust is needed before people publicly reveal their innermost thoughts and feelings, and great skill is required to present the complexity and nuance of character. A deep understanding of human nature is rightly attributed to good novelists but they are also free to let their imagination roam. They are spared the demands, both practical and ethical, of gaining a person's trust and drawing an accurate portrait from life.

It is widely believed, thanks to the rhetorical force of Tom Wolfe's manifesto *The New Journalism* (Wolfe 1975), that the use of fictional techniques in journalism was his idea, but it has a much longer history. Novelists and journalists have been borrowing from each other since at least the eighteenth century. Novelists envy journalists' power of the real and journalists resent the limitations of news, both its rigid form and the shadow of restrictive libel laws. The early novelists cloaked their pioneering efforts in other literary forms and in varying degrees acted as if their stories were true. Daniel Defoe presented *Robinson Crusoe* in 1719 as a 'just history of fact', Samuel Richardson posed as the editor of a series of letters between friends in publishing *Pamela* in 1741, and the following year Henry Fielding claimed in his preface to *Joseph Andrews*: 'everything is copied from the book of nature, and scarce a character or action produced which I have not taken from my own observations and experience'.

Journalists with any more than a few years newsroom experience start to chafe against the limitations of daily news; they realise that the *form* of the standard news story may be tailor-made for conveying information but flounders under the weight of emotion or subtlety. As Norman Mailer once said, hard news is 'forever munching nuances like peanuts' (Stephens 1988, p. 255). Journalists find out things about people that are libellous and in frustration some, like Australian author Frank Hardy in *Power Without Glory* and more recently Anonymous (aka political columnist Joe Klein) in *Primary Colors*, turn to the roman-à-clef (novel in which real people and events are disguised as fiction). As Robert Drewe, an award-winning Australian journalist and novelist, puts it:

> In my experience, journalism has enough trouble with the libellous, the abstract and the subjective. Its attention span is too short. Anyway, its space limitations prevent the true and continuous tracking of connections. Journalism shies away from psychology. For all its nosy reputation it mostly ignores the private life and rarely sees the larger truth. (in Conley 1998, p. 54)

Defoe is known to generations of schoolchildren as the pioneer of the modern novel but in recent years he has been claimed as a pioneer of literary journalism. Kevin Kerrane wrote:

> Defoe built a writing career in the zone between fiction and fact. His novels, rich in realistic detail, read like documentary reports, while his journalism shines with literary quality. This generic ambiguity is typified by *A Journal of the Plague Year* (1722), which purports to be a survivor's memoir of the 1665 London epidemic: in fact, the book is a clever composite of Defoe's family history, early childhood memories, and very extensive reading. (Kerrane and Yagoda 1997, p. 23)

The historical anthology makes rich reading, belying the usual distinction between literature as the province of fiction and journalism as hastily composed hackwork. Though deeply entrenched, this view has been threatened in recent years, notably from an Oxford English professor, John Carey, who says literature is not an objectively ascertainable category where certain works naturally belong, but a term used by institutions and other culture-controlling groups to dignify those texts to which, for whatever reasons, they wish to attach value (Carey 1987a, p. 36). Accordingly, he says, arguments about whether reportage (his term) can be literature are neither interesting nor meaningful, which may be true, but successful literary journalism shares two qualities with those traditionally ascribed to literature — it deeply moves the reader, whether to tears or laughter or outrage, and it endures over time.

The power of a true story

To tell their true stories more powerfully, historians, biographers and journalists have long drawn on a range of techniques normally claimed by novelists. Some, like Mark Twain and Stephen Crane in the nineteenth century and Ernest Hemingway, George Orwell, Truman Capote, and Joan Didion in the twentieth, have been novelists themselves. However, many others have sought, as another critic, Thomas Connery, wrote, to go beyond journalism's facts but stop short of fiction's creations; literary journalists fuse the role of observer and maker to find a third way of depicting reality (Sims 1990, p. 18). One of the extracts in Kerrane and Yagoda's anthology is Boswell's *The Life of Johnson* (1791). Its status as the first great biography and Boswell's reputation for eccentricity have obscured his achievement as an early literary journalist. Boswell prefigures by almost two centuries Tom Wolfe and the New Journalists in creating dramatic scenes, recording salty dialogue, listing 'status details', and shamelessly drawing attention to himself in the narrative.

Some writers have used fictional techniques to examine momentous historical events; the effect can be electrifying. In 1946 John Hersey meticulously reconstructed the bombing of Hiroshima through the eyes of six survivors, narrating what each one did from the moment the bomb dropped at 8.15 a.m. on 6 August 1945, to six months later when the effects of delayed radiation began to be known. Hersey's 31 000-word piece occupied an entire issue of the *New Yorker* — a first in the magazine's life — and sold out within hours. Broadcast companies in several countries cancelled regular radio broadcasts on four successive evenings to read aloud the whole article. Albert Einstein bought 1000 copies of the magazine and the US army ordered reprints for its education service. The Book-of-the-Month Club distributed hundreds of thousands of copies to its subscribers free. Hersey's achievement (shared with his *New Yorker* editors, Harold Ross and William Shawn) was to be the first of the Second World War's victors to tell what had actually happened to the vanquished and show them not as evil but as fellow human beings. Equally important, he had resisted the huge pressure he must have felt to give free rein to his horror at the dropping of the first atomic bomb. Instead he wrote clinical, almost detached prose that enabled readers to see with chilling clarity the bomb's impact (Kunkel 1995, Yagoda 2000).

More recently, John Simpson covered the students' democracy protests in China in June 1989 and in the next few months wrote a piece for *Granta*, the quarterly English magazine of new writing, that was later reprinted (and is still in print) in *The Best of Granta Reportage* (Buford 1993, pp. 257–66). Simpson, the BBC's foreign editor, described how he and his crew watched in horror as an army tank charged and veered through Tiananmen Square, crushing several people, not students but factory workers from the outskirts of Beijing. Besieged by the workers' petrol bombs, the tank crashed into a block of concrete and got jammed, its engine whirring wildly. A terrible shout of triumph came from the chanting mob, who charged the burning tank. As first one and then a second soldier tried to escape their inferno, the mob grabbed them by the hair and ears and skin on their faces, and within seconds beat them to death. Just as a third soldier was dragged out of the tank, a bus screamed up and some students got out to try to save the soldier. Simpson wrote:

> I had seen people die in front of me before. But I had never seen three people die, one after the other, in this way. Once again the members of the crowd closed around the soldier, their arms raised over their heads to beat him to death. The bus and the safety it promised were so close. It seemed to me then that I couldn't look on any longer, a passive observer, watching another man's skin torn away or his head broken open, and do nothing. I saw the soldier's face, expressing only horror and pain as he sank under the blows of the people around him, and I started to move forward. The ferocity of the crowd had entered me, but I felt it was the crowd that was the animal, that it wasn't properly human. The soldier had sunk down to the ground, and a man was trying to break his skull with a half-brick, bringing it down with full force. I screamed obscenities at the man — stupid obscenities, as no one except my colleagues could have understood them — and threw myself at him, catching him with his arm up, poised for another blow. He looked at me blankly, and his thin arm went limp in my grasp. I stopped shouting. He relaxed his grip on the brick, and I threw it under the bus. It felt wet. A little room had been created around the soldier, and the student who had tried to rescue him before could now get to him. The rest of the mob hadn't given up, but the students were able to pull the soldier away and get him on to the bus by the other door. He was safe. (in Buford 1993, pp. 265–5)

Simpson's piece is important for two reasons. First, it broadens the reader's understanding of what happened in Tiananmen Square by showing that soldiers too were victims of the violence and that it was the students who helped save the third soldier's life. This does not mean there was no massacre in Tiananmen

Square, as the Chinese government has persuaded some to believe, but Simpson forces the reader to see beyond the headlines to consider the complexities and nuances of the event. Second, and perhaps more importantly, Simpson's piece has a real impact. It is almost impossible not to be moved by it, so sickening are its images and so compellingly is it written. Simpson is rare among journalists in that he is equally accomplished in both broadcast and print journalism. Literary journalism is mostly found in the print medium but it is worth noting that fictional techniques have been applied to television and film, usually in documentaries. In Australia, Chris Masters' great storytelling skills have been applauded less than his investigative reporting, and Bob Connolly and Robin Anderson showed in *Rats in the Ranks* how artful a fly-on-the-wall documentary could be.

Rats in the Ranks points to the second strand of literary journalism: true stories about people and issues that are neither historic nor even especially newsworthy. Few people outside Leichhardt would normally be interested in a local council power struggle, but Connolly and Anderson's storytelling abilities made the documentary universally appealing. Similarly, the American literary journalist, Tracy Kidder, spent a year sitting at the back of Mrs Zajac's grade five classroom in Holyoke, Massachusetts, to write a 340-page book in 1989 entitled *Among Schoolchildren*. As a news story it had the appeal of a mouldy school lunchbox, but a decade later on the other side of the world an experienced teacher came across the book by chance and was so engrossed he sat up all night reading it and then ordered a copy from a bookshop to pass on to his colleagues. He told Lauren Anderson, an RMIT University journalism student studying the book for an assignment, that he felt as if he was reading about himself, so compellingly were Mrs Zajac's experiences presented. Few people have the skill, literary or journalistic, to fashion an absorbing narrative out of such threadbare dramatic material. Kidder seems to revel in such topics; in 1985 he wrote a book about the building of a house.

It is not surprising, then, that literary journalism commonly appears in book form — books that often began life as lengthy magazine articles. William Finnegan's *Cold New World: Growing Up in a Harder Country*, about the underclass of young Americans, first appeared in the *New Yorker* before its publication in 1998. Magazines are the seedbed of literary journalism: they provide a bridge between daily journalism and books, giving writers the time and space to learn the narrative skills needed to hold a reader's interest through 10 000 or 15 000 words. The United States has long had a strong culture of magazine journalism (at *Harper's*, *The Atlantic Monthly*, *Esquire* and, of course, the *New Yorker*). So too has the United Kingdom; *Granta*, as John Carey noted, has published 'some of the most powerful journalism of recent years, transmitting excitement and intelligence that would be hard to match' (Buford 1993, back cover). In recent years, literary journalism has percolated through to the daily media according to Chris Harvey in *American Journalism Review*, becoming 'as commonplace as the pie chart in many newspapers, ranging from the *New York Times* to the *Oregonian* to the weekly *Washington City Paper*' (p. 41). Jon Franklin, a Pulitzer Prize-winning journalist and author of an influential textbook, has set up a website where literary journalism is showcased and sold (Weinberg 1998, p. 58).

Australia has a vibrant magazine industry, but, because of the country's vastness and its small population, has been unable to sustain support for the kind of publications that run literary journalism. Magazines like *Australian Society* and the *Independent Monthly*, and weekly newspapers such as *Nation Review* and the *National Times* (all now defunct) sometimes ran literary journalism but either did not have the money to support the research time literary journalists needed or the know-how to train journalists in this demanding form. It has largely fallen to individual journalists to do their own experiments. Evan Whitton and Craig MacGregor were influenced by the New Journalists, and their efforts in the 1970s to transplant literary journalism to Australia rewarded them both with Walkley Awards, but spurred only a small number of imitators and successors. The rising popularity of literary journalism overseas over the past decade has sparked a similar, more muted resurgence in Australia. A few writers have published books that could be termed literary journalism; namely, Helen Trinca and Ann Davies' *Waterfront: the Battle that Changed Australia*. Helen Garner also controversially staked a claim to this territory in *The First Stone* (see the case study below). In the 1990s, newspapers such as the *Age, Sydney Morning Herald, Australian Financial Review* and the *Australian* have run only a few pieces of literary journalism but have made greater use of narrative to tell the stories of major news events in a way that makes sense of them for readers. The *Age* has done this most often, notably with a Walkley Award-winning narrative of the Port Arthur tragedy in 1996. the *Australian* has set up a regular feature, 'Inside Story', to run less ambitious but still narrative-driven pieces that background news events.

The elements of literary journalism

A body of critical literature has been emerging in the past decade, developed by practitioners such as Jon Franklin and Mark Kramer, as much as by critics. Between them, they have delineated the following elements of literary journalism:

1 Documentable subject matter chosen from the real world as opposed to 'invented' from the writer's mind. This means no composite characters, no invented quotes and no attributing thoughts to sources unless they can be verified.

2 Exhaustive research, whether through conventional sources such as documents and interviews, or by 'saturation' reporting; that is, by immersing

yourself in the world of your subject, often for weeks or months at a time to get beneath surface realities. This implies a higher standard of accuracy.

3 Novelistic techniques: with this bedrock of research it is possible legitimately to use a range of techniques borrowed from fiction, such as creating whole scenes, quoting passages of dialogue, describing the social milieu in detail, and writing interior monologues for subjects (based on interviews with the subject). Literary journalists are restricted mostly to techniques drawn from socially realistic fiction.

4 Voice: daily journalism is tyrannised by the institutional voice. This form gives the writer freedom to be ironic, self-conscious, informal, hectoring, self-aware, and so on. It is mainly through the authorial voice that literary journalists can move beyond a socially realistic portrayal of events and people. Hunter S. Thompson is the most extreme example of the individual voice. Sometimes indulgent, he can be highly effective too; one of George McGovern's advisers said Thompson's account of the 1972 presidential campaign was the least accurate and most truthful he had ever seen. (Carroll 1993, p. 153)

5 Literary prose style, both in the attention paid to structuring the narrative and choosing the words themselves.

6 Underlying meaning. The purpose of all this work and style is to go beyond the constraints of daily journalism and find the underlying meanings in issues and events. This implies greater intellectual rigour in mounting an argument about the subject, even if that argument is embedded in an artfully constructed narrative.

What emerges from this list of elements is that literary journalism stands or falls on the quality of the reporting and research work. Without that, all the fine prose in the world has little meaning. In literary journalism the research is the iceberg, the polished prose its tip. Everybody sees the tip and it can be a truly impressive sight. Bulking below the surface is the iceberg, unseen and largely unknown. Literary journalists themselves understand the need for strong research. As Tom Wolfe put it in an overlooked section of his infamously self-promoting manifesto:

> They had to gather all the material the conventional journalist was after — and keep going. It seemed all-important to *be there* when dramatic scenes took place, to get the dialogue, the gestures, the facial expressions, the details of the environment. The idea was to give the full objective description, plus something that readers had always had to go to novels and short stories for: namely, the subjective or emotional life of the characters. (Wolfe 1975, p. 41)

Wolfe cited numerous journalists to build his case, but before and since there have been many examples showing the importance of reporting and research work in literary journalism. John Hersey interviewed about forty A-bomb survivors in Japan before choosing six as representative for his *New Yorker* piece (Yagoda 2000); John McPhee traversed the United States several times with geologists before writing *Basin and Range* (1980); John Bryson said his account of the Azaria Chamberlain case occupied him 'day and night' for four years; Adrian Nicole Blanc tracked the chaotic life of a teenage drug-addicted prostitute over two years for a piece in *The Village Voice* (reprinted in Sims and Kramer 1995, pp. 209–33); Gay Talese interviewed hundreds of *New York Times* people during two and a half years for his 1969 book *The Kingdom and the Power*; Ian Jack took the best part of a year to research and write for *Granta* his 20 000-word account of the killing of three IRA terrorists at Gibraltar in 1987; and Ryszard Kapuscinski journeyed 60 000 kilometres through remote villages in the Soviet Union as it collapsed for his 1993 book *Imperium*.

Keeping faith with the reader

If the reporting work earns literary journalists the freedom to borrow fictional techniques to write the story, there is just one problem: how does the reader *know* that the events described are real? The simple answer is they do not; they trust the writer. But some writers are not trustworthy. They envisage all those months of research, gaining people's trust, hanging around waiting for things to happen, recording minute details, asking endless questions and they start to think: *Why don't I simply make it up?* Or else, they amass all the material and are horrified by the gaps and lumps and mess of real life. They are tempted: *Why don't I make this read better?* The freedom of literary journalists to borrow from fiction to tell their true stories better comes at a price; to keep faith with the reader. Postmodern literary theory shows us it is important to question notions of the inviolability of objective truth (Eagleton 1996, pp. 190–208). It is important for journalists to be aware that they bring cultural and psychological baggage to every assignment. It is important to understand that the act of storytelling frames the world in a particular way and portrays people through a particular lens. But all this does not mean journalists should give up trying to find out what is going on in the world, and trying to make sense of it and communicate it as widely and strongly as possible.

If at one level theorists preach the kaleidoscopic nature of representation, at another, like everyone, they distinguish between truth and falsehood; no postmodernist enjoys being misquoted in the media. More seriously, truth and lies carry weight. The number of people killed in Tiananmen Square is not simply a rarefied academic debate — as was underscored by the Chinese government's censoring of any coverage of the massacre's tenth anniversary. Closer to home, try telling Aborigines it is unimportant whether they were stolen from their families or 'rescued', as former Liberal federal minister Peter Howson claimed in the June 1999 issue of the conservative monthly, *Quadrant*. Claims about the importance of truth-telling may sit oddly with the contemporary news media's crumbling credibility and obsession with entertainment. Some critics, like Jack Fuller, an American former newspaper executive and now a novelist, believe literary journalism actually aggravates this problem as it blurs the lines between fact and fiction. It is harder, he says, for readers to assess the veracity of literary journalism than conventional journalism with its attributed quotes and sources (Fuller 1996, p. 132). It is a fair point, and although literary journalism has won a devoted readership and acceptance among many journalists and is hammering out a body of critical literature, Fuller's scepticism remains common in news-rooms.

Paradoxically, literary journalists have more time than colleagues on daily deadlines to ensure a higher standard of factual accuracy and to plumb underlying meanings in events, as is shown in Hersey's *Hiroshima* or Bryson's *Evil Angels*. The key point is that fictional furnishings are built on factual foundations. Labelling a work correctly becomes more important. If a writer wants to blur fact and fiction because they could not get the full story or because it suits their literary purposes, then they should label their work accordingly, and not call it a true story. Muddying these waters confuses or angers readers. As American journalism professor Norman Sims wrote:

> As a reader, I react differently to literary journalism than to short stories or standard reporting. Knowing *this really happened* changes my attitude while reading. Should I discover that a piece of literary journalism was made up like a short story, my disappointment would ruin whatever effect it had created as literature. (Sims 1984, p. 5)

It is probably time Sims and other scholars reassessed *In Cold Blood*. Truman Capote made great play of the five years he had spent researching and writing the book, retracing the killers' journey across America as they fled the law and spending countless hours interviewing them on death row in Kansas. The book has been hailed as a masterpiece of literary journalism, translated into twenty-five languages and remains in print after thirty-four years; in 1998 it was included in the Penguin Essentials series. Two biographies of Capote reveal that he either made up or massaged certain key events (Clarke 1988; Plimpton 1998). He could not bear to end the book with the executions so he invented a redemptive scene, a chance meeting between two characters at the murdered family's graves. Capote painted one of the killers, Dick Hickock, as a 'sex fiend . . . just to make a better story,' according to the Kansas jail chaplain, James Post. This came out after Hickock's son, who was a baby when his father had murdered the Clutters, and had taken his stepfather's name after his mother's remarriage, was studying *In Cold Blood* at school. The boy was shocked when he eventually worked out his relationship to the notorious killer. Post was called in to help the teenager sort fact from fiction. One of the detectives on the case also believed Capote and the other killer, Perry Smith, had become lovers while Smith was in jail. In the book Capote describes the executions in detail but while he watched Hickock hang he fled the room when Smith was led to the scaffold. If these statements are true, they spoil the book or at the least diminish it.

In 1994 the critic Edmund White described John Berendt's *Midnight in the Garden of Good and Evil* as 'the best non-fiction novel since *In Cold Blood* and a lot more entertaining.' From the blurb on the book's front cover, his description is significant, though perhaps not as he intended it. Berendt's book, a blend of gripping courtroom drama and evocative travelogue about Savannah, Georgia, *is* more entertaining than *In Cold Blood* and therein lies the germ of its problems. Berendt is a former *Esquire* editor who attended the Melbourne Writers' Festival in 1995 when his book had become a bestseller — it eventually sold over a million copies. In a newspaper interview he laid out in detail the meticulousness of his research; he spent five years on the project, spending months at a time living in Savannah, and filling a bookshelf with notebooks of his interviews (Ricketson 1995). Such diligence was a sign, he said, of his respect for the raw material. He did acknowledge that concerns about some of his fictional devices had led the Pulitzer Prize non-fiction committee to deny him an award. By 1998, with *Midnight* still on the *New York Times* bestseller list, a growing number of people were questioning its accuracy (Dufresne 1998, pp. 78–9). Two key issues emerged: first, Berendt placed himself in the narrative of events years before he arrived in Savannah. He reconstructed an argument between the alleged murderer and his victim through interviews, but then put himself in the room at the time as if he actually witnessed the argument.

Second, Berendt's description of events at times beggars belief. For example:

> He put his arms around her and stroked her back with both hands, caressing her throat lightly with kisses, and sending a shiver down her spine. She reached down to remove her shoes, but before she could do it, he was pressing against her, probing with his fingers gently and insistently. With the other hand, he unzipped his fly; he took her buttocks tightly in his hands and pulled her towards him as he thrust into her. She breathed the salty smell of his t-shirt and felt his belt buckle rubbing against her stomach. Their rising body heat enclosed them like a steamy towel.

The man concerned, Danny Hansford, described elsewhere in the book as 'a walking streak of sex', was the murder victim and so Berendt's account relied on one party, a woman named Corinne, who, he insisted, described the encounter in blow-by-blow detail, right down to the belt buckle rubbing against her stomach. It still beggared belief, adding to the suspicion that Berendt may have gathered a prodigious amount of reporting detail but his desire to create a suspenseful, entertaining narrative overrode his duty to the truth of the story.

Conclusion

In conclusion, the use of fictional techniques in journalism throws up a host of complex and subtle issues. It offers readers much more than they customarily get and the best literary journalists create pieces that, unlike most daily journalism, stand the test of time. John Hersey's *Hiroshima* is as moving to read today as it was on publication over half a century ago. But literary journalism requires considerably more skill and work than most daily journalism. It is hard for journalists to master its demands, and it requires substantial time and resources, two things that are increasingly squeezed in newsrooms. If literary journalism seeks to get at underlying meanings in issues and events, it also makes it far harder for readers to determine what is fact and what is fiction, making it all the more important that its practitioners keep faith with their readers. In a world where spin doctors put more turn on the truth than Australian spin-bowling cricketer Shane Warne could even imagine, and simple notions of objective truth are rightly questioned, literary journalism does not pretend to have all the answers. It does, however, ask good questions, and with a persistence and flair that is easily lost in the helter skelter of daily journalism.

Case study

In March 1995 one of Australia's leading novelists, Helen Garner, created a literary storm with the publication of a book about a sexual harassment case at Melbourne University's Ormond College. Garner was alternately applauded for writing a beautiful, brave book that asked long overdue questions about punitive feminism and political correctness, or vilified for prostituting her undoubted literary skills in a cynical exercise that plugged into sexist stereotypes.

Amid the furore over *The First Stone*, which sold well over 60 000 copies, Garner's initial aims were lost. Garner had made her reputation as a novelist but had also produced a body of freelance journalism over twenty years, including a Walkley Award-winning feature about child abuse victim Daniel Valerio. Garner admired Janet Malcolm, whose superbly written books had dissected the underpinnings of psychoanalysis, journalism, and biography with surgical skill, and she lamented the lack of opportunities in Australia to create the same kind of literary journalism. *The First Stone* was her attempt to start filling this void.

In an author's note in the book she said she had conceived it as an extended piece of reportage but 'soon encountered obstacles to my research that forced me to write a broader, less "objective", more personal book. They also obliged me to raise the story on to a level where, instead of its being just an incident specific to one institution at one historical moment, its archetypal features have become visible.' Accordingly, she changed the names of those involved. It was a confusing note. Was it only the names that had been changed? What were the mysterious obstacles? And where did the reporting of real events end and the archetypal feature begin? Some answers lay within the book; others became public months after its release.

Garner reprinted in her book a letter she wrote in 1992 to Dr Alan Gregory, the Ormond College master who had been accused of sexual harassment by two female students. Garner expressed deep sympathy for Gregory, saying whatever the truth, he had been dealt with in an 'appallingly destructive, priggish and pitiless way'. Not surprisingly, the two young women refused her interview requests when she began her research, believing her to have already made up her mind on the case. Dr Jenna Mead, a senior woman in the college to whom the young women had originally turned for advice and support, refused to speak to Garner for the same reason. In the book Garner shrilly criticised all three for their refusal. Shortly before the book's release, the publisher's lawyers advised Pan Macmillan that Mead might sue for defamation. The choices presented to Garner were to drop the project, publish and be damned, or disguise Mead's identity. Garner reluctantly took the last choice, splitting Mead into between six and nine people in the book.

This did not become public until after Garner delivered a stinging address at the Sydney Institute in August 1995, again savaging Mead for blocking her research efforts. Mead revealed in the *Age* that Garner had split her into at least six people. 'The effect,' Mead wrote, 'is to suggest Garner is reporting the existence of a real conspiracy.' Reading this, numerous people suddenly felt the book's power collapsing inside them. Mead was variously described as a 'thin-faced, thin-bodied woman in her forties,' a headmistress working over a fourth-former, and a rude, secretive woman who 'mined and ambushed' Garner's path to the complainants. How could this Hydra actually be a solitary articulate feminist who offered legitimate arguments as to why she had decided not to cooperate with Garner's research; namely, that Garner had sabotaged any authentic project by writing, on the strength of a solitary newspaper report, an impassioned letter of support to Alan Gregory?

In March 1996 a collection of Garner's journalism, *True Stories*, was published, and a curious transformation unfolded. Suddenly Garner was recognised as a premier journalist by literary critics like Peter Craven and respected journalists like Gideon Haigh, the latter fashioning a fresh image of the established novelist as an elder of the journalistic tribe. Fiona Capp, a journalist turned novelist, favourably compared Garner's journalism with her fiction. Later in 1996, *True Stories* was short-listed in the Victorian Premier's literary awards: category, non-fiction.

Nobody disputed that Garner was a fine writer, but did that make her a fine journalist? *The First Stone was* a work of journalism, though a seriously flawed one. Garner's approach and the fact that many people read the book as if it was a novel underscored the belief of prominent non-fiction writers that the successful use of fictional techniques in journalism demanded not *less* but *more* skill and care. Some readers felt *The First Stone* was closer to autobiography than journalism; it did contain autobiographical elements, but what autobiography would take something *other* than the writer as its starting point? What autobiography covered only a couple of years of the subject's life, and only a small part of it, at that? If the book was primarily autobiography, then the writer really was left open to the charge that they had preyed on other people's suffering for their own edification.

The stony fact was that the book dealt with real events in a real place at a real point in time. Simple notions of objective truth are rightly questioned, but the students and staff at Ormond College never doubted that it was *their* college and *their* disastrous 'smoko' night at the centre of *The First Stone*; nor did anyone — including Helen Garner — who commented publicly after the book's release. Amid the glad-handing over *True Stories* and minting of a new reputation for Garner as the nation's major literary journalist, no one seemed to notice a telling change in the 1995 speech that Garner had given to the Sydney Institute. In *True Stories* a new paragraph was added near the end. It read:

> One thing I do regret, however, is that my publisher's defamation lawyers obliged me to blur the identity of a certain woman who was the young complainants' chief supporter in the college. I did this in a simple way: I didn't invent anything, but each time that the words or actions of this woman appeared in the text, I called her by a different name, thus splitting her into half a dozen people. Months after the book came out, the woman identified herself publicly, to my relief, since I had divided her with the greatest reluctance. This is the only ruse I engaged in, but has given some people the idea that the book is 'fictionalised' — that it's a novel. It is not a novel. Except for this one tactic to avoid defamation action, it is reportage (p. 178).

This was a remarkable paragraph. To start with, it was the first time Garner had publicly expressed regret at splitting up Mead. Second, where Mead had previously been chopped up, in *True Stories* she was made whole again, but rendered anonymous. This is more significant now than then because anyone looking at *The First Stone* controversy will probably read Garner's speech in *True Stories* rather than the original, which was what Kerryn Goldsworthy did in her recent study of Garner's work, thereby missing the change. Third, Garner violated her contract with readers that she laid out in the introduction to *True Stories*:

> A reader of non-fiction counts on you to remain faithful to the same 'real' world that both reader and writer physically inhabit. As a non-fiction writer you have, as well, an implicit contract with your material and with the people you are writing about: you have to figure out an honourable balance between tact and honesty. You are accountable for the pain you can cause through misrepresentation: you have a responsibility to the 'facts' as you can discover them (pp. 6–7).

Her words echoed Janet Malcolm's oft-quoted line about the non-fiction writer being a renter in the House of Actuality. Fourth, Garner failed to discuss the potential effects of her 'ruse'.

Garner had previously offered a sketchy defence of her actions in a post-script to her Sydney speech before it was published in the institute's journal, the *Sydney Papers*:

> I do not, of course, believe — it would be an absurd suggestion — that Mead was the sole supporter or adviser of the two young women. But this does not mean that I think there was 'a conspiracy' at work. At no point have I ever believed, nor have I suggested, that the Ormond events were fomented by 'a conspiracy' of feminists. I quote in my book other people who think that they were, but I myself do not (pp. 39–40, vol. 7, no. 4, spring 1995).

Taking these points one by one, she could not pretend that inflating on six to nine occasions the number of women blocking her research would have no impact on how the reader perceived the case, especially when she had made this issue central to the book's narrative. Second, there were at least twenty-five passages in the book that directly or indirectly suggested a feminist conspiracy in the Ormond case. There were other flaws in Garner's book, notably its thin research, but it was also persuasively written and by some measures Garner is an outstanding journalist; she has an astonishing ability to unlock the minutiae and meaning of unexamined everyday events and, of course, she is a fine stylist. In the end this was not enough to outweigh the book's careless rupturing of the faith between writer and reader. John McPhee, regarded by his peers as a scrupulous, gifted literary journalist, has said he gets irritated by writers who take short cuts and 'hitchhike on the credibility of writers who don't' (Sims 1984, p. 15). Helen Garner's *The First Stone* was exactly the kind of book that would raise his ire.

DISCUSSION QUESTIONS

1 What is fact and what is fiction? Can they ever be blended?
2 Does a purely 'factual' account of an event or person convey the full truth of it?
3 How can a reader assess the truth-telling claims of a piece of literary journalism? What can literary journalists do to help readers assess their work? Compare this with how readers assess similar claims in standard daily journalism?
4 What does the reader get in literary journalism that is usually denied them in daily journalism?
5 Are there any areas that literary journalism cannot tackle or treat?

Further reading

Buford, B. (ed.) 1993, *The Best of Granta Reportage*, Granta Books, London. Reprinted in 1998 with a new title *The Granta Book of Reportage* and an introduction by Granta's recently appointed editor, Ian Jack.

Carey, J. (ed.) 1987, *The Faber Book of Reportage*, Faber Books, London.

Franklin, J. 1986, *Writing for Story: Craft Secrets of Dramatic Nonfiction by a Two-time Pulitzer Prize Winner*, Plume Books, New York.

Kerrane, K. and Yagoda, B. 1997, *The Art of Fact: A Historical Anthology of Literary Journalism*, Scribner, New York.

Sims, N. (ed.) 1990, *Literary Journalism in the Twentieth Century*, Oxford University Press, New York.

11

Putting the public back into journalism

ANGELA ROMANO AND CRATIS HIPPOCRATES

People power has been an important part of journalistic vernacular since the dying days of the Marcos era, when reporters brought the world pictures of Filipino nuns forming human barricades in the path of oncoming tanks, and other dramatic images of mass political activism. Journalists are easily enchanted with evidence of people power in foreign contexts, from the Velvet Revolution in the former Czechoslovakian republic to the anti-Suharto student demonstrations in Indonesia. The struggle of common people to take control of their lives makes powerful news.

However, journalists appear less enraptured by consciousness-raising, community building, and empowerment at home. Admittedly, they are almost always content to throw their support behind obviously philanthropic campaigns that involve public engagement, such as anti-AIDS, anti–drink-driving and *slip-slop-slap* skin-cancer promotions. But apart from these occasional public-spirited gestures, journalists who work the political, police, and other well-worn news beats more commonly aim to remain detached and keep at arm's length from their subjects, their sources, and their audiences, in the name of objective, impartial reporting. Their maxim seems to be: *Tell it as it is, and let the chips fall as they may*.

Proponents of a new style of journalism, public journalism, have challenged such attitudes in an attempt to respond to declining audience levels and increasing community alienation from old-style news and traditional political processes. Public journalism acknowledges that, although many news organisations have catchy slogans along the lines of 'news you can use', most news has little direct relevance or use to Mr or Ms Average. The media bombards the audience with claims and counter-claims from political and other vested-interest groups, leaving the community with a poor understanding about what choices 'the little people' can make to influence public life, or how politicians and other leaders can be compelled to act on these choices.

The coverage of the political activities of independent Australian Senator Brian Harradine in late 1998 and early 1999 exemplifies this phenomenon. The balance of numbers in the Senate made Harradine's voting decisions critical to the success of many of the coalition government's legislative initiatives. The increasing numbers and power of independents in the preceding decade could be seen as an opportunity to invigorate public debate, as independents can voice a range of opinions seldom heard from members of large, mainstream political parties who are conventionally obliged to faithfully reiterate the policies reached through party-room decisions. Many journalists, however, stereotyped Harradine's complex and often intriguing negotiations over a range of political issues as a stoush between Prime Minister John Howard and Harradine — a clash between two opposing titans. Despite this, much of the news — on topics ranging from the screening of the controversial film *Lolita*, to attempts to privatise the national Telstra telecommunications carrier, native-title legislation, and the format of the new Goods and Services Tax — was often reduced to a simplistic Harradine versus Howard formula.

Why reporting needs reform

It is classic journalistic technique to use conflict between different groups or powerful personalities as the spice to flavour news stories, but over-reliance on the *A versus B* recipe can make it difficult for the public to understand the costs, consequences, and trade-offs involved in different policies or programs. Nor can citizens determine how decisions or actions on their part can influence politicians, policies, or public programs. Public disengagement with the media has consequences not only for media profitability but also for public participation in wider political processes. There are clear implications for political life and policymakers if the 'little people' feel they have no power apart from giving a tick or cross on the electoral report card once every three years. With traditional-style media political reportage often criticised as resembling coverage of horse races, it is little wonder that many frustrated Australians do not get involved in politics, many only voting because they are required by law to do so.

Beyond habitually recycling cliched approaches to story-telling, conventional journalism often fails the community by approaching news as a series of simple, discrete events rather than complex, ongoing processes. Today's *Daily Drivel* might carry a story about an environmental group warning that much of the earth's pastoral land will be rendered unproductive due to global warming. Tomorrow, one might expect the *Drivel* to report a scientist's claims that his or her research proves there is no such thing as global warming. A few weeks later, the *Drivel* might feature another scientist from a rival organisation, saying that her research on polar icecaps has shown that average daily temperatures have increased by 1.2°Celsius in the past thirty years. News audiences can expect that journalists will regularly serve up a cacophony of contradictory claims from competing sources. This is partly because no one source can articulate all significant variables on a given issue, so journalists must provide a variety of perspectives from a range of relevant sources. The *Drivel*, however, typifies the error of modern journalism in that each day's claims and counterclaims are presented without background or context on the issue and how it has developed. Readers can only obtain the complete picture if they diligently monitor the media, closely following all information exchanges from all sides over an extended period of time.

This style of journalism is in one sense consistent with the philosophies that underlie liberal democracy. The founding fathers of liberal democratic thought — John Milton, John Erskine, Thomas Jefferson, and John Stuart Mill — assumed that people were rational beings who could exercise reason to distinguish between right and wrong among the mass of competing, conflicting opinions, and information that circulated in 'the open market place of ideas'. Siebert (1963, p. 51) was one of the earlier theorists who noted that the impact of such assumptions was that media should subject the public:

> ... to a barrage of information and opinion, some of it possibly true, and some of it possibly false, and some of it containing elements of both. Ultimately the public could be trusted to digest the whole, to discard that not in the public interest and to accept that which served the needs of the individual and of the society of which he is part. (1963, p. 51)

However, maintaining such assumptions is inappropriate considering that more than five decades of studies have indicated that audiences consume news in a sporadic way (Schramm 1947; Burgoon and Burgoon 1980; Bogart 1989; Stone and Boudreau 1995). Somewhat like butterflies, they flit from one story to another without following issues or stories to their completion. Audiences are often only attracted to stories that reflect their worldview, and may only read, listen to, or watch *part* of any given story. This is reflected in the training of aspiring young newspaper reporters, who are taught to write in the classic inverted-pyramid story structure. This structure puts all the most important information in the first few sentences, on the assumption that the reader has a low attention span, generally skimming through only the first few lines of a story (Granato 1991; Keeble 1994; Mencher 1994; Conley 1997). The reader then flits off to the next story, and the next, and the next again, scanning the first few lines of many stories but settling only occasionally to read at any length.

This is fine for most stories, because their impact on society is ephemeral. Stories about a hit-and-run car accident in the suburbs or an earthquake on the Nullarbor Plain do not normally require extensive backgrounding or context. But more significant social, cultural, economic, or political issues — such as race relations, industrial reform, or constitutional change — might require careful mediation of debate to make the information meaningful for news audiences.

More than style

It is relatively easy to train journalists to improve the style and context of their reporting, but it may require a major shift in organisational and professional culture to address the most grass-roots problem — the relevance and interest of news topics to the audience. On an average day, most reporters will sift through the details of the major activities that have occurred or issues that have emerged in the public institutions of power. With the aid of conventional rules about traditional news values, they make value judgments about which of these events or problems is most important to their audiences and then investigate them further. These reporters may feel they have done their duty if they probe and pry and successfully wrestle with public relations spin-doctors to obtain a fair account of the activities and utterances of those in institutions of power. However, the best of efforts to represent an issue or event in a balanced and accurate style are wasted if audience members simply stop reading or switch off because the information is not pertinent to them.

Innumerable sociological studies have shown that, to a large degree, news agendas revolve around the agendas set by public servants, politicians, and business leaders, rather than those of the ordinary person on the street. This is because most news organisations base their journalists at the centres of political and economic power, where they can guarantee that authoritative sources will provide regular flows of information. If the information comes from sources seen as credible experts in their given field, then their statements require little labour-intensive fact-checking before they are crafted into news stories. (Such ideas are discussed in Sigal 1973, pp. 120–5; Hall et al. 1978, p. 58; Gans 1979, p. 128; Fishman 1980, pp. 51–2; Herman 1986, p. 172; Herman and Chomsky 1988, pp. 18–25; Tiffen 1989, chapter 2; Tuchman 1997, pp. 173–92; McNair 1998, chapter 4.) While this enables the news organisations to satisfy their unremitting need to find constant supplies of fresh news in a cost-effective and efficient manner, it also means that news agendas more commonly reflect the interests of the government and economic élite than the 'average Joe' in the audience.

Public journalism differs from the standard approach to news in three major ways. First, it works to allow the public to drive the agenda of what is reported in the news, rather than to allow the 'big boys' of business, bureaucracy, and politics unlimited control of the wheel. Second, it attempts to include the public in a discussion rather than merely throw information at the audience as it comes to hand. Third, it aims to help the public in making decisions about significant community issues, and conveys those decisions to policymakers, the captains of industry and commerce, and society at large.

Sources of inspiration for public journalism

As Gunaratne (1996) notes, the foundational philosophies of public journalism bear strong similarities to those of development journalism, a style of journalism promoted in Third World countries since the mid-1960s. Development journalism was started in The Philippines by journalists, educators, and practitioners hoping to improve reporting and writing skills, to enable journalists to cover complex development processes in language simple enough for poorly educated audiences with low literacy levels (Lent 1977, p. 17; Chowdhury 1978, p. 10; Lent 1979, pp. 66–7; Stevenson 1994, p. 239; Loo 1995, p. 4). The concept rapidly spread, taking on different meanings in different political contexts. In many countries, development journalism was often seen as spreading *positive news*. Positive news, which often does not fit in a *hard news* framework, explores the struggle for stability and progress, emphasising attempts to improve society, successful initiatives and individuals, or institutions that have contributed to their communities (Szende 1986, p. 38; Idid and Pawanteh 1989, p. 80; Galtung and Vincent 1992, p. 156; Ali 1994, p. 90). Other theorists and practitioners, drawing from liberation theorists such as Paulo Freire, defined development journalism as an interactive, advocative, educational, and often ethnographic medium that aimed to build self-reliance and participant democracy in the community. This style of journalism gives the marginalised, the minorities, and the under-privileged the opportunity to share information not just with those at the heights of political and economic power, but also fellow citizens (Hedebro 1982, pp. 103–17; Hester 1987, p. 9; Ponteñila 1990, pp. 22–4; Galtung and Vincent 1992, pp. 163–5; Dixit 1994, pp. 23–4; Loo 1996, p. 122). The concept of development journalism was virulently opposed by many Western liberal journalists and theorists, particularly those in the United States (see Righter 1978, pp. 189–92; Sussman 1978, p. 77; Lent 1979, p. 67) because of indications that some nations wanted journalists to engage in self-censorship to protect social stability and political order of fragile developing nations (see Mahathir 1985, p. 215; Suharto 1989, p. 132; Lee 1992, p. 29).

Ironically, despite the hostility of many US journalists to development journalism, similar aspirations to develop community life through community-centred reporting shaped the germinal philosophies underpinning public journalism in the United States decades later. Public journalism emerged in the

United States in the late 1980s as an innovative philosophy and technique that positioned media organisations as catalysts rather than mere recorders of public debate. The founders of the philosophy were concerned by a measurable nose-dive in public involvement in both political and civic organisations. They argued that journalism had contributed to a decline in public life by destroying confidence in public institutions and not making any counterbalancing efforts to revitalise community involvement in the public sphere (Hoyt 1992; Kurtz 1993; Rosen 1993b; Rosen and Meritt 1994; Carey 1995; Denton and Thorson 1995; MacNeil 1995; Merritt 1995; Fallows 1996). Public journalism proponents often unconsciously revived earlier concepts developed by the 1947 Commission on Freedom of the Press, commonly known as the Hutchins Commission, in calling for journalists to develop codes of responsibility that would enable journalism to develop democratic participation (Altschull 1997; Parisi 1998).

Two men who helped initiate the public journalism concept, Davis 'Buzz' Merritt and Jay Rosen, began experimenting with New Journalism techniques in the late 1980s in response to indications that Americans had withdrawn from civic life and were not engaging in news on politics and significant societal issues. Their ideas resonated with those of other media researchers and scholars, who developed empirical data to support their assertions that the media lacked community connection. The Pew Research Center for Public Journalism, the Poynter Institute for Media Studies, and the scholars they gathered together were pivotal in nurturing and developing the theory of public journalism. The Pew Research Center produced a body of statistical evidence to support Merritt and Rosen's thesis about the disintegrating connection between the community and the news media during the late 1980s and 1990s. A 1999 Pew Research Center survey, for example, found that 38 per cent of respondents found the news media were immoral, an increase of 25 per cent since 1985, while 32 per cent described news organisations as unprofessional, a rise of 21 per cent. Thirty-eight per cent also said the news media hurt democracy, compared with 23 per cent in 1985. In other telling findings, 58 per cent of the public doubted the general accuracy of news reports, 31 per cent thought press criticism kept political leaders from doing their jobs, and 72 per cent felt the media propagated scandals rather than merely reported them (Pew Research Center 1999). Other Pew Research Center surveys have similarly found consistent declines in the public confidence and credibility ratings of both broadcast and print news media.

Rosen (1993a, pp. 4–5) credits three key figures with helping to develop and legitimise the fledgling public journalism movement in 1990 through high-profile endorsements of its philosophies. These were *Knight-Ridder, Inc.* chief executive James K. Batten, *Dallas Morning News* editor Burl Osborne, and the *Washington Post* columnist David Broder. In a lecture at the University of Kansas, Batten (in Rosen 1993a, p. 13) emphasised the importance to newspapers of community spirit, which he defined as 'the willingness of people to care about where they live and to wade in to help solve its problems'. After noting an escalating sense of disinterest and disconnectedness of people to their communities and community responsibilities, Batten (in Rosen 1993a, p. 15) asked: 'If communities continue to erode, how can we expect newspapers to continue to prosper, over the long term?' He argued that those 'who feel a real sense of connection to the places they live' are twice as likely to become newspaper readers (in Rosen 1993a, p. 13). A month later, Osborne, then the incoming president of the American Society of Newspaper Editors, similarly described Americans as being 'isolated from public life, from the self-governing process, and from the source of our public institutions' (Rosen 1993a, p. 5). Finally, and perhaps most influentially, Broder published a series of columns in which he urged his colleagues to take more responsibility for the deteriorating quality of political discussion.

> We cannot allow the 1990 election to become another exercise in public disillusionment and political cynicism. It is time for those of us in the world's free-est press to become activists, not on behalf of a particular party or politician, but on behalf of the process of self-government. We have to help reconnect politics and government to what happens in the campaign and what happens afterward in public policy if we are to have accountability and genuine democracy in this country. (Rosen 1993a, p. 5)

In contrast to the old standards of journalistic professionalism, which revolve around objectivity and detachment, the new philosophers talked about connectivity and conversation (as opposed to mere debate) that allow people to find solutions through democratic participation (for example, Anderson, Dardenne and Killenberg 1994, 1997; Carey 1995, 1997e; Lauterer 1995; Benesh 1998). Such journalism described audiences as citizens and participants rather than consumers, and endeavoured to explore processes through which things might 'go right', rather than merely pointing out things that had 'gone wrong' (Merritt 1998, pp. 113–14).

Public journalism in practice

Public journalism practitioners have used a variety of techniques to tap into public sentiments, to reflect these sentiments in their news stories, and to ensure these stories influence political processes. Public journalism may involve a range of market research style techniques — such as focus groups, qualitative and quantitative opinion polls, public forums, and other survey instruments — to enable community members to discuss what topics are important to them. On a smaller scale, some organisations oblige their reporters to spend time at information booths at local fairs, having brown-paper bag lunches in shopping malls, visiting meetings of community groups, and similar techniques. In this way, it is evident that public journalism is not a new technique *per se*. It merely returns to the spirit of journalism as practised in the 1950s and 1960s, before big news rounds and beats were established with constant flows of PR-originated information feeds. It recreates an era when journalists' news values were more prone to be influenced by conversations with ordinary people in pubs, church fetes, school meetings, and the like.

Once a focus for news is established, journalists gather information based on consideration of the choices that the public might make in response to a particular issue and the consequences of such choices. Rather than allowing politicians and businesspeople to set the news agenda through press conferences and other activities, journalists present the source with the questions and issues advanced by the audience. The focus of interviewing also changes. Journalists often think they are being objective, accurate, complete reporters by asking side A and side B what they think the problem or issue is. Public journalism is directed to asking A, B, community members, and other relevant stakeholders what potential solutions might be. Instead of asking A and B why they think each other's side is wrong, they are asked what values they have in common and what issues they might be able to work together on. Public journalism also recognises the expertise of ordinary people as news sources. Reporters go beyond *the usual suspects* of big business and politics by cultivating sources in a wide range of community groups or inviting the community to attend discussion forums and similar events.

Public journalism prioritises background and context that enables the public to dip into a story and follow the currents of the debate without being experts on the issue. Solutions to problems are not presented as black and white, since no *one* policy or action is all good or all bad. By providing details of the pluses and minuses, public journalism helps people to pick the solution that has the most positive elements in the final balance. Public journalists have also been creative in using story-telling techniques, graphs, and other graphics to clearly spell out the competing interests and the respective pros and cons of different ideas in ways that help the public make decisions. Good public journalists are awake to the risk that the findings of this research might eventually sound like a dry sermon or dull morality tale. Stories are enlivened by the opinions and life stories of a range of community members, tales of human struggle, failure, triumph, and achievement among the 'battlers', and other techniques. Bringing the stories, opinions, and experiences of ordinary people into the limelight also prompts politicians, bureaucrats, and businesspeople to react to their concerns.

Early international forays into public journalism

One example of a successful public journalism project was the *Akron Beacon Journal*'s 1994 'A Question of Colour' series, published thirty years after Martin Luther King's 'I have a dream' speech about equality in America. The year-long project, which won that year's Pulitzer Prize for public-service journalism, was broken into four segments, with three-day instalments run each quarter, followed by focus groups, and other qualitative research. For example, the segment entitled 'The streets where we live' used state and federal government data and information from schools, the police, and courts to examine disparities between the races in housing, education, economic opportunity, and crime. The aim was not simply to trot out contrasting statistics but also to examine the human face behind the reasons that substantial gaps still persisted in the 1990s despite decades of effort to close those disparities. Reporters went to follow-up focus groups to observe what went on and to write stories to provide qualitative research to complement the quantitative data. The paper invited community organisations to volunteer to establish projects addressing race relations, and hired facilitators to aid in project planning. The segment put a human face on statistics by including interviews with blacks and whites from low-, middle-, or high-income backgrounds, describing their attitudes to each other, and the streets in which they lived. In the last part of the series, the paper invited readers to send in a coupon pledging to fight racism: more than 22 000 people responded, and 10 000 of those were actively engaged in race relations projects by mid-1994.

The philosophies of community-centred reporting have spread from the United States to other developed nations. One of the early adopters of public journalism was New Zealand. During the 1993 NZ general election campaign, for example, politicians led the change by shifting away from traditional relations with political reporters, showing considerable frustration with journalistic reliance on 'bad news', ten-second grabs, and the adversarial *A versus B* storytelling mode (McGregor 1994, pp. 94–6). Politicians began bypassing the traditional manufacture of news, making unprecedented use of talkback radio, and talkshow television. This allowed them to appeal directly to the public instead of working through the filters of mainstream journalism. The talkback format facilitated techniques often used in public journalism. These included the opportunity for audiences to ask politicians what they were *for* rather than just what they were *against*, and what politicians agreed about with their opposition (and by implication, what they would be willing to compromise and co-operate on (McGregor 1994, pp. 96–8)).

The period also marked the beginning of experimentation in public journalism by two major newspapers, The *Evening Standard* and *Waikato Times*. The push to public journalism escalated in the 1996 election campaign, when the electoral system shifted from first-past-the-post to proportional representation, leading to widespread concerns that old methods of political reportage were not adequate tools for reporting the complex new political system (McGregor, Comrie and Campbell 1998, pp. 2–3). The *Evening Standard*, *Waikato Times* and a third paper, the *Press*, each recruited university researchers to conduct public opinion polls asking readers to identify the campaign issues. Among techniques used to measure public opinion were telephone surveys, readers' panels, and 'deliberative opinion polls', in which a random sample of citizens was brought together for intensive briefings, discussion, exchange of ideas, and debate. Instead of merely following politicians and waiting for them to proclaim their policy announcements and campaign promises, journalists took control of the agenda, writing stories and asking questions based around the issues that the community prioritised. Journalists tried to help the public compare the policies of one party against another by using techniques such as printing tables outlining each party's position on a particular question. When parties failed to answer questions before the deadline, the newspapers printed a block of white space with the words 'No response' under the party's name. This happened once when the National Party, rejecting the newspapers' attempt to drive the campaign, refused to answer questions. After the *Press* printed white space under the National Party's name, which appeared next to the answer of the rival New Zealand First party, the Nationals never missed another deadline (McGregor, Comrie and Campbell 1998, pp. 13–14).

These activities involved considerable re-education of not just politicians, but also of journalists, who had to use different news-gathering and writing techniques. Once these were mastered, editing and reporting staff were elated at their ability to take greater control of campaign coverage. However, there was also much hostility and resentment about the labour and resource-intensive nature of the public journalism projects, in which some journalists were dedicated to special public journalism teams while the remainder struggled to complete all the remaining reporting and editorial work (McGregor, Comrie and Campbell 1998, pp. 12, 14).

Australian initiatives

In Australia, a variety of journalists and media educators have attempted to build community-centred journalism. Among the proponents was Eric Loo, strongly influenced by the principles of development journalism in The Philippines, India, and other developing countries in the 1960s. He argues that the US concept of public journalism merely crystallises the 'community-oriented' reporting functions developed in the Third World under a new label (pers. comm., 13 May 1999). Since the mid-1990s, he has attempted to teach journalism students that they must go beyond seeing themselves as scribes — waiting to report and discover some one *objective* reality — to an understanding of themselves as tools for constructive change. Loo also warns journalism educators that they risk becoming irrelevant if they continue to teach journalism students only the inverted pyramid and mould them in an event-oriented reporting mindset based on conventional news values (Loo 1994, p. 7).

Several public journalism projects have been run in Australia, including one pioneering effort at the Australian Broadcasting Corporation (ABC) in

Queensland in 1997. An ABC think tank decided to hold a series of public forums, working with municipal councils to identify issues of local significance, going on location, listening to the community, and addressing the issues at public meetings broadcast on radio and television. Anna Reynolds, then an ABC talk-back host involved in the project, describes the rationale as to revive a slow downward trend in ratings. By physically being among different communities, touching people's lives in a constructive way, the station hoped to convince them to become regular listeners or viewers. Two forums were conducted: one in Ipswich, the birthplace of the right-wing One Nation party; the other in the inner-Brisbane suburb of Fortitude Valley, which is characterised by an eclectic combination of nightclubs, needle-exchange centres, primary schools, and prostitutes. The ABC led up to each forum by gathering information through field research, community consultation, and a commissioned survey that questioned residents about local issues including crime, politics, race, and availability of government services. Armed with this data, the ABC invited the public to the forums to discuss town planning and social issues affecting the two areas. The Fortitude Valley forum was broadcast live on the ABC's Brisbane radio station, 4QR, and the Ipswich event was edited into a half-hour program for ABC TV. Although these forums were not labelled public journalism at the time, they clearly exhibited many of the same motivations, objectives, and practices (Reynolds 1998).

The PJ Project

In the following year, the Public Journalism (PJ) Project was established by the Queensland University of Technology (QUT) and the University of Wollongong. Drawing direct inspiration from overseas initiatives, most particularly the *Akron Beacon Journal* project, the PJ Project called on the public to help set the agenda for debate on race relations issues such as immigration and Aboriginal reconciliation. Unlike other public journalism projects, in which extensive surveys or other market-research techniques were used to establish a topic, the project partners settled on race relations as a fraught issue in the fore of public consciousness. The issue was directly connected with numerous public demonstrations, occasionally characterised by violence, logjams of calls to talk-back programs, surging numbers of letters to editors, and increasing membership in almost all party-political groups. Race had become a hot topic, in part because of the *Mabo* and *Wik* High Court decisions on Indigenous land rights. The problem was compounded by the incessant, fractious debate stimulated by independent federal MP Pauline Hanson's statements on Aboriginal issues, immigration, ethnic diversity, multiculturalism, and similar topics. Hanson, who went on to found One Nation, tapped into popular sentiments by associating her self-avowedly politically incorrect statements on race and other issues as representative of 'the real Australians' who were locked out of public debates by politicians and other large, vested interests. For a public disenfranchised with political institutions, including the media, Hanson's constant declarations that she was a parliamentarian and not a politician had a palpable appeal.

The first phases of the Public Journalism Project — involving a collaboration between QUT, the Ethnic Communities Council, the Australians for Reconciliation Project and Brisbane's daily newspaper, the *Courier-Mail* — invited community input on complex social issues that journalists often avoid as 'not sexy enough' or unpopular. Project activities included two public forums, focus groups, a telephone hotline, questionnaires, and consultations with various community leaders. The two forums, called 'Reconciliation: Local Solutions' and 'Immigration Beyond 2000', attracted 600 people. These events stimulated extensive media reportage, including two eight-page, tabloid-size lift-out supplements plus another 1392 column centimetres of coverage in the *Courier-Mail*. Material published included news articles, feature and colour articles, opinion pieces, editorials, letters to the editor, hotline comments, fact boxes, and even one fiction story. These described the experiences of different ethnic groups, represented a diverse range of perspectives on race-related policy issues, and detailed various public initiatives towards building racial harmony and a better community life (Tickle and Hippocrates 1999).

Reportage of the project contrasted sharply with other media coverage of Indigenous and immigration issues during Hanson's 1996 to 1998 term in Parliament, when journalists often reported the statements of prominent political figures and lobby groups in simplistic and knee-jerk style, without mediating or focusing the debate. This kind of 'objective' reportage, letting the chips fall as they may, was condemned by a range of community stakeholders, including Hanson herself. Journalists *told it as it was*, and the community appeared more inclined to spit chips than to disinterestedly watch them fall. The response suggested that while journalists had developed many techniques of objectivity and detachment from the news, they had been less sophisticated in their techniques of connection with their audiences.

Not all went smoothly with the project, with the newspaper spiking several stories, which had involved much effort from the community partners, because the articles were not seen as sufficiently newsworthy. The newspaper also faced commercial pressures to find well-known figures and 'big names' to talk about issues of national or state significance, rather than to represent the initiatives of small people operating at a local level. Follow-up focus groups also had some criticisms, including that the forums had not concentrated enough on local issues, there had been insufficient time to discuss the issues fully, and the debate at the immigration forum was too polarised. However, there were many measures of strong community satisfaction with the project efforts, including positive responses to surveys conducted at each forum, high levels of input to the telephone hotline (which received three times as many calls as a hotline for the looming federal election), an influx of letters to the editor related to the project, and increasing community inquiries to the project's community-group partners.

In the wake of these activities, there was no indication that newspaper circulation increased significantly in the short term. Since both of the forums coincided with a state or federal election campaign, the overall effect on circulation is difficult to measure. However, it does not appear that circulation exceeded the levels normally expected during election-campaign periods. It would be premature to expect that these projects on reconciliation and immigration — with coverage between them lasting a total of five weeks — would immediately or radically alter community orientation towards the *Courier-Mail*. As Merritt (1998, p. 7) warns, doing a little public journalism here and there will not produce quick answers for publishers and broadcasters seeking the solution to declining audiences. Even in US experiments in which public journalism philosophies and techniques have been scrupulously followed, some US public journalism innovators have seen higher circulations but others have not. There is more indication that such newspapers have recorded increases in readership satisfaction rather than direct circulation rises in the initial periods following the introduction of public journalism activities (Charity 1995, p. 156).

The second phase of the Public Journalism Project, based at the University of Wollongong, took a different approach in its programs, which engaged the community in media debates in regional and rural New South Wales. The NSW phase operated in collaboration with five daily newspapers from the Rural Press publishing group. The newspapers had strong networks with local communities in Bathurst, Dubbo, Maitland, Mudgee, Orange, and Tamworth, so they started from a strong base for acting as community-building institutions. After consultation with the local communities, the newspapers conducted 'Project Y', examining issues important to young people in central and western NSW. Through focus groups in youth centres and schools, the newspapers identified key discussion topics, which set the agenda for subsequent forums and media coverage.

Other Australian projects

These early and imperfect steps of the Public Journalism Project stimulated other public journalism initiatives. The largest have been the efforts of the Victorian Local Government Association (VLGA), comprising four projects involving the community, local government, and the media. One VLGA project in the Latrobe Valley stands out for particularly strong use of public journalism principles. The *Latrobe Valley Express*, the Latrobe Shire Council, and representatives of the Shire's community consultative forums formed a partnership committed to using public journalism techniques. The area has a high youth population, and the partners attempted to assess whether lack of public transport was an issue for young people, and, if so, how the issue could be addressed. The first stage of the project was a seminar that attracted almost 100 representatives from across the community — from private bus companies to high-school students and their parents — who identified a set of needs to be fulfilled. The second stage explored the progressive steps required to meet those identified needs.

This contrasts with the three other VLGA projects, which resulted in positive relations between the partners but ultimately did not move beyond traditional relations between the community, councils, and the media. A Moreland City Council project was committed to involving young people in council activities, organising a 'Voices of the Future' youth summit and following through on recommendations arising from the summit. However, the effort expended in ensuring that young people could work in a power-sharing arrangement left little time for increasing the access of youth to the media. Another project involved community groups in Cardinia negotiating with the shire council to donate land, with the council collaborating in lobbying the state government to provide assistance in building housing for families with special needs. Although the groups were pleased that the media supported their case by publicising various stages of the project, they realised that many levels of the negotiations were best conducted without the pressure of continual media scrutiny. Buloke Shire Council and its partners were similarly satisfied by the media coverage of a new program to ensure community groups that catered for their members and supporters (for fundraising and other purposes) were accredited to meet certain food-handling and hygiene standards. However, beyond publicising the initiative and raising the issues in the public arena, the media were not integrally involved in the overall process as had initially been planned.

There have been other public journalism projects in Australia, although many have not been labelled as such. These include the *Australian* newspaper's poll on the 1999 referendum to consider whether Australia should become a republic and whether a preamble should be added to the Constitution. The activity, Australia's first deliberative poll, was designed to show how people would choose if they had the opportunity to ask the questions for themselves and to consider issues in depth. After the poll, which was broadcast live on ABC TV and radio, the 347 participants had changed their intended voting behaviours markedly (the *Australian*, 25 October 1999). The newspaper, however, pragmatically noted that most people had other priorities than following the issue and that many would 'continue to block out the messages the weekend participants heard' (McGregor 1999, p. 7). It should be noted that the poll supported the *Australian*'s strongly pro-Republican stance and its attitude that people who were educated on the issues were more inclined to support a Republic. Despite this, the poll can be considered as one of a number of special features and series run by the *Australian* that have told the previously unheard tales and expressions of concern of community members.

Criticisms

Despite the positive outcomes of some public journalism projects, the journalistic community has not been unanimously supportive of this new approach. The philosophy and associated journalism techniques have attracted stringent criticism, most particularly from US journalists and theorists. Some have questioned the underlying philosophy, blaming public journalism for excessive political correctness and erosion of basic journalistic standards. Such critiques have commonly been based on conservative liberal philosophies that the concept of loyalty to the community can conflict with the duty of journalists to serve the truth (Barney 1997, p. 82–6). Senior academics, such as John Merrill and William Lawbaugh, support devotion to *truth* rather than community service, claiming that *serving the public* is a dangerous term that has been misused in the past by the Nazis and Soviets to rationalise oppressive actions that obstruct rather than strengthen democracy (Merrill 1997; Corrigan 1998–99). There have been additional criticisms that there is no hard evidence that public journalism techniques increase public understanding of issues, political participation, or civic engagement (McMasters 1997), and that public journalism proponents ignore research that has suggested some communities have remained unchanged after public journalism projects (Diamond 1997).

Others have condemned public journalism as a sloppy technique. They point to examples of journalists using person-in-the-street quotes and other techniques in circumstances that do not add to public debate or knowledge (Diamond 1997; Waddell 1997; Corrigan 1998–99). Some have questioned why journalists might consider it a virtue to be blindly devoted to opinion polls and other market research mechanisms, while they condemn such devotion among politicians (McMasters 1997). It should be understood here that any journalism technique can be used sloppily, and that such critics have neglected to note that the problem may have been more one of lazy or misguided practitioners applying the techniques in inappropriate contexts rather than a flaw in public journalism itself.

Finally, some have noted how public journalism does not suit the commercial needs of news organisations, which need to gather information quickly from sources seen as reliable experts. Public journalism projects have sometimes acted as a black hole in news organisations, sucking resources such as journalists' labour, newspaper space, or airtime with little direct return (Waddell 1997). One case that exemplifies this problem is that of the *Columbus Ledger-Enquirer* in Columbus, Ohio. In 1988 the newspaper conducted a formal survey of 400 residents, and more informal journalistic research aimed at uncovering the fears and concerns of residents. With little community response, editor Jack Swift intensified his efforts, sponsoring backyard barbecues, town hall meetings, and other activities. After almost two years, with reporters working twelve to fourteen hours a day, the project had absorbed almost all the newsroom resources, leaving little left for regular journalism. Swift was harshly criticised, a factor that is believed to have contributed to his suicide in 1990 (Waddell 1997, pp. 94–5).

Conclusion

Public journalism techniques must still be understood as experimental. Journalists are yet to perfect any formula that enables them to connect deeply with the public while also fulfilling their news organisations' needs to produce accurate, reliable, and interesting news about public affairs on a daily basis. A major challenge for public journalism proponents has been to organise public journalism activities to suit the production routines of daily newspapers or to bend those production routines sufficiently to suit public journalism. An ongoing aim is to inculcate public journalism philosophies as part of the daily working experience of the bulk of reporting and editorial staff, rather than to simply try out techniques in one-off experiments every once in a while. Even true believers can expect difficulties in organising forums and other activities that enable community stakeholders to participate fully in political processes.

It is possible to propose five keys to successful public journalism:

1 *Establishing the agenda*: if journalists are to fulfil their role as 'professional problem-solvers and public sense-makers' (Dennis 1989, p. 182), they must first find out which issues community members believe should be scrutinised. If discussion on these topics is not mediated properly, then the community will quite probably have to grope its way through the disorienting labyrinth of ten-second TV-news grabs, splash headlines, columnists' opinions, and sensationalist reporting. Public journalism should be user-friendly, as it defines issues that are important to the community and should structure the arguments on these issues in a meaningful way.

2 *Dedicating the resources*: any news organisation that commits itself to the principles of public journalism must also be willing to commit significant editorial resources. These include a guarantee from a senior editor for editorial space in the form of stories and pictures. Both reporting and editorial will require initial training in the requirements of the new approach. Reporters must dedicate time towards discussion with different grass-roots elements of the community. This may not return immediate story benefits, but should have long-term implications for the story ideas they pursue and how they pursue them. Interested community groups and community members might pledge to assist in helping to organise forums or other forms of public consultation.

3 *Setting the timetable*: after identifying the issues to be explored, a program
   for public journalism activities, for example, forums and other 'community
   conversations' on those topics, should be determined by deliberation between
   senior editors and different community groups, including a range of relevant
   stakeholders.
4 *Obtaining feedback*: feedback on public journalism projects is important.
   Members of the public should be able to express their feelings through letters
   to the editor, e-mail, telephone hotlines, surveys, focus groups, and other
   feedback mechanisms.
5 *Analysing the activities and outcomes*: the project team should measure how the
   focused coverage of a particular socio-political issue impacts on public perceptions. The team should measure both the social benefits that accrue and
   public satisfaction with the different kinds of public journalism techniques
   that were used. Measuring public satisfaction is a difficult task. However, project teams can evaluate through analysis of the feedback to the newspaper,
   audience surveys, quantitative and qualitative analysis of editorial coverage,
   focus groups with community stakeholders, focus groups with those journalists who worked on the project and those who didn't, and by monitoring the
   level of enquiries to any community groups involved with the project.

The use of public journalism by VLGA partners in the Latrobe Valley indicates the extent to which communities can adopt and adapt different public journalism techniques. However, the decision of participants in three other VLGA
projects not to take this approach underlies a pragmatic reality, recognised even
by public journalism proponents, that such techniques are not necessarily useful
for solving all community problems in all places at all times. Some problems may
be best solved by negotiations between parties outside the glare of the media
spotlight. Simplistic adoption of public journalism techniques cannot be seen
as a panacea for all social ills. Those attempting to initiate public journalism
projects may initially copy activities tried by other media and community organisations in other contexts, but partners must be sophisticated enough to experiment with different styles of interaction to determine those that best suit local
needs and conditions. They must also be astute enough to know when the media
should withdraw to enable problems to be resolved through other forms of
democratic participation.

As mentioned above, the activities organised by public journalism practitioners have required considerable commitment of resources in terms of financial
costs, the commitment of staff time, and the space dedicated in the newspaper
to public journalism activities. Attempts to inculcate a new working culture have
been neither cheap nor easy. Although there have been many challenges and substantial costs, proponents have been driven by an assurance that the struggle of
everyday Australians to take control of their lives can make powerful news, even
at home.

Case study

Eric Loo, a long-term proponent of public journalism-type techniques in both developing and developed countries, describes public journalism as an Americanisation of practices that have been developed with less fanfare in poorer nations. He argues that all journalists can work for constructive change, although he uses the term *community-service reporting* in favour of *public* or *development* journalism. An abridged summary of his framework for community-service reporting is listed below (from Loo 1994, 1995).

1　Don't just look on events from afar. Be a participant observer of events and issues.
2　Critically assess the needs and interests of the audience and the wider community.
3　Develop your cognitive and experiential knowledge of the issues reported.
4　Be aware of the way the story can affect the development of community resources.
5　Shift news emphasis from policymakers to those affected by the policies (that is, the community).
6　Shift news focus from economic figures and other facts and statistics to look at concrete personal life experiences of community members.
7　Personally connect with a wide cross-section of the community.
8　Treat audiences as communities with needs and concerns rather than as information markets.
9　Provide the community with open access to the media.
10　Pay fair attention to mainstream and minority views, including minority views on mainstream issues.

DISCUSSION QUESTIONS

1　Many journalists feel uncomfortable with the public journalism goals of seeking to direct the public agenda and community debate, arguing that journalists should merely report the news and not try to shape it. What are the strengths and weaknesses of such an argument?
2　Is the aim of building greater connections between journalists and the community inconsistent with the goal of journalists to cover news topics in an *objective* fashion?
3　Identify a socio-political issue that is significant to your community, and determine whether it requires a public journalism approach. Imagine that you are working for a news organisation and plot how you would go about

developing a commercially viable proposal for a public journalism project on the issue you have identified.

4 Public journalism aims to allow the public greater voice in expressing their interests, ideas, concerns, and desires, and allowing these to set the agenda for public debate. How should journalists respond if surveys, public forums, or other public journalism mechanisms reveal that a significant portion of the community wants to pursue a racist or other undesirable agenda?

5 Are there any topics that should not be reported with public journalism techniques?

6 Is public journalism significantly different to the way that many alternative and community media outlets operate? Analyse the contents of one community or alternative publication in your area to ask how much it prioritises the agendas of its target community, helps its readers to make decisions on important issues, and incorporates community opinion on matters of public concern.

Further reading

Corrigan, D. 1998, 'Public journalism's sugar daddy offers short cuts on the intellectual journey', *The St Louis Journalism Review*, September, *http://www.webster.edu/%7Ereview/pjconcepts.html#sugardaddy*, 3 November 1999.

Hippocrates, C. 1998, 'Public journalism: Will it work in Australia?', *http://www.dcita.gov.au/crf/papers98.htm*, 3 November 1999.

McKnight, D. 1996, 'Public journalism, citizenship and strategies for change', *http://www.gu.edu.au/centre/cmp/McKnight.html*, 3 November 1999.

Meyer, P. 1995, 'Public journalism and the problem of objectivity', *http://www.unc.edu/~pmeyer/ire95pj.htm*, 3 November 1999.

Steele, R.M. 1995, 'The ethics of civic journalism: independence as the guide', *http://www.poynter.org/research/me/me_civic.htm*, 3 November 1999.

Internet resources

Details of the Brisbane-based Public Journalism Project's activities and findings are available at http://www.maj.arts.qut.edu.au/Journalism/pj/index.html.

The Washington-based Pew Research Center describes itself as an incubator for civic journalism experiments that enable news organisations to create and refine better ways of reporting the news to re-engage people in public life. Its website is at *http://www.pewcenter.org/index.php3*.

The Reporter's Notebook: Civic Journalism provides citations and links to sites dedicated to civic, public, or citizen-based journalism. It is at *http://www.ntu.edu.sg/home/tblmassey/civicj/cj.htm*.

Part 6

Moral minefields, legal landmarks

Journalism sometimes seems like an eternal journey through a minefield of moral, legal, and ethical choices and challenges. This section considers journalism's moral and legal rights and responsibilities, and examines the balance between the interests of the public and the *public interest*. It looks at the ethical and legal tightrope that stretches between an individual's right to privacy and the media's right to publish, exploring notions of privacy, journalistic justifications for intrusion, and the impact of corporate influences on media ethics. It examines the journalist's precarious, liberating, comfortable, and negotiable relationship with the law, and the balance between the media's rights and its responsibilities. The legal and moral issues surrounding journalism can no longer be viewed from a purely parochial perspective. The global village is a reality, with new communications technologies carrying journalism across borders within seconds. Media ownership is shrinking, and a handful of trans-national media giants dominate the world stage. New problems are emerging as local laws struggle to respond adequately to the technological and commercial might of global media organisations.

12

Public interest, private lives

IAN RICHARDS

On 17 August 1998, the *Age* newspaper in Melbourne carried a dramatic front-page colour photograph to illustrate its report of a brutal incident in which two policemen had been murdered the previous weekend. Taken from the air, the photograph of the crime scene clearly showed the body of one of the policemen lying prone beside a pool of blood. In an interview published several days later, the *Age* editor Michael Gawenda stated he would not describe the photograph as 'particularly graphic'.

> What happened was confronting and shocking. I think this reinforced in people's minds the horror of what happened. If I had the choice again, I'd publish that photograph. (*Weekend Australian* 1998, p. 29)

Certainly, it is possible to view the publication of such a photograph as striking a blow for uncompromising journalism, a means of 'telling it how it is' and bringing home to the paper's readers the full impact of the horrific event. But it can also be interpreted as an act of crass insensitivity towards the family, friends, and former colleagues of the dead policeman. It can be portrayed as a cheap attempt to grab attention and provoke debate, possibly in the hope of stimulating sales at a time when the paper's circulation was under sustained attack. And, in a wider context, it could be seen as an increasingly common form of media behaviour that is, at best, confronting to many readers and, at worst, disturbing to others, especially children.

The dilemma

Undoubtedly, incidents such as the slaying of the two policemen are the material of real news. They contain many of the key elements of genuine human drama, they combine major news values, and they are of significance to major sections of the public. Yet at the same time they invariably provoke controversy. Sometimes this controversy attaches to the words that are used to describe what actually happened to the victim of a brutal incident, sometimes to the way the news was gathered in the first place, and often to the images used to accompany such reports.

Complaints about media insensitivity to survivors and witnesses are not new, and some of these criticisms arise from behaviour that is simply the product of poor training. There is a considerable literature on dealing with bereaved individuals, which provides many insights into appropriate ways for journalists to interact with them. While some complaints might be alleviated by better education and training of journalists (Richards 1996), many of the major controversies arising from media treatment of such incidents are the product of a fundamental dilemma in the vexed field of journalism ethics. This is the uncertain boundary between the public's right to information and the individual's right to privacy. At what point does legitimate public interest become crass public prurience? What, indeed, do 'public' and 'private' mean? Both are notoriously ambiguous concepts, a situation that, no doubt, helps explain why many people who object to governments gathering information on private citizens see nothing wrong with reading or viewing material that has been gathered by hidden cameras or by photographers who have invaded someone else's privacy.

Hanson (1970) argues that, historically, the emergence of city–states and theories of sovereignty led to the idea of a distinctly public realm, and that the emergence of a notion of democracy involving a citizenry and a public arena led to the associated notion of 'the private'. While there is still an ongoing debate over what these notions mean, the literature contains many echoes of Parent's view that privacy is 'the condition of not having undocumented personal knowledge about one possessed by others' (Parent 1992, p. 92) although, as Kieran (1997, p. 75) points out: 'it is not merely particular information about our lives that is private but those areas of our lives that the information concerns'. In other words, 'the notion of the private delineates a sphere within which we are free to be intimate with others and pursue goals and interests we have without being subject to the public gaze' (Kieran 1997, p. 76).

While the concept of rights has a long and respectable history going back via Mill, Milton, Paine, and Jefferson to Locke, who argued (1689) that individuals have rights to 'life, health, liberty and possessions', today it is frequently used to mean something that an individual regards as his or her entitlement regardless of how significant or trivial it might sometimes be. However, as Wasserstrom, among others, points out, 'the things to which one is entitled as a matter of right are not usually trivial or insignificant' (Wasserstrom 1971, p. 99). Broadly, a right means a guarantee of protection from certain actions of others, or an entitlement to a positive concept such as 'liberty' or a tangible phenomenon such as a secret vote. As far as journalism is concerned, it would seem self-evident that citizens do not have a 'right' to all information — facts, rumours, gossip, salacious material, and so on — that journalists might acquire in the course of their daily routines. The fundamental issue is to which information citizens have a right of access. In ethical terms, the arguments in favour of publication need to be weighed against the arguments against publication.

Notions of privacy

Central to this debate is the right to privacy, which has been interpreted in many ways — the right to be left alone, the right to control unwanted publicity about one's affairs, the right to withhold any and all information that one does not want made public. As a legal concept, the contemporary notion of privacy appears to date from an article in the *Harvard Law Review* in 1890 in which the authors proposed legal recognition for 'the sacred precincts of private and domestic life' (Warren and Brandeis 1890) as a counter to mounting newspaper violations of what they regarded as common standards of decency. Today, privacy law generally has four distinct interpretations — intrusion, meaning an unwarranted violation of one's physical solitude; publication of embarrassing private facts; publication of information that places someone in false light; and appropriation, meaning use of an individual's name, picture or likeness without that person's permission, usually for commercial exploitation (Day 1997, p. 118).

In ethical terms there is a strong argument, derived from deontological (duty-based) theory, that autonomy is necessary for moral agency. After all, it is difficult to see how an individual can behave ethically unless that individual has the freedom to choose to behave so. And, once the necessity of autonomy is acknowledged, the door to privacy opens. 'Autonomy implies control over one's person, and therefore, one's privacy' (Winch 1996, p. 205). The underlying point is that the ability to maintain confidentiality with regard to one's personal affairs is the hallmark of an autonomous individual, and breaching this principle means an undermining of any sense of autonomy. As Cram states:

> ... the idea of privacy or a protected sphere of private life within which the individual is free from interference from others and can determine who has access (and in which circumstances) to personal information — seems a useful means of promoting autonomy and thereby the conditions needed for human flourishing. The converse position, in which the individual has little or no control over the disclosure of personal information may diminish the prospects for entering into meaningful relationships with others and playing a fuller part in community life. (1998, p. 98)

Lack of control by individuals over the disclosure of personal information by journalists is, of course, the reason why this issue arouses so much heat in the field of journalism ethics. Journalists are propelled in the direction of revelation rather than concealment, of disclosure rather than protection. Consequently, intrusion into privacy forms the basis of some of the most common ethical dilemmas facing journalists. And portrayal of the dead, as in the *Age* photograph described earlier, raises some particularly difficult questions. Is an individual entitled to less, the same, or more privacy after death? To what extent should journalists be guided by compassion for relatives, friends, and colleagues of the deceased? What weight should be given to basic audience perceptions of 'good' and 'bad' taste? And what does that well-worn phrase 'dying with dignity' mean in this context?

From the perspective of the working journalist, the starting point to answering these questions is usually that the inclusion of such material in news and current affairs should be able to be justified according to the same criteria as any other material. This means that, at the very least, it should be newsworthy and it should be essential to the story in the sense that it provides significant information or understanding that would otherwise be absent. In practice, however, except where the law forbids it, it is very difficult for individual journalists to know where to draw the line. In the United Kingdom, the former Thatcher Government set up an inquiry into the treatment of privacy by sectors of the media, and the subsequent report identified at least three ways in which individual privacy can be invaded — entering private property without consent; placing surveillance devices; and taking unauthorised photos or voice recordings with a view to publication (Report of the Committee on Privacy and Related Matters 1990). Yet the UK journalists' code of practice states only that 'Everyone is entitled to respect for his or her private and family life, home, health and correspondence. A publication will be expected to justify intrusions into any individual's private life without consent'. In Australia, the Media, Entertainment and Arts Alliance ethics review committee (MEAA 1997) noted that privacy can involve the person (bodily privacy), conversations (eavesdropping), seclusion (surveillance), and personal information (unauthorised disclosure). Clause 11 of the Alliance's revised Code of Ethics advises journalists to 'Respect private grief and personal privacy', and the third clause of the Australian Press Council's (APC) statement of principles states that news and comment should be presented 'honestly and fairly, and with respect for the privacy and sensibilities of individuals', with the caveat that 'the right to privacy should not prevent publication of matters of public record or obvious and significant public interest'.

While such provisions provide some guidance, they are of limited benefit to someone trying to decide whether or not to publish graphic photographs such as the one that appeared in the *Age* in August 1998. Nor, for that matter, are they of much use to a journalist who is, say, trying to decide whether to publish details about someone's terminal illness, the names of victims of a major crime, or the details of a suicide.

The journalistic response

Journalists themselves have put forward a number of justifications for favouring intrusion over respect for privacy. These can be summarised as follows:

- by entering public life, individuals surrender any claim to personal privacy: accordingly, they are 'fair game' for enquiring journalists;
- journalists have a duty to report private situations when these details could have relevance to the public performance of an individual or group;
- individual journalists are simply conduits for information, and it is up to the readers/listeners/viewers to decide the limits;
- if it is not illegal, it must be permissible.

Most of these journalistic defences derive from the notion of the greater good. In other words, the unspoken assumption behind them is that it is valid for journalists to invade someone's privacy because this serves the interest of the greater good by passing important information on to the citizenry. Variations of this argument have been put forward for a wide range of journalistic activity, from reporting the sexual peccadilloes of celebrities to intrusion into grief and the portrayal of the dead. But this defence raises a number of difficulties. For one thing, the concept of 'public figure' is exceedingly vague and ill-defined. For another, to argue that journalists simply 'report the facts' ignores the role of the individual as moral agent.

The journalistic defence of the greater good rests on a common underlying view of the role of the media in democracy. This is hinted at in the introduction to the MEAA's revised Code of Ethics when it states that 'Respect for the truth and the public's right to information are fundamental principles of journalism'. It receives a slightly longer exposition in the APC's statement of principles that observes:

> . . . the freedom of the press to publish is the freedom of the people to be informed. This is the justification for upholding press freedom as an essential feature of a democratic society. This freedom, won in centuries of struggle against political and commercial interests, includes the right of a newspaper to publish what it reasonably considers to be news, without fear or favour, and the right to comment fairly on it. (APC 1998, p. 4)

While many have disputed this interpretation (see, for example, Keane 1991; Ward 1995; Curran and Gurevitch 1996) even the many journalists who base their ethical approach on it would have difficulty applying such provisions because they are so vaguely worded. It seems clear that 'additional determinants are needed to distinguish gossip and voyeurism from information necessary to the democratic decision-making process' (Christians et al. 1998, p. 116).

One provision often espoused in journalism ethics is the desire to minimise harm. Even if one were able to define precisely what constitutes 'harm' (and this is seldom possible), a complex dilemma remains — is one ever justified in allowing harm to some in order to prevent greater harm to others? And, if so, under what circumstances? In journalistic terms, how should the harm of concealment of information (from the wider society), for example, be weighed against the harm of publication (to relatives and friends of victims)? In short, while this principle is central to journalism ethics, it is not sufficient in itself to be a single guiding principle.

Day (1997, p.132) puts forward three additional principles that could form a basis for ethical guidance. These are respect for individuals as autonomous beings entitled to dignity, which should not be compromised for the sake of slogans such as the 'public's right to know'; social utility, which implies that the journalist as moral agent must decide what information is essential to enable the audience to understand what is being communicated; and the notion of justice, which must be applied to all parties to the situation.

Individual autonomy

The notion of individual autonomy is, in fact, fundamental. It is regularly invoked to defend a wide range of rights, from the right to vote to the right to freedom of religion. Brison (1998) identifies six different accounts of autonomy in the literature on free speech:
- freedom from government interference;
- the individual as autonomous moral agent;
- a good consisting of the actual ability to be rationally self-legislating;
- the right to moral independence;
- freedom of both thought and action in the relevant domain;
- the range of goals one is aware of having as real options.

Of these, the first two are particularly relevant to journalism — the so-called 'watchdog' role of the press and its part in keeping citizens free from government interference, which can be traced directly to Mill; and the notion that information conveyed via the media is essential if individuals are to be equipped to operate as autonomous moral agents. The idea of a rational, moral, autonomous self, drawing together the main elements of classical liberal press theory, has been central to the concept of the role of the press since the eighteenth century. Freedom of expression came to be seen as a natural right essential to the preservation of individual autonomy, and freedom of the press as 'a personal and universal prerogative to publish one's views freely' (Christians et al. 1993, p. 28). Inherent in this theory is a negative concept that equates liberty with freedom from external and arbitrary restraint. This remains the case today in discussions about journalism, where individuals are often considered to have a (negative) right not to have their privacy invaded by having personal information or images published, rather than a (positive) right to be able to demand that material about themselves must be published.

Individual autonomy underlies many of the ethical questions raised over intrusion into privacy. How far should journalists go in providing individuals with a forum for free speech in controversial areas such as those involving racism and sexism? How can the individual autonomy of journalists be balanced against the individual autonomy of media proprietors? To what extent should the demands of individual subjects of news stories be given precedence over wider notions of justice or fairness for the wider community? While some attention has been directed at trying to answer such questions, a more fundamental concern is now being raised with increasing frequency. Has Western society gone too far in the direction of personal autonomy, and are notions of community and the common good suffering in the process? As Wolpe (1997), Manne (1998), and others argue, there has been a slow but steady drift 'from classical Millsian liberalism (non-interference in the freedom of the individual unless that freedom causes harm) to the libertarian principle of no interference no matter what harm flows' (Manne 1998, p. 15). While this might be something of an over-statement of the situation, the fact remains that, as Callahan argues, autonomy 'should be a moral good, not a moral obsession. It is *a* value, not *the* value' (1984, p. 42).

Corporate influences

This trend has implications for journalism ethics. One of the most significant is that the focus on ethical decision-making by individual journalists has diverted attention from the issue of institutional accountability. Yet there are dramatic differences of ethical consequence between an individual's behaviour and that of a corporation. While journalists are ultimately responsible as individuals, it is as individuals in a setting where their roles are at least in part defined by their place in the corporate organisation. As discussed elsewhere in this book, most journalists work for large media corporations operating in highly competitive commercial environments. One consequence is that they are not so much competing in a news market, as is often claimed, but in a market for public attention. In other words, 'a person who watches the evening news for the entertaining situations, the drama, and the pictures counts just as much on a Nielson People Meter as someone watching to become informed' (McManus 1997, p. 197). Faced with this reality, media outlets have increasingly changed their approach to news and current affairs, despite the inherent conflict between serving the public and serving the market.

There is considerable evidence that what the media defines as news has changed substantially (Bogart 1991, Stepp 1991). An American study (MNS 1998), for example, examined 6020 stories in sixteen news outlets over twenty years, and detected a demonstrable shift towards lifestyle, celebrity, entertainment, and crime/scandal in the news and away from government and foreign affairs, with an even more pervasive shift towards 'people-oriented approaches to the news, away from traditional straight news accounts'. This trend is evident in Australia, and is reflected in such statements as the 1998 observation by a senior media executive that:

> In terms of content, there is no doubt that the consumer is more promiscuous than ever before, and that the only way to ensure that your relationship with him or her is more than a one-night stand is to make the experience compelling. If all we do is report the news fairly and accurately, we haven't got a chance. (O'Reilly 1998)

In Australia, the situation is exacerbated by the fact that, as former editor-in-chief of the *Sydney Morning Herald* John Alexander states, the economic expectations of media owners are changing:

> Proprietors once owned newspapers for reasons other than making money. The late Sir Warwick Fairfax felt he had a duty to make the world as good and as pious as he was, while his successor as chairman of Fairfax, James Fairfax, thought his city paper should be run in the interests of the people of New South Wales. Lord Beaverbrook, the Canadian behind *The Daily Express* empire, and one of the most influential publishers of this century, once said he owned newspapers to have fun ... Newspapers, like all forms of media, have always been businesses, which in spite of an increasingly economic literate world I think many of today's journalists seem to have trouble coming to terms with. Media, and especially the quality media, is a high-cost business, and there is a clear link between quality and commercial success. But newspaper companies will increasingly have to make tougher decisions than they have in the past about the allocation of capital. (Alexander 1998)

As far as privacy is concerned, the combined effect of these various forces has been an increasing tendency to reveal details of the private lives of individuals, and publish more graphic images such as the *Age* photograph described at the beginning of this chapter and the multitude of evening television news bulletins that regularly carry footage of crime scenes, dead bodies, and bloody pavements. In the process, the journalists and photographers who have been required to gather this material have come under increasing pressure to compromise ethical standards.

Conclusion

The growth in corporate dominance of the media has undermined traditional arguments in favour of press freedom as it is harder to mount these arguments to defend an institution that is simply meeting consumer demand for lively descriptions of, say, the private lives of celebrities or graphic details of a bizarre crime. As Lichtenberg asserts, arguments for press freedom seem increasingly to amount to an assertion of the property rights of those who control the media. By arguing strenuously against regulation, the press:

> ... appears to be claiming special rights not possessed by the rest of us, and these require special justification. If press institutions or their agents have special rights, it is because the people as a whole have granted them; if the people have granted them, it is because doing so is to the benefit of us all. (Lichtenberg 1987, p. 332)

It is difficult to see how many of the media's intrusions into individual privacy are to the benefit of us all. Nor is the fact that much of the public debate about the propriety of media intrusion is actually conducted via the media. In other words, the parameters of the debate are largely being determined by those who have a strong vested interest in the outcome.

This is not to say that there are not forces working against the trend towards intrusion. For one thing, many journalists are themselves resisting pressures for ethical compromise, including intruding into privacy. Studies such as Cooper's (1989) examination of more than 100 journalist codes of ethics and codes of practice support Elliott's argument that at least three principles have remained consistently non-negotiable — that news reports should be accurate, balanced, relevant, and complete; that reporting should be of information that an audience needs to know; and that reporting should avoid harm (Elliott 1988). The last has particular relevance to arguments about privacy.

But while journalistic adherence to these principles is encouraging, it would be unrealistic to expect individual journalists to be able to carry the prime respon- sibility for withstanding the forces discussed earlier. Paradoxically, the greatest hope for doing this seems to lie with the same commercial pressures that have done so much to erode media respect for privacy in the first place. As US media commentator Steve Brill, among others, observes: 'the most valuable newspapers in the world are, by and large, the newspapers that have the best reputation for quality' and, further, that 'there's no inconsistency between good business and good journalism' (Brill 1998). This correlation is supported by such develop- ments as the rise of public journalism. Despite the many difficulties associated with public journalism — it has been described as everything from a 'gimmick' (Gartner 1998, p. 229) to 'a cover of respectability' to enable newspapers to pursue greater financial returns (Jackson 1997, p. 105) — the fact remains that its many supporters are making a genuine attempt to deal with some of the defi- ciencies in the way journalism operates, including ethical deficiencies. Significantly, much of the support for public journalism is at senior management level. As a result, when public journalism's supporters argue that good journalism must be ethical journalism and that, for example, intrusion into privacy should be carefully monitored, their arguments have a good chance of being heard and acted on (see Chapter 11 for a more detailed discussion of public journalism).

In short, the debate over media intrusion into individual privacy is far from over. While the constant publication of information gained by journalists who have intruded into someone's privacy sometimes seems never-ending, there are at least grounds for hope that the tide will eventually be turned. Or, if not turned, at least prevented from washing all before it.

Case study

In August 1988, former South Australian police drug squad head Barry Moyse was sentenced to twenty-seven years' jail after pleading guilty to charges involving the sale and supply of heroin and cannabis resin. His sentence was reduced on appeal, with a non-parole period of sixteen years.

In January 1999, South Australians learnt via the media that Moyse was serving out the final part of his sentence on home detention in the Eyre Peninsula fishing and tourist centre of Port Lincoln. Under the heading 'He's out: Ex-drug squad boss tastes freedom', the *Advertiser* (19 January 1999) reported on page one that Moyse was living with his girlfriend in a house in Port Lincoln.

The *Advertiser* report began with a description of Moyse umpiring junior cricket — 'Out in the middle of the country cricket ground, he looked like any other umpire. But the face was unmistakably that of disgraced former drug squad chief Barry Moyse' — before moving on to describe, among other things, Moyse's situation and his response to attempts to interview him.

When the *Advertiser* asked Moyse for an interview during the lunch break in the cricket match, he replied curtly: 'You've got two chances — Buckley's and f... all'.

But after lunch he was a little more friendly.

'What brings you over here?' he asked. 'There are thousands of other people far more interesting than me.'

Asked how he enjoyed life out of jail, he said: 'I get up in the morning and go to bed at night. It's a nice place to live. Nice weather.'

Publication of the article was followed by a media rush to interview Moyse, during which some reporters 'staked out' the house where he was living, and a number of reports similar in tone to the *Advertiser* report followed.

Public interest or public prurience?

As a result of this media coverage:
- The South Australian public was informed about the way in which their system of justice deals with convicted former policemen.
- Newspapers and news bulletins were able to include a story that aroused the interest and curiosity of many readers/viewers.
- Moyse's attempt to adopt a low profile was destroyed and his past revealed to local people in Port Lincoln.
- Those close to him were subjected to media scrutiny and intrusion.

DISCUSSION QUESTIONS

1 Was the media justified in reporting Moyse's situation?
2 Does the media have a duty to 'tell it how it is'?
3 Should media reports be modified to minimise any possible harm to those who are the subjects of those reports?
4 Is media attention really just part of the price that people should expect to pay if they befriend people who have been convicted?
5 To what extent should journalists respect attempts by those who have been convicted to start a new life for themselves?
6 What do 'public' and 'private' mean in a context such as the one described here?
7 At what point does legitimate public interest become crass public prurience?

Further reading

Archard, D. 1998, 'Privacy, the public interest and a prurient public', in M. Kieran (ed.), *Media Ethics*, Routledge, London, pp. 82–96.

Belsey, A. and Chadwick, R. (eds) 1992, *Ethical Issues in Journalism and the Media*, Routledge, London.

Bok, S. 1980, *Lying: Moral Choice in Public and Private Life*, Quartet, London.

——1982, *Secrets: On the Ethics of Concealment and Revelation*, OUP, Oxford.

Day, L. 1997, *Ethics in Media Communications: cases and controversies* (2nd edn), Wadsworth, Belmont.

Gordon, D. and Kittross M. 1999a, 'Data privacy', in D. Gordon, M. Kittross, and J. Merrill (eds), *Controversies in Media Ethics*, Longman, New York, pp. 164–81.

——1999b, 'Private lives, public interests', in D. Gordon, M. Kittross, and J. Merrill, *Controversies in Media Ethics*, Longman, New York, pp. 148–63.

Parent, W. 1992, 'Privacy, morality and the law', in E. Cohen (ed.), *Philosophical Issues in Journalism*, Oxford University Press, New York.

13

A question of legality

MARK PEARSON

The journalist's relationship with the law is occasionally precarious, sometimes liberating, usually comfortable, and almost always negotiable. It ranges across this terrain because it involves the balance of rights and responsibilities in a complex, ever-changing social climate. It is precarious where journalism challenges the boundaries of the law, particularly when a new law is being tested or law-enforcement agencies are under political pressure to rein in the behaviour of the media. It can be liberating when journalists can work under the protection of a legal Trojan horse to bring to light some great wrongdoing or social injustice. It is comfortable when the day-to-day routines of journalists are carried out with confidence because they are working within the bounds of known, predictable laws. And it is negotiable because the law, far from being a clinical science, is subject to the whims and machinations of powerful individuals and the affordability of wise counsel.

Journalism law

What, exactly, is 'journalism law'? Like many other aspects of journalism as an academic field covered in this book, the study of the legalities of journalism had already been colonised by scholars in another field, in this case the law. Only in the past decade or so has the field attracted serious attention in its own right, first by legal scholars such as Professor Sally Walker (1989) and Professor Mark Armstrong (1995), and more recently from the journalist's perspective by Pearson (1997). Walker (1997, p. 91) recalls that, when her book was written in the late 1980s, her legal colleagues were sceptical about whether there was even a distinct field of 'media law'. In some ways they were correct, because technically there are very few laws that apply exclusively to journalists. Usually they apply to all citizens — it is just that journalists' work practices bring them into contact with such laws on a daily basis. However, as Walker (1989) demonstrated in her book, *The Law of Journalism in Australia*, there was indeed a body of law that could be deemed 'journalism law' in that it constituted all the legal implications that arose from the act of news reporting and publishing. Such laws included those related to defamation, court reporting, contempt of court and parliament, obscenity, media regulation, freedom of information legislation, intellectual property, trespass, and breach of confidence, among others.

The positioning of the law within the theory of journalism is more a question of approach than a question of content. As mentioned above, legal scholars had developed, over centuries, treatises on each of the areas of law that might impact on journalists' work, for the purpose of guiding lawyers and judges in their deliberations. While such a legalistic approach might be useful, indeed necessary, for such a purpose, it can be far removed from the needs of working journalists as they report and publish. While some legal principles may be pertinent, the facts of many hallmark historical cases are far removed from the practices of modern journalists and the likelihood of them ever applying to present-day journalism is slim. Further, the legalistic approach is preoccupied with advice on what behaviours a journalist may *not* carry out, rather than presenting legal avenues for safe and sound reporting. Finally, the approach normally ignores the reality of the modern legal environment, with its emphasis on negotiated out-of-court settlements, and by so doing deprives the journalist of useful examples from this vibrant, fruitful, and highly relevant domain.

An alternative, preferable, approach is to view journalism law from the perspective of the reporter and publisher rather than that of the lawyer. This opens the way for journalists to examine 'journalistic cases', as well as legal cases — situations that possibly escaped the courtroom and thus the attention of legal scholars, but nevertheless hold some important lesson for journalists in how they might adjust their reportage to navigate a legal minefield. It is an approach that encapsulates the ethos of educationalist Donald Schon (1991), who coined the expression 'reflection-in-action' to describe the ability of the professional to reflect on some problem in the midst of action in the workplace. Students and journalists need such an ability to reflect on their knowledge of journalism law while reporting if their education in media law is to be useful, and the use of real-life journalistic case studies helps develop that ability.

Rights, responsibilities and the public interest

A common technique used by judges and educators to view the legal position of the journalist is to frame it in terms of the range of rights and responsibilities of journalists. Put simply, journalists have no rights beyond those of ordinary citizens, although they are given some special privileges in order to facilitate their role in bringing information to the wider citizenry. For example, journalists are given special privileges in the courtroom, such as the provision of special seating, note-taking and access to court documents that would not be afforded to ordinary citizens. Also, they are sometimes allowed the privilege of withholding the name of a source during preliminary proceedings in a defamation trial under a judicial discretion known as the 'newspaper rule'. However, such special privileges granted to journalists are rare. Theirs are normally the rights of the ordinary citizen, issued only on the proviso that they are not abused. Examples include the right to publish without fear of retribution, to photograph from public places, and to attend court proceedings. Yet each of these so-called 'rights' has been afforded by the courts and legislators with the proviso that they do not overly infringe on other citizens' rights. Therefore, the right to publish without fear of retribution is limited by the laws of defamation in recognition that other citizens have the right to their good reputations being untarnished by false accusations. The right to photograph from public places is weighed up against citizens' rights to privacy. And the right to attend court proceedings is balanced against the right of an accused to a fair trial. Thus, the legal position of the journalist is the result of the legal system's navigation of these competing rights and responsibilities. Put simply, journalists are afforded such rights if they perform their roles responsibly. When they begin to perform them irresponsibly, the balance of the law normally shifts in favour of the other citizens whose rights are being infringed.

A term often used in such balancing is the expression the 'public interest'. Judges and legislators will allow journalists certain privileges if it seems it is in the public interest to do so; if it is performing greater public good by being allowed to continue. This tension is also discussed in Chapter 12. Early on, the courts had to distinguish between what might be considered in the public interest from this perspective and what an over-enthusiastic editor might consider in the public interest. In the case of *Chappell v. TCN Channel Nine Pty Ltd* [1988] 14 NSWLR 153, the NSW Supreme Court held that the private behaviour of the Australian cricket captain was not a matter of public interest on which a defamation defence could be based. What might be interesting to the public and good for circulation and ratings was not necessarily in the public interest. It needed to be a matter of serious concern to audiences as citizens, not just as curious consumers (Pearson 1997, p. 125). The public interest test does not just apply in defamation law. It appears in various forms in several laws, including those of contempt, confidentiality, trespass, and copyright. The common factor is a requirement that the courts consider whether the infringement of other citizens' rights by journalists is justifiable because a greater public interest is served by them carrying on their reporting or publishing. This balancing process reflects the journalist's general relationship with the law, which, as noted at the outset of this chapter, is 'occasionally precarious, sometimes liberating, usually comfortable, and almost always negotiable'. It is now opportune to take up examples of each of these guises of the relationship — the precarious, the liberating, the comfortable and the negotiable.

Sub judice

The journalist's legal position after the arrest of a suspected criminal can be a precarious one. Publication interfering with an individual's right to a fair trial is known as 'sub judice' contempt, from the Latin meaning 'under a judge'. It is just one version of the ancient law of contempt of court, which renders illegal any behaviour impairing or threatening the administration of justice. Other kinds of contempt affecting journalists include contempt in the face of the court (controlling behaviour in the court room), scandalising the court (allegations undermining public confidence in the judicial system), and disobedience contempt (refusal to answer a question in court). Journalists in Australia have been jailed for both sub judice contempt (when they have caused trials to be aborted) and disobedience contempt (when they have refused to reveal their sources in court).

Sub judice contempt is particularly precarious for journalists because the law imposes heavy restrictions on publications the instant an individual has been arrested in relation to a crime. The law of sub judice contempt is designed to prevent the practice of 'trial by media', where excessive media commentary on a case stands to prejudice the deliberations of prospective jurors and the recollections of witnesses (Pearson 1997, pp. 25–6). The law of sub judice represents an attempt by the courts to balance at least two competing interests: an individual's right to a fair trial and the public interest served by the opening of the justice system to media coverage so that citizens can witness the process of justice taking its course. That balance is a delicate one, and is dependent on journalists undertaking their role professionally, with a clear understanding of their legal position. Unfortunately, that position is not always as clear as one might hope.

Journalists should consider an individual's passage through the criminal justice system as a series of time zones that guide them in the extent to which they can report on the matter. These time zones are fairly clear-cut in their determination of a journalist's reportage. However, they vary markedly as to the nature of the material the courts will allow media outlets to publish. In the period before a suspect has been arrested for a crime, contempt law presents no legal restrictions on what the media may report, although other laws such as defamation might. Once an individual has been arrested for a crime, a series of quite precise sub judice restrictions apply. Until the individual has appeared in court, the media are restricted to reporting only the 'bare facts' of the crime, described in Packer's case (1912, p. 588) as being 'extrinsic ascertained facts to which any eyewitness could bear testimony, such as the finding of a body and its condition, the place in which it is found, the persons by whom it was found, the arrest of a person accused, and so on'. This effectively prevents journalists reporting on any facts that might be contested in court, particularly those that go to the guilt or innocence of the accused, and the identification of the accused if this might be at issue in the trial. Once the accused has appeared in court, journalists may publish a fair and substantially accurate report of the court proceedings, along with an account of the bare facts of the crime as mentioned earlier. Such restrictions apply until the case concludes, with all sub judice restrictions lifted after an individual has been acquitted of the charge, or the appeal period has expired (Pearson 1997, p. 47).

The problematic time zone is at the point where maximum media attention is likely to be focused in the most sensational crimes: the point at which the suspect is about to be arrested over a serious crime. The media attention relating to a major crime can be intense, particularly if the arrest follows a criminal incident such as a siege or mass shooting, or an extended hunt for a murderer or rapist in an atmosphere where members of the public fear for their safety. Such an atmosphere existed in Port Arthur, Tasmania, in 1996, when thirty-five people were killed in a shooting rampage. Media coverage should have been toned down to the 'bare facts of the crime' the instant a suspect was arrested, badly burnt, after he fled a fire he had lit at the scene. Instead, there was considerable coverage in local and national media outlets featuring photographs of the suspect, Martin Bryant, and extended details about his background, which might have prejudiced an upcoming trial. Media coverage was only 'toned down' after Bryant was formally charged with murder at his hospital bed the following day (Williams 1996, p. 87).

Legal authorities had been at odds for some decades over whether or not sub judice restrictions applied at the point of arrest. As is so common in the law, much depends on the definition of a single word. In this situation that crucial word is 'pending'. Matters become sub judice when criminal proceedings are 'pending', it was decided in the High Court case of *James v. Robinson* (1963). There, the court held that an article published while a 'manhunt' was in progress after a double murder was not sub judice because the proceedings were not 'pending' because no warrant had been issued for an arrest. The court ruled that 'curial procedures, and not merely police activity, must have commenced' (at p. 605).

The uncertainty was resolved in a NSW case in 1990, known at the Mason case. There, the NSW Supreme Court determined once and for all that the sub judice period started at the time of arrest in a criminal matter (Mason 1990, p. 378). That case centred on Channel Nine's footage of an accused murderer walking around the scene of the killing of a woman and her young child in southern NSW *after* he had been arrested but *before* he had appeared in court for official charging. The arrest followed an intensive manhunt, and the Channel Nine coverage identified the accused man clearly, showing him pointing to the place he had hidden the murder weapon and reporting he had confessed to the murder. The television station was convicted of contempt. Its argument that the coverage was in the public interest to quell community fears about a killer on the loose was rejected by the court, which said any such public interest could be served by a less offensive report (Mason 1990, p. 384).

Journalists covering the Port Arthur shootings might have been unaware of the current law on sub judice coverage, believing the sub judice period did not operate until a suspect had been charged (Williams 1996, p. 87), or perhaps they thought some greater public interest was being served by the coverage. Tasmanian authorities threatened sub judice contempt charges against media outlets that covered the matter in a sensational style during the period the alleged killer lay in his hospital bed before he had been charged (Zanotto 1998). However, charges were never laid against those outlets.

Another instance took place in NSW with the arrest of former detective Harry Blackburn in 1989 on a series of sexual assault charges dating back more than two decades. In an ill-considered publicity stunt the police paraded Blackburn past the press corps on his way to being charged after he had been arrested and questioned (Lee 1990). The ensuing media coverage ignored any presumption of innocence and publicly identified and damned Blackburn as a serial rapist. The charges were later dropped for lack of evidence after Blackburn supplied several alibis to the alleged incidents and the whole matter was exposed as a police bungle. A royal commission into the mistaken arrest included criticism of the media coverage during the sub judice period (Lee 1990).

Thus, the journalist's position in covering such a major crime can indeed be a precarious one. The law of sub judice positions the point of restricted coverage at a moment when maximum media attention might be focused on a major crime. The highly charged atmosphere of a competitive news occasion, the hunger of news audiences for more information, and the pressure of news directors and editors for the story make it easy to appreciate the temptation of enthusiastic reporters to misjudge or overstep the mark in the race for the 'scoop'.

Freedom of information

While sub judice contempt laws might be precarious for journalists, some laws can function as a liberating force for journalism. Freedom of information (FOI) legislation is one example. It is a law designed to allow greater public access to information held by government departments. While it has been labelled 'freedom from information' by some cynics because of the number of exemptions to release allowable under the legislation, it has been used to effect on numerous occasions by investigative journalists.

Freedom of information was a legislative reform promised in Australia in the first days of the first Whitlam Government in December 1972. The *Freedom of Information Act 1982* (FOI Act) of the Commonwealth came into operation on

1 December 1982. The states and territories followed with their own FOI legislation over the ensuing decade. While the legislation and its method of administration varies across jurisdictions, the Commonwealth Act is a useful indicator of the ground covered.

The preamble to the FOI Act 1982 encapsulates its spirit in its initial section:

(1) The object of this Act is to extend as far as possible the right of the Australian community to access to information in the possession of the Government of the Commonwealth by:

  (a) making available to the public information about the operations of departments and public authorities and, in particular, ensuring that rules and practices affecting members of the public in their dealings with departments and public authorities are readily available to persons affected by those rules and practices; and

  (b) creating a general right of access to information in documentary form in the possession of Ministers, departments and public authorities, limited only by exceptions and exemptions necessary for the protection of essential public interests and the private and business affairs of persons in respect of whom information is collected and held by departments and public authorities. (Section 3 (1) (b)

Again, this important area of media law represents a balance between certain rights and interests. The legislation actually creates a general right of access to government information, but balances that against the protection of 'essential public interests and the private and business affairs of persons'. The main exemptions to FOI release are government documents dealing with national security, defence, international and interstate relations; cabinet documents; law enforcement and public safety; secrecy provisions of other Acts; personal privacy; business affairs; confidentiality; national economy; contempt of court or parliament; legal professional privilege; property interests and agency operations; and electoral rolls and related documents (Armstrong et al. 1995, pp. 186–8). While this appears to be a wide-spanning list of exemptions, most documents would only be exempt under the provisions if their disclosure would be against the public interest because of a 'substantial adverse effect' on that aspect of government operations. It is worth noting that the right applies to all citizens, not just journalists.

A down side to the execution of a request for information under FOI legislation is that it can be costly. Prices vary slightly across jurisdictions; however, an initial application normally costs $30 and processing charges for locating documents are $15 per hour (Coulthart 1999). Agencies charge a further $20 per hour for their decision-making and consultation time and 10 cents per photocopy. A fee of $6.25 per half hour applies to supervised inspection of documents in a departmental office. An appeal for an internal review of a decision will cost another $40. Fee remissions might be granted on the basis of financial hardship or public interest (Coulthart 1999).

Channel Nine's *Sunday* program reporter Ross Coulthart (1999) suggests journalists use FOI as an ancillary to investigative research rather than as 'a search tool to trawl for general information on a subject or issue'. In advice to prospective sources on the program's website, Coulthart advises bureaucratic whistleblowers to provide a description of an offending document so reporters can make a specific request for it under FOI legislation. Such an approach allows journalists to use the legislation to effect without entering into confidentiality agreements with sources. It also minimises the expense outlayed in making an application. In other words, journalists will usually use the FOI mechanism to request a document they already know exists or to legitimise the ownership of one that has 'fallen from the back of a truck' rather than as a broader search facility.

Nevertheless, the legislation is remarkably under-utilised by Australian journalists. Coulthart (1999) bemoans the fact that despite liberal FOI laws in the Australian Capital Territory, only 0.5 per cent of all FOI requests in 1994–95 in the ACT were from journalists. Patching (1998, p. 348) laments that at the height of the 'Travel Rorts' affair in Canberra in 1997, the nation's top political journalists failed to use FOI legislation to pursue the story. However, some have used it effectively. A good example was the *Redland Times* newspaper in Brisbane, which applied to the Redland Shire Council for access to geotechnical reports relating to canal wall stability at Raby Bay Canal Estate, a subdivision that had been plagued for some years by rumours of subsidence (OIC 1998). The application was initially refused by the council after an objection from the estate developer on the grounds that it would reveal information concerning its financial affairs. On appeal, the Information Commissioner ordered the documents be released to the newspaper after deciding that disclosure would, on balance, be in the public interest. The commissioner agreed with the newspaper's submission that the release of the documents was in the public interest because it could reveal future liability for compensation over subsidence, as a warning to prospective buyers in the estate and that the disclosure would be useful in dispelling rumours that had been circulating. A greater public interest was served through the release of the report than would be served by its suppression, he ruled. The case demonstrated that FOI legislation could be quite liberating for journalists and the audiences they served in that it provided a mechanism for public documents to become truly that: 'public'.

Defamation law

Most other areas of media law provide comfort to journalists through their predictability in balancing the public interests at stake. Certain parts of defamation law offer this level of comfort to journalists, allowing them to go about the daily business of reporting, confident that they are probably safe from legal action if they follow certain rules. That is not to say defamation law is simple or that it is always predictable. To the contrary, each jurisdiction has its own body of defamation law, amounting to eight different defamation laws in Australia alone, and some areas of its operation are quite complex and dynamic. One such field of complexity evolved in the 1990s with High Court decisions introducing, and then amending, an implied constitutional freedom to communicate on matters of politics and government. Cases such as Theophanous (1994) and Lange (1997) have combined to offer a much more liberal standard of commentary on political matters; however, the operation of this new defence is only being determined as new cases are brought before the court to test its boundaries. Journalists will only find comfort in such a new area of the law as its finer details are determined by ensuing court decisions.

However, some other areas of defamation law are quite predictable and, to that extent, quite comforting to journalists working to daily deadlines in certain fields of reporting. These include the defences of fair report and fair comment, each of which offers a straightforward protection against defamation action if journalists follow certain rules.

Fair report is the standard defence relied on by journalists reporting on court and parliament. It stems from an absolute protection against defamation action afforded to anyone speaking in court or parliament and to any documents tabled in those institutions, known as 'absolute privilege'. This privilege has been granted to the proceedings of court and parliament because society deems them so important that citizens should not feel intimidated by defamation laws when they are in session (Pearson 1997, p. 127). In other words, society values freedom of speech in court and parliament as more important than the reputations of individual citizens. Journalists have been granted a lesser protection for their reports of the proceedings of court and parliament, reflecting the view that it is in the public interest that the broader citizenry is fully informed about the goings-on in parliament and the justice system. However, while politicians in parliament and witnesses in court can state what they like, knowing their words are absolutely protected from defamation action, journalists need to follow some simple rules in order to win that protection. The law requires their reports of court or parliamentary proceedings be 'fair' and 'accurate'. Fairness in reporting requires that stories about court or parliament reasonably reflect the tenor of the proceedings, with the views of all sides gaining some representation in the story. For example, a newspaper's coverage of the prosecution case presented on the first day of a criminal trial should be followed by a story covering the defence case when it is presented. In fact, 'fairness' requires coverage of the complete trial and of any ensuing appeals. The accuracy requirement stipulates that the facts in the story must be substantially accurate, or at least an accurate report of what occurred in the proceedings. For example, the misspelling of an accused's name in a court report might destroy the defence of a defamation action brought by another individual whose name is spelt that way. While journalists should strive to ensure the accuracy of all facts, they will only lose the defence if the error is a 'substantial inaccuracy'. The journalist's position becomes difficult in complex cases, such as those involving intricate corporate relationships, because the simplifying of facts for media reports might render them unfair or inaccurate in the eyes of the court (Eisenberg 1998). However, the protection means journalists reporting on court or parliament on a daily basis can go about their work knowing their stories will be protected against defamation action as long as they have done their jobs properly.

Similarly, the defence of fair comment offers protection to journalists whose writing involves the publication of an opinion about a public matter. This defence applies to commentaries such as editorial columns, book reviews, sports reports, and letters to the editor. It is based on the principle that matters which occur in the public domain, or which seek to profit from the public, should be open to fair criticism. In other words, individuals who trade off their public reputation should not be able to sue for defamation if that reputation is fairly criticised. The requirements for meeting the fair comment defence are more extensive than those needed for the fair report defence. To earn the defence, the defamatory statement must be one of opinion, not fact; the comment must be based on true facts stated in the material; it must be fair; it must be the honest opinion of the commentator; and it must be on a subject of public interest (Pearson 1997, pp. 130–2). Of course, each of these criteria has its own precise definition emanating from judicial decisions, but each is straightforward enough to provide a structured framework for those working in the field. Thus, an individual writing a book review is protected from defamation action for expressing a low opinion of the author's writing style as long as the view is supported by actual examples taken from the work, he or she truly holds that opinion (and is not motivated by some other purpose), and the comment is fair in that readers could appreciate how the critic arrived at that opinion.

Occasionally, however, the comfort zone seems to evaporate, as happened when *Sydney Morning Herald* food critic Leo Schofield wrote a scathing review of a meal at the Blue Angel restaurant in Sydney (Blue Angel Restaurant 1989). But Schofield's problem was that he had not followed one of the key rules of the defence in that he could not prove the facts on which his criticism was based: he had literally eaten the evidence. The case showed the difficulties of applying the defence to restaurant reviews, but did not reflect on its operation in other areas of criticism. Therefore, while defamation is recognised as a complex field, journalists are able to perform most of their daily tasks, confident that the sound practices will keep them on the right side of the law.

Negotiation and political influence

While some legal scholars treat media law as an exact science, it is in fact a very negotiable human enterprise, subject to the vagaries of its players and the inequities of society generally. That is not to suggest that the judicial system is corrupt or that significant proportions of the judiciary or the legal fraternity have improper motives. However, so much more comes into play in the field of media law than the legislation or precedents on which the courts rely in reaching their decisions. Power, politics, and money also wield substantial influence and often become the negotiating chips in a media law matter.

Negotiability of media law happens at many levels. There is negotiation in the newsroom between journalists and their editors over the meaning of words and the legal risk that might attach to them. Negotiation takes place between journalists and complainants once material has been published. It occurs between journalists and their lawyers once legal action is threatened. And it takes place at the highest level of news and political organisations as executives and law-makers negotiate the substance of law reforms and the determination of governments to prosecute over media transgressions.

In defamation, for example, most cases are settled out of court after negotiations between the parties. Defamation actions are beyond the means of most ordinary citizens. They can cost tens of thousands of dollars to launch and the appeal process can cost tens of thousands, perhaps hundreds of thousands, of dollars more. Also, the government provides no legal aid to those suing for defamation. And the media defendant is normally a large conglomerate with the best legal advice and ample experience in this area of the law. Therefore, many potential defamation actions never even get off the ground because of the scale of the task facing the plaintiff (Pearson 1997, p. 98). The converse can also apply. Smaller media defendants can suffer at the hands of powerful organisations and corporations that can use defamation threats as a weapon to wield influence over the media outlet. As Pearson notes:

> Too often smaller media groups and individuals have agreed to make some payment in out of court settlements because they could not afford to defend a quite winnable defamation suit. Such an attitude creates a 'chilling' effect in the media, with journalists not pursuing stories to their limits for fear of being sued. Thus, the rich and powerful can use defamation as a weapon against the media without ever having to go to court. (1997, p. 99)

Edgeworth and Newcity (1992, p. 43) studied the sociology of defamation actions and found that most defamation plaintiffs were from the business and professional classes or from the media, arts, or sports. Politicians constituted the largest single group of plaintiffs (14.8 per cent), followed by company owners and managers (13.4 per cent), and other professionals (5.8 per cent). Interestingly, those who held other positions of power were also prominent litigants, with union officials constituting 4.5 per cent of plaintiffs in the study.

Political influence can also play a role in media law on two levels at least. First, politicians are responsible for proposing and enacting legislation that can impact greatly on the rights and responsibilities of journalists. The legislative process involves considerable consultation and lobbying by interest groups, including media corporations, industry groups, regulators, and journalists' unions in favour of more liberal media laws, and, countering this, pressure from other interest groups seeking more restrictions on the media or the advancement of other civil rights at the expense of press freedom. For example, the NSW Law Reform Commission (1995) received submissions from thirty-two parties in conducting its inquiry into the reform of defamation laws. These included media groups such as the Australian Press Council, the Australian Broadcasting Corporation, Channel Nine, the Media Entertainment and Arts Alliance, Australian Consolidated Press, and other interested parties including the Communications Law Centre, the NSW Council of Churches, and the Australian Securities Commission.

Second, governments can exercise their political will to bring pressure on the media by insisting their law enforcement agencies focus their attention on media transgressions. The Attorney-General in each jurisdiction, as the chief legal officer, can initiate prosecutions in some instances or direct a public prosecutor to do so. For example, the Attorney-General's consent must be sought in almost all jurisdictions for someone to prosecute the rare offence of criminal defamation (Walker 1989, p. 219). Similarly, it is the Attorney-General or the Director of Public Prosecutions who can instigate proceedings for contempt of court (Walker 1989, p. 37), such as those threatened against the Tasmanian media for sub judice contempt in the wake of the Port Arthur mass murder mentioned earlier. While such powers might be exercised responsibly on most occasions, it is easy to see the potential for their partisan use, particularly when there is political mileage to be gained from 'cracking down' on the media or some perceived advantage in targeting a particular media outlet. Conversely, there is the potential for media organisations to avoid legislative reform or even prosecutions by bringing their own corporate pressure to bear on the politicians who might be driving such initiatives. This has become a particular concern in the wake of the enormous concentration of Australian media interests that has occurred over the past two decades, leaving the chief executives of corporations such as News Limited (Murdoch) and Publishing and Broadcasting Limited (Packer) in particularly powerful positions of influence. Thus, the very formulation of media law and, to some extent, its enforcement become points of negotiation between key players while the judiciary attempts to handle equitably and clinically the individual cases that come before it. (Further implications of this are discussed in the next chapter.)

Conclusion

So, where has this foray into media law led? And what is its link with a broader discussion of journalism theory? The chapter has covered considerable terrain in what is often seen as a complex field. It has used a range of strategies to portray the journalist's curious relationship with the law in an attempt to distinguish the reality of that relationship from the theory of it portrayed by legal scholars. As discussed, some areas of the law such as sub judice contempt can leave journalists in a precarious, uncertain legal position. Others such as freedom of information legislation can be liberating for journalists, providing them with tools to help them find the truth about public affairs. Most areas of media law, such as key defamation defences, leave journalists in a comfortable position, able to go about their daily reporting routines confident that their work falls within acceptable legal bounds. And negotiation is an important, yet under-rated, component of media law at a range of levels.

In discussing these issues, some key principles of media law have arisen that surface regularly in both media and legal rhetoric. One is the issue of the 'public interest', a notion that many an editor and publisher claims to defend, but which the judiciary often interprets in a different way. While journalists might argue that anything interesting to the public is in the 'public interest', the courts prefer to weigh up the relative social benefits of a given situation. They ask whether the public interest served by allowing the media to publish or report in a particular way is greater than the other interests that are affected by the action. Another key principle is the idea of viewing journalists' relationship with media law as a series of rights and responsibilities. While journalists might be allowed to behave in a certain way in their reporting and publishing, they also have a corresponding range of responsibilities to society in doing so. The weighting of such rights and responsibilities will vary as the courts and legislators tinker with media law in response to changes in social attitudes. It highlights the sheer negotiability of much media law, at a range of levels from newsroom discussions through to the machinations of power and politics at the highest levels.

Perhaps most important to the theoretical principles that constitute this book has been the approach to this discussion. It has been a journalist-centred perspective, viewing media law from the position of the journalist. If there is a distinctive theory of journalism law, its essence is in the adoption and articulation of that position as a journalistic one, fundamentally different from the legal approach in recognition of the different needs it serves.

Case study

The Hinch case (1987) provides a useful example of the balance between journalists' rights and responsibilities, and the notion of the 'public interest'.

Derryn Hinch was a Melbourne radio journalist running a campaign against the abuse of power by people in positions of trust, particularly abuses of a sexual nature. It came to Hinch's attention that a former Catholic priest, Father Michael Glennon, was facing charges relating to the molestation of children in his care at a youth foundation. Hinch went to air on his prime-time talkback program, naming Glennon and detailing previous charges he had faced, including some for which he had been jailed and others on which he had been acquitted. Hinch asked why someone with such a record should be allowed to continue in his role as governing director of the foundation when these further charges were pending. The thrust of the three broadcasts mentioning the matter implied Glennon was guilty of the charges he faced.

Hinch was charged with sub judice contempt, since the broadcasts were made during the most sensitive time zone in a criminal matter, the period after someone has been charged with a crime but before the matter has been tried in court. It is the period when witnesses and jurors are most likely to be influenced by media commentary.

Hinch attempted to defend the charge using a public interest defence, arguing that the public interest in protecting children in Glennon's care from suffering harm outweighed the public interest in Glennon's right to a fair trial. However, on appeal the High Court held that Hinch had gone too far in his commentary to be granted such a public interest defence. The court found Hinch had overstepped the mark by prejudging Glennon's guilt, and jailed him for twenty-eight days and fined him $10 000. Justice Deane was alone in entertaining the notion that the revelation of someone's past convictions might be excusable in the public interest in extreme circumstances. He suggested that Hinch might have sustained the public interest defence if he had just called for Glennon's removal from office while the charges were pending.

Ironically, Hinch's attempts to see justice done almost led to it becoming badly unstuck. Glennon later appealed against his conviction on the sexual charges on the grounds that Hinch's radio reportage would have adversely influenced the jurors' judgment in his trial. Only by a 4–3 majority did the High Court uphold Glennon's conviction. Hinch's actions had almost resulted in the guilty escaping conviction (R v. Glennon 1992).

The Hinch case demonstrates the conflicting rights and responsibilities facing journalists in their reportage. They have a right to report fairly and accurately on the commission of a crime and the subsequent judicial process. In fact, they have a responsibility to make the community aware of the workings of the justice system. But at the same time they have a responsibility to society to allow individuals their right to a fair trial. The public interest is served in both ways: in the judicial process being publicised and in it being allowed to operate unhindered.

DISCUSSION QUESTIONS

1 Is it a journalist's role to publish material that is 'in the public interest' or material that is 'interesting to the public'? Discuss.
2 Discuss the pressures that might lead journalists to publish material that might be sub judice.
3 What strategies can be put in place so that journalists make more use of freedom of information legislation in their reporting?
4 Explain which is more important: the public's right to know about a criminal matter or an individual's right to a fair trial?
5 List three rights of journalists and three corresponding responsibilities of journalists.

Further readings

Coulthart, R. 1999, 'Freedom of information',
    http://sunday.ninemsn.com.au/, 17 February.
Pearson, M. 1997, The Journalist's Guide to Media Law, Allen and Unwin, Sydney.
Walker, S. 1997, 'Changing journalism in a changing world: the changing legal environment', Australian Journalism Review, vol. 19, no. 1, pp. 91–7.
Williams, R. 1996, 'Port Arthur: some contempt of court issues', Australian Media Law Reporter, vol. 3, no. 6, pp. 86–9.

14

Journalism in the global village

RHONDA BREIT

The media revolution, discussed elsewhere in this book, has created an environment of uncertainty for journalists struggling to keep pace with changing technology and work practices. The effects of this revolution (not the media
revolution) are also being felt in legal circles, as domestic laws struggle to control
global issues. Two crucial social monitors — the media and the law — are forced
to re-evaluate their roles to take account of their global responsibilities.
Television, radio, satellites, direct-dial telephones, mobile phones, digital technology, and modems have radically affected 'the actions of the media and . . .
the messages they present' (Kirby 1998a, p. 1). Now the Internet is posing even
greater challenges to journalists and to the domestic legal regimes that regulate them.

The latest technological advances have taken place in an environment of commercialisation, with the formation of 'super-powerful' media giants, known as
transnational corporations or TNCs (McChesney 1997, p. 1). These TNCs and
their global audiences are regulated by local laws, the powers of which are limited
to geographical borders. The power and independence of the domestic judiciaries throughout the world are being challenged by 'the dynamic growth and
enormous power of the modern media of communications' (Kirby 1998a, p. 5).
At the same time, many local laws are being seen as irrelevant as new technologies
make their application almost ridiculous.

While freedom of speech may flourish in this environment, other rights such
as personal privacy are suffering. Freedom of speech is only one of the fundamental human rights (albeit the 'most powerful') that are balanced by the legal
system to ensure a strong and vibrant society. The combined effect of technology
and corporatisation is undermining the ability of domestic laws to act as a social
watchdog. At the same time, journalists (the other major social watchdog) face
uncertainty about the application of local laws, the legality of publication and

their roles in society. The independence of society's two most important watch-dogs, the media and the judicial system, is being undermined.

Legal and professional reforms are needed to create more certainty for journalists in the global environment. The first step is to identify the problems created by globalisation.

Globalisation and the global village

The term 'global village' was first used in the 1960s to describe the 'linking of humanity in all parts of the world' (Kirby 1998a, p. 3). Developments such as cheap print, electricity, radio, television, satellites, direct-dial phones, and mobile phones have helped to break down borders to create a global media audience. The Internet has accelerated this process.

> The media's messages are no longer confined to a particular village, town, city or even a particular country. The technology now takes them, instantaneously across jurisdictional borders. The powerful, opinionated media can thereby play an important role in the assertion of freedom and in the undermining of autocratic government. It was, to some extent, the global media which brought the concerns ... from the docks of Gdansk, Poland remorselessly through Hungary and Czechoslovakia. It swept from there to Bulgaria, Mongolia and Romania. It consumed the Baltic States. It eventually destroyed the old Yugoslavia. In the space of a couple of years, it brought the Berlin Wall crashing down. Ultimately, it destroyed one of the two global mega-powers: the Soviet Union. (Kirby 1998a, pp. 1–2)

Technology has given the media a global audience, but corporatisation has given them power, with ten 'super corporations' dominating the global media: Time Warner, Disney, Bertelsmann, Viacom, Rupert Murdoch's News Corporation, Sony, TCI, Universal (Seagram), NBC (GE), and Polygram (Herman and McChesney 1997, pp. 70–94). These corporations have total annual sales of more than $115 billion, netted from a diverse range of media-related businesses, including 'film production, book publishing, music, TV channels and networks, retail stores, amusement parks, magazines and newspapers' (McChesney 1997, pp. 1, 3–11). Herman and McChesney (1997, pp. 95–104) also identify a 'second tier' of media corporations that dominate the niche markets. Included in this group is Kerry Packer's Publishing and Broadcasting Limited (PBL).

Opinions are divided on the effects of increasing concentration of media ownership. The *Age* publisher and editor-in-chief Steve Harris argues 'diversity of ownership and diversity of source has never guaranteed diversity of opinion, and ... independent ownership has never guaranteed quality, just as group ownership does not guarantee the absence of quality' (in Grattan 1998, p. 9). McChesney (1997, p. 1) claims, however, that the concentration of global media ownership in the ten transnational corporations (TNCs) is 'disastrous' for two reasons:

- the diversity of interests held by the transnational corporations;
- the alliances and joint ventures formed within this group, creating an 'oligopoly' of mainly US media corporations, which is supported by a second tier of multi-million dollar corporations that dominate the niche markets within specific areas (McChesney and Herman 1997, pp. 95–103).

The Australian media scene is dominated by two such corporations: Rupert Murdoch's News Limited — the Australian arm of News Corp (one of the ten media TNCs) — and Kerry Packer's PBL — a second-tier corporation. These two corporations have now joined forces to acquire a 40 per cent interest in the telecommunications company One.Tel (The *Age* Business 16 February 1999, p. 1), setting them up to dominate Internet and multi-media markets, at least within Australia.

News Corporation is seen as the archetypal twenty-first-century global media firm, with holdings in 132 newspapers (predominantly in Australia, Britain, and the United States), Twentieth-Century Fox, US Fox broadcasting including Fox News, twenty-two US television stations, twenty-five magazines, book publishing interests and much more (Herman and McChesney 1997, pp. 70–1; McChesney 1997, pp. 8–9). News Corporation has alliances with other major media owners and telecommunications corporations, including equity joint ventures, equity interests, or long-term exclusive strategic alliances with these first-tier media firms: Time Warner, the world's largest media corporation; Viacom, ranked number four in the world; TCI, ranked seventh; Universal, ranked eighth; PolyGram; Sony, ranked sixth; and Bertelsmann, ranked third (Herman and McChesney 1997, p. 72). It also has strong ties with second-tier media firms including EMI, Canal Plus, Softbank, Granada, Globo Televisa, MGM, BBC, Carlton, telecommunication/informatics firm Concert (BT-MCI) (Herman and McChesney 1997, p. 72) and Kerry Packer's PBL (The *Age* Business 16 February 1999, p. 1).

Herman and McChesney's prediction of media alliances being formed to position the TNCs to dominate the Internet and other multi-media services seems well founded. In addition to the News–PBL alliance, one of the most powerful TNCs, Time Warner, joined forces with America On-line (AOL) in January 2000 to take the prime position in the global media. Technology is giving the media a global audience and strategic alliances are giving the media immense power, but this has not created a global voice. As discussed elsewhere in this book, news and information have become commodities that must be packaged and sold in a cost-effective way (*Media Report* 1996; Grattan 1998, p. 5), resulting in the 'homogeneity' of information that is pitched at a predominantly middle-class and Western audience (Gerbner in *Media Report* 1996). Globalisation has resulted in a 'standardisation' of information and audience (Gerbner in *Media Report* 1996), with large sections of the world left under-represented.

Major corporations also use exclusive deals and local laws such as copyright to obtain a competitive advantage. Journalists have no right of access to private property. To obtain a story, they must have permission from the venue manager or owner of the property to enter the premises. The owner/manager's right to deny access to venues can be used to exclude journalists from competing news services. This becomes particularly relevant in major sporting events, when event organisers and venue managers enter exclusive broadcast arrangements or operate their own websites. If journalists from a competing news service are denied access to the venue, they are limited to producing a text report of the event based on the live broadcast of their competitor. They cannot provide visual images or analytical commentary of the whole event. Their interpretation of the event is coloured by the impressions of the crew filming the event.

Thus commercial considerations are tainting the news agenda in the global media, as they have done in the national media (for example, coverage of cricket, motor-racing, tennis, and so on). But commercialisation is also undermining the fundamental tenets of local laws — such as laws of contract, copyright, and trade practices — as media managers try to get around exclusive deals. The on-line division of one major newspaper got around copyright restrictions on some audio-visual material by creating a 'hotlink' to a site that had consent to reproduce the material.

Event organisers had refused the newspaper permission to use the material, but the newspaper sidestepped the copyright by negotiating a 'deal' with an organisation with the requisite permission. Instead of using copyright to protect creative endeavour, copyright owners are using it to exclude some competitors, while their competitors are entering into deals to avoid the consequences of the copyright laws. The copyright laws aim to balance two competing interests: the rights of the creator of original works to profit from their creative endeavour and the public's interest in accessing original works at a fair price. Commercialisation and new technology are distorting this balance, making application of the copyright laws almost ridiculous.

Commercialisation also has brought management strategies that are merging the commercial and editorial sides of news services (Grattan 1998, p. 1). This convergence is particularly obvious in Australian newspapers, which are struggling to understand their role in the increasingly commercial world (Grattan 1998, p. 3). But the biggest threat to newspapers comes 'from within'.

> As newspaper managements struggle to please both shareholders and readers, it is journalism which suffers. Proprietors, increasingly conglomerates or with aspirations to be so, want maximum returns, while readers have a right to expect their

papers, particularly broadsheets, to fulfil their accepted societal role. Both these demands are entirely understandable. But are they reconcilable? At the very least they are creating a kind of identity crisis in newspapers ... For the sake of circulation, or profit, we are being urged to compromise our journalistic integrity. We might win short-term circulation gains, or a better looking bottom line, but we do our own industry's reputation long-term harm. (Guthrie in Grattan 1998, pp. 7–8)

Concentration of media ownership into the hands of a few TNCs is threatening the integrity of journalism. At the same time it threatens the legal systems that regulate the media and balance basic human rights. Some journalists might view the 'vulnerability' of local laws as a positive step for freedom of speech, but this is more aptly described as freedom of the powerful — predominantly US — media giants to spread their interpretation of world events; not freedom to report matters of public interest that affect the global village.

Most journalists acknowledge that freedom of speech is not an absolute right. Even in the United States, where the First Amendment provides a Constitutional guarantee of freedom of speech, this right must be balanced against other fundamental human rights, including the right to privacy, the right to protect reputation and honour, the right to protect information disclosed in confidence, the right to a fair trial, and the right to protect creative endeavours. The local laws of defamation, privacy, confidential information, copyright, contempt of court, and the criminal justice system set out rules that balance these fundamental human rights to ensure an ordered society. If the domestic legal regimes that balance these rights are undermined, society will become increasingly more dependent on the media as a social watchdog. But the media watchdog is dominated by TNCs, part of whose business it is to 'sell news' (*Media Report* 1996, p. 2; Grattan 1998, p. 5). Journalists operating within that regime are 'vulnerable and uncertain' (Grattan 1998, pp. 5, 7–8). How can they tackle the might of the conglomerates that are the major employers within the industry, particularly given the alliances formed between them?

The media must have power to influence legal and social change, but the legal system must also be capable of regulating the media where they abuse their power and ignore fundamental human rights, especially if the power to determine what is news is vested in the hands of a few TNCs. This can only be achieved where there is a balance of power between the media and the legal regimes that regulate them. At present, the media wield international power while the legal regimes wield only local power. As Kirby observed:

If the global media can invade the privacy of Royal Families of several countries and the personal lives of presidents, if it can effectively override local laws established for local cultural, linguistic or moral objectives, if it can set the agenda of national and international concerns for its viewers and listeners, promote its own causes and turn issues on and off at will, we have on our hands an important challenge to the rule of law. The very instrument which is potentially such a defender of human rights, and the vehicle for one of the most important and precious of those rights, the media, can become a threat to other basic rights and interests — to reputation, to privacy, to fair trial, to effective democracy. (Kirby 1998a, p. 13)

Commentators, such as techno-visionary Nicholas Negroponte, claim the dominance of the TNCs will be short-lived because the Internet, 'with its 500 million channels', will diffuse their power. Negroponte, among others, believes the Internet will give the 'global village' a global voice. This optimism is not shared by Herman and McChesney (1997, p. 134), who argue that convergence and market pressures will see the 'global media oligopoly ... gradually evolve into a far broader global communication oligopoly over the next several decades'. They predict the media giants 'will link with the handful of telecommunication "global gangs" ... and they will strike deals with the leading computer firms' (Herman and McChesney 1997, p. 134). Joint ventures such as those formed by News Limited/PBL and Time Warner–AOL indicate that the TNCs are forming alliances and acquiring interests in telecommunications and multi-media organisations, allowing them to dominate these markets.

If Herman and McChesney are correct (and the evidence suggests they are), an individual's power to publish and collect information will be limited by the types of services available and the ability to advertise the message. Given that the ten super powers all have 'numerous media industries, such as film production, book publishing, music, TV channels and networks, retail stores, amusement parks, magazines, newspapers and the like' (McChesney 1997, p. 1), the TNCs are ideally poised to dominate the multi-media world. The information available will be dominated by the 'homogenised' message of the corporations that are able to present their message in an easily accessible manner.

Effect of globalisation on journalism

Commercialisation and technology have combined to alter the media, with the packaging of news as a commodity that can be bought and sold being one of the greatest changes facing journalists.

In her book *Reviving the Fourth Estate: Democracy, Accountability and the Media*, journalist and academic Julianne Schultz interprets empirical research on the attitudes of Australian journalists. Schultz (1998, p. 150) finds that 'journalists are critical of the pressures and demands of commercialism of the news media'. Based on her study, which canvassed both news and investigative journalists, she reports that 'commercial priorities actively' intrude on the 'idealised nature of the Fourth Estate'.

Schultz's study also considers the ability of Australian journalists to understand public opinion. Her findings 'highlight the limits on the newsgatherers' ability to know, understand and represent public opinion' (Schultz 1998, p. 155).

> ... (the) process of communicating with the public was considered by many of the respondents as an onerous aspect of their work ... (and) many of the journalists surveyed demonstrated that other news media organisations and journalists had a major impact in their understanding of public opinion and their decisions about what to report and how. (Schultz 1998, p. 156)

Media operators and others in the industry are setting the news agenda, as journalists put commercial interests before the public's right to know, traditionally seen as the motivation to break stories. But, given the commercial environment and the standardisation of the media's message and target audience, journalists must consider whether a 'right to know' still accommodates the public interest. They must distinguish between the concepts of information, knowledge, and understanding.

Information is 'something told; knowledge; items of knowledge; news' (Moore 1997, p. 684). Knowledge is 'awareness/familiarity gained by experience; a person's range of information; a theoretical or practical understanding of a subject; the sum of what is known' (Moore 1997, p. 743). Understanding is 'the ability to understand or think; the power of abstract thought; individual's perception or judgement of a situation' (Moore 1997, p. 1490).

In a world dominated by US-based media owners, and considering this book's previous discussion of 'truth' in storytelling, is it enough that journalists 'communicate facts, truths or principles' obtained from their study or investigation? Given the commercial pressures on journalists and the standardisation of the message and audience, it is vital that journalists rethink their functions in society. To adequately fulfil their role, their stories must help their audiences to understand (*Media Report* 1996). Journalists should halt the standardisation of news and prevent the further marginalisation of non-Western, non–English-speaking cultures lacking the wealth or power to create independent media. They must look beyond profit at how issues actually affect the global audience, and must aim to help the various publics in their audience to comprehend each other's meaning.

To aid understanding, journalists must pursue their investigative role and not give in to the commercial pressures that, in the late 1990s, saw investigative journalism as an embarrassing 'side-effect of newspaper ownership' (Guthrie in Grattan 1998, p. 8). Preservation of public broadcasting institutions such as the ABC is also important to restoring the integrity of journalism.

By reviewing their function to take account of 'public understanding' rather than 'public knowledge', journalists will preserve the integrity of 'news'. They must confront the blurring of news and entertainment and news and public relations. Movie stars have always been big news, but now the movies themselves are being incorporated into the news. Newsreaders and journalists are becoming the 'stars' and, in turn, the news. For journalists to fulfil their role, they must do more than simply tickle the interest of the public. Their job is to foster public understanding of *all* issues, including their proprietor's interest in promoting certain films, books, software, and even journalists.

If journalists aim to build public understanding they must look beyond the daily news fodder. Press releases and promotional grabs/videos, which are increasingly setting the news agenda and determining the content of the news, may accommodate the public right to know, but much of this 'information' does not necessarily facilitate understanding. The journalist must do more.

Of course, the 'bottom-line' determines the numbers of journalists employed in any news organisation and affects the types of stories that are presented to the public. This just reinforces the need for journalists to reappraise their role in society and aim to 'aid understanding'.

Journalists also must be aware that public-relations firms have a vested interest in maintaining the perception of an independent media so that the PR message is accepted by the audience and not viewed as hype. The investigative function of journalists might be under threat from commercial pressures, but PR firms have a vested interest in promoting journalism as the independent watchdog (*Background Briefing* 1997). A simple refocusing of journalism's role in society should help raise public perception of journalists in the global environment and help them resist some of the pressures of new employment practices in the media, such as the trend to employ journalists on contracts rather than under awards. This fuels the environment of uncertainty that has developed in conjunction with commercialisation, and it also limits the ability of the MEAA (the journalists' union) to exert pressure where management practices conflict with the MEAA's Code of Ethics.

Schultz suggests that neither the journalists she surveyed 'nor the corporate news media seem to value the importance of diversity highly' and 'the journalists surveyed are reluctant to accept accountability mechanisms that may intrude on their professional judgement and the exercise of their duties' (1998, pp. 160–5). Journalists must accept a transparent system of accountability if they are to restore public confidence in their role as social watchdog.

Corporatisation and commercialisation of the media have resulted in an environment where media owners increasingly set the news agenda. The public's 'right to know and understand' is substantially ignored in favour of the commercial interests of the media owners, and accountability processes (such as self-regulatory bodies and the rule of law) are being undermined by employment practices and commercial reality.

Technology also has brought changes to the role of journalists. First, it has expanded dramatically the journalist's reach, with the Internet creating a truly global audience. But the Internet has brought changes to the physical nature of the traditional media. For example, broadcast (radio and television) has traditionally been considered a transient form of communication. This transient nature of a radio program was one factor taken into account by the court in *Morosi v. Broadcasting Station 2GB* (1980; p. 418n) in deciding the defamatory nature of a program. But many radio and television news and current affairs programs are now available on the Internet. The *Media Report* and the *Sunday Program* are examples of how 'transient' publications can be downloaded from the Internet in permanent textual form. Other news programs are webcast or can be downloaded in their original form (audio or video) on demand. Newspapers, which have always been regarded as permanent publications, are also on the Internet. But they are changing character as their on-line services look to incorporate moving images to accompany Internet stories.

Internet publication does give the audience greater power to decide what is 'news', but the pool of information from which the audience selects is being filtered by the TNCs that are beginning to dominate the Internet. The standardised message of the TNCs is limiting the power of the audience to set the agenda, even in a public forum such as the Internet.

Immediate technology also has put pressure on journalists to 'get news first'. Competition to break the story compromises 'the observance of best practice: with the checking of sources and the consideration of values that compete with the repetition of unattributed, unsubstantiated rumour, gossip and salacious innuendo' (Kirby 1998b, p. 11). It also means that corporations are looking to the law to prevent competitors accessing information or to gain a competitive edge, as described in the examples cited earlier in this chapter. The independence and integrity of the legal system are being undermined by these practices.

Legal implications of globalisation

The judiciary performs two fundamental functions: protecting society from 'misuse of legislative and executive power' and promoting 'fundamental rights and principles' (Toohey 1993, p. 174):

> Some principles are fundamental and it is the role of an independent judiciary to give effect to those principles, within the rule of law, as best it can. Thus, although the relationship in our society between the authority of the legislature and the rule of law fluctuates over the course of time, the rule of law is the dominant factor in the relationship. This explains the efficacy of the rule of law as a means both of protection against misuse of legislative and executive power and promotion of fundamental rights and principles. (Toohey 1993, p. 174)

A domestic judiciary can only perform these two functions in the 'jurisdiction' granted to it by the government it 'oversees'. Unless relying on some international treaty or covenant, the power of a domestic judiciary is strictly local and its rules that regulate publication and the media apply only within its designated jurisdiction. When publishing material globally, the media must comply with the publication laws of each jurisdiction in which they publish. For the journalist who writes the stories, this is an onerous task.

Given that the 'footprint' of the modern media is global, not local, 'the capacity of the local laws to control such media — and to insist on local public policy in matters of culture, language, and morality — is reduced accordingly' (Kirby 1998a, p. 4). Two factors are undermining domestic laws — the global reach of the media brought about because of technological and economic changes, and the power of the transnational corporations (Kirby 1998a, pp. 5–14).

The Internet has brought many challenges to local laws because it is a unique communication medium that was not envisaged when the laws that regulate it were enacted or decided. One major problem for journalists who use the Internet for publication and to gather information is uncertainty about the legality of material given the diverse range of local laws that regulate the Internet. This situation also applies to global print and broadcast services that must contemplate the legality of material in every jurisdiction where the material is read, seen, or heard.

Protected speech in the United States could be defamatory in Australia. As Kirby observes, 'local laws, which worked quite well when defamation was local, work less well now that the same defamation can spread across many borders' (1998a, p. 7). The principles of defamation, designed to protect a person's reputation from unjustified attack, the contempt of court rules that protect the administration of justice, privacy principles, and the right to protect information communicated in confidence are all suffering in the global media environment.

Defamation is problematic because each domestic jurisdiction differs in the way it protects an individual's reputation. Within Australia, the defamation laws of each State and territory are different. A national publication in Australia must take this into account. In the global context the issue is further complicated by differing levels of freedom of speech.

Privacy is another area where local laws throughout the world vary greatly, despite a considerable amount of international agreement on the need to respect privacy. Australia, for example, has no general tort of privacy, whereas the United States does. These differing levels of privacy protection fuel the uncertainty of journalists publishing globally.

Domestic laws apply established legal principles while relying on 'common decency and good manners' to respect basic human rights. If the global media ignore 'common decency' in their reporting, especially regarding individual privacy, and local laws are found deficient in providing any consistent global regulation, confidence in the legal system to effectively control the media will be undermined. Unless someone challenges the media's right to publish, they remain unchecked, creating an expectation of more of the same among their audience and sending a message that the law cannot restrain the media.

Examples of the media undermining public confidence in the justice system abound in Australia. Reports of the Port Arthur massacre (mentioned in earlier chapters), the Jaidyn Leskie murder,[1] the Thredbo disaster, and the charging of Liam Gallagher with assault of a fan are all examples where the Australian media have challenged the fundamental legal principles that protect basic human rights.

These examples illustrate the media's over-reporting of information they claim is in the public interest — reporting that exceeds what is necessary to fulfil the public's right to know and understand. Another such example involves reports about a man questioned regarding the murder of three women who went missing on separate occasions after visiting nightclubs in Perth's Claremont area.

Virtually every news service ran the story, and reports varied in content. One news service named the man and showed his face. Some identified where he worked and lived, while others interviewed his parents about his state of mind. One report even speculated on his ability to kill by outlining how he fitted the serial killer profile (*Media Watch* 1998). Because the man had not been charged or arrested, the sub judice period was not operating. Many journalists believed this meant a 'free for all' where anything could be said. The ABC's *Media Watch* program highlighted the confusion about what can and cannot be reported about people who have been questioned by police. This confusion was summed up by the comment: 'Well there's [sic] no rules and that's the problem ... maybe there should be' (*Media Watch* 1998). (See the previous chapter for a discussion of sub judice.)

But what of the man's fundamental right to a fair trial? What about the presumption of innocence? What about common decency and respect for individuals' privacy? Do these basic rights not exist? What of the journalists' ethical obligations to respect a person's privacy? What about the man's right to protect his reputation and honour? It seems these 'rules' were forgotten as the major media scrambled for a new angle. Although the story was not in contempt of court, the media had other legal and ethical obligations. In this situation, a person was almost tried and found guilty of murder without being charged with any crime. This highlights Kirby's claim that the power of the media is challenging the independence of domestic judiciaries, increasingly ignoring the rules and conventions, and the basic common decency on which domestic judiciaries rely to protect basic human rights.

When balancing the competing factors and determining what is necessary to aid public understanding, journalists must weigh the public interest in warning people of a potential serial killer against other fundamental rights. The reports mentioned above went beyond what was necessary to warn the public and to aid understanding.

One example of a publisher using local laws to undermine rules that restrict the ability to publish is the *Spycatcher* case (Kirby 1998a, p. 8). The *Spycatcher* litigation arose when the British government tried to suppress publication of the memoirs of a former officer of the British Secret Service. The British government instituted litigation in several countries, including Australia, claiming the book revealed confidential information. But the book had been freely available in America and Europe for some time. The British government's attempts to suppress the information failed for a variety of reasons. One factor was the 'undesirability of the courts offering their aid to a struggle so futile as the endeavour to suppress the book in a particular jurisdiction' when it had been freely available in Europe and the United States (Kirby 1998a, pp. 8–9).

This situation might be construed as a breakthrough for freedom of speech, but it represents a skewing of basic human rights that further empowers the transnational media corporations and undermines the legal regimes designed to protect basic human rights and protect against misuse of executive power.

Corporatisation is also undermining the public's ability to access information. As discussed in the previous chapter, each State and territory in Australia and the Commonwealth government has freedom of information laws. The FOI Acts give individuals the right to access government information, but the sale of government-owned utilities such as state electricity corporations means that much of the information previously available to public scrutiny under FOI is now unavailable because of commercial confidentiality.

The rules of commercial confidentiality create the ridiculous situation where material that is publicly available in a company's annual report to shareholders in the jurisdiction where the company is incorporated is actually unavailable to the public in Australia via FOI. This anomaly also undermines the credibility of domestic laws.

Schultz (1998, p. 163) reports that 'most ... journalists surveyed fervently believe that defamation and contempt laws act as a major impediment to freedom of speech and investigative journalism'. Recent contempt decisions highlight the importance placed on freedom of speech by the courts in balancing basic human rights. The Supreme Court of New South Wales found Television and Telecasters (Sydney) were not guilty of contempt of court despite reporting on proceedings that had taken place in the absence of the jury (*Attorney-General for the State of New South Wales v. Television and Telecasters (Sydney) Pty Ltd*, 1998). In reaching his decision, Justice Greg James relied on the views of Kirby P (as he then was) in *Director of Public Prosecutions (Cwlth) v. United Telecasters Sydney Ltd*:

> Out of deference to the competing demands of free discussion in an open media in a society informed about public issues, courts must beware of over-sensitivity to the mere possibility of interference in a criminal trial. If they are not cautious

in this regard, the development of the law of contempt will not only impose burdens on media personnel in a particular case seeking to achieve a just resolution of the identified conflict. The orders for punishment will have a chilling effect, leading to excessive caution by those engaged in the media, with the consequence that too much weight will be given to the protection. (*A-G for NSW v. Television and Telecasters (Sydney) Pty Ltd 1998*, pp. 9–10)

Mindful of this caution, James J. stressed that 'material is contemptuous only if it is proved ... beyond reasonable doubt that the publication of it is of a character which might, as a matter of practical reality, have a substantial or real risk of serious prejudice to a fair trial' (A-G for NSW 1998, p. 10). He found that, although undesirable, the material was not contemptuous because it did not pose a 'substantial or real risk of serious prejudice to the trial' (A-G for NSW 1998, p. 10). This approach has also been adopted by the Perth District Court when Judge Michael O'Sullivan found a journalist's 'polite but deliberate' refusal to answer questions about who had given him certain information had not significantly impacted on the course of justice to be in contempt of court. These cases suggest that the courts will look at the actual, rather than perceived, effect of the publication on the course of justice.

Given the threat posed by globalisation, the media and the judiciary should work towards global solutions, which could help restore these important estates to their 'ideal' watchdog status. There is no simple solution to the problems facing journalists and domestic judiciaries in the global village. The adverse effects of media globalisation must be addressed from both fronts in a variety of ways.

Looking forward

No one global body has the power to impose change, so any steps to restore public confidence in these two institutions must take place in the individual nation-states. But there must be global cooperation if changes are to have any real effect. Reforms such as a cyber-jurisdiction, shrinkwrap and clickwrap licences, which include a choice-of-law clause and nominate the jurisdiction of original publication as the domestic jurisdiction, are problematic in that they require global cooperation, and they further complicate the laws of publication that apply globally.

A cyber-jurisdiction would overcome the problem of which law to apply regarding the publication of material on the Internet, but it would not simplify the law's application to global publications. A situation could arise where a publication could be illegal in broadcast and print, because of the domestic laws that apply, but legal on the Internet. What law would be applied where a person received their information via television with the aid of the Internet?

A cyber-jurisdiction would not overcome the choice-of-law problems (which domestic law applies to publication) of an international multi-media service. It simply creates another layer of laws that would have to be considered when publishing material, adding to the journalist's confusion.

Shrinkwrap/clickwrap licences, which include a choice-of-law clause, are another option for Internet users, particularly regarding e-commerce and copyright issues. But these licences are not suitable to overcome all problems arising from international publication. Shrinkwrap licences include terms and conditions under the shrinkwrap (the clear plastic wrap) around the packaged goods. Opening the package signifies acceptance of the terms and conditions set out under the shrinkwrap, including a choice-of-law clause that identifies the jurisdiction in which disputes will be resolved. The electronic version — clickwrap licences — work similarly, with the consumer indicating consent to the terms and conditions that appear on screen by clicking on an 'I agree' button.

It is highly likely that these licences will be upheld in a court of law if the consumer is fully aware of the conditions of sale before consenting to them. At least one court in the United States has upheld a clickwrap agreement (*Hotmail v. Van$ Money Pie Inc et al.* 1998). These types of licences could be used to incorporate a choice-of-law clause in international publications, where a person must accept the terms and conditions of sale by removing the packaging or clicking 'I agree'. While this may work well for copyright and contractual issues, it would not be an effective solution to the choice-of-law problems facing publishers of material that is defamatory or in contempt of court. Shrinkwrap/clickwrap licences rely on the parties' consent to be enforceable.

Under defamation law every person involved in the publication of defamatory material is liable unless they are an innocent disseminator. The choice-of-law licence would only protect the party with whom the reader had contracted, and not those in the publication line who were not a party to the licence. Taking media publishing as an example, the shrinkwrap choice-of-law licence would protect the publisher, but not the journalist who wrote the story, unless he or she were specifically made a party to the agreement. The other problem with these licences is that they would further empower the TNCs. This would effectively allow the TNCs to nominate the jurisdiction most favourable to them.

This is also a problem with nominating the jurisdiction of original transmission/creation as the domestic law to be applied in resolving legal disputes arising from international publications. The TNCs could then select the most favourable jurisdiction in which to originate publication, further disempowering the public (in much the same way as some shipping companies register their vessels in countries with the least stringent laws).

Given the problems with implementing global rules of publication, domestic judiciaries need to 'internationalise' the rule of law (Kirby 1998a, p. 7) and support an international initiative to 'devise principles as global as the technology itself' (Kirby 1998b, p. 10). 'The rule of law, in the future, will increasingly be international in its content. This is merely a reflection, in the law, of problems presented to society by international technology and the powerful interests which control or direct it' (Kirby 1998a, p. 7).

This approach has been accepted in the United States. When the US Supreme Court, in *Reno v. American Civil Liberties Union*, was called on to decide whether the Communication Decency Act 1996 violated the First Amendment because it prohibited the transmission of indecent and patently offensive material to minors over the Internet, the US judiciary took account of the global effects of its decision. In finding that 'indecent speech on the Internet is entitled to the same full First Amendment protection as other indecent speech', the court discussed the effect of its decision on the global village (Reno 1997, p. 3). It also took into account the need for greater 'self-regulation' and the systems that have been developed 'to help parents control the material that may be available on a home computer' (Reno 1997, p. 3). The court found that:

> As a matter of constitutional tradition, in the absence of evidence to the contrary, we presume that governmental regulation of the content of speech is more likely to interfere with the free exchange of ideas than to encourage it. The interest in encouraging freedom of expression in a democratic society outweighs any theoretical but unproven benefit of censorship. (Reno 1997, p. 15)

This case illustrates three important things:
1 Local laws are starting to take account of their global obligations, an essential step towards restoring judicial independence.
2 If it could be proved the global media are restricting freedom of speech, laws could be enacted to redress this situation.
3 The need for 'consumers' to take greater responsibility for their own actions.

Rather than developing another set of local laws to regulate the Internet, reformers favour nation-states reviewing their local laws to take account of technological changes, while industry and consumers adopt practices that reflect 'common decency and respect'. As the Internet is being integrated into the traditional media's publication stream, this is probably the most suitable approach.

The Internet Industry Association in Australia has devised an Internet Industry Code of Practice for users, which 'is designed to achieve a sensible and workable range of solutions to challenges ... of concern to Australian Internet users, (particularly) issues such as privacy, unsuitable and illegal content and consumers' rights in the context of transactions over the Net' (IIA 1998b, p. 1).

Self-regulation, supported by local laws, is the favoured approach to regulating the Internet, and it may be the most appropriate way of regulating the globalised media. Unfortunately, journalism does not have a healthy track record in terms of self-regulation (Calcutt 1993), and Schultz's study (1998, p. 165) suggests that Australian journalists, at least, do not support a system of further accountability.

Australia has no central body to regulate journalism. Complaints about journalistic practice can be made to organisations including the MEAA, the Australian Press Council and the Australian Broadcasting Authority. There is a move towards individual organisations developing their own codes of ethics and conduct and regulatory schemes, such as those introduced at the Melbourne *Age* and the Herald and Weekly Times. The power to discipline journalists for ethical/professional breaches lies with employers (who have the power to sack an employee who does not comply with a code of practice), the MEAA (whose power is dependent on membership), and specialist bodies such as the press council and the ABA. The employers, the MEAA, and the specialist bodies make their own interpretations of when the public interest in receiving information outweighs the ethical obligations of journalists. The diverse approaches within these regulatory schemes increase the uncertainty for journalists, reinforcing the need for a central review body to provide a clear and transparent system of accountability. Such a body could look at the track record of an owner or journalist when considering media complaints. It could also provide a clear framework by which journalists could interpret the public interest that justifies ethical breaches, and offer a hotline to advise journalists on ethical rights and obligations.

Workplace codes of conduct may be the key to future self-regulation of journalism, but only if the disciplinary adjudication process is taken out of the hands of employers and the codes are sanctioned by an independent central body. These prerequisites are essential to ensure the independence and integrity of journalism in the globalised media. Any arbitration or mediation process must be conducted by an independent body that considers all interests, not just those of the employers. The public must be informed of the complaints process and have immediate access to it.

Any adjudication process should take account of the rights and obligations of media consumers, as well as journalists. Consumers are under an onus, to some extent, to seek a balanced view, instead of relying on headlines and pictures to glean a story. Kirby states (Chakravarti 1998, p. 337) that modern communication practices mean the media should exercise special care with 'prominently published material (including) . . . headlines, captions and photographs and their digital equivalents'. Kirby suggests that the contemporary journalist needs to encapsulate a story in three or four words, instead of looking at the publication as a whole to determine whether it gives rise to a defamatory meaning. This approach completely exonerates the information consumer from any responsibility, imposing a higher burden of care on the journalist, who is facing stricter deadlines in a shrinking workplace. In an information age should people who have access to diverse sources of information have some responsibility to be informed? Journalists are the vehicle by which the public right to know (and understand) is asserted and it is acknowledged this brings with it many obligations. But should the public be completely free from obligations themselves? If it is accepted that a key role of journalists is to promote understanding, then the public cannot be free from responsibility, particularly on the Internet, which is giving the public greater editorial control over the information it consumes. They must 'think' and 'abstract' issues to understand. This requires them to be informed, which in turn requires them to consider different sources of information. Thus it is suggested that steps taken by information consumers could be one of the factors taken into account by a central review body determining whether a consumer had a valid complaint against a journalist or media outlet. Information consumers, who have access to diverse sources of information, can play a key role in refocusing media owners and journalists on the public agenda.

Restoration of public confidence in the media is dependent on an adequate system of accountability that involves the public. Decentralising the regulatory scheme but centralising the process could create a system of accountability that considers the different functions of the media and the publics they serve. This would provide a local scheme that could take account of the global village while also educating the public as to its responsibilities concerning its membership of the global community.

Given journalism's historical resistance to systems of accountability, any moves to implement such a scheme will face a huge challenge. But unless journalists do implement a transparent system of public accountability, journalism in the new millennium will be just another word for public relations.

Conclusion

Media globalisation is threatening society's two most important watchdogs — the judiciary and journalism. Trans-national corporation dominance of modern communications makes it imperative that journalism and the judiciary are not at loggerheads. They need to internationalise their response and work together wherever possible to pressure the TNCs to introduce work practices and ethical guidelines that reflect high journalistic standards, such as the *Age* Charter, which outlines the ethical obligations of management. Journalists must consent to a transparent system of accountability, supplemented by internationalised local laws that acknowledge the changing role of the global journalist.

Case study

Sporting news is a valuable commodity and many organisers, venue managers and promoters are capitalising on the public's desire to be informed.

Components of the news are being sold off: broadcast and photographic rights are being sold to the highest bidder while organisers are packaging statistics for sale to various outlets. Now each major sporting event has its own website and newspapers and other organisations operating on-line sporting news services must compete with the official body for an audience.

The creators of original material can rely on the law of copyright to protect their works, but they can sell off any of their exclusive rights on whatever conditions they like. Recently, a major newspaper was precluded from using audio-visual material of a major sporting event. The paper avoided the owner's copyright by creating a 'hotlink' to a site that had permission to use the audio-visual material.

This 'creative' approach to the copyright laws is not in the spirit of the Copyright Act. However, the use of copyright to exclude a competitor is not in the spirit of section 46 of the Trade Practices Act, which precludes a corporation from:

- eliminating or substantially damaging a competitor;
- preventing the entry of a person into a market;
- deterring or preventing a person from engaging in competitive conduct in any market.

This example illustrates a number of points made in this chapter:

- the blurring of what is news with entertainment and public relations;
- the commodification of news and information;
- the commercial pressures on the role of journalists;
- the pressures placed on local laws by the commodification of news;
- the pressures placed on local laws by new technology.

DISCUSSION QUESTIONS

1 Select three daily newspapers and compare the major stories. Identify how they vary: are they telling the same story in different ways?

2 Using the same three papers, identify how the major stories will aid public understanding. When doing this, keep in mind the different publics the paper services.

3 Now have a look at your local newspaper and obtain a copy of another paper produced by that publisher. Compare the content of these two papers and identify any 'standardisation' of information.

4 Identify five areas where the public right to know and understand must give way and discuss why these interests outweigh the public interest in freedom of speech.

Further reading

Background Briefing 1997, 'Corporate PR: a threat to journalism', 30 March, *http://www.abc.net.au/rn/talks/bbing/stories/s10602.htm*, 15 January 1999.

Herman, E. and McChesney, R. 1997, *The Global Media: the New Missionaries of Corporate Capitalism*, Cassell, London.

Kirby, M. 1998a, 'The globalisation of the media and judicial independence', *Foundation Law*,
http://www.fl.asn.au/resources/kirby/papers/19980601_speakfre.html,
9 October 1998, pp. 1–17.

Kirby, M. 1998b, 'International dimensions of cyberspace law: protection of privacy and human rights in the digital age', *Foundation Law*,
http://www.fl.asn.au/resources/kirby/papers19980630_unespriv.html, 17 August 1998, pp. 1–16.

Note

1   Fourteen-month-old Jaidyn Leskie disappeared in June 1997 while in the care of his mother's boyfriend Mr Greg Domaszewicz. The circumstances of his disappearance were quite unusual, with a pig's head being found in the front yard of Mr Domaszewicz's Newborough home on the morning of the child's disappearance. Jaidyn's body was found in Blue Rock Lake on 1 January 1998. Mr Domaszewicz, who was charged with Jaidyn's murder and was in prison at the time the child's body was discovered, was subsequently acquitted of the boy's murder.

Part 7

Technological talespinning

Technology is changing the face of journalism, but does it sound the death knell for traditional news media? How do journalists, the media, and the public make sense of a society that seems inundated with technological change, caught in an ever-increasing spiral of techno-claims and counterclaims? This section explores the potential impact of the Internet and on-line journalism on older forms of print and broadcast news, and examines the possible future of journalism in a converged, digital environment. Must all journalists become multi-skilled, multiple-media performers who deliver text, sound, vision, and on-line copy for a global audience? Should they? Will the result be improved access to information for the public, and a better level of understanding of news events? Or will the technological revolution prove to be little more than cosmetic surgery on the crumbling face of contemporary Australian journalism?

15

The media is the message[1]

SUELLEN TAPSALL

The mobile journalist's workstation of the future was unveiled in mid-1999 at a Berlin street festival (Clayton Powell 1999). Developed by a consortium of European television producers, Deutsche Telekom, and Avid Technology, the 'Urban Jungle Pack' (URP) is a wearable set of computers that stream audio, video, and text from the field reporter back to the newsroom.

The URP includes a global positioning system, head-mounted video camera, electronic compass, head-mounted display (with options to see the recorded vision through either a translucent image in front of the reporter's eyes, or to move across a solid ten-inch display screen), battery, and Linux computer. By no means the first futuristic technological solution for news-gathering of the future (see, for example, Williams' 1993 description of 'journocam'), the URP epitomises perceptions of working life and reality for the twenty-first-century journalist.

The convergence of communications and information technologies (CIT), the growth in on-line media, and the relative decline of both print and broadcast news journalism in Australia have encouraged prophetic statements about the future — or lack thereof — of the 'traditional' news media. But are the traditional news media under threat from technology (as opposed to the challenges presented by commercialisation and corporatisation as discussed elsewhere in this book)? How likely is it that the average journalist of 2010 will be a multi-skilled, multiple-media performer, individually delivering high-quality and effective text, sound, vision, and on-line copy for a global audience? More importantly, how desirable is this vision of the future newsroom? Will the result be improved access to information for the general public, a better level of understanding of news events, or just more of the 'same old, same old'?

Out with the old . . .

On-line news journalism and multiple-media newsrooms became realities in the late 1990s. *American Journalism Review*'s *Newslink* site contained links to 9000 newspaper, magazine, broadcast, and news bureau sites around the world — with links to nearly 5000 on-line newspapers alone (Meyer 1999a). The premiere twenty-four-hour cable television news network, *CNN*, was one of the most popular news sites on the World Wide Web (the *most* popular, according to a 1997 *PC Magazine* survey of 5000 Internet users). The site, which averaged about fifteen million users a month, brought together news from more than 3500 news practitioners working in thirty-six bureaus and more than 600 broadcast affiliates.

In Australia, more than 1.5 million households were connected to the Internet by May 1999 ('Aussies warm to the web' 1999). Australia's major metropolitan newspapers (The *Age*, the *Australian* and the *Sydney Morning Herald*) ran comprehensive news websites that paralleled their daily print publications. The ABC's news site offered text, video, and audio news and features, updated frequently throughout the day. *ABC Online* had won numerous awards, and was accessed by more than 2.5 million users a week. Text transcripts of news programs were available on-line and News Radio was available in streamed audio format for those who wanted to listen to the news station through a computer. Newspaper journalists (for example, employed by the *Age*) were putting together audio and video grabs to go on the paper's websites, while ABC reporters were writing text stories and getting photographs for the public broadcaster's on-line site. And, while many news organisations flirted playfully with the notion of an on-line presence, or simpered shyly in the corner waiting to see whether everyone else had a good time at the on-line publication party, the majority of the world's news organisations had established a WWW presence that allowed them to repackage their news product and advertise their wares.

Proclamations about the death of traditional news media are nothing new — although it is worth noting that most of these prophetic statements do not originate with the traditional media themselves. As Katz (1999) argues, newspapers have traditionally been slow to change and react to outside challenges, and the latest prophecies of doom have had little impact on many news editors:

> They've heard it before. The newspaper industry has a deeply sado-masochistic streak. It goes to extraordinary lengths, and sometimes even great expense, to arrange for speakers to dump on newspapers and pronounce their downfall, even as they go to even greater lengths to take little or none of the advice they get.

The rhetoric suggests that traditional print media — primarily newspapers are most under threat, with newspapers portrayed as 'relics of the past':

Of course, this isn't the first time the pundits have written obituaries for newspapers. In the 1950s and 60s most of them were convinced that television would be the death of newspapers, and in the '70s and early '80s it was videotext. In each case, technology and economics were thought to favor electronic media. Yet far from killing them, new technologies actually helped to save newspapers and make them even more profitable. Now the pundits are wringing their hands again. (Fidler 1991, p. 115)

However the convergence of CITs and the shift to digitisation have also called into question the future of radio and television journalism.

Like earlier predictions, the present forecasts of the death of traditional news media are firmly grounded in an implacable — and often unspoken — belief in the determinist nature of technology. Technological convergence *has* taken place, digital and Internet technologies *do* provide options to package text, sound, and vision in one easy-to-access — from home or work — product. Increasing numbers of Australian and overseas citizens *are* connecting on-line and to cable and satellite services in order to access the deluge of material — both gold and dross — available in digital format. And most traditional news organisations continue to struggle to stay afloat while weighed down by such problems as shrinking audiences, increased costs, and the challenges of corporatisation and commercialism. This volatile mix of technological possibility and evolutionary environmental factors provides a fertile feeding ground for perceptions of revolutionary change. However, the fundamental premise of the paradigm-changing nature of technology is in itself fatally flawed, reflecting what media theorists label a *technological determinist* perspective of technology and the world around it.

Technological determinism

Technological determinism (occasionally referred to as media determinism) is the most popular and influential theory of the relationship between technology and society (Carey and Quirk 1992; MacKenzie and Wajcman 1993; Chandler 1995). The theory has a number of proponents — present-day and historical — such as Marx, Ellul, Innes, McLuhan, Postman, Stoll, and Negroponte. Yet much of society — including many whose attitudes towards technology are epitomised by this approach — would be unaware their beliefs have a theoretical label.

Technological determinists adhere to a central tenet that technology, in and of itself, causes social and cultural change. Technology is reified, presented as a *thing* that exists and has just been waiting to be discovered and used — and it will be discovered. Technology is pictured as a tsunami — a massive, inescapable wave waiting to sweep all in its path. Its directions and effects are unpredictable and immeasurable.

Technological determinists interpret technology in general and communications technologies in particular as the basis of society in the past, present and even the future. They say that technologies such as writing or print or television or the computer 'changed society'. In its most extreme form, the entire form of society is seen as being determined by technology: new technologies transform society at every level, including institutions, social interaction and individuals. At the least a wide range of social and cultural phenomena are seen as shaped by technology. 'Human factors' and social arrangements are seen as secondary. (Chandler 1995)

Technological-determinist statements may be optimistic or pessimistic in nature. They easily translate into prophetic and visionary statements — they capture the imagination and headlines, they echo anxieties already present in society, they capitalise on self-evident and taken-for-granted assumptions.

Technological utopianism / dystopianism

Individual theorists may consider the impact of technology-driven change to be either positive or negative. However, regardless of their analysis of the final outcome, they reflect a common belief that technological change drives social change. Their responses vary from those who believe that any technology-inspired outcome is a positive one, making the world a better place to live in (utopianism) to those who consider the opposite — that technological change leads to the loss of all traditional values and beliefs (dystopianism).

Those who are optimistic about the impact of technology see it as solving such social and economic woes as unemployment and poverty, while lifting humans to new planes of creativity and innovation. More pessimistic theorists consider that the technology can exacerbate the very problems it endeavours to solve:

The optimistic approach sees the march of technology as bringing about unprecedented human benefit. With the advent of new technology, according to the optimists, far more jobs will be created than will be lost. Not only will there be more jobs but these jobs will be at a higher intellectual level ... In contrast, the pessimistic view of technological change sees the advance of technology as inevitably leading to massive unemployment. But the pessimist argues that, even in those jobs which do remain, there is still present an unremitting tendency for the jobs to be continually deskilled and degraded. (Watkins 1986, p. 6)

The optimistic technological determinist view of the future of journalism and the news media, for example, would see technological convergence as the solution to current problems inherent in the news. Thus, the Internet provides free and open access for all to a global communications and information medium, allowing unprecedented space for in-depth news articles and coverage of important world and local events. The pessimist, on the other hand, might cite the mechanisation of news-gathering and sub-editing processes as further ammunition in the hands of those debasing and devaluing traditional news practices, such that content is simply regurgitated and the journalist becomes little more than a word-processor. Rather than heralding a brave new world, new technologies limit and reduce available opportunities:

> ... contrary to conventional wisdom, new technologies do not, by and large, *increase* people's options but do just the opposite ... new technologies drive old technologies out of business; which is to say that there is an imperialistic thrust to technology, a strong tendency to get everyone to conform to the requirements of what is new. Now, this is not always a bad thing, although sometimes it is very bad ... I bring it up to call attention to the fact that what we too easily call 'progress' is always problematic. The word comes trippingly off the tongue, but when you examine what it means, you discover that technology is always a Faustian bargain. It giveth and it taketh away. (Postman 1993a)

Modern modes of transport have signalled the end of international travel by boat. CDs replaced LPs and decimated the record market. On-line or a converged form of news media would presumably signal the inevitable decline, and eventual disappearance, of traditional news media.

Regardless of the inherently optimistic or pessimistic view of technology, a technological determinist perspective is consistent with a disempowering of the stakeholders in the technology-affected situation.

The technological imperative

This disempowerment is linked to notions of the inevitability and inescapability of technological change. The technological imperative diverts attention away from questions of whether or not technology is necessary or desirable through an acceptance that it is unstoppable. The focus of any consideration becomes dealing with the impact and effect of the technology, adjusting to life in the new age, or moving on to the next stage.

> The doctrine of the technological imperative is that because a particular technology means we *can* do something (it is technically possible) then this action either *ought* to (as a moral imperative), *must* (as an operational requirement) or inevitably *will* (in time) be taken. (Chandler 1995)

Thus, journalists and news organisations are challenged to articulate their plans to cope in the converged digital media age, rather than considering whether or not on-line, virtual, or converged media forms are preferred or even desired options. News organisations are more likely to be asked 'how will you compete on-line?', rather than 'do you need or want to maintain an on-line presence?' Technology becomes both question and answer:

> ... the answers to the media's future lie in understanding and managing conver-
> gence — the coming together of all forms of communication technologies and
> functions into a single system, a blurring and integration of traditional print and
> electronic media that has *already* occurred, especially at the ownership level. Wall
> Street understands this, and corporate chieftains at some large media enterprises
> do too, but this is where it stops. Others who head media operations like news-
> papers and television networks continue to work and think in a vacuum, dealing
> mostly with the conditions of their own subset of the industry and regarding com-
> petition and challenges from other media as 'threats' in a sort of Cold Warriorish
> fashion. (Dennis 1991, pp. 64–5)

For Australian journalists, this disempowerment further compounds existing pressures that in themselves result in feelings of powerlessness or inability to effect change and maintain quality of news product. These pressures (as discussed elsewhere in this text) include the corporatisation and commercialisation of the media and concerns about the nature and shape of contemporary journalistic work.

Technology as autonomous and neutral

Closely associated with notions of the technological imperative is that of the uncontrollability or autonomy of technology. Technology is no longer subject to the agency of humans, it 'thus reveals itself at once destroyer and creator, and no one wishes or is able to master it' (Ellul 1964, p. 85). Technology might be an independent variable, operating outside society, or a dependent factor. It might also be considered to be 'neutral' or 'value free' — its positiveness or negativity determined by the use to which it is put rather than the nature of the technology itself.

> This is the 'cargo cult' view of technology: we wake up one morning to find a com-
> puter in the garden, it has arrived impersonally and we must take it or leave it as
> we find it. Technological determinists argue that if we reject high technology we
> will be punished: if we accept it, the prerecorded birds will sing all day, and artificial
> lighting will abolish night. (Jones 1996, p. 219)

One view presents technology as a force operating totally outside human con-trol, changing under its own momentum and 'blindly' shaping society. The fact that it is *possible* to do something, therefore, becomes the justification for doing it. It is now possible for the journalist to be simultaneously camera operator; sound recordist; interviewer; technician; sub-editor; and presenter for television, radio, and on-line news products. The possibility therefore justifies the fulfilment of this technological vision. The contrasting view sees technology as neither autonomous nor value free, and seldom introduced in neutral fashion.

> ... it is unlikely that technology has been introduced in a neutral or random fashion ... technology can always be seen as beneficial to some and detrimental to others. Who benefits and who is disadvantaged reflects in turn the conscious decisions of those in power, which give rise to the particular time and extent of technological innovation. (Watkins 1986, p. 9)

However, those who accept the notion of technological autonomy tend to argue in support of the '*non*-neutrality' of technology as an agent of social change, 'arguing we cannot merely "use" technology without also, to some extent, being influenced or "used by" it' (Chandler 1995).

This latter view positions technologies as not inherently neutral. In a political sense, they may be designed to enable or dismiss social options, or may, of themselves, be more in keeping with various social options (Winner 1993). Every technology 'carries with it a program, an agenda, and a philosophy, that may or may not be life-enhancing and that therefore requires scrutiny, criticism, and control' (Postman 1993b, p. 185).

Acceptance of the assumption that technology is neutral or autonomous carries with it similar problems as the acceptance of the notion of the technological imperative — that it leads to a pressure to respond to, rather than a questioning of, the role of technology in society.

Technocracy and progress

The coupling of technology and progress is linked in the narratives surrounding social development and historical change. Thus humankind has survived the 'print revolution', the 'electric revolution', and the 'technological revolution', while moving from the 'machine age' to the 'industrial age' and the 'information age'. Theorists acknowledge the equation of technology and progress: 'in this popular context technological change is viewed as progress while progress is defined in terms of technological change' (Watkins 1986, p. 3). Those who fail to accept, adopt, and implement the technological advances available to them — such as new converged electronic forms of news-gathering and publication — are viewed as Luddites, attempting to stand in the path of progress.

This mythos has been especially evident in America, the birthplace of the Internet and home of many major communications empires, including News Corporation, Time Warner, and Microsoft. Carey and Quirk, for example, argue that forecasts of the American future always suggested wealth, power, and productivity would derive from mechanics and industrialisation and that 'a special importance was attached periodically to specific technologies that performed key services' (Carey and Quirk 1992, p. 119), namely printing technologies and a free press. They trace this awe of, and belief in, the progressive power of technology through the development of print, steam engines, machines, electricity, and CITs.

Towards a social determination of technology

Technological determinism has its critics. Any mono-causal approach, or as Chandler suggests, the *billiard-ball model* of technology and society is inadequate to deal with the complexities of political, social, and economic change. Any vision of technology as a distinct entity divorced from its social context is misconceived.

> The way in which technology is designed, developed and utilised is a reflection of the intellectual and creative energy of human beings ... technology can only be properly understood by placing it in its human context and questioning the present and potential forms of technological innovation. (Watkins 1986, pp. 8–9)

The social contexts of technology must be taken into account (Marvin 1988; Winston 1990). The theory of technological determinism is inadequate and incomplete, failing to explain why developments occur at a particular time, instead presenting simplistic accounts that either hail the 'great man' behind the invention or detail a 'seamless sequence of technical events' that resulted in the new technology (Winston 1990).

Information revolutionists argue the technological imperative — that if technology makes something possible then it will inevitably happen — and yet history is full of evidence that contradicts this position (Winston 1986).

In Australia, for example, access to the Internet is relatively inexpensive (although not as cheap as in the United States) and easy to organise. Yet the uptake of desktop Internet access is still not routine in many of Australia's newsrooms. 'It's a bit embarrassing actually that it's not more widespread in the media,' Sales (1998) said. 'It's getting to be so widespread in the corporate world that people do ask you for your email, and if you don't have one you feel a bit of a goose'. The technology itself is available and more than adequate, so what has caused its scanty adoption in the fiercely competitive news media? The answer might be a combination of factors — the heavy investment in and reliance of newsrooms on made-to-measure news systems that predate the late 1990s rapid growth of Internet services; prioritisation of investments in digital recording and editing technologies or printing systems; concerns about the economic and time costs of Internet use; and a lack of knowledge about ways to maximise the Internet as a communications, information, and publication medium (Kingston 1998b; Sales 1998; Walsh 1998). Walsh says the slow move to incorporate the Internet is 'crazy':

It's just bad management basically. It's mean, stingy bad management. There's no other explanation for it. It's downright stupidity. I wouldn't say that by and large your average newsroom's on the cutting edge of technology . . . I've been staggered by the slow uptake of the Net by journalists.

Another example of technological change that failed to conform to a technological determinist charting of its adoption is the development of sound on film (Winston 1990). The technological determinist view focuses on the mechanical and technical history of this technological advance. Sound recording devices had been developed by the turn of the twentieth century, but these were mechanical, with no amplification, and so did not work well in the theatre. By 1906, advances in electric and electronic devices had resulted in specialised tubes that could record and amplify electrical sound signals. Eventually, twenty years later, the technology was applied to silent films, and in turn this led to the introduction of faster film stock, with sound and vision recorded on the one film.

Alternative accounts situate the technological change that led to 'talking pictures' in the struggle of a corporation to maintain and grow its business. Warner Brothers, a small studio in the mid-1920s, borrowed money to expand its business by 'vertically integrating' — buying theatre chains to distribute its movies and a radio station to promote them. At that time, Warner Bros was a smaller player than the five major studios and it introduced sound in an attempt to gain a competitive advantage and bring a larger audience into its theatres. Another smaller player, Fox, later showed that sound news films were popular with the public. It was this possible threat to the silent movie business that eventually led other major studios to introduce sound. Until the threat posed by Warner Bros, the 'technology was available, but the commercial desire and need were not' (Winston 1990). Significantly, the major studios then agreed on a common system, sound on film, which was complex, expensive, and slightly different from the techniques employed by Warner Bros and Fox; the latter two organisations were forced to come into line with the dominant standard.

While the two accounts are not mutually exclusive, the technological determinist view ignores crucial information that influenced the role, pace, and form of the technological change. Nor is the second view complete as it assumes the 'main engines of change are the corporation and the market and that the corporation's motive will always be to increase the bottom line' (Winston 1990). Innovation can be designed specifically to safeguard existing corporations and markets, and technological innovation can proceed independently of corporate interest. The key to Winston's argument is that:

> . . . all technological communication innovation can be thought of as a series of events taking place in the realm of technology, but influenced by and reacting to

events taking place (a) in the realm of pure science and (b) in society in general.(Winston 1990)

Commercial interests had also played a significant role in the development and eventual massification of the motion picture. Thomas Edison had produced the necessary technology in the early 1890s, but failed to see any viable market in the commercial projection of films, instead promoting the Kinetoscope, which allowed one person at a time to view short moving images. The most successful of the early picture projectors, the Vitascope, was developed by Edison and Thomas Arnat, after French and English groups projected films in 'salons' and had standing-room only crowds (De Fleur and Ball-Rokeach 1982, pp. 56–7). Similarly, the Westinghouse Electric and Manufacturing Company established Station KDKA in Pittsburgh in 1920, and began regular broadcasts, in order to sell more radio receiver sets (De Fleur and Ball-Rokeach 1982, pp. 81–2).

The development of television exemplifies the complex social, cultural, and corporate factors influencing technological development (Winston, 1990). The process known as television was a technical possibility from the turn of the century, but it apparently had no practical use. It was considered of no account because there was no social need for it; theatrical circuits took theatre to the masses, and film was mechanising the process. Nor was there any perception of a market demand for the entertainment in the home: 'the masses, given the long hours they worked and the poor pay they received, had not yet the means to use it' (Winston 1990). Film studios and radio corporations were also uninterested, seeing TV as a threat to current business (although with potential for the future), despite the emergence of the basic TV camera tube (and associated technology) in the mid-1920s. By the end of the Second World War, the consumer society was emerging, the radio market was saturated, and there was a significant electronic manufacturing capacity. Winston (1990) suggested it is the emergence of 'supervening social necessity' that accelerates the development of media and technology, and that this process is influenced by various factors — including individuals, economic forces, politics, and social and cultural forces.

The first mass medium to successfully enter the home and conquer boundaries between the private and the public was the telephone. Yet, it was originally envisaged as an alternative to the dominant communications medium of the time. Alexander Graham Bell saw the telephone as a mass medium, 'transmitting music, Sunday sermons and important public speeches to a paying network of wired up subscribers' (Sterling 1995, p. 34). However, Bell's system struggled to be taken seriously, viewed as a novelty compared with the established communication network of the telegraph system. Faced with the market dominance of telegrams, Bell and his backers determined the real 'selling point' of the telephone was as a personal technology, allowing users to speak to each other (Sterling 1995, pp. 34–5). Once established, the telephone was used both as a medium for personal speech and a mass medium for public spectacle (Marvin 1988, pp. 209–16).

A range of social and environmental factors shape technology, including — but not limited to — economics, gender, war, social relations, and ideology (MacKenzie and Wajcman 1993). The social shaping of technology approach allows one to look at factors that influence the speed and direction of technological change, together with causes and effects (Edge 1995, p. 14) in a holistic way that does not attempt to understand technology in isolation. Television systems, for example, differ because of their development in specific social, economic, cultural, and technological contexts, and the same is true of other technologies:

> Certainly the capabilities of these technologies to deliver more channels, avoid state control and turn the TV set into a place for shopping, banking and game playing are significant developments, but the driving forces are commercial and political rather than simply technological. (Barker 1997, p. 56)

A multi-causal understanding of the shaping of society provides an alternative to the single-mindedness of technological determinism. Technological and social change –which may be simultaneously positive and negative in impact — are influenced by various considerations, not least of which are corporate and economic factors. It is far more likely that all these elements interact in a complex and intricate pattern that may be impossible to codify and unravel. In some situations, at some stage, technology may influence society in expected or unexpected ways. At other times, the technology will be a response to various political, economic, commercial, or social demands.

> Technology is often seen as a whole which is more than the sum of its parts, or various manifestations ... the umbrella term 'mass communication' covers a multitude of very different media. And even categories such as 'writing', 'print', 'literacy', 'television', or 'the computer' encompass considerable diversity. Referring loosely to such abstract categories is hazardous. Some technologies may ... be less determining than others; the flexibility or 'openness' of tools varies. And of course a technology cannot be cut off as a separate thing from specific contexts of use: technology has many manifestations in different social contexts. A single technology can serve many quite different purposes. (Chandler 1995)

Different forms of journalism: competition or complement?

Having identified a technological determinist theme underlying many prophetic statements about the future of news media, which has focused attention on the inevitability and necessity of technological change, it is important to restate and reconsider notions of the future interplay of broadcast, print, and on-line journalism. This re-examination of the issues does not presuppose that technological convergence will *not* take place, as Fidler acknowledged in 1991:

> That's not to say newspapers can survive by remaining as they are, or that alternative electronic and information services will not threaten established newspaper companies in the future. Technology and economics *do* favor electronic media. The convergence of print, broadcast and computer technologies is already apparent in the array of multimedia products on the market. (Fidler 1991, p. 116)

Nor does a re-examination of the issues ignore current audience or practitioner dissatisfaction with some or many contemporary news products and processes. However, solutions to these concerns might have little to do with technology.

This book has already acknowledged the fragmentation of the news audience and increasing competition for news consumers. The answer, according to some in the news industry, is for news products to become more alike. Witness the current tendency for newspapers to impose arbitrary word limits on all stories — nothing over fifteen centimetres long — or to increase the proportion of news briefs in a vain attempt to compete with television, radio, or on-line news. The very notion of a converged digital format suggests that one medium can provide a complete or whole picture of any one news event or situation. Is this a valid assumption, or is it more useful to consider the various media as complementing each other? Radio, print, television, and now on-line journalism might be more correctly viewed as telling different stories — or different parts of the story — of the one news event or happening. There might well be a central core of journalistic principles that all hold to — truth, fairness, factual recounting, and so on. However, at times this is, and perhaps should be, questionable —the views, voices, and techniques the different formats employ to tell their stories vary enormously.

This discussion should not be considered an exercise in *ranking* the various media on a best to worst scale (although it is here that much of the present literature can be found), but rather an attempt to identify the unique attributes of various media forms of news.

Broadcast media

While radio and television share some similarities — both involve audience engagement beyond the textual — they are distinctly different. Radio engages the sense of sound and gives free rein to the imagination. It is immediate and informational, providing in the briefest possible time — usually thirty seconds or less — the bare bones of a story — what, where, when, why, who, and how. Masterton and Patching (1990, p. 7) argue that as a medium, 'radio has many advantages over its "big brothers" newspapers and television' because it is less expensive to set up and operate, is more immediate, and the equipment is cheaper and easier to use.

> While newspapers and television are visual media, in that you see what you read or view, radio is the medium of the imagination. The mix of words and sounds in a radio program stimulates the audience into creating mental pictures, whether the program is news, current affairs or entertainment. The radio reporter is limited only by his or her power to describe, and the listeners' ability to imagine. Radio is a warm, emotional medium. (Masterton and Patching 1990, p. 7)

Radio is also problematic. Radio listeners tend to be engaged elsewhere at the same time as they partake of its wares. Reliance on the aural sense alone limits the quantity and type of information that can be conveyed. There is no double-dipping in the radio news barrel. Those listeners who miss the story first time around probably have to wait for the next news bulletin in order to hear the story again and by then their attention might be on other things or they might not be near a radio.

Television takes the audience *to* the news event or happening (in a limited way in news, but more so in the current affairs or lifestyle programming). Its engagement of the senses of sight and sound gives the viewer some idea of the actual look of the news event. Television has become the mass medium and harbinger of life-changing news events — a role it has taken over, at least in the developed world, from radio. In an era of instantaneous communications and satellite feeds, a worldwide audience clusters around television screens to watch history unfold — the Gulf War and Kosovo, the death of Princess Diana, the rescue of Thredbo survivor Stuart Diver, the mass murder at Columbine high school in Colorado. The development of *wall-to-wall* television coverage of major news events may still be in an evolutionary phase — accompanied by questions concerning the behaviours, ethics, and necessity of swarms of reporting packs descending on the already traumatised players in the latest unfolding news drama — but it would appear nonetheless to be here to stay.

Like radio, television is a transitory medium and there is no 'second reading' or 'slackening of speed for individual comprehension rates. If it is not understood on first hearing, it is not understood at all. However, the printed word can not match radio for speed or television for clarity and total impact in stories of action' (Masterton and Patching 1990, p. 19). Still, the majority of people in the developed world are turning to television as their sole source of news. This is problematic in itself. The voracious appetite of television for moving images means stories that might otherwise barely register on the newsworthiness scale are likely to gain precedence. And, like radio, some stories are difficult to adequately tell on television news:

> ... some news items are easier to present on radio or television than others. Radio requires no pictures other than that engendered by the words themselves in the listener's head; television's task of providing pictures is both a huge advantage and a massive impediment to accurate and balanced reporting. But it is difficult in either broadcast medium to tell accurately and interestingly the detail required in a story about a budget, an involved debate in parliament or any other story in which complex structure is involved (Masterton and Patching 1990, p. 19).

All media are forced to package information in a way that engages the audience, but for television especially, the line between entertainment and information has blurred considerably (Cave 1998, Sales 1998). Cave, a former bureau chief in the United States, says it is amazing to see what has happened to network news there:

> It's very much a source of gee whiz and titillation, it is certainly not a source of comprehensive news — and doesn't even pretend to be any more ... it's an entertaining source of gee whizzery, it's certainly not a comprehensive news source.

Print and on-line media

And what of the traditional newspaper? Print should provide a depth of information, analysis, and comment that the broadcast media cannot. There are those who suggest newspapers need to take on the broadcast media at their own game (such as Fidler, arguing in 1991 that newspapers needed to undergo a 'media-morphosis' — creatively transforming into a new electronic medium). Yet newspapers are unable to compete with the immediacy of radio, television, and on-line news. New technologies in the print newsroom and printing presses have seen daily copy deadlines brought forward, leading to longer lag times between the writing of stories and their publication. As a result, unless the newspaper is breaking an exclusive story (or scoop), it is unlikely to contain major new facts about a particular news event. Newspapers can provide a depth of coverage, analysis, and comment that the broadcast media are unable to match. Newspaper coverage allows the telling of stories that might be summed up in one sentence on radio or a few frames on television. This recasting of newspapers as explainers, interpreters, or contextualisers of news, rather than merely papers of record, demands a depth of financial and time commitment to reporting that is not evident in many Australian newsrooms. It also requires a level of journalistic experience and skill that takes the reporter far beyond the role of news transcriber. Katz (1999) argues that 'nobody knows if a radical return to context, writing and storytelling' is enough to 'save' newspapers, adding 'but wouldn't it be nice to find out?'

On-line journalism combines some elements of all its predecessor forms of news. On-line journalism can be immediate, providing frequently updated stories of news events. It gives news consumers some sense of control, allowing them to explore news events and related issues at their own pace. If one aspect of the story is particularly intriguing the consumer can head off and explore that without waiting for the story-teller to get around to the information — providing, of course, that someone has previously identified that element of interest and published related information on the World Wide Web. While on-line news is still in its infancy, Meyer (1999b) argues 'what you see now (re on-line publishing) may be all you ever get'. He suggests there is no 'untapped generation of non-readers' waiting to grab hold of the on-line news lifeline, but that the 'dominant audience is composed of voracious readers who seek out the net as a source of augmentation for other material already available to them in traditional form'. He further argues that committed on-line news consumers (as opposed to itinerant net surfers) might want their audio-visual taste buds whetted, but are far more interested in efficient access to, and delivery of, on-line news.

Radio, television, print, and on-line news provide a smorgasbord of information that ultimately should serve up a balanced and more complete picture of any news happening or event. While they compete within their own medium, they should be seen as complementary across media. 'In many respects today's television news is a great advertisement for tomorrow's newspaper' (Masterton and Patching 1990, p. 20). By extension, any news consumer who fails to access the news in more than one medium is likely to wind up with an inadequate or incomplete understanding of the news — a challenge Masterton and Patching recognise for television news:

> The audience is a bigger problem for television news editors . . . every year a larger proportion of the public receives its news of the day from television. To more and more people television is the sole source of information on what is happening around the world. (1990, p. 8)

This recognition of the necessity for diverse media forms of news and acceptance of the further fragmentation of news markets and need for niche products provides the best hope that journalism across all media will survive as a meaningful service.

Medium specialist or media generalist?

Despite the convergence of the technology, it seems that the practice of journalism in the various media is fragmenting, as are media products and audiences. Just as newspapers have diversified to meet the needs of multiple publics within the pages of one daily newspaper, news products — on radio, television, and the Internet — will reflect increasing fragmentation. Walsh (1998) says there is no doubt television will get 'sliced up in salami style' as well. 'There'll always be very large free-to-air stations, the way there are very large newspapers surviving, but there are nowhere near as many newspapers surviving as there were, or in the same form.' Such a scenario was also envisaged by Williams (1993, p. 94), who predicted fragmentation of the role of television journalists.

Aside from the common core of activities that define journalistic endeavour, the medium-linked skills have become more specialised and demanding. Radio journalism might have started out as the aural expression of print reporting and television news was originally radio on a television screen (complete with close-ups of talking heads immobilised in front of the camera), but both forms of reporting have evolved far beyond those beginnings. The ideal contemporary television journalist is as much actor as news-gatherer, entertainment personality as reporter. The ideal radio journalist is also a sound engineer, capable of doubling as talkback announcer or disc jockey. And the ideal print reporter has an unparalleled mastery of the written word.

The language of the various media differs. Each has developed its own distinctive style. Print still is likely to require a more formal approach to language and grammar, while radio and television journalism capitalises on the spoken word — being written for the ear, not the eye. The ability to effectively interweave words and pictures (for television) or words and sound (radio) is far removed from writing a summary lead for a traditional print news story. In the limited time available to the broadcast journalist, sound and vision become separate narrative and descriptive tools, cleverly crafted with the spoken word to tell the most complete story possible. In the same way, those working in on-line journalism quickly realised that to move text successfully and effectively from the printed page to the computer screen requires a transformation of copy, rather than a mere transferral of information from one medium to the next.

Jobs become even more distinct, and roles more specialist. In Chapter 1 this dichotomy was discussed with regard to content — the same holds true when it comes to the medium of delivery. Just as the gulf is likely to grow between the generalist journalist — jack of all trades and master of none — and the specialist reporter who is an authoritative source in a specific area of news, a similar gulf is likely to develop between the specialist radio, television, or print journalist, and the multiple-media reporter. The generalist, or multiple-media reporter, is likely to be seen in those places where roles have always converged — small alternative publications, rural areas, and the like. There will be journalists who simultaneously report across media — because they have to or want to. The medium specialist is more likely to be seen in larger news markets that are supporting niche publications in diverse media. At the same time, natural linkages, partnerships, and new specialities will emerge. Thus, for example, it is easy to forecast a growth in video-journalism that will probably parallel the continued rising interest in photo-journalism.

Television journalists may also be confronted with the removal of the process layers between the gathering of news and its broadcast, in the same way that compositors have disappeared from newspaper print rooms. Sales (1998) envisages a future in which television journalists are multi-skilled and where, within fifteen or twenty years, 'journalists will be shooting and cutting their own stories'.

Conclusion

The popular rhetoric that envisages converged news media forms appears to ignore one major change to journalism already obvious in Australian newsrooms. Technological change, corporatisation, commercialisation, and other pressures have ushered in an *unbundling* or disaggregation of the journalistic role. This development is not unique to reporting — similar trends are also evident in teaching, for example. No longer is the journalist responsible for the entire reporting process from interview to written story. While accustomed to the intervention of a sub-editor in the end stages of news publication, journalists have traditionally been responsible for the reporting process until that stage. The unbundling of the journalist's role sees the further breaking down of the news process to a series of steps or component parts — with the ownership of each up for grabs. News *content* and *packaging* are more clearly segregated. One person or group is responsible for getting interviews, sound, or vision (the content) that is then distributed to partners or purchasers for packaging into print, radio, television, or on-line news stories. The packaging might precede the gathering of content — with news forced to *fit* the size, shape or style of the package regardless of its inherent quality and values (Kingston 1998b, Osmond 1998).

> Content becomes less and less important, whereas for a traditional journalist the content is what matters and what should be given priority. But these days ... a great deal of effort goes into the look, rather than content. And the look is becoming all-important. (Osmond 1998)

The reliance on packaging is not surprising, given the 'pack mentality' of journalists (Sales 1998) and limited resources available to many newsrooms, though it favours media managers and those who have the resources to pre-package their own materials. This unbundling might also be a natural outcome of the growth of news bureaus, agencies, and national networks.

Where do these developments leave the Urban Jungle Pack, the mobile journalist's workstation of the future? The technology is available, it works, and it reflects a considerable investment and commitment from European CIT and media corporations. It presents potentially a tremendous tool for the foreign correspondent or roving reporter of the twenty-first century. Alternatively, it provides the means to turn any person in any location into a remote-controlled walking content generator. And what of the traditional news media? There is every reason to suggest they will survive, alongside on-line news and yet-to-be-developed forms of technology-mediated journalism. Their continued success might involve changes in the way news media do business. The Internet, for example, has revived and extended the reach of radio news, with live coverage of events and real-time broadcasting of news products delivered, using audio streaming software, through the desktop computer. The ABC's publication of transcripts and real-time delivery of its premiere news programs demonstrate this potential.

> The ABC's product is available now on the Internet, it's available anywhere in the world, and very shortly the output of my program *AM* will be available in FM quality on the Internet, and there will be the ability to look at the rundown of our program and say 'I want that, that, and that story', put it into a browser and either download it to listen to it when you want to, or to do your own filtering and filter out those stories you're not interested in and listen to them real time. (Cave 1998)

The continued success of a medium-diverse journalism will certainly require news organisations to identify their niche and build on the strengths of their medium. More importantly, it will require a willingness to look beyond the technological determinist visionaries and doomsayers to consider strategically and realistically the promises and challenges posed by technology and convergence.

Finally, if Australian journalists are going to deliver a news that matters, regardless of the medium in which it is delivered, they, their audiences, media owners, and governments need to actively engage in, and respond to, the existing challenges of commercialisation, competition, and corporatisation. Newsmakers and owners might believe technological solutions present a made-for-measure response to existing challenges, but new technological forms will prove, at best, a temporary panacea, unless underlying issues are confronted and resolved. Journalism will continue to struggle for respectability and acceptance, and attempts to maintain and increase audiences are most likely to fail in the long term, unless journalists, and their publics, are convinced that there is a genuine and passionate commitment, at all levels of the news organisation, to the delivery of news in the public interest.

DISCUSSION QUESTIONS

1   Obtain a copy of television and radio news programs (public and commercial) and the local newspaper (all from the same day). What similarities or differences are apparent? (Be aware that you do not have to prove one program is better than another.)
2   How does the medium of delivery affect the content of the program?

3   Compare the coverage of the same issue in all programs. How does the story differ across the various media?

Further reading

AJR Newslink 1999, 'Digital Feed', *http://ajr.newslink.org/ajrwww.html*, 27 September.

Media Studies Journal 1991, 'Media at the millennium', vol. 5, no. 4, The Freedom Forum Media Studies Center, Columbia University, New York.

The Freedom Forum On-line, 'Technology' 1999, *http://www.freedomforum.org/technology/welcome.asp*, 27 September.

Notes

1   This chapter will not debate the relative strengths and weaknesses of McLuhan's and Fiore's (1967) mantra 'the medium is the message': that *content* is insignificant, the *technology* or *medium of delivery* is the real determinant of the message received by the audience. Countless books, articles, stories, and essays have already done that. Instead, this chapter will consider the future prospects of broadcast and print journalism, and the potential impact of technological convergence on more traditional forms of news.

2   This bears elements of Marxist accounts of progress, where technological progress is an expression of the constant need of capital to extract profit (surplus value) from the labour/technology process. These accounts are the subject of significant analysis and discussion in *The Social Shaping of Technology* (Mackenzie and Wajcman, 1993).

Bibliography

AAP. See Australian Associated Press.

ABA 2000a, *ABA decides to impose licence conditions on 2UE* (press release), 7 February 2000, *http://www.aba.gov.au/about/public_relations/newsrel_2000/7nr2000.htm*, 16 June 2000.

——2000b, *ABA imposes licence conditions on 2UE* (press release), 21 March 2000, *http://www.aba.gov.au/about/public_relations/newsrel_2000/20nr2000.htm*, 16 June 2000.

ABC News Online 1999, 'Aussies warm to web', 6 September, *http://www.abc.net.au/news/1999/09/item19990906160024_1.htm*, 6 September.

ABC News Online 1999, 'Radio station limits endorsements for broadcasters', 18 July, *http://www.abc.net.au/news/1999/07/item19990718081653_1.htm*, 24 September.

Aboriginal and Torres Strait Islander Commission 1997, *A Plain English Guide to the Wik Case*, ATSIC, Canberra.

Adam, S. 1990, 'Journalism and the university: reporters, writers and critics', in Kathleen Jaeger (ed.), *The Idea of the University: 1789–1989*, University of King's College, Halifax.

——1993, *Notes Towards a Definition of Journalism: Understanding an Old Craft as an Art Form*, The Poynter Papers, No. 2, The Poynter Institute for Media Studies, St Petersburg, Florida.

Adkins, B. 1992, 'Arguing the point: the management and context of disputatious challenges in radio current affairs interviews', *Australian Journalism Review*, vol. 14, no. 2, pp. 37–48.

Age 1992, *Charter*, carried as an insert in the *Age*, Melbourne, 10 March.

AJR Newslink 1999, 'Digital feed', *http://ajr.newslink.org/ajrwww.html*, 27 September.

Albers, R. R. (n.d.), Profiles in journalism: the 'lone cowboy' gives way to the modern journalist, *http://www.naa.org/presstime/96/PTIME/modjour.html*, 27 September 1999.

Alexander, J. 1998, Andrew Olle Memorial Lecture, *The Media Report*, ABC Radio National, 19 November.

Alford, P. and Stewart, C. 1998, 'The scoop that was scuppered', the *Weekend Australian*, 20–21 June, Review section, pp. 6–8.

Ali, O. A. 1994, 'Roundtable', *Media Asia*, vol. 21, no. 2, p. 90.

Alleyne, M. D. 1997, *News revolution: political and economic decisions about global information*, Macmillan, London.

Altschull, J. H. 1984, *Agents of Power: The Role of the News Media in Human Affairs*, Longman, New York.

——1995, *Agents of Power: The Media and Public Policy*, Longman Publishers, White Plains.

——1997, 'A crisis of conscience: is community journalism the answer?', in J. Black (ed.), *The Public/Civic/Communitarian Journalism Debate*, Lawrence Erlbaum Associates, New Jersey, pp. 140–59.

——1998, 'A crisis of conscience: is community journalism the answer?', in J. Black (ed.), *Mixed News: The Public/Civic/Communitarian Journalism Debate*, Lawrence Erlbaum, New Jersey, pp. 141–2.

Anderson, B. 1984, *Imagined Communities: Reflections on the Origin and Spread of Nationalism*, Verso, London.

Anderson, R., Dardenne, R. and Killenberg, G. M. 1994, *The Conversation of Journalism: Communication, Community and the News*, Praeger, Westport.

——1997, 'The American newspaper as the public conversational commons', in J. Black (ed.), *Mixed News: The Public/Civic, Communitarian Journalism Debate*, Lawrence Erlbaum, New Jersey, pp. 96–117.

Andrews, A. R. 1997, 'Just what is a journalist?', *http://www.toad.net/~andrews/journalist.html*, 27 September.

APC. See Australian Press Council.

Archard, D. 1998, 'Privacy, the public interest and a prurient public', in M. Kieran (ed.), *Media Ethics*, Routledge, London, pp. 82–96.

Archer, J. 1996, *The Fourth Estate*, Harper Collins, London.

Armstrong, M., Lindsay, D. and Watterson, R. 1995, *Media Law in Australia* (third edn), Oxford University Press, Melbourne.

Arvidson, C. 1998, 'Matt Drudge says Internet will save news business', *http://www.freedomforum.org/professional/1998/6/3drudge.asp*, 23 September.

Associated Press 1996, 'Edison speaks', *Telegraph Herald*, 18 February, *www.thonline.com/th/news/1996/th0218/stories/3136.htm*, 23 September.

Atallah, P. 1991, 'Of homes and machines: TV, technology, and fun in America, 1944–1984', *http://kali.murdoch.edu.au/cntinuum/4.2/Atallah.html*, 5 March 1996.

ATSIC. see Aboriginal and Torres Strait Islander Commission.

Attorney-General for the State of New South Wales v. Television and Telecasters (Sydney) Pty Ltd (1998), *http://online.butterworths.com.au/unrep/98/9805428.htm*, 8 December 1998, pp. 1–10.

Australian Associated Press 1998, 'TV journalist avoids contempt charges over Halden', 22 December, *http://online.butterworths.com*, 11 January 1999, 1.

Australian Press Council 1998, *Aims, Principles and Complaints Procedure*, Archer Press, Sydney.

Australian 1999, 'Search for meaning, not just slick sloganeering', 25 October, p. 4.

Background Briefing 1995. 'Hindmarsh Island Royal Commission', 17 September, *http://www.abc.net.au/rn/talks/bbing/stories/s10792.htm*, 13 November 1999

——1997, 'Corporate PR: a threat to journalism', 30 March, *http://www.abc.net.au/rn/talks/bbing/stories/s10602.htm*, 15 January 1999.

Bacon, W. 1999, 'What is a journalist in a university?', *Media International Australia Incorporating Culture and Policy*, no. 90, pp. 79–90.

Baker, I. 1980, 'The gatekeeper chain: a two-step analysis of how journalists acquire and apply organisational news priorities', in P. Edgar (ed.), *The News in Focus: The Journalism of Exception*, Macmillan, Melbourne.

Bardoel, J. 1996, 'Beyond journalism: a profession between information society and civil society', *European Journal of Communication*, vol. 11, no. 3, pp. 283–302.

Barker, C. 1997, *Global Television: An Introduction*, Blackwell Publishers, Oxford.

Barney, R. D. 1997, 'A dangerous drift? The sirens' call to collectivism', in J. Black (ed.), *The Public/Civic/Communitarian Journalism Debate*, Lawrence Erlbaum Associates, New Jersey, pp. 72–93.

Baxter, J., Emmison, M. and Western, J. (eds) 1991, *Class Analysis and Contemporary Australia*, Macmillan, Melbourne.

Belay, G. 1996, 'The (re)construction and negotiation of cultural identities in the age of globalisation', in H. B. Mokros (ed.), *Interaction and Identity. Information and Behaviour*, vol. 5. Transaction, New Brunswick, NJ, pp. 319–45.

Bell, P. 1992, *Multicultural Australia in the Media: A Report to the Office of Multicultural Affairs*, Australian Government Publishing Service, Canberra.

Belsey A. and Chadwick R. (eds) 1992, *Ethical Issues in Journalism and the Media*, Routledge, London.

Benesh, S. 1998, 'The rise of solutions journalism', *Columbia Journalism Review*, March–April, *http://www.cjr.org/year/98/2/solutions.asp*, 2 November, 1999.

Berendt, J. 1994, *Midnight in the Garden of Good and Evil*, Vintage, London.

Berkowitz, D. (ed.) 1997, *Social meanings of news: A text-reader*, Sage, California.

Bird, R. 1997, *The End of News*, Irwin Publishing, Toronto.

Birkerts, S. 1987, 'Docu-fiction', in *An Artificial Wilderness: Essays on Twentieth Century Literature*, William Morrow and Company, New York.

Blue Angel Restaurant v. John Fairfax and Sons Ltd (1989), *Gazette of Law and Journalism*, vol. 11, p. 13.

Blythe, F. 1988, *Native Americans and the Press: Accurate Coverage or Stereotype?* tape transcript from AEJMC Conference, Portland, Oregon, 2–5 July.

Bogart, L. 1989, *Press and Public: Who Reads What, When, Where and Why in American Newspapers*, Lawrence Erlbaum Associates, Hillsdale, New Jersey.

——1991, *The American Media System and its Commercial Culture*, Columbia University, New York.

Bok, S. 1980, *Lying: Moral Choice in Public and Private Life*, Quartet, London.

——1982, *Secrets: On the Ethics of Concealment and Revelation*, OUP, Oxford.

Bordieu, P. 1998, *On Television and Journalism*, Pluto Press, London.

Boreland, M. and Smith, L. 1996, *Community Relations in Media Education: Representations of Ethnic Communities in Australian Print and Broadcast Media*, Deakin University, Geelong.

Bostock, L. 1997, *The Greater Perspective: Protocol and Guidelines for the Production of Film and Television on Aboriginal and Torres Strait Islander Communities*, Special Broadcasting Service, Sydney.

Bowman, D. 1988, *The Captive Press: Our Newspapers in Crisis and the People Responsible*, Penguin, Melbourne.

Bowman, L. 1993, 'Interviewing: establishing the context', *Australian Journalism Review*, vol. 15, no. 2, pp. 123–30.

——1994, 'How journalists' cultural dispositions affect news selection', *Australian Journalism Review*, vol. 16, no. 2, pp. 25–30.

Bowman, L. and McIlwaine, S. 1997, *Regional Journalism Education and Training Information Gathering Unit Three*, Regional Dailies Association, Sydney.

Bowman, L., McIlwaine, S. and Tapsall, S. 1996, *Regional Journalism Education and Training, RJET Information Gathering, Unit One*, Regional Dailies Association, Sydney.

Bowman, L., McIlwaine, S., Tapsall, S. and Hippocrates, C. 1996, *Regional Journalism Education and Training Information Gathering, Unit Two*, Regional Dailies Association, Sydney.

Boyd-Barrett, O. 1998, ' "Global" news agencies', in O. Boyd-Barrett and T. Rantanen (eds), *The Globalization of News*, Sage, London.

Boyd-Barrett, O. and Rantanen, T. (eds) 1998, *The Globalization of News*, Sage, London.

Braverman, H. 1974, *Labor and Monopoly Capital: The Degradation of Work in the Twentieth Century*, Monthly Review Press, New York.

Breed, W. 1955, 'Social control in the newsroom: a functional analysis', in D. Berkowitz (ed.) (1997) *Social Meanings of News: A Text-reader*, Sage Publications, Thousand Oaks, California, pp. 107–122.

Brennen, B. 1995, 'Cultural discourse of journalists: the material conditions of newsroom labor', in H. Hardt and B. Brennen (eds), *Newsworkers: Towards a History of the Rank and File*, University of Minnesota Press, Minneapolis.

Brill S. 1998, *The Media Report*, ABC Radio National, 19 November.

Brison S. 1998, 'The autonomy defense of free speech', *Ethics* vol. 108, January, pp. 312–39.

Broder, J. K. 1993, 'Newspapers and community', in J. Rosen (ed.), *Community Connectedness: Passwords for Public Journalism*, Poynter Institute for Media Studies, St Petersburg, Florida, pp. 13–16.

Brown, M. 1998, 'News consumption in the Internet age: audience shifts that can't be ignored', *Editor and Publisher*, *http://www.mediainfo.com/ephome/news/newshtm/minfocom/0398b.htm*, 27 September 1999.

Bryson, J. 1985, *Evil Angels*, Viking, Ringwood.

Buford, B. (ed.) 1993, *The Best of Granta Reportage*, Granta Books, London (reprinted as *The Granta Book of Reportage*, 1998 with Ian Jack as the new editor).

Burgoon, J. and Burgoon, M. 1980, 'Predictors of newspaper readership', *Journalism Quarterly*, Autumn, pp. 589–96.

Calcutt, Sir D. 1993, *Review of Press Self-Regulation*, Department of National Heritage, London.

Callahan, D. 1984, *Autonomy: A Moral Good, Not a Moral Obsession*, The Hastings Centre Report, October, Hastings Institute, New York.

Callaghan, G. 1998, 'Why seeing is not believing', *The Weekend Australian*, 4–5 April, pp. 4–5.

Callinicos, A. and Harman, C. 1989, *The Changing Working Class: Essays on Class Structure Today*, Bookmarks, London.

Cameron, D. and Lagan, B. 1999, 'John Laws admits $1m deal to stop radio attacks', *The Sydney Morning Herald*, 14 July, *http://www.smh.com.au/news/9907/14/pageone/pageone1.html*, 27 September 1999.

Capote, T. 1965, *In Cold Blood*, Random House, New York.

Carey, J. 1980, 'The university tradition in journalism education', *Carleton University Review*, vol. 2, no. 6, Summer, pp. 3–7.

——(ed.) 1987a, *The Faber Book of Reportage*, Faber Books, London.

——1987b, 'The press and public discourse', *The Center Magazine*, vol. 21, p. 14.

——1993a, 'Foreword' in *Notes Towards a Definition of Journalism: Understanding an Old Craft as an Art Form*, by G. S. Adam, The Poynter Papers: No. 2, The Poynter Institute for Media Studies, St Petersburg, Florida.

——1993b, 'May you live in interesting times', *Australian Journal of Communication*, vol. 20, no. 3, pp. 1–12.

——1995, 'The press, public opinion, and public discourse', in T. Glasser and C. Salmon (eds), *Public Opinion and the Communication of Consent*, The Guildford Press, New York.

——1997a, 'The press, public opinion, and public discourse: on the edge of the post-modern', in E. Stryker Munson and C. A. Warren (eds), *James Carey: A Critical Reader*, University of Minnesota Press, Minneapolis, pp. 228–57.

——1997b, 'The communications revolution and the professional communicator', in E. Stryker Munson and C. A. Warren (eds), *James Carey: A Critical Reader*, University of Minnesota Press, Minneapolis, pp. 128–43.

—— 1997c, 'Afterword/The culture in question', in E. Stryker Munson and C. A. Warren (eds), *James Carey: A Critical Reader*, University of Minnesota Press, Minneapolis, pp. 308–39.

——1997d, 'Communications and economics', in E. Stryker Munson and C. A. Warren (eds), *James Carey: A Critical Reader*, University of Minnesota Press, Minneapolis, pp. 60–75.

—— 1997e, 'Community, public, and journalism', in J. Black (ed.), *The Public/ Civic/Communitarian Journalism Debate*. Lawrence Erlbaum Associates, New Jersey, pp. 1–15.

Carey, J. and Quirk, J. 1992, 'The mythos of the electronic revolution', in Carey, J. (ed.), *Communication as Culture: Essays on Media and Society*, Routledge, New York, pp. 113–41.

Carroll, E. J. 1993, *Hunter: The Strange and Savage Life of Hunter S. Thompson*, Plume, New York.

Cavallin, J. 1998, 'European policies and regulations on media concentration', *International Journal of Communications Law and Policy*, *http://www.digital-law.net/IJCLP/1_1998/ijclp_webdoc_3_1_1998.html*, 26 August 1998.

Cave, P. 1998, personal interview with S. Tapsall, 19 November, Sydney.

Chadwick, P. 1998a, 'Breathing new life into journalism ethics', keynote address, Journalism Education Association Annual Conference, Yeppoon, 3 December.

Chadwick, P. 1998b, 'We all deserve privacy – even you, Rupert', the *Age*, 16 October, p. 17.

Chakravarti v. Advertiser Newspapers Ltd 1998, 154 ALR 294.

Chandler, D. 1995, *Technological or Media Determinism*, *http://www.aber.ac.uk/~dgc/tecdet.html*, 23 September 1999.

Charity, A. 1995, *Doing Public Journalism*, Guildford Press, New York.

Cheney, T. A. 1987, *Writing Creative Nonfiction*, Ten Speed Press, California.

Chibnall, S. 1977, *Law and Order News: An Analysis of Crime Reporting in the British Press*, Tavistock Publications, London.

Chowdhury, A. 1978, 'Development reporting: it gives us the chance to manoeuvre with honour', *IPI Report*, April–May, pp. 8–10.

Christians, C. and Carey, J. 1981, 'The logic and aims of qualitative research', in G. H. Stempel and B. H. Westley (eds), *Research Methods in Mass Communication*, Prentice-Hall, Englewood Cliffs.

Christians, C., Ferre, P. and Fackler, M. 1993, *Good News: Social Ethics and the Press*, Oxford University Press, New York.

Christians, C., Rotzoll, K. and Fackler, M. 1998, *Media Ethics: Cases and Moral Reasoning*, (fifth edn), Longman, New York.

Clarke, G. 1988, *Capote: A Biography*, Hamish Hamilton, London.

Clayton Powell III, A. 1998, 'What's wrong with new media? Same things as old media', *http://www.freedomforum.org/technology/1998/4/24newmedia.asp*, 23 September 1999.

——1999, 'Reporter's "work station of the future" debuts in Europe', *http://www.freedomforum.org/technology/1999/7/29urbanjunglepack.asp*, 20 September 1999.

Cohen, B. C. 1963, *The Press and Foreign Policy*, Princeton University Press, Princeton, New Jersey.

Committee of Concerned Journalists 1997, *Changing definitions of news*, *http://www.journalism.org/lastudy.htm*, 27 September 1999.

Conley, D. 1997, *The Daily Miracle: An Introduction to Journalism*, Oxford University Press, New York.

——1998, 'Birth of a novelist, death of a journalist', *Australian Studies in Journalism*, no. 7, pp. 46–73.

Connery, T. B. 1992, *A Sourcebook of American Literary Journalism: Representative Writers in an Emerging Genre*, Greenwood Press, New York.

Connolly, B. and Anderson, R. 1997 *Rats in the Ranks*, ABC, Sydney.

Connolly, C. 1998, 'Internet code of practice takes shape', *Internet Law Bulletin*, vol. 1, no. 2, pp. 17–18.

Cooper, T. 1989, *Communication Ethics and Global Change*, Longman, New York.

Corrigan, D. 1998–99, 'Professors say public journalism undermines SPJ ethics', *The St. Louis Journalism Review*, December–January, *http://www.webster.edu/%7Ereview/pjconcepts.html#ethics*, 2 November 1999.

Coulthart, R. 1999, 'Freedom of information', *http://sunday.ninemsn.com.au*, 17 February 1999.

Council for Aboriginal Reconciliation 1996, *Making the Grade: News Media and Indigenous Australia* (videotape), Council for Aboriginal Reconciliation, Canberra.

Craig, G. 1997, 'Plastic vision: an analysis of Reuters Financial television', paper presented at the Cultural Crossroads Conference organised by the Australian Key centre for Cultural and Media Policy, Sydney, November.

Cram, I. 1998, 'Beyond Calcutt: the legal and extra-legal protection of privacy interests in England and Wales', in M. Kieran (ed.), *Media Ethics*, Routledge, London.

Crang, M. 1998, *Cultural Geography*, Routledge, London.

Cronau, P. 1995, 'Manufacturing dissent', *Reportage*, Autumn, pp. 24–6.

Croteau, D. and Hoynes, W. 1994, *By Invitation Only: How the Media Limit the Political Debate*, Common Courage Press, Monroe.

——1997, *Media/Society: Industries, Images, and Audiences*, Pine Forge Press, Thousand Oaks, California.

Cryle, D. 1987, 'Snakes in the grass: the press and race relations at Moreton Bay 1846–47', in R. Fisher (ed.), *Brisbane: Aboriginal, Alien, Ethnic*, Brisbane History Group Papers, no. 5, pp. 23–34.

——1996, 'Stability or stagnation?: the regional press', in D. Cryle, G. Griffin and S. Stehlik (eds), *Futures for Central Queensland*, Central Queensland University, Rockhampton.

——1997, 'Journalism and status: an historical case study approach', *Australian Journalism Review*, vol. 19, no. 1, pp. 171–9.

Cudlipp, H. 1980, *The Prerogative of the Harlot: Press Barons and Power*, Bodley Head, London.

Culhane, D. 1998, *The Pleasure of the Crown: Anthropology, Law and First Nations*, Toronto, Talonbooks.

Cunneen, C. 1999, *Racial Stereotypes Kill*, *www.austlii.edu.au/au/other/media/Australian%20Courts/Free%20Speech%20Comentary/1257.htm*, 29 November.

Cunningham, S. and Flew, T. 1998, 'Journalism versus culture: a pointless game', *The Australian*, 25 March, p. 41.

Cunningham, S., Tapsall, S., Ryan, Y., Stedman, L., Bagdon, K. and Flew, T. 1998, *New Media and Borderless Education: A Review of the Convergence between Global Media Networks and Higher Education Provision*, Department of Employment, Education, Training and Youth Affairs, Canberra.

Curran, J. and Gurevitch, M. 1996, *Mass Media and Society*, Arnold, New York.

Curthoys, A. 1991, *Television before Television*, *http://kali.murdoch.edu.au/~cntinuum/4.2/Curthoys.html*, 15 September 1999.

Davis, G. 1998, 'Witness: the verdict', *The Bulletin*, 17 November, pp. 42–5.

Dawkins, R. 1989, *The Selfish Gene*, Oxford University Press, Oxford.

Day, L. 1997, *Ethics in Media Communications: Cases and Controversies*, Wadsworth, New York.

De Fleur, M. L. and Ball-Rokeach, S. 1982, *Theories of Mass Communication* (fourth edn), Longman, New York.

Dennis, E. 1989, *Re-shaping the Media*, Sage, London.

Dennis, E. 1991, 'Media at the millennium', *Media Studies Journal*, vol. 5, no. 4, pp. 51–66.

Denovan, C. 1998, personal interview with S. Tapsall, 18 November, Melbourne.

Denton, F. and Thorson, E. 1995, *Civic Journalism: Does it Work?*, Pew Center for Civic Journalism, Washington DC.

Desbarats, P. 1996, *Guide to Canadian News Media*, Harcourt and Brace, Toronto.

Diamond, E. 1997, 'Civic journalism: an experiment that didn't work', *Columbia Journalism Review*, July–August, *http://www.cjr.org/year/97/4/civic.asp*, 2 November 1999.

Director of Public Prosecutions (Commonwealth) v. United Telecasters Sydney (in liquidation) (1992) 7 BR 364, quoted in *Attorney-General for the State of New South Wales v. Television and Telecasters (Sydney) Pty Ltd* (1998), *http://online.butterworths.com.au/unrep/98/9805428.htm*, 8 December 1998, 1–10.

Dixit, Kunda 1994, 'Global news: a view from the south', *Who's Telling the Story: A Conference on Media and Development in Australia and the Region*, Community Aid Abroad, Melbourne, pp. 20–5.

Doheny-Farina, S. 1995, 'The Glorious Revolution of 1971', *http://sunsite.unc.edu/cmc/mag/1995/oct/last.html*, 23 September 1999.

Dombkins, M. 1993, 'The impact of technology and environmental factors on newspaper organisational design', *Australian Journalism Review*, vol. 15, no. 1, January–June, pp. 29–51.

Dougary, G. 1994, *The Executive Tart and Other Myths: Media Women Talk Back*, Virago, London.

Drucker, P. F. 1989, *The New Realities*, Mandarin, London.

Duffy, M. 1998, 'Kroger bias charge a sad reflection on the ABC', *The Weekend Australian*, p. 25, 14–15 February.

Dufresne, M. 1998, 'Why midnight may be darker than you think', *Columbia Journalism Review*, May/June, pp. 78–9.

Durkheim, E. 1964, *The Division of Labor in Society*, translated by George Simpson, The Free Press, New York. First published 1933.

Eagleton, T. 1996, *Literary Theory: An Introduction* (second edn), Basil Blackwell, London.

Edge, D. 1995, 'The social shaping of technology', in N. Heap, R. Thomas, G. Einon, R. Mason and H. Mackay (eds), *Information, Technology and Society*, Sage Publications, London.

Edgeworth, B and M. Newcity 1992, 'Politicians, defamation law and the "public figure" defence', *Law in Context*, vol. 10, no. 1, pp. 39–62.

Eggerking, K. and Plater, D. (eds) 1993, *Signposts: A Guide to Reporting Aboriginal, Torres Strait Islander and Ethnic affairs*, Australian Centre for Independent Journalism, University of Technology, Sydney.

Eggerking, K., Scott, P. and Sheridan Burns, L. 1998, *The Media and Indigenous Australians Project*, Department of Journalism, University of Queensland, St Lucia.

Eisenberg, J. 1998, 'Strictness rules', *Gazette of Law and Journalism*, no. 47, pp. 4–10.

Elliott D. 1988, 'All is not relative: essential shared values of the press', *Journal of Mass Media Ethics*, vol. 3, no. 1, June, p. 29.

Ellul, J. 1964, *The Technological Society* (translated by J. Wilkinson), Alfred A. Knopf, New York.

Engel, M. 1996, *Tickle the Public: One hundred Years of the Popular Press*, Victor Gollancz, London.

Epstein, E. J. 1974, *Between Fact and Fiction: The Problem of Journalism*, Vintage, New York.

Ericson, R. V., Baranek, P. M. and Chan, J. 1987, *Visualising Deviance: A Study of News Organisation*, Open University Press, Milton Keynes.

——1989, *Negotiating Control*, University of Toronto Press, Toronto.

Ewart, J. 1997a, 'Journalists, readership and writing', *Australian Studies in Journalism*, no. 6, University of Queensland, pp. 83–103.

Ewart, J. 1997b, 'The scabsuckers – regional journalists' representation of Indigenous Australians', *Asia Pacific Media Educator*, no. 3, July–December, pp. 108–17.

Fallows, J. 1996, *Breaking the News: How the Media Undermine American Democracy*, Pantheon, New York.

Feola, C. J. 1995, 'Making the cut: enhance your job opportunities by developing your computer skills,' *Quill*, vol. 83, no. 2, pp. 24–6.

Ferguson, R. 1998, *Representing Race: Ideology, Identity and the Media*, Arnold, London.

Fidler, R. 1991, 'Newspapers II: mediamorphosis, or the transformation of newspapers into a new medium', *Media Studies Journal*, vol. 5, no. 4, pp. 115–25.

Fifer, S. and Sacks, M. 1997, 'The price of international free speech: nations deal with defamation on the Internet', *Depaul Journal of Art and Entertainment Law*, vol. 8, no. 1, pp. 1–22.

Fishman, M. 1980, *Manufacturing the News*, University of Texas Press, Austin.

Forde, S. 1997, 'A descriptive look at the public role of the Australian independent alternative press', *Asia Pacific Media Educator*, no. 3, July–December, pp. 118–30.

——1998, 'The development of the alternative press in Australia', *Media International Australia*, no. 87, pp. 114–33.

Franklin, B. 1997, *Newszak and News Media*, Arnold, London.

Franklin, J. 1986, *Writing for Story: Craft Secrets of Dramatic Nonfiction by a Two-time Pulitzer Prize Winner*, Plume Books, New York.

Freedom Forum Online, the 'Technology', *http://www.freedomforum.org/technology/welcome.asp*, 27 September 1999.

Freedom of Information Act 1982 (Cwlth), *http://www.austlii.edu.au/au/legis/cth/consol_act/foia1982222/*, *http://www.austlii.edu.au/au/legis/cth/consol_act/foia1982222/* (last accessed 13 June 2000)

Fuller, J. 1996, 'News and literary technique', in *News Values: Ideas for an Information Age*, University of Chicago Press, Chicago.

Galtung, J. and Vincent, R. C. 1992, *Toward a New World Information and Communication Order?*, Hampton Press, Cresskill, New Jersey.

Gandy, O. 1998, *Communication and Race: A Structural Perspective*, Arnold, Great Britain.

Gans, H. 1979, *Deciding What's News*, Pantheon, New York.

Garner, H. 1995, *The First Stone*, Pan Macmillan, Sydney.

——1996, *True Stories*, Text Publishing, Melbourne.

Garson, B. 1988, *The Electronic Sweatshop: How Computers are Transforming the Office of the Future into the Factory of the Past*, Simon and Schuster, New York.

Gartner, M. 1998, 'Public journalism – seeing through the gimmicks', in E. Lambeth, P. Meyer and E. Thorson, *Assessing Public Journalism*, University of Missouri Press, Columbia, Missouri, pp. 226–31.

Gaunt, P. 1990, *Choosing the News: The Profit Factor in News Selection*, Greenwood Press, New York.

Geimann, S. 1996, Acceptance Speech by Steve Geimann, SPJ President, National Convention of the SPJ, 21 September 1996, Washington, DC. *http://idi.net/dcspj/resources/data/geiman.html*, 27 September 1999.

Glasser, T. and Craft, S. 1997, 'Public journalism and the prospects for press account-
    ability', in J. Black (ed.), *Mixed News: The Public/civic/communitarian Journalism
    Debate*, Lawrence Erlbaum, New Jersey.
Goldsworthy, K. 1996, *Helen Garner*, Australian Writers Series, Oxford University Press,
    Melbourne.
Goodall, H. 1993, 'Constructing a riot: television news and Aborigines', *Media Information
    Australia*, no. 68, pp. 70–7.
Gordon D. and Kittross M. 1999a, 'Data privacy', in D. Gordon, M. Kittross and C. Reuss
    (eds), *Controversies in Media Ethics*, Longman, New York, pp. 164–81.
——1999b, 'Private lives, public interests' in D. Gordon, M. Kittross and C. Reuss,
    Controversies in Media Ethics, Longman, New York, pp. 148–63
Gordon D., Kittross, J. and Reuss, C. 1999, *Controversies in Media Ethics*, Longman, New
    York.
Grabosky, P. and Wilson, P. 1989, *Journalism and Justice: How Crime is Reported*, Pluto
    Press, Sydney.
Gramsci, A. 1971, *Selections from the Prison Notebooks*, edited and translated by Q. Hoare
    and G. Nowell Smith, Lawrence and Wishart, London.
——1988a, *The Antonio Gramsci Reader: Selected Writings 1916–1935*, translated and edited
    by David Forgacs, Shocken Books, New York.
——1988b, *A Gramsci Reader: Selected Writings 1916–1935*, translated and edited by David
    Forgacs, Lawrence and Wishart, London.
Granato, L. 1991, *Reporting and Writing News*, Prentice Hall, Melbourne.
Grattan M. 1998, *Editorial Independence: An Outdated Concept?*, Australian Journalism
    Monographs, no. 1, Department of Journalism, University of Queensland.
Green, K. 1994, 'Computer-assisted reporting — sources from cyberspace', *Australian
    Studies in Journalism*, vol. 3, pp. 219–30.
Greenwall, H. J. 1957, *Northcliffe: Napoleon of Fleet Street*, Wingate, London.
Griffin, G. 1998, 'Theorising photojournalism', in M. Breen (ed.), *Journalism Theory
    and Practice*, Macleay Press, Sydney, pp. 301–29.
Guerke, L. and Hirst, M. 1996, 'Across the genres: how journalism is changing in the
    1990s', *Australian Journalism Review*, vol. 18, no. 1, pp. 117–33.
Guerke, L. and Hirst, M. 1996, 'Across the genres: how journalism is changing in the
    1990s', *http://www.csu.edu.au/faculty/arts/commun/jea/ajr/hirst.htm*, 1 December
    1997.
Guissani, B. 1997, 'A new media tells different stories',
    http://www.firstmonday.dk/issues/issue2_4/giussani/index.html, 27 September 1999.
Gunaratne, S. 1996, 'Old wine in a new bottle: public journalism movement in the United
    States and the erstwhile NWICO debate', paper presented to the IAMCR
    Conference, Sydney, 18–22 August.
Hackett, R. and Zhao, Y. 1998, *Sustaining Democracy? Journalism and the Politics of
    Objectivity*, Garamond Press, Toronto.
Hall, S. 1975, 'Introduction', in A. C. H. Smith (ed.), *Paper Voices: The Popular Press and
    Social Change*, Chatto and Windus, London.
——1981, 'The whites of their eyes: racist ideologies and the media', in G. Bridges and
    R. Brunt (eds), *Silver Linings: Some Strategies for the Eighties*, Lawrence and Wishart,
    London.

——1982, 'The rediscovery of "ideology": return of the repressed in media studies', in M. Gurevitch, T. Bennett, J. Curran and J. Woollacott (eds), *Culture, Society and the Media*, Methuen, London, pp. 56–90.

——1983a, 'Ideology and the modern world: an address by Stuart Hall', La Trobe University, Department of Sociology and Department of Legal Studies, 4 April.

——1983b, 'The problem of ideology: Marxism without guarantees', in B. Matthews (ed.), *Marx 100 Years On*, Lawrence and Wishart, London.

——1992, *Discourse and Power*, Polity Press, London.

Hall, S., Crichter, C., Jefferson, T., Clarke, J. and Roberts, B. 1978, *Policing the Crisis*, Macmillan, London.

Hallin, D. C. 1986, *The 'Uncensored War': The Media and Vietnam*, Oxford University Press, New York.

——1994, *We Keep America on Top of the World: Television Journalism and the Public Sphere*, Routledge, London.

Hannan, E. 1998, 'United Kennetts ask for privacy', the *Age*, 9 October, p. 3.

Hanson D. 1970, *From Kingdom to Commonwealth*, Harvard University Press, Cambridge, Massachusetts.

Hardt, H. and Brennen, B. (eds) 1995, *Newsworkers: Toward a History of the Rank and File*, University of Minnesota Press, Minneapolis.

Harrington, W. 1997, *Intimate Journalism: The Art and Craft of Reporting Everyday Life*, Sage Publications, California.

Hartley, J. and McKee, A. 1996, *Telling Both Stories: Indigenous Australia and the Media*, Conference Proceedings of the National Media Forum, Arts Enterprise, Edith Cowan University, Perth.

Hartley, J. 1982, *Understanding News*, Methuen and Co., London.

——1992, *The Politics of Pictures: The Creation of the Public in the Age of Popular Media*, Routledge, London.

——1995, 'Journalism and modernity', *Australian Journal of Communication*, vol. 22, no. 2, pp. 20–30.

——1996, *Popular Reality: Journalism, Modernity and Popular Culture*, Arnold, New York.

——1997, *Popular Reality: Journalism, Modernity and Popular Culture*, Arnold, London.

—1999, 'What is journalism? The view from under a stubbie cap', in *Media Wars, Media International Australia incorporating Culture and Policy*, no. 90, p. 26.

Harvey, C. 1994, 'Tom Wolfe's Revenge', *American Journalism Review*, September/October, pp. 40–6.

Hausman, C. 1994, 'Information age ethics: privacy ground rules for navigating in cyberspace', *Journal of Mass Media Ethics*, vol. 9, no. 3, pp. 135–44.

Hedebro, G. 1982, *Communication and Social Change in Developing Nations: A Critical View*, Iowa State University Press, Ames, Iowa.

Heinich, R., Molenda, M., Russell, J. and Smaldino, S. 1996, *Instructional Media and Technologies for Learning* (fifth edn), Prentice-Hall, New Jersey.

Henderson, I. 1998, 'Harradine ups ante on Wik poll', the *Australian*, 21 June, p. 1.

Henningham, J. 1990, 'Is journalism a profession', in J. Henningham (ed.) *Issues In Australian Journalism*, Longman Cheshire, Melbourne.

——1993, 'How journalists lean', *Independent Monthly*, March, p. 21.

——1998, 'The Australian journalist', in Breen, M. (ed.), *Journalism: Theory and Practice*, Macleay Press, Paddington.

Herbert, J. 1997, 'Journalism education at the tertiary level', *Australian Journalism Review*, vol. 19, no. 1, pp. 7–18.

Herman, E. and McChesney, R. 1997, *The Global Media: The New Missionaries of Corporate Capitalism*, Cassell, London and Washington.

Herman, E. S. 1986, 'Gatekeeper versus propaganda models: a critical American perspective', in P. Golding, G. Murdock and P. Schlesinger (eds), *Communicating Politics: Mass Communications and the Political Process*, Holmes and Meier, New York, pp. 171–95.

Herman, E. S. and Chomsky, N. 1988, *Manufacturing Consent: The Political Economy of the Mass Media*, Random House, New York.

Hersey, J. 1989, 'The legend on the license', in *Killing the Messenger: 100 Years of Media Criticism*, Columbia University Press, New York.

Hester, A. L. 1987, 'The role of the Third World journalist', in A. L. Hester and W. L. J. To (eds), *Handbook for Third World Journalists*, University of Georgia, Athens, Georgia, pp. 5–12.

Hinch's case. *Hinch v. Attorney-General* [Vic.] (1987) 164 CLR 15.

Hippocrates, C. 1998, 'Public journalism: will it work in Australia?', *http://www.dcita.gov.au/crf/papers98.htm*, 3 November 1999.

——1999, 'Public journalism: the media's intellectual journey', *Media Information Australia*, no. 90, February, pp. 65–78

Hippocrates, C. and Meadows, M. 1996, *Race Reporter: A Report on an Investigation into the Media and the Representation of Race Relations*, Queensland Anti-Discrimination Commission, Brisbane.

Hirst, M. 1993, 'Class, mass media and the 1993 election', *Australian Journal of Communication*, vol. 20, no. 2, pp. 28–43.

——1997, 'MEAA Code of Ethics for journalists: an historical and theoretical overview', *Media International Australia*, no. 83, February, pp. 63–77.

——1998a, 'Raymond Williams: the godfather of media studies', proceedings Journalism Education Association Annual Conference 1997, University of Western Sydney, Sydney.

——1998b, 'From Gonzo to PoMo: hunting new journalism', in M. Breen (ed.), *Journalism Theory and Practice*, Macleay Press, Sydney.

Hoagland, J. H. 1997, 'Some perspectives on the changing media', paper delivered at The Journalist in Cyberspace Conference, 11–12 October 1997, organised by the Warsaw Journalism Centre, text supplied by author.

Hogan, A. 1997, 'It's popular more than vulgar', *The Australian*, 21 November, p. 15.

Hollis, P. 1970, *The Pauper Press: A study in the Working-class Radicalism of the 1830s*, Oxford University Press, Oxford.

Holub, R. 1992, *Antonio Gramsci: Beyond Marxism and Postmodernism*, Routledge, London.

Horne, D. 1994, 'A market place of ideas?', in Julianne Schultz (ed.), *Not Just Another Business: Journalists, Citizens and the Media*, Pluto Press, Sydney.

Houston, B. 1996, *Computer-Assisted Reporting: A Practical Guide*, St Martin's Press, New York.

Hoyt, M. 1992, 'The Wichita experiment: what happens when a newspaper tries to connect readership and citizenship?', *Columbia Journalism Review*, vol. 31, no. 2, pp. 42–7.

HREOC Race Discrimination Unit 1996,*The Racial Hatred Act: A Guide for People Working in the Media*, Canberra.

Hume, E. 1995, 'Tabloids, talk radio and the future of news: technology's impact on journalism', The Annenberg Washington Program in Communications Policy Studies of Northwestern University, *http://www.annenberg.nwu.edu/pubs/tabloids*, 27 September 1999.

Hunter, P. 1997, 'The Wik decision: unnecessary extinguishment', in G. Hiley (ed.), *The Wik Case: Issues and Implications*, Butterworths, Sydney.

Hurst, J. 1988, *The Walkleys: Australia's Best Journalists in Action*, John Kerr Press, Richmond.

Hurst, J. and White, S. 1994, *Ethics and the Australian News Media*, Macmillan Education Press, South Melbourne.

Idid, S. A. and Pawanteh, L. 1989, 'Media, ethnicity and national unity: A Malaysian report', *Media Asia*, vol. 16, no. 2, pp. 78–85.

Internet Industry Association 1998a, *Submission to the Select Committee on Information Technologies in Respect of Self-Regulation in the Information and Communication Industries*, *http://www.iia.net.au/news/980102.html*, 24 August 1998, pp. 1–8.

Internet Industry Association 1998b, *IIA Code to form Central Element of Industry Self-governance in Australia*, media release, *http://www.iia.net.au/news/981207.html*, 15 January 1999, pp. 1–2.

Internet Industry Association 1998c, *Internet Industry Code of Practice 8 December*, *http://www.iia.net.au/Code4.html*, 15 January 1999, pp. 1–17.

Itule, B. and Anderson D. 1991, *News Writing and Reporting* (fourth edn), Wm C. Brown, Dubuque.

Jackson, W. 1997, 'The press cops out', *New York Times*, 7 October, p. 105.

Jakubowicz, A. 1990, *Racism, Racist Violence and the Media*, Human Rights and Equal Opportunity Commission, Sydney.

Jakubowicz, A., Goodall, H., Martin J., Mitchell, T., Randall, L. and Seneviratne, K. 1994, *Racism, Ethnicity and the Media*, Allen & Unwin, St Leonards.

Jakubowicz, A. and Seneviratne, K. 1996, *Ethnic Conflict and the Australian Media*, Australian Centre for Independent Journalism, University of Technology, Sydney.

Jakubowicz, K. 1997, 'Does journalism have a future? A few preliminary answers', paper delivered to The Journalist in Cyberspace Conference, 11–12 October, Warsaw Journalism Centre, *http://www.uiowa.edu/wjcc/wjckj.html*, 1 December 1997.

James v. Robinson 1963, 109 CLR 593.

Jervis, R. 1987, *News Sense*, Adelaide Newspapers Pty Ltd, Adelaide.

Jhally, S. 1993, 'Communications and the materialist conception of history: Marx, Innis and technology', *http://kali.murdoch.edu.au/~cntinuum/7.1/Jhally.html*, 15 April 1996.

Johnston, G. 1964, *My Brother Jack*, Fontana Modern Novels, London.

Johnson, J. T. 1994, 'Applied cybernetics and its implications for education for journalism', *Australian Journalism Review*, vol. 16, no. 2, pp. 55–66.

Jones, B. 1996, *Sleepers, Wake!* (fifth edn), Oxford University Press, Melbourne.

——1998, 'What kind of Web? The risks of exclusion', paper presented at the 7th International World Wide Web conference (WWW7), 17 April, Brisbane, Australia.

Jopson, D. 1999, 'Hindmarsh fallout: a bridge writ large', *Sydney Morning Herald*, 2 March, *http://www.smh.com.au/news/9903/02/features/features1.html*, 12 November 1999.

Katz, J. 1999, 'Newspapers losing core business that they could keep', *The Freedom Forum Online*, *http://www.freedomforum.org/technology/1999/4/20katz.asp*, 23 September 1999.

Keane J. 1991, *The Media and Democracy*, Polity, Cambridge.

Keeble, R. 1994, *The Newspapers' Handbook*, Routledge, New York.

Kelly, P. 1994, 'Bound for disappointment on the highway from heaven to hell', in Julianne Schultz (ed.), *Not Just Another Business: Journalists, Citizens and the Media*, Pluto Press, Sydney.

Kerrane, K. and Yagoda, B. 1997, *The Art of Fact: A Historical Anthology of Literary Journalism*, Scribner, New York.

Kieran M. 1997, *Media Ethics: A Philosophical Approach*, Praeger, Westport.

——1998, *Media Ethics*, Routledge, London.

Kilminster, R. (1997), 'Globalization as an emergent concept', in Alan Scott (ed.), *The Limits of Globalization: Cases and Arguments*, Routledge, London and New York.

King, J. 1997, 'Principles, professionalism and philosophy', *Australian Journalism Review*, vol. 19, no. 1, pp. 19–33.

Kingston, M. 1998a, Keynote address, Journalism Education Association Annual Conference, 2 December, Yeppoon.

——1998b, personal interview with S. Tapsall, C. Varley and C. Jenkins, 6 December, Yeppoon.

Kirby, M. 1994, 'Press freedom – a very fragile right', *Foundation Law*, *http://www.fl.asn.au/resources/kirby/papers/19940503_pressf.html*, 17 August 1998, pp. 1–5.

——1998a, 'The globalisation of the media and judicial independence', *Foundation Law*, *http://www.fl.asn.au/resources/kirby/papers/19980601_speakfre.html*, 9 October 1998, pp. 1–17

——1998b, 'International dimensions of cyberspace law: protection of privacy and human rights in the digital age', *Foundation Law*, *http://www.fl.asn.au/resources/kirby/papers19980630_unespriv.html*, 17 August 1998, pp. 1–16.

Koch, T. 1990, *The News as Myth: Fact and Context in Journalism*, Greenwood Press, New York.

Koppel, T. 1997, 'They take the risks, yet WE are afraid', *http://www.cpj.org/awards97/koppel.html*, 23 September 1999.

Krause, T. 1999, 'Goodbye to all that', *Media*, the *Australian*, 29 April, p. 7.

Kunkel, T. 1995, *Genius in Disguise: Harold Ross of the New Yorker*, Random House, New York, pp. 369–74.

Kurtz, H. 1993, *Media Circus: The Trouble with America's Newspapers*, Time Books, New York.

Lange v. Australian Broadcasting Corporation (1997) 71 ALJR 818; 145 ALR 96.

Langton, M. 1993, '*Well, I Heard it on the Radio and I Saw it on the Television': An Essay for the Australian Film Commission on the Politics and Aesthetics of Filmmaking by and about Aboriginal People and Things*, Australian Film Commission, Sydney.

Lappin, T. 1995, 'Deja Vu all over again', *Wired, 3.05*, http://www.hotwired.com/wired/3.05/features/dejavu.html, 30 May 1995.

Lauterer, J. 1995, *Community Journalism: The Personal Approach*, Iowa State University Press, Ames, Iowa.

Lawson, S. 1998, 'Sidelined—but not entirely lost in translation: some lessons from Indonesia on writing and the press', *Southern Review*, vol. 31, no. 1, pp. 74–87.

Lee, J. A. 1990, *Report of the Royal Commission of Inquiry into the Arrest, Charging and Withdrawal of charges against Harold James Blackburn and Matters Associated Therewith,* NSW Government Printer, Sydney.

Lee, K. Y. 1992, 'Discipline versus democracy', *Far Eastern Economic Review*, 10 December, p. 29.

Lent, J. A. 1977, 'A Third World news deal? Part one: the guiding light', *Index on Censorship*, vol. 6, no. 5, September–October, pp. 17–26.

——1979, *Topics in Third World Mass Communication: Rural and Development Journalism, Cultural Imperialism, Research and Development*, Asian Research Service, Hong Kong.

Lichtenberg J. 1987, 'Foundations and limits of freedom of the press', *Philosophy and Public Affairs*, vol. 16, no. 4, Fall, pp. 329–55.

Lippmann, W. 1929, *Public Opinion* (originally published 1922, Macmillan, New York) George Allen & Unwin, London.

Lloyd C. and Hippocrates C. 1997, 'Public journalism, public participation and Australian citizenship', *Culture and Policy*, vol. 8, no. 2, pp. 9–21.

Locke J. 1689, in Yolton J. (ed.) 1977, *The Locke Reader: Selections from the Works of John Locke*, Cambridge University Press, London.

Loo, E. 1992, 'It's still black and white', *The Koori Mail*, 18 November.

——1994, 'Teaching development journalism in the reporting of cultural diversity', *Australian Journalism Review*, vol. 16, no. 2, pp. 1–10.

——1995, 'Teaching community service reporting values as an identifiable component of Asian-centred journalism', Asian Values in Journalism conference, AMIC, Kuala Lumpur, 24–25 August.

——1996, 'Value formation in journalism education in Asia', in *Asian Values in Journalism*, ed. M. Masterton (ed.), AMIC, Singapore, pp. 114–23.

Lounsberry, B. 1990, *The Art of Fact*, Greenwood Press, Connecticut.

Lounsberry, B. and Talese, G. (eds) 1995, *Creative Nonfiction: The Literature of Reality*, Harper Collins, New York.

Love, M. 1997, 'The farmgate effect', *Native Title News*, vol. 3, no. 1, March, pp. 11–12.

Mac An Ghaill, M. 1999, *Contemporary Racisms and Ethnicities*, Open University Press, Birmingham.

MacKenzie, D. and Wajcman, J. 1993, 'Introductory essay', in D. MacKenzie and J. Wajcman (eds), *The Social Shaping of Technology*, Open University Press, Milton Keynes, pp. 2–25.

Mahathir, M. 1985, 'A prescription for a socially responsible press', *Media Asia*, vol. 12, no. 4, pp. 212–15.

Malcolm, J. 1990, *The Journalist and the Murderer*, Bloomsbury, London.

——1994, *The Silent Woman*, Picador, London.

Mander, J. 'Four arguments for the elimination of television', *http://www.hrc.wmin.ac.uk/campaigns/ef/dt/elimtv.html*, 5 February 1998.

Mann, F. 1998, ' "New media" brings a new set of problems', *http://www.poynter.org/research/nm/nm_mann98.htm*, 27 September 1999.

Manne, A. 1998, 'Autonomy vs obligation', *The Australian's Review of Books*, 3–4 July, pp. 12–16.

Marshall, S. 'Prelude to Vegas: Neil Postman gets interviewed', *http://www.channel-zero.com/issue1/postman1.html*, 5 February 1998.

Marvin, C. 1988, *When Old Technologies Were New: Thinking About Electric Communication in the Late Nineteenth Century*, Oxford University Press, New York.

Marx, K. 1993, 'The machine versus the worker', in D. MacKenzie and J. Wajcman (eds), *The Social Shaping of Technology*, Open University Press, Milton Keynes, pp. 79–80.

Mason case. *Attorney-General for NSW v. TCN Channel Nine Pty Ltd* (1990) 20 NSWLR 368.

Masterton, M. and Patching, R. 1990, *Now the News in Detail* (second edn), Deakin University Press, Melbourne.

McChesney, R. 1997, *The Global Media Giants: The Nine Firms that Dominate the World*, *http://www.fair.org/extra/9711/gmg.html*, 16 December 1998, pp. 1–13.

McCormick, C. 1995, *Constructing Danger: The Mis/representation of Crime in the News*, Fernwood Publishing, Halifax.

McGregor, C. 1983, *Soundtrack for the Eighties*, Hodder and Stoughton, Sydney.

McGregor, J. 1994, ' "New" news and the 1993 general election in New Zealand', *Australian Journalism Review*, vol. 16, no. 2, pp. 93–101.

McGregor, J., Comrie, M. and Campbell, J. 1998, 'Public journalism and proportional representation: the New Zealand experiment', *Australian Journalism Review*, vol. 20, no. 1, pp. 1–22.

McGregor, R. 1999, 'Not a true pointer to main event', *The Australian*, 26 October, p. 7.

McKee, A. 1998, 'Suggestions and advice for reporting on Indigenous issues', unpublished report from the Reporting on Indigenous Affairs Workshop of the National Media Forum at Clontarf Aboriginal College, Perth, Western Australia, March, Department of Communications, Edith Cowan University.

McKeen, W. 1995, *Tom Wolfe*, Twayne's United States Authors Series, No. 650, Twayne Publishers, New York.

McKnight, D. 1996, 'Public journalism, citizenship and strategies for change', *http://www.gu.edu.au/centre/cmp/McKnight.html*, 3 November 1999.

McLuhan, M. and Fiore, Q. 1967, *The Medium is the Message*, Penguin Books, Middlesex.

McManus, J. 1994, *Market-Driven Journalism: Let the Citizen Beware*, Sage, California.

——1997, 'Serving the public and serving the market: a conflict of interest', *Journal of Mass Media Ethics*, vol. 7, no. 4, pp. 196–208.

McMasters, P. 1997, 'Providing answers or raising questions', in *The Case For and Against Civic Journalism*, *http://www.fac.org/publicat/campaign/lth96sb3.htm*, 12 June 2000.

McNair, B. 1998, *The Sociology of Journalism*, Arnold, London.

MacNeil, R. 1995, 'Regaining dignity: let's get back to being journalists', *Media Studies Journal*, vol. 9, no. 3, Summer, pp. 103–111.

McQuail, D. 1994, *Mass Communication Theory* (third edn), Sage Publications, London.

McQueen, H. 1977, *Australia's Media Monopolies*, Widescope, Melbourne.

MEAA. See Media, Entertainment and Arts Alliance.

Meade, A., Boreham, T. and Spencer, M. 1999, 'Laws row worsens as MPs intervene', the *Australian*, 17 July, *http://www.theaustralian.com.au/masthead/theoz/state/4405121.htm*, 27 September 1999.

Meadows, M. 1987, 'People power: reporting or racism?' *Australian Journalism Review*, vol. 9, nos 1 and 2, pp. 102–12.

——1988, 'Getting the right message across: inadequacies in existing codes make imperative the development of a code of conduct for Australian journalists reporting on race, *Australian Journalism Review*, vol. 10. January–December, pp. 140–53.

——1993, 'The way people want to talk: media representation and Indigenous media responses in Australia and Canada', unpublished PhD thesis, Faculty of Humanities, Griffith University, Brisbane.

——1994a, 'Lost opportunities: the media, land rights and Mabo', *Media Information Australia*, no. 71, pp. 100–9.

——1994b, 'At the cultural frontier', in J. Schultz (ed.) 1994, *Not Just Another Business: Journalists, Citizens and the Media*, Pluto Press, Australia, Leichhardt.

——1995, 'Sensitivity not censorship: reporting cultural diversity in Australia', *Australian Journalism Review*, vol. 17, no. 2, pp. 18–27.

——1997a, 'Perfect match: the media and Pauline Hanson', *Metro*, no. 109, pp. 86–90.

——1997b, 'Taking a problem-based approach to journalism education', *AsiaPacific MediaEducator*, no. 3, July–December, pp. 89–107.

——1998a, 'Making journalism: the media as cultural resource', *Australian Journalism Review*, vol. 20, no. 2, pp. 1–23.

——1998b, 'A 10-point plan and a treaty', paper presented at the Unmasking Whiteness Conference, Brisbane, 17–18 September.

Meadows, M. and Oldham, C. 1991, 'Racism and the dominant ideology: Aborigines, television news and the bicentenary', *Media Information Australia*, no. 60, pp. 30–40.

Meadows, M., Hippocrates, C. and van Vuuren, K. 1997, 'Targeting the media: comparing television and print coverage of Indigenous affairs', *Australian Journalism Review*, vol. 19, no. 2, pp. 73–87.

Media, Entertainment and Arts Alliance 1996, *Ethics Review Committee Final Report*, MEAA, Sydney.

——1997, *Ethics in Journalism*, Melbourne University Press, Melbourne.

——1998, 'Recommended code of ethics', *The Alliance*, Autumn, MEAA, Sydney, p. 11.

——1999, Journalists' Code of Ethics, *http://www.alliance.aust.com/3-3.htm*, 24 September 1999.

Media Report 1996, 'Globalisation and Mass Communication' 29 August, http://www.abc.net.au/rn/talks/8.30/mediarpt/mstories/mr290896.htm 4 July 1997, pp. 1–8.

——1997, 'Journalism and self-regulation', 13 March, *http://www.abc.net.au/rn/talks/8.30/mediarpt/mstories/mr970313.htm*, 4 July 1997, pp. 1–8.

——1998a, 'The Power of the media', 13 October, *http://www.abc.net.au/rn/talks/8.30/mediarpt/mstories/mr980813.htm*, 12 October 1998, pp. 1–8.

——1998b, 'Conflict in journalism education', 10 December, *http://www.abc.net.au/rn/talks/8.30/mediarpt/mtalks/mr981210.htm*, 15 March 1999.

Media Studies Journal 1991, 'Media at the millennium', vol. 5, no. 4, Fall, The Freedom Forum Media Studies Center, Columbia University, New York.

Media Watch 1998, ABC TV, 7 September.

——1999, ABC TV, 12 July, *http://abc.net.au/mediawatch/transcripts/990712.htm*, 27 September 1999.

Medill News Service 1998, *Project for Excellence in Journalism*, Medill News Service, Washington.

Medsger, B. 1996, *Winds of Change: Challenges Confronting Journalism Education?*, *http://www.freedomforum.org/FreedomForum/resources/journalism/journalism_edu/winds_of_change/WOCwelcome.html* , 27 September 1999.

Mencher, M. 1987, *News Reporting and Writing*, W.C. Brown Co., Dubuque, Iowa.

——1994, *News Reporting and Writing*, Brown and Benchmark, Dubuque.

Mercer, C. 1989, *Antonio Gramsci: E-Lavorare, or the Work and Government of Culture*, paper delivered at TASA '89, La Trobe University, Melbourne, December.

Merrill, J. 1997, 'Communitarian's rhetorical war against enlightened liberalism', in J. Black (ed.), *Mixed News: The Public/Civic/Communitarian Journalism Debate*, Lawrence Erlbaum, New Jersey, pp. 54–69.

Merritt D. 1998, Public Journalism and Public Life: Why Telling The News is Not Enough (2nd edn), Lawrence Erlbaum, New Jersey.

Meyer, E. 1999a, 'An unexpectedly wider web for the world's newspapers', *AJR NewsLink*, 14–20 September, *http://ajr.newslink.org/emcol10.html*, 24 September 1999.

——1999b, 'The 10 Myths of online publishing', *AJR NewsLink*, 14–20 September, *http://ajr.newslink.org/emcol3.html*, 24 September 1999.

Meyers, C. 1993, 'Justifying journalistic harms: right to know vs interest in knowing', *Journal of Mass Media Ethics*, vol. 8, no. 3, pp. 133–46.

Mickler, S. 1992, *Gambling on the First Race: A comment on Racism and Talk-Back Radio*, Centre for Research in Culture and Communication, Murdoch University, Perth.

——1997a, 'Talk-back Radio and Indigenous Citizens: Towards a Practical Ethics of Representation', *UTS Review*, vol. 3, no. 2, pp. 46–66.

——1997b, 'The "Robespierre" of the air: talk-back radio, globalisation and Indigenous issues', *Continuum*, vol. 11, no. 3, pp. 23–34.

——1998, *The Myth of Privilege: Aboriginal Status, Media Visions, Public Ideas*, Fremantle Arts Centre Press, Fremantle.

Mills, C. W. 1959, *The Sociological Imagination*, Oxford University Press, New York.

Mitford, J. 1979, *The Making of a Muckracker*, Joseph, London.

MNS. See Medill News Service.

Moore, B. (ed.) 1997. *The Australian Concise Oxford Dictionary* (third edn), Oxford University Press, Melbourne.

Morgan, H. 1999, 'He's out: Ex-drug squad boss tastes freedom', the *Adelaide Advertiser*, 19 January.

Morgan Poll 1995, 'Medical profession most honest and ethical', Morgan Poll finding no. 2749, Roy Morgan Research.

Morosi v. Broadcasting Station 2GB (1980) 2 NSWLR 418n

Mumford Jerding, C. 1998, 'Ex-Poynter chief attacks 9 bad habits of journalism', *http://www.freedomforum.org/education/1998/8/10haiman.asp*, 24 September 1999.

Munson, E. S. and Warren, C.A. (eds) 1997, *James Carey: A Critical Reader*, University of Minnesota Press, Minneapolis.

National Inquiry into Racist Violence (Australia) 1991, *Racist Violence: Report of the National Inquiry into Racist Violence in Australia*, AGPS, Canberra.

Negroponte, N. 1995a, *Being Digital*, Alfred A. Knopf, New York.

——1995b, *Being Digital*, Coronet Books, London.

Nelson, D. 1994, 'Context: going beyond anecdotal reporting', *The IR Journal*, vol. 17, no. 2, pp. 4–5.

Ness, S. 1997, 'From hype to reality in the emerging digital age', *http://www.fcc.gov/speeches/ness/spsn721.html*, 15 February 1998.

Nettheim, G. 1997, 'Wik: on invasions, legal fiction, myths and rational responses', *University of New South Wales Law Journal*, vol. 3, no. 2, pp. 5–8.

Newport, F. and Saad, L. 1998, 'A matter of trust', *American Journalism Review*, July/August, *http://www.newslink.org/ajrgallup98.html*, 24 September 1999.

Noack, D. 1998a, 'Bias against online news reporters: the second class citizens of journalism', *Editor and Publisher*, January, pp. 13–14, 44.

Noack, D. 1998b, 'America's newsrooms bend to the Internet', *Editor and Publisher*, 21 February, p. 13.

NSW Law Reform Commission 1995, *Report 75 — Defamation*, October 1995, *http://www.austlii.edu.au/au/other/nswlrc/rpt75*, 18 February 1999.

O'Reilly C. 1998, *The Media Report*, ABC Radio National, September 3.

Oakham, K. M. 1998, 'Kick it, Karl: a jump start for journalism theory', *Australian Journalism Review*, vol. 20, no. 2, pp. 24–34.

Office of the Information Commissioner 1998, Decision No. 98002, 25 March 1998, Queensland Community Newspapers Pty Ltd and Redland Shire Council, *http://www.slq.qld.gov.au/infocomm/decision/98002.html*, 17 February 1999.

OIC. See Office of the Information Commissioner.

Olin-Wright, E. 1985, *Classes*, New Left Books, London.

O'Neill, J. 1992, 'Journalism in the market place', in A. Belsey and R. Chadwick (eds), *Ethical Issues in Journalism and the Media*, Routledge, London.

Onufrijchuk, R. 1993, 'Introducing Innis/McLuhan concluding: the Innis in McLuhan's "System"', *http://kali.murdoch.edu.au/~cntinuum/7.1/Onuf.html*,15 April 1996.

O'Regan, T. 1992, 'Radio daze: some historical and technological aspects of radio', *http://kali.murdoch.edu.au/cntinuum/6.1/O'Regan.html*, 7 March 1996.

Osmond, W. 1998, personal interview with S. Tapsall, 20 November, Sydney.

Outing, S. 1997, 'Are "passionate amateurs" journalists?', *Editor and Publisher Interactive*, *http://www.mediainfo.com/ephome/news/newshtm/stop/st042897.htm*, 24 September 1999.

Packer v. Peacock (1912) 13 CLR 577.

Page, C. 1997, 'A credit to his race', NewsHour with Jim Lehrer, 1 May, *http://www.pbs.org/newshour/essays/page_5-1.html*, 1 November 1999.

Paletz, D. L. and Entman, R. M. 1982, *Media*Power*Politics*, Free Press, New York.

Palmer, J. 1998, 'News production: news values', in Briggs, A. and P. Cobley, P. (eds), *The Media: An Introduction*, Longman, Edinburgh Gate.

Parent, W. 1992, 'Privacy, morality and the law', in Cohen E. (ed.), *Philosophical Issues in Journalism*, Oxford University Press, New York.

Parisi, P. 1998, 'Toward a "philosophy of framing": news narratives for public journalism', *Journalism and Mass Communication Quarterly*, vol. 74, no. 4, pp. 673–86.

Patching, R. 1998, 'The preparation of professional journalists', in M. Breen (ed.), *Journalism Theory and Practice*, Macleay Press, Paddington.

Paul, N. 1995, 'Content: a revisioning. Production in the electronic products newsroom', *http://www.poynter.org/research/nm/nm_revision.htm*, 24 September 1999.

Pavlik, J.V. 1997, 'The future of online journalism: bonanza or black hole?', *Columbia Journalism Review*, July/August, pp. 30–6.

Pearl, C. 1977, *Wild Men of Sydney*, A&R Non-fiction Classics, Sydney (first published by W. H. Allen, London, 1958).

Pearl, D. 1995, 'Futurist schlock: today's cyberhype has a familiar ring', *Wall Street Journal*, 9 July, p. A1.

Pearson, M. 1994, 'Journalism education: taking up the challenge of a changing world', *Australian Journalism Review*, vol. 16, no. 1, pp. 99–107.

——1997, *The journalist's guide to media law*, Allen & Unwin, Sydney.

Pettman, J. 1999, On Boundaries and Institutions, *www.austlii.edu.au/do/disp.pl/au/other/media/Australian+Courts/Free+Speech+Comentary/1258.htm?query=royal%20commission%20into%20aboriginal*, 29 November.

Pew Research Center 1999, 'Big doubts about news media's values: public votes for continuity and change in 2000', survey of 18–21 February, *http://www.people-press.org/feb99que.htm*.

Phipps, J. L. 1998, 'Are journalism schools lost in cyberspace? The frustrating search for Internet-savvy writers', *Editor and Publisher*, March, pp. 26–9.

Pilger, J. 1992, *Distant Voices*, Vantage, London.

Plater, D. 1992, 'Guidelines on reporting Aboriginal and Torres Strait Islander issues', in K. Eggerking and D. Plater (eds), *Signposts: A Guide to Reporting Aboriginal, Torres Strait Islander and Ethnic Affairs*, Australian Centre for Independent Journalism, Sydney.

——1999, 'Guidelines on Reporting Aboriginal and Torres Strait Islander Issues', *www.austlii.edu.au/do/disp.pl/au/other/media/Australian+Courts/Free+Speech+Comentary/1260.htm?query=royal%20commission%20into%20aboriginal*, 29 November.

Plimpton, G. 1998, *Truman Capote: In Which Various Friends, Enemies, Acquaintances, and Detractors Recall His Turbulent Career*, Doubleday, New York.

Pontenila, R. 1990, 'Development communication and total human development', in F. Imperial-Soledad (ed.), *Monograph on Development Communication*, Communication Foundation for Asia Media Group, Manila, pp. 19–33.

Postman, N. 1992, 'Deus machina', *Agency for Instructional Technology Journal*, vol. 1, no. 4, *http://www.technos.net/journal/volume1/4postman.htm*, 27 September 1999.

——1993a, 'Of Luddites, learning and life', *Agency for Instructional Technology Journal*, vol. 2, no. 4, *http://www.technos.net/journal/volume2/4postman.htm*, 27 September 1999.

——1993b, *Technopoly: The Surrender of Culture to Technology*, Vintage Books, New York.

Poynter Institute 1999, *Competence in the Newsroom: A Poynter Conference*, *http://www.poynter.org/comp/comp_index.htm*, 24 September 1999.

——1999, *Cultural Competence*, *http://www.poynter.org/comp/comp_cult.htm*, 12 August.

Putnis, P. 1993, 'A day in the life: the Channel Ten Brisbane newsroom', *Australian Journalism Review*, vol. 15, no. 2, July–December, pp. 112–22.

Quinn, S. 1997, 'Australian journalists and the Internet', *Australian Journalism Review*, vol. 19, no. 2, pp. 1–13.

R v. Glennon (1992) 173 CLR 592.

Rakow, L. 1986, 'Feminist approaches to popular culture: giving patriarchy its due', *Communications*, vol. 9, no. 1, pp. 19–41.

Rantanen, T. 1998, 'The struggle for control of domestic news markets', in O. Boyd-Barrett and T. Rantanen (eds), *The Globalization of News*, Sage, London, pp. 35–48.

Raysman, R. and Brown, P. 1998. 'Clickwrap licence agreements', *Law Journal Extra*, *http://www.ljx.com.internet/0811clickwrap.html*, 4 January 1999, pp. 1–7.

RCADC. See Royal Commission into Aboriginal Deaths in Custody.

Real, M. 1989, *Super Media: A Cultural Studies Approach*, Sage, Newbury Park.

Reddick, R. and King, E. 1997, *The Online Journ@list: Using the Internet and Other Electronic Resources*, Harcourt Brace College Publishers, Fort Worth.

Reno, Attorney-General of the United States, et al., *Appellants v. American Civil Liberties Union et al.* (1997), Citizens Internet Empowerment Coalition, *http://www.ciec.org/SC_appeal/opinion.shmtl*, 4 January 1999, pp. 1–20.

Report of the Committee on Privacy and Related Matters 1990, Cmnd. 1102, HMSO, London.

Reynolds, A. 1998, 'Between the theory and the reality: a practical assessment of public journalism', a paper delivered to the JEA conference, Capricorn International Resort, Yeppoon, 1–4 December, *http://www.maj.arts.qut.edu.au/Journalism/pj/research/anna.html*, 3 November 1999.

Reynolds, H. 1989, *Dispossession—Black Australians and White Invaders*, Allen & Unwin, St Leonards.

——1996, 'Native title and pastoral leases', *Aboriginal Law Bulletin*, vol. 3, no. 85, October, pp. 14–15.

Richards I. 1996, 'Dealing with death: intrusion into grief and journalism education', *Australian Journalism Review*, vol. 18, no. 1, pp. 99–105.

Richardson, J. 1998, personal interview with S. Tapsall, 19 November, Sydney.

Richon, O. 1996, 'Representation, the harem and the despot', in the *Block Reader in VisualCulture*, Routledge, London, pp. 242–57.

Ricketson, M. 1995, 'After midnight' interview with John Berendt, *Herald-Sun*, 4 November.

——1997, 'Helen Garner's *The First Stone*: hitchhiking on the credibility of other writers', in Jenna Mead (ed.) *Bodyjamming: Sexual Harassment, Feminism and Public Life*, Random House, Sydney.

Righter, R. 1978, *Whose News? Politics, the Press and the Third World*, Andre Deutsch, London.

Robertson, L. 1998, 'Shattered glass at the new republic', *American Journalism Review*, 16–22 June, *http://ajr.newslink.org/ajrby78.html*, 2 September 1999.

Rogers, E. M. 1995, *Diffusion of Innovations* (fourth edn), The Free Press, New York.

Rosen, J. 1993a, *Community Correctedness: Passwords for Public Journalism*, Poynter Institute for Media Studies, St Peters burg, Florida.

——1993b, *Getting the Connections Right: Public Journalism and the Troubles of the Press*, Twentieth Century Fund Press, New York, *http://www.tcf.org/publications/media/getting_the_connections_right/Preface.html*, 4 June 1998.

Rosen, J. and Merritt, D. 1994, *Public Journalism: Theory and Practice*, Kettering Foundation, Dayton, Ohio.

Royal Commission into Aboriginal Deaths in Custody (1991), *Regional report of inquiry into underlying issues in Western Australia*, Australian Government Publishing Service, Canberra, *http://www.austlii.edu.au/au/special/rsjproject/rsjlibrary/rciadic/regional/wa_underlying/99.html*, 13 June, 2000.

Said, E. 1978, *Orientalism*, Routledge & Kegan Paul, London.

Salcetti, M. 1995, 'The emergence of the reporter: mechanization and the devaluation of editorial workers', in H. Hardt and B. Brennen (eds), *Newsworkers: Towards a History of the Rank and File*, University of Minnesota Press, Minneapolis, pp. 48–74.

Sales, L. 1998, personal interview with S. Tapsall, 20 November, Sydney.

Schattscheider, E. E. 1960, *The Semisovereign People: A Realist's View of Democracy in America*, Holt, Rinehart and Winston, New York.

Schlesinger, P. 1978, *Putting Reality Together*, Methuen, London.

Schon, D. 1991, *Educating the Reflective Practitioner*, Jossey-Bass, San Francisco.

Schramm, W. 1947, 'Measuring another dimension of newspaper readership', *Journalism Quarterly*, winter, pp. 4–12.

Schudson, M. 1991, 'The Sociology of News Production Revisited' in James Curran and Michael Gurevitch, *Mass Media and Society*, Edward Arnold, Great Britain.

——1995, *The Power of News*, Harvard University Press, Cambridge, Massachusetts.

——1997, 'The sociology of news', in Dan Berkowitz (ed.), *Social Meanings of News: A Text-Reader*, Sage, California, pp. 7–22.

Schultz, J. 1989, 'Failing the public: the media marketplace', in Helen Wilson (ed.) *Australian Communications and the Public Sphere: Essays in Memory of Bill Bonney*, Macmillan, Melbourne.

——1992a, 'Our future: media and democracy', *The Journalist*, September/October, pp. 5–8.

——1992b, 'Investigative reporting tests journalistic independence', *Australian Journalism Review*, vol. 14, no. 2, pp. 18–30.

——(ed.) 1994, *Not Just Another Business: Journalists, Citizens and the Media*, Pluto Press, Leichhardt.

——1998, *Reviving the Fourth Estate: Democracy, Accountability and the Media*, Cambridge University Press, Melbourne.

Scott, A. 1997, 'Globalization: social process or political rhetoric?', in A. Scott (ed.) *The Limits of Globalization Cases and Arguments*, Routledge, London and New York.

Scott, P. and Sheridan Burns, L. 1997, 'The media and Indigenous Australian Project: time to act', *TIME for Journalism*, proceedings of the Journalism Education Association Annual Conference, Journalism Education Association, Australia.

Sekuless, P. 1999, *A Handful of Hacks*, Allen & Unwin, Sydney.

Sepstrup, P. 1981, 'Methodological developments in content analysis', in K. E. Rosengren (ed.), *Advances in Content Analysis*, Sage, Beverly Hills.

Shalev, N. and Leon, Y. 1997, *Primetime War*, video documentary, SBS.

Shawcross, W. 1993, *Rupert Murdoch: Ringmaster of the Information Circus*, Pan Books, London.

Sheehan, P (1997) *Among the Barbarians* Random House, Sydney.

Sheridan Burns, L. and McKee, A. 1999, 'Reporting on Indigenous issues: some practical suggestions for journalists', *Australian Journalism Review*, vol. 21, no. 2, pp. 103–16.

Shohat, E. and Stam, R. 1994, *Unthinking Eurocentrism: Multiculturalism and the Media*, Routledge, London.

Siebert, F. S. 1963, 'The libertarian theory', in F. Siebert, T. Peterson and W. Schramm (eds), *Four Theories of the Press* (second edn), University of Illinois, Urbana, pp. 39–71.

Sigal, L. 1973, *Reporters and Officials: The Organisation and Politics of Newsmaking*, Heath, Lexington, Massachusetts.

Silk, M. 1991, 'Who will rewire America?', *Columbia Journalism Review*, May–June, pp. 45–8.

Simons, M. 1999, *Fit to print: Inside the Canberra Press Gallery*, UNSW Press, Sydney.

Simper, E. 1997a, 'Wendt's wisdom under a bushel', the *Weekend Australian*, 15–16 November, p. 3.

——1997b, 'Jana's theme: beating up current affairs', the *Australian*, 21 November, p. 15.

——1998, 'Kennett saga: first in, best press', the *Australian*, 9 October, p. 6.

Sims, N. (ed.) 1984, *The Literary Journalists*, Ballantine Books, New York.

——1990, *Literary Journalism in the Twentieth Century*, Oxford University Press, New York.

Sims, N. and Kramer, M. (eds) 1995, *Literary Journalism: A New Collection of the Best American Nonfiction*, Ballantine Books, New York.

Singer, J. B. 1996, 'Virtual anonymity: online accountability on political bulletin boards and the makings of the virtuous virtual journalist', *Journal of Mass Media Ethics*, vol. 11, no. 2, pp. 95–106.

——1998, 'Online journalists: foundations for research into their changing roles', *http://lamar.colostate.edu/~jsinger/online.htm*, 24 September 1999.

Smart, B. 1976, *Sociology, Phenomenology and Marxian Analysis*, Routledge and Kegan Paul, London.

SMH. See *Sydney Morning Herald.*

Smyth, C. 1999, personal communication, 11 September, Perth.

Smythe, M. 1998, *An Analysis of the Media Coverage of Bringing Them Home: the Report of the National Inquiry into the Separation of Aboriginal and Torres Strait Islander Children from their Families*, pp. 3–5, Australian Institute for Aboriginal and Torres Strait Islander Studies, Sydney.

Snoddy, R. 1992, *The Good, the Bad and the Unacceptable*, Faber and Faber, London.

Spurgeon, C. 1989, 'Challenging technological determinism: Aborigines, Aussat and remote Australia', in H. Wilson (ed.), *Australian Communications and the Public Sphere*, Macmillan, Sydney, pp. 27–45.

Sreberny-Mohammadi, A., Winseck, D., McKenna, J. and Boyd-Barrett, O. (eds) 1997, *Media in Global Context: A Reader*, Arnold (Hodder Headline Group), London.

Stam, R. and Spence L. 1983. 'Colonialism, racism and representation', *Screen*, vol. 24, no. 2.

Stephens, M. 1988, *A History of News: From the Drum to the Satellite*, Viking Books, New York.

Stepp, C. 1991, 'When readers design the news', *Washington Journalism Review*, April, pp. 20–4.

——1996, 'Public journalism: balancing the scales,' *American Journalism Review*, vol. 18, no. 4, pp. 38–40.

Sterling, B. 1995, 'The hacker crackdown: evolution of the US telephone network', in N. Heap, R. Thomas, G. Einon, R. Mason and H. Mackay (eds), *Information, Technology and Society*, Sage Publications, London, pp. 33–40.

Sternberg, R. J. 1995, *In Search of the Human Mind*, Harcourt Brace and Company, Orlando, Florida.

Stevenson, B. 1997, 'The Wik decision and after', *Queensland Parliamentary Library Research Bulletin*, no. 4.

Stevenson, R. L. 1994, *Global Communication in the Twenty-First Century*, Longman, New York.

Stoll, C. 1996, *Silicon Snake Oil: Second Thoughts on the Information Highway*, Pan Books, London.

Stone, G. and Boudreau, T. 1995, 'Comparison of reader content preferences', *Newspaper Research Journal*, fall, pp. 123–8.

Streeter, T. G. 1986, Technocracy and Television: Discourse, Policy, Politics and the Making of Cable Television, unpublished PhD Speech Communication, University of Illinois, Urbana-Champaign.

Streeter, T. G. 1997, 'Blue skies and strange bedfellows: the discourse of cable television', *http://www.uvm.edu/~tstreete/newfable.htm*, 27 September 1999.

Suharto 1989, 'Role of the press in national development', in A. Mehra (ed.), *Press Systems in ASEAN States*, AMIC, Singapore, pp. 131–4.

Sussman, L. R. 1978, 'Development journalism: the ideological factor', in P. C. Horton (ed.), *The Third World and Press Freedom*, Praeger Publishers, New York, pp. 74–92.

Swing, R. 1964, *'Good Evening!' A Professional Memoir*, Harcourt, Brace and World, New York.

Sydney Morning Herald 1999. 'Maybe I'm stupid, but I won't give in.' 20 July, *http://www.smh.com.au/news/9907/20/pageone/pageone10.html*, 27 September 1999.

Szende, A. 1986, *From Torrent to Trickle: Managing the Flow of News in Southeast Asia*, Institute of Southeast Asian Studies, Singapore.

Tapsall, S. 1997, 'Can Australian journalists drive the US CAR?', *Australian Journalism Review*, vol. 19, no. 1, pp. 69–75.

——1998, 'Technological talespinning', Masters thesis, Queensland University of Technology.

——1999, 'Spreadsheets and databases', in S. Quinn *Newsgathering on the Net: An Internet Guide for Australian Journalists*, Macmillan Education, Australia, pp. 123–8.

Tapsall, S. and Granato, L. 1997, 'New CAR curriculum will influence the practice of journalism', *Australian Journalism Review*, vol. 19, no. 2, pp. 14–23.

Tarnas, R. 1991, *The Passion of the Western Mind: Understanding the Ideas that have Shaped our World View*, Harmony Books, New York.

Theophanous v. the Herald and Weekly Times Ltd (1994) 182 CLR 104.

Tickle, S. and Hippocrates, C. 1999, 'Australian public journalism in practice: the Holy Grail or just another cheap cocktail?', paper delivered to the ANZCA Annual Conference, Sydney, 7–9 July.

Tiffen, R. 1989, *News and Power*, Allen & Unwin, Sydney.

——1994, 'The media and democracy: reclaiming an intellectual agenda', in J. Schultz (ed.), *Not Just another Business: Journalists, Citizens and the Media*, Pluto Press, Sydney.

Toohey, J. 1993, 'A Government of Laws, and Not of Men?' *Public Law Review*, vol. 4, pp. 158–74.

Torre, S. (ed.) 1990, *The Macquarie Dictionary of Australian Quotations*, The Macquarie Library, Sydney.

Trigger, D. 1995, ' "Everyone's agreed, the West is all you need": ideology, media and Aboriginality in Western Australia', *Media Information Australia*, vol. 75, pp. 102–22.

Tucher, A. 1997, 'Why Web warriors might worry', *Columbia Journalism Review*, July/August, p. 35.

Tuchman, G. 1978, *Making News: A Study in the Construction of Reality*, Free Press, New York.

——1997, 'Making news by doing work: routinizing the unexpected,' in D. Berkowitz (ed.), *Social Meanings of News: A Text-Reader*, Sage, Thousand Oaks, pp. 173–92.

Turner, G. 1993, 'Media texts and messages', in S. Cunningham and G. Turner (eds), *The Media in Australia: Industries, Texts, Audiences*, Allen & Unwin, St Leonards, NSW.

——1996, 'Post journalism: news and current affairs from the late '80s to the present', *Media International Australia*, no. 82, pp. 78–91.

Underwood, D. 1993, *When MBAs Rule the Newsroom: How Markets and Managers are Shaping Today's Media*, Columbia University Press, New York.

United Kingdom Journalists' Code of Practice 1997, *http://www.uta.fi/ethicnet/uk2.html*, 2 September 1999.

United Nations Committee on the Elimination of Racial Discrimination 1999, *Committee on Elimination of Racial Discrimination Examines Situation in Australia, Adopts Decision*, United Nations news release, 16 August.

van Dijk, T. A. 1991, 'The interdisciplinary study of news as discourse', in K. B. Jensen and N. W. Jankowski (eds), *A Handbook of Qualitative Methodologies for Mass Communication Research*, Routledge, London.

Varley, C. 1997, 'Legislating from within', *Australian Journalism Review*, vol. 19, no. 1, pp. 105–18.

Vatsikopoulos, H. 1998, personal interview with S. Tapsall, 19 November, Sydney.

Waddell, L. 1997, 'Voices: in the beginning there was Columbus', in J. Black (ed.), *The Public/Civic/Communitarian Journalism Debate*, Lawrence Erlbaum, New York, pp. 94–5.

Walker, M. 1998, 'The power of the media', *The Media Report*, ABC Radio National, 13 October, *http://www.abc.net.au/rn/talks/8.30/mediarpt/mstories/mr980813.htm*, 15 February 1999.

Walker, R. B. 1976, *The Newspaper Press in New South Wales, 1803–1920*, Sydney University, Sydney.

Walker, S. 1989, *The Law of Journalism in Australia*, Law Book Company, Sydney.

——1997, 'Changing journalism in a changing world: the changing legal environment', *Australian Journalism Review*, vol. 19, no. 1, pp. 91–7.

Walsh, M. 1998, personal interview with S. Tapsall, 20 November, Sydney.

Ward, I. 1991, 'Who writes the political news? Journalists as hunters or harvesters', *Australian Journalism Review*, vol. 13, nos 1 and 2, pp. 52–8.

Ward I. 1995, *Politics of the Media*, Macmillan, Melbourne.

Ward, O. 1989, 'The media and human rights', *Broadcaster*, March–April, p. 28.

Warren S. and L. Brandeis 1890, 'The right to privacy', in *Harvard Law Review*, vol. 4, no. 5, December 15, pp. 193–220.

Warren, A. 1995, *The Media Report*, ABC Radio National, 21 December.

Watkins, P. 1986, *High Tech, Low Tech and Education*, Deakin University Press, Geelong.

Wasserstrom R. (ed.) 1971, *Morality and the Law*, Wadsworth, Belmont, California.

Weber, R. (ed.) 1974, *The Reporter as Artist: A Look at the New Journalism Controversy*, Hastings House, New York.

Weber, R. 1980, *The Literature of Fact: Literary Nonfiction in American Writing*, Ohio University Press, Athens, Ohio.

Weinberg, S. 1998, 'Tell it long, take your time, go in depth', *Columbia Journalism Review*, January/February, pp. 56–61.

Weston, M. 1996, *Native Americans in the News: Images of Indians in the Twentieth Century Press*, Greenwood Press, Westport, Connecticut.

White, S. 1996, *Reporting in Australia*, Macmillan Education Australia, South Melbourne.

——1998, *The Media Report*, ABC Radio National, 12 March.

Williams, K. 1997, *Get Me a Murder a Day! A History of Mass Communication in Britain*, Arnold, London.

——1977, *Marxism and Literature*, Oxford University Press, London.

Williams, R. 1988, *Key Words: A Vocabulary of Culture and Society*, Fontana Press, London.

——1993, 'Journocam and beyond: a look into the future of ENG', *Australian Journalism Review*, vol. 15, no. 1, pp. 93–8.

——1996, 'Port Arthur: some contempt of court issues', *Australian Media Law Reporter*, vol. 3, no. 6, pp. 86–9.

Wilson, D. 1992, 'Charters of editorial independence', *Australian Journalism Review*, vol. 14, no. 2, pp. 31–6.

Wilson, J. 1996, *Understanding Journalism: A Guide to Issues*, Routledge, London.

Winch S. 1996, 'Moral justifications for privacy and intimacy', *Journal of Mass Media Ethics*, vol. 11, no. 4, pp. 197–209

——1997, *Mapping the Cultural Space of Journalism*, Praeger Publishers, Westport, Connecticut CT, USA.

Windschuttle, K. 1986, 'Education, high technology and the future economy', in R. Castle, D. Lewis and J. Mangan (eds), *Work, Leisure and Technology*, Longman Cheshire, Melbourne, pp. 107–13.

——1988, *The Media: A New Analysis of the Press, Television, Radio and Advertising in Australia* (third edn), Penguin, Melbourne.

——1998, 'The poverty of media theory', *Quadrant*, March, pp. 11–18.

Winner, L. 1993, 'Do artifacts have politics?', in D. MacKenzie and J. Wajcman (eds), *The Social Shaping of Technology*, Open University Press, Milton Keynes, pp. 26–38.

Winston, B. 1986, *Misunderstanding Media*, Routledge and Kegan Paul, London.

——1990, 'How are media born?', in J. Downing, A. Mohammafi and A. Sreberny-Mohammadi (eds), *Questioning the Media: A Critical Introduction* (as reproduced in *http://www.uwindsor.ca/faculty/socsci/comstudies/Costclasses/winston.htmled*, Sage Publications, Newbury Park.

Wolfe, T. 1975, *The New Journalism*, with an anthology edited by T. Wolfe and E. W. Johnson, Picador, London.

——1988, 'Stalking the billion-footed beast', reprinted as an introduction to *The Bonfire of the Vanities*, Picador, London.

Wolpe P. 1997, 'The triumph of autonomy in American bio-ethics: a sociological view' in R. DeVries and J. Subedi (eds), *Bioethics and Society*, Prentice Hall, New Jersey.

World Today 2000, Aboriginal athletes facing added pressures, ABC Radio, *http://www.abc.net.au/worldtoday/s104046*, htm_28 February.

Yagoda, B. 2000, *About Town: The New Yorker and the World it Made*, Scribner, New York, pp. 183–94.

Zanotto, J. 1998, 'Contempt laws: are we headed for a crackdown?', paper presented to the Journalism Education Association Conference, Yeppoon, December.

Zawawi, C. 1994, 'Sources of news — who feeds the watchdogs?', *Australian Journalism Review*, vol. 16, no. 1, pp. 67–72.

Zelizer, B. 1992, 'CNN, the Gulf War, and journalistic practice', *Journal of Communication*, Winter, pp. 66–81.

Index